RECKONING WITH LAW IN EXCESS

Reckoning with Law in Excess offers a ground-breaking approach to understanding the relationship between law and social and political transformation in a changing and uncertain world. The book's authors examine a wide range of case studies in which social movements pursue justice and social change within, against, and beyond the law. The interdisciplinary research at the heart of the volume reveals patterns in the ways in which law and legality are invested with heightened importance during certain historical moments, a process of over-loading that most often gives way to disenchantment with the ultimate limits of law. In reflecting critically and synthetically on these complicated dialectics of reckoning with law, the book shines a light on one of the most important, and consequential, dynamics in an era of climate crisis, rising populism across the political spectrum, and social conflict. This title is also available as Open Access on Cambridge Core.

MARK GOODALE is Professor of Cultural and Social Anthropology and Director of the Laboratory of Cultural and Social Anthropology (LACS) at the University of Lausanne. One of the pioneers in the anthropology of human rights, he is the author or editor of a number of books on law, human rights, and justice, including *Reinventing Human Rights* (2022).

OLAF ZENKER is Professor of Social and Cultural Anthropology at the Martin Luther University Halle-Wittenberg. His research deals with political and legal issues such as statehood, bureaucracy, the rule of law, normative pluralities, inequality and justice. His latest book publications include *Beyond Expropriation Without Compensation: Law, Land Reform and Redistributive Justice in South Africa* (2024).

RECKONING WITH LAW IN EXCESS

Mobilization, Confrontation, Refusal

Edited by

MARK GOODALE

University of Lausanne

OLAF ZENKER

Martin Luther University Halle-Wittenberg

CAMBRIDGE UNIVERSITY PRESS

CAMBRIDGE
UNIVERSITY PRESS

Shaftesbury Road, Cambridge CB2 8EA, United Kingdom

One Liberty Plaza, 20th Floor, New York, NY 10006, USA

477 Williamstown Road, Port Melbourne, VIC 3207, Australia

314–321, 3rd Floor, Plot 3, Splendor Forum, Jasola District Centre, New Delhi – 110025, India

103 Penang Road, #05-06/07, Visioncrest Commercial, Singapore 238467

Cambridge University Press is part of Cambridge University Press & Assessment, a department of the University of Cambridge.

We share the University's mission to contribute to society through the pursuit of education, learning and research at the highest international levels of excellence.

www.cambridge.org
Information on this title: www.cambridge.org/9781009499545

DOI: 10.1017/9781009499552

First published 2025

Cover image: *Angles of Elevation*, Vans the Omega

A catalogue record for this publication is available from the British Library

A Cataloging-in-Publication data record for this book is available from the Library of Congress

ISBN 978-1-009-49954-5 Hardback
ISBN 978-1-009-49959-0 Paperback

CONTENTS

NOTES ON CONTRIBUTORS

PENELOPE ANTHIAS is Associate Professor in Human Geography at Durham University. Her work explores the relationship between colonial racial formations, extractive geographies and the politics of rights, using ethnographic and audiovisual methods conducted in collaboration with Indigenous and campesino communities in Southern Bolivia. Her monograph *Limits to Decolonization: Indigeneity, Territory, and Hydrocarbon Politics in the Bolivian Chaco* (Cornell University Press, 2018) won the 2019 American Political Science Association Best Book Award in the field of Race, Ethnicity and Politics. Penelope has co-edited two books and three special issues on extractive geographies, ethnic territories and (de)colonial natures, among other publications. She is currently working on a book manuscript and documentary film examining the political and legal geographies of gas development in Bolivia's Tariquía National Reserve of Flora and Fauna.

MATTHEW C. CANFIELD is Assistant Professor of Law and Society & Law and Development at the Van Vollenhoven Institute for Law, Governance, and Society at Leiden Law School. He is the author of *Translating Food Sovereignty: Cultivating Justice in an Age of Transnational Governance* (Stanford University Press, 2022), as well as the principal investigator of the ERC Consolidator Grant funded project, DIGIFOOD: Data Governance for Equitable and Sustainable Digital Food Systems.

LYNETTE J. CHUA is Professor of Law at the National University of Singapore. She is a law and society scholar who specializes in the study of legal mobilization, legal consciousness, and rights and resistance. She has received multiple awards for her research and writing, including the International Prize of the Law & Society Association. She is the author of *The Politics of Rights and Southeast Asia* (Cambridge University Press, 2022), *The Politics of Love in Myanmar: LGBT Mobilization and Human*

Rights as A Way of Life (Stanford University Press, 2019), and *Mobilizing Gay Singapore: Rights and Resistance in an Authoritarian State* (Temple University Press, 2014), as well as co-editor of *The Asian Law & Society Reader* (Cambridge University Press, 2023, with David Engel and Sida Liu), *Out of Place: Fieldwork and Positionality in Law and Society* (Cambridge University Press, 2024, with Mark F. Massoud), and *Contagion, Technology, and Law at the Limit* (Hart Publishing, 2024, with Jack Jin Gary Lee).

KAMARI MAXINE CLARKE is a Distinguished Professor of Transnational Justice and Sociolegal Studies at the University of Toronto at the Centre for Criminology & Sociolegal Studies. Over the past twenty-five years Professor Clarke has conducted research on issues related to international legal domains, sociolegal studies, religious transnationalism, the politics of globalization and race, and decolonial approaches to anthropology. She has spent her career exploring theoretical questions of culture and power and, in the field of law and anthropology, detailing the relationship between new transnational formations and contemporary problems. She is the author of nine books and over fifty-five peer-reviewed articles and book chapters, including her 2009 publication of *Fictions of Justice: The International Criminal Court and the Challenge of Legal Pluralism in Sub-Saharan Africa* (Cambridge University Press, 2009), and *Affective Justice* (Duke University Press, 2019), which won the finalist prize for the American Anthropological Association's 2020 Elliot P. Skinner Book Award for the Association for Africanist Anthropology, and was the recipient of the 2019 Royal Anthropological Institute's Amaury Talbot Book Prize. Recently, she was a recipient of the 2021 Guggenheim Prize for career excellence in Anthropology, and in 2024 was inducted as a fellow into the Royal Society of Canada Academy of Social Sciences.

JULIA ECKERT is Professor for Political Anthropology at the University of Bern. Her research focuses on the transformation of democracy and law under conditions of global entanglement. She is interested in the relationship between moral and legal responsibility, citizenship and political participation, security and border regimes, and the juridification of social protest. Currently, she leads a research project on the relationship between law, democracy, and fascization in India. Her publications include *The Charisma of Direct Action* (Oxford University Press, 2003),

The Social Life of Anti-Terrorism Laws (Transcript, 2008), *Law against the State* (Cambridge University Press, 2012), *The Bureaucratic Production of Difference* (Transcript, 2020), and recently, *Just Sharing; The (Potentially) Radical Politics of Helping.* She is co-editor of *Anthropological Theory.*

MARK GOODALE is Professor of Cultural and Social Anthropology and Director of the Laboratory of Cultural and Social Anthropology (LACS) at the University of Lausanne. Between 2023 and 2024 he was a Leverhulme Trust visiting professor in the School of Anthropology and Museum Ethnography (SAME) and a member of St Antony's College at the University of Oxford. His wide-ranging publications and public scholarship include seventeen sole-authored, edited, and co-edited books. His most recent include *Extracting the Future: Lithium in an Era of Energy Transition* (University of California Press, 2025), *Reinventing Human Rights* (Stanford University Press, 2022), and *A Revolution in Fragments: Traversing Scales of Justice, Ideology, and Practice in Bolivia* (Duke University Press, 2019). In addition to his academic writing, his nonfiction essays have appeared in literary journals such as *The Paris Review* and *Boston Review*, and he has been quoted as an expert in publications including *The New York Times, The Guardian, The Washington Post, The Nation*, and *Le Monde.*

AGATHE MORA is Assistant Professor in Anthropology and International Development at the University of Sussex. She is also an editor at *Allegra Lab* and a research associate at the Universities of Lausanne and Basel. As a legal and political anthropologist, Mora conducts research within international organizations in Kosovo, the EU, and the UN. Her research interests include human rights, international law and legal practice, international interventionism, property restitution, postconflict reconstruction and transitional justice, and climate justice. Her first monograph is forthcoming with Stanford University Press.

ARZOO OSANLOO is a Professor in the Department of Law, Societies, and Justice at the University of Washington. She is a legal anthropologist and previously worked as an immigration and asylum and refugee law attorney. Her books include *Forgiveness Work: Mercy, Law, and Victim's Rights in Iran* (Princeton University Press, 2020), and *The Politics of Women's Rights in Iran* (Princeton University Press, 2009). She is also co-editor of *Care in a Time of Humanitarianism: Stories of Refuge, Aid, and Repair in the Global South* (Berghahn Books, 2024).

KIRI SANTER is a postdoctoral researcher and lecturer at the Institute of Social Anthropology at the University of Bern. Her work and research interests cover the anthropology of policy and regulation, border regimes, valuation, and transnational law. Her first book *Bordering Responsibility* (working title) on the outsourcing of migration control in the central Mediterranean is under preparation with Duke University Press. Her current research tracks the implementations of reforms being carried out on the European Union's emissions trading system, with a focus on the Carbon Border Adjustment Mechanism (CBAM) and their effects on the global production networks of steel and aluminum. She is one of the editors of the journal *Anthropological Theory*.

NITZAN SHOSHAN is a Professor at the Centro de Estudios Sociológicos at El Colegio de México. He received his PhD in cultural anthropology from the University of Chicago. His work has focused on nationalism, populism, and the far right in Germany and beyond, as well as on urban processes in Berlin and Mexico City, and on questions of ethics and methods in ethnographic research. Recently, he has conducted research on polarization and youth mobilization in Latin America, as well as on the social life of *Heimat* (home, homeland) in Germany and its historical and contemporary intertwinements with right-wing nationalism.

RACHEL SIEDER is Senior Research Professor at the Centre for Research and Graduate Studies in Social Anthropology (CIESAS) in Mexico City, where she teaches legal and political anthropology. She is a research associate at the Chr. Michelsen Institute in Bergen, and global fellow of LawTransform, the Centre for Law and Social Transformation at the University of Bergen. Her research focuses on the judicialization of Indigenous peoples' rights and Indigenous justice systems, specifically in Guatemala, where she continues to collaborate with Indigenous lawyers' associations. She has also worked extensively on gender and Indigenous justice systems. Her most recent books include *The Handbook of Law and Society in Latin America* (Routledge, 2019, ed. with Karina Ansolabehere and Tatiana Alfonso, published as *Manual de Derecho y Estado en América Latina*, Uniandes/Siglo del Hombre, 2024), *Demanding Justice and Security: Indigenous Women and Legal Pluralities in Latin America* (Rutgers, 2017). Her publications can be found at www.rachelsieder.com.

OLAF ZENKER is Professor of Social and Cultural Anthropology at the Department for Anthropology and Philosophy at Martin Luther University Halle-Wittenberg. His research deals with political and legal issues related to justice, inequality, land reform, the rule of law, normative pluralities, postliberal affordances, postcolonial statehood, and bureaucracy in South Africa and beyond. His latest publications include the special issues *Justice in the Anthropocene* (*Zeitschrift für Ethnologie | Journal of Social and Cultural Anthropology*, 2024), and *Collaborations and Contestations in Publicly Engaged Anthropologies* (*Public Anthropologist*, 2023), as well as *Beyond Expropriation Without Compensation: Law, Land Reform and Redistributive Justice in South Africa* (Cambridge University Press, 2024), and *The Oxford Handbook of Law and Anthropology* (Oxford University Press, 2022). He is the convenor of the annual *ANTON WHILHEM AMO ~~LECTURES~~* at Martin Luther University Halle-Wittenberg, and the editor of the eponymous open-access series (Universitätsverlag Halle-Wittenberg).

ACKNOWLEDGMENTS

This volume began its life as a weeklong research seminar at the University of Lausanne. We gratefully acknowledge the financial and logistical support of a number of institutions that made this June 2022 event possible, including the Swiss National Science Foundation, which provided funding for both the weeklong event and this Open Access volume; the Institute of Social Sciences and the Laboratory of Cultural and Social Anthropology (LACS) at the University of Lausanne; and the Institute for Social and Cultural Anthropology at Martin Luther University Halle-Wittenberg. The project also benefitted from the research assistance of Amelia Veitch, PhD student in LACS. Finally, although she didn't contribute a chapter, Andrea Freeman participated in all phases of the weeklong seminar in Lausanne and her timely and insightful interventions were much appreciated.

At Cambridge University Press, editor Tom Randall supported the idea of transforming the June 2022 research seminar into an edited volume from early on. After Tom moved to a new position at the press, the responsibility for the book passed to Marianne Nield, who shepherded it through many of the most important stages. Finally, Natasha Burton took over as our editor while the book moved into production and provided excellent guidance and oversight toward the end of the process.

Our warmest thanks go to the participants themselves, who agreed to come together at the end of the academic year to reflect on the contested status of law in a world of confrontation and crisis. During a week of intensive debate, disagreement, and, finally, something like a working consensus, this interdisciplinary group of scholars proved equal to the formidable task: to take the measure of law against a backdrop of rising populism, a continued weakening of the postwar international system, and a sharpening of political divisions within – and beyond – democratic states. Despite this daunting wider context, the group managed to enjoy many productive and congenial hours together, a week of intellectual work enriched by the welcoming spirit of the city of Lausanne and its different attractions.

Finally, on a personal note, Mark would like to acknowledge the loving support of his family, Romana, Dara, and Isaiah, who have been there through the trials and tribulations of now seventeen books. Olaf is grateful for a fellowship at the Käte Hamburger Kolleg Münster "Legal Unity & Pluralism" that facilitated finalizing the co-authored Introduction to this volume as well as his chapter. Over the years, his thoughts on transformative constitutionalism in South Africa have also benefitted greatly from spirited discussions with Cherryl Walker, Zsa-Zsa Boggenpoel, Andries du Toit, and Michaela Hailbronner. Last but not least, he wishes to acknowledge the ongoing support, patience, and encouragement of his family, Julia, Nele, and Max.

Mark Goodale and Olaf Zenker

NOTE ON THE TEXT

Published with the support of the Swiss National Science Foundation.

Introduction

Social and Political Transformation within, against, and beyond the Law

MARK GOODALE AND OLAF ZENKER

I.1 Juristocracy and the Dialectics of Reckoning

In light of pervasive critiques of human rights, constitutionalism, international and transnational justice mechanisms, and even the rule of law itself, what remains of the status of law as a framework for justice-seeking and social change? Relatedly, given the fact that diverse movements for social and political change around the world were "juridified" or reframed through legal categories during the key first decade of the post-cold war, which UN Secretary-General Kofi Annan described in 2000 as the "Age of Human Rights," how do social and political movements view their relation to law in the present, after this "Age of Human Rights" has passed away? And if law and legal categories no longer form the obvious basis for social and political mobilization across the ideological spectrum, has any other transversal framework come to replace them?

As a contribution to these and related debates over the status of law against a background of "neoliberal maelstrom" (Moyn 2018), populist insurgence, planetary heating, and other global crises, *Reckoning with Law in Excess* explores the divergences and complexities of a generalized process we describe as "juristocratic reckoning." Derived from legally, politically, and culturally diverse case studies from around the word, the category of juristocratic reckoning builds on, yet critically modifies and reappropriates, the notion of "juristocracy." Ran Hirschl introduced this framework in 2004 to describe something more limited: the post-cold war emergence of "new constitutionalism" as an ideology and practice in which political demands were transformed when they were absorbed into constitutional bills of rights. Juristocracy was also used to describe the newly expansive role accorded to judicial review exercised by theoretically independent judiciaries. Hirschl focused on a number of signal moments in the historical shift "toward juristocracy," most importantly, the juridification of South Africa's post-apartheid transition, in which longstanding demands for land redistribution, economic and political equality, and racial justice, among others, were both reframed and incompletely expressed through law, notably through the country's landmark 1996 Constitution (see Zenker, this volume; Klug 2000; Wilson 2001).

However, despite the broader importance of key historical moments, our claim is that these do not completely circumscribe the meaning or significance of juristocracy, which should be understood as both a more diffuse and transhistorical phase in law's social, discursive, and institutional lives and afterlives. At a more definitional level, we see "juristocracy" as a process of transformation – sometimes subtle and implicit, in others accompanied by different forms of intentionality – through which law and legal categories are invested with unusual weight and responsibility beyond their more conventional roles in conflict resolution, government regulation, and the social response to wrongdoing. In this sense, we understand "juristocracy" as a process of sharpening and concentration – for a variety of reasons and, more importantly, with a variety of consequences – through which the law, broadly conceived, is freighted with demands and expectations that overflow its normal institutional, instrumental, and normative carrying capacity.

From this expanded perspective, we can say that passages into juristocracy have taken place quite often and at different levels: transnational, international, regional, national, and local. But regardless of the empirical and historical diversity, there is another dimension to juristocracy that is essential to understanding its generalized importance. This is the fact that the over-freighting of law, the way law and legal categories are charged with functions that go well beyond their conventional limits, typically involves a *dialectics of reckoning*. This is a two-part process of coming to terms, of critical evaluation, and of social response, which helps to explain why law is elevated during certain moments in time, but also, equally important, what happens when the law and legal categories fail to usher in the often-utopian future that the always-temporary juristocratic transformation promises.

In the first phase of juristocratic reckoning, law is amplified as a privileged mechanism for coming to terms with both past and ongoing injustice, either through the struggle for the equal application of existing laws, or through novel and expansive applications of existing law, or through the fight for new legal instruments, new legal protections, and new legally recognized rights. This initial transition into juristocracy is thus a form of reckoning with the relative failures of nonlegal approaches to justice-seeking and transformative change, a form of reckoning that has as a consequence – despite its various specificities and variances – the corresponding elevation of legal institutions (courts, commissions, regulatory bodies) to positions of even greater centrality and political importance than they otherwise would occupy. And, during this first part of the dialectics of reckoning, social and political movements that had previously taken to the streets or otherwise pursued revolutionary violence, direct action, or other nonlegal strategies for change, now experience a relative decline in legitimacy that corresponds to the rise of law in its heightened forms.

Yet almost inevitably, the sharpening of law and legal categories into instruments that promise widespread transformation, or reconciliation, or reparation, or social leveling, give way – historically and ideologically – to a second phase in the dialectics of reckoning: a coming to terms with the perceived failures or incapacities of juristocracy itself, an often-drawn-out process of unraveling marked by critique, skepticism, and eventual disenchantment. The disillusionment with the ultimate limits of social, political, and economic transformation *through* law doesn't last forever, since the underlying legacies of past injustice, and the pressing realities of ongoing injustice, remain; indeed, the urgent need to address injustice is often heightened as the dialectics of juristocratic reckoning unfold. This is because the elevation of law into an overestimated framework during the initial transition into juristocracy often masks the persistence, if not expansion and deepening, of social, economic, environmental, and other forms of conflict. At the same time, given the ironic if not paradoxical potential of law *as law* to reveal its intrinsic limits and even inevitable failures *in and of itself*, that is, of inviting having its bluff called given the stark contrast between its promise and practice, the framework of juristocratic reckoning offers a new analytical lens through which to appreciate the urgency of these ongoing injustices *despite* the stubborn historical presence of law.

In part as a recognition of the ever-present need to confront injustice, and in part as a critical acknowledgement of the structural limits of law and legal categories in light of the pressing demand for more effective action, social and political movements *remobilize* beyond the boundaries of law, either by drawing on past ideological or organizational models or by launching new models for change – or, it must be added, through hybrid mobilizations that involve reimaginings or reinventions of existing models within historical moments that are themselves hybrid. Where this subsequent phase of a relational "return to politics" (Postero & Elinoff 2019) leads to in the dialectics of reckoning remains an open empirical and historical question, and we don't want to make over-broad claims about its cross-cultural and transhistorical similarities. Nevertheless, as the chapters in the volume demonstrate, processes of juristocratic reckoning – that is, the ebbs and flows of relative transitions into and then against legal apotheosis – can be seen across a surprisingly wide range of otherwise diverse contexts.

In addition to the widespread, if diverse, persistence of juristocratic reckoning, there is another dimension to the phenomenon that is examined in different chapters. Even if, at a more general level, the transition into and then against juristocracy shares commonalities across different historical and ethnographic case studies, certain instances of juristocratic reckoning are invested – both in the moment and then in retrospect – with greater degrees of importance. Returning to the work of Ran Hirschl, this fact allows us to create a theoretical bridge between Hirschl's original use of juristocracy and the ways in which the volume appropriates and expands it. This theoretical bridge is grounded in the recognition that certain histories of juristocratic reckoning are imbued with what might be thought of as an "iconic indexicality," in which their supposed historical significance itself enters into the process of juristocratic elevation and then unraveling. Even more, the fact of being invested – by various actors, for various reasons – with iconic importance, especially during the transition *into* juristocracy, has the corresponding effect of heightening the affective consequences of the relative disenchantment that follows and of rendering more violent the mobilizations to which this intense social disenchantment frequently gives way.

For example, the historical case of South Africa's post-apartheid transition is taken as a paradigmatic example of first the elevation of law, especially constitutional law, as a coming to terms with the illegitimacy or impracticability of pursuing other forms of social transformation and justice-seeking, and then a reckoning – which is ongoing – with the relative failures of law to fulfill the utopian promises of South Africa's rights-based "rainbow revolution" (Zenker, this volume; Klug 2018; Zenker, Walker & Boggenpoel 2024). Although the process of reckoning *against* the law in South Africa has taken a variety of forms, it is also seen as an iconic model for other contemporary backlashes against the post-cold war liberal constitutional order, backlashes that have been driven by both right-wing and left-wing populism, both of which depend heavily on the weaponization of national, religious, racial, and other categories of identity. But despite the fact that populist mobilization is partly justified as a response to the failures of human rights, international law, and even the rule of law itself, the sources of populist discontent remain, arguably, largely political-economic. As Martin Krygier (2022: 21) has argued, the underlying causes of injustice are to be found "outside the law," "in besieged domains of life that [law] often can't reach, and even if it does, where it has limited sway."

In critically examining these and related problems, the chapters in the volume endeavor to trace the contours of juristocratic reckoning through a diverse and global range of case studies, which include those that are marked by an iconic indexicality and those that are not. The end result is a broad account of what we describe as "taxonomies of reckoning," which crystallize around different modalities, focal points, and driving forces behind context-specific and situational transitions into and out of elevated legalities. As we discuss in Section I.3 against the backdrop of a broader contextualization of our contemporary moment, the taxonomies that emerge from our case studies coalesce around concerns with "states of juristocracy," "alter-legal reckonings," as well as "juristocracies against the state," attesting to the persisting centrality – if always contested, variable, and fragmented – of the state form. These different forms include situations in which mobilization takes place more formally against law, and contexts in which the possibility of recourse to law is strategically preserved as one among a number of different strategies of political confrontation and logics of resistance.

I.2 Juristocratic Reckoning in an Era of Crisis and Confrontation

In proposing the concept of juristocratic reckoning as a framework through which the wider transhistorical relationship between law, social change, and politics is given new meaning and significance, *Reckoning with Law in Excess* must be located with respect to a number of legal, political, and social contexts, as well as academic debates that reflect on these contexts. First, the postwar international order, embodied in the United Nations and its various institutions and monitoring bodies, which arguably rose to its greatest level of power and legitimacy during the first post-cold war decade, continues its apparently inevitable descent into impotence in the face of a range of global crises (Koskenniemi 2011;

Hopgood 2013; McNeilly 2017; Goodale 2022). At the same time that different super-sovereign permanent members of the UN Security Council – from the United States to China to Russia – refine a long tradition of manipulating the mechanisms of international law and politics as a tool for advancing national interest, a tradition that stands in utter contempt of the ideological grounding of the UN itself (Terretta 2012; Roberts 2015; Allen & Yuen 2022), the UN's actual incapacity to respond meaningfully to global problems such as climate change, socio-economic inequality, global pandemic, and, more recently, military invasion, remains as stark as ever (Posner 2014; Slaughter 2015; An-Na'im 2016; Moyn 2018).

The comparative irrelevance of the UN system has important implications for the study of the relationship between law, politics, and social change, because so many of the legal forms at the center of key instances of juristocratic reckoning, such as human rights, can be traced back to legal treaties and doctrines with origins in international law. This means that the kinds of specific case studies of juristocratic reckoning examined in this volume *cannot* be framed against a transnational or international legal order in which the rule of law actually meets its expansive objectives – for example, "to maintain international peace and security" – since such a well-functioning international legal order doesn't exist, and never has (Mattei & Nader 2008; Stark 2015; Morales 2017; Meierhenrich & Loughlin 2021; but see Pirie 2021).

Second, even as the chapters in *Reckoning with Law in Excess* explore the ways in which both international and national legal orders are characterized by shifts between legal apotheosis, political disenchantment, and political mobilization, there are nevertheless other related dynamics that must be acknowledged, dynamics that reflect on the core problem of juristocratic reckoning, but more indirectly. One of these dynamics that has received scholarly attention recently is the emergence of investigative communities that work in the shadows of formal legal processes but in terms of radically different organizational and technological logics. For example, across a diverse number of regions, everyday citizens have become involved in using social media to document mass violence in collaboration with communities of citizen-scientists, who use digital technologies to locate clandestine graves, identify sites of ethnic cleansing, and otherwise gather evidence of mass atrocities that remain hidden to national or international legal institutions (Bishr & Kuhn 2007; Rubin 2020). And beyond their "para-legal" applications, scholars have described the ways that new communication technologies have shaped social movements as a form of "bio-constitutionalism" (Jasanoff 2011; Agathangelou 2017, 2019) animated by an ideology of "hashtag activism" (Ristovska 2016; Clarke 2017; Niezen 2020). For purposes of the volume, the rise of hashtag activism and crowdsourced forensic investigations raises questions about whether these new technologies should be seen as a way of preserving a semblance of legal legitimacy, given that their use often takes place in relation to ongoing legal procedures, or whether they should be included within the catalogue of political backlash *against* the inadequacies of law. In many contexts, it seems, they ambiguously oscillate between both modes.

And finally, despite the fact that the framework of *Reckoning with Law in Excess* is meant to shed light on a more general, transhistorical phenomenon – the dialectical relationship between the alternating rise and fall of law and politics as mechanisms for justice-seeking and social change – it is important to take stock of a number of recent examples of juristocratic reckoning by way of underscoring the complexity in the relative movements from law to politics and back again. This can best be appreciated with reference to several notable contemporary social and political movements whose ongoing practices of mobilization and refusal illustrate an argument made collectively across the book's chapters: that the political reckoning with law takes a range of forms, some of which are more clearly framed – situationally or as a matter of principle – as a backlash against law, while others maintain a more strategic or ambiguous relationship with it.

For example, important contemporary mobilizations against the unfolding climate crisis are being undertaken by groups such as Just Stop Oil and especially Extinction Rebellion, a decentralized environmental justice movement that has national and local branches in over eighty countries, giving it global scope. Organized around the principle that extractive industrial capitalism is the driving factor behind global warming, biodiversity loss, and ecological collapse, Extinction Rebellion activists engage in various strategies of civil disobedience, monkey-wrenching (the destruction of equipment used for extractive activities), and symbolic acts of often spectacular public protest (Extinction Rebellion 2023). But in demanding a "just energy transition," and in insisting that governments around the world "act now" to undo the economic and social structures that contribute to the climate crisis, Extinction Rebellion has little use for law or legal categories; it neither justifies its claims as flowing from rights or legal entitlements nor looks to legal institutions – at whatever level – to oversee the "just energy transition."

The relationship between law and politics is equally revealing for another transnational movement: Black Lives Matter (BLM). BLM is a similarly decentralized social and political movement that has less of a global imprint than Extinction Rebellion, although BLM-inspired organizations, which mobilize for racial justice and against systemic and institutional racism, have been established in different countries beyond the United States, where BLM was founded in 2013. As a social and political movement working for racial justice and the end of what they perceive as a pervasive culture of white supremacy, BLM activists use a variety of direct-action strategies, including mass public protest, naming-and-shaming, and online media campaigns (Célestine & Martin-Breteau 2016). But much like Extinction Rebellion, BLM is manifestly *not* a movement whose claims are framed through legal categories. With reference to BLM's origins and continuing base of highest visibility in the United States, it is notable that a contemporary movement for racial justice *does not* position itself as a civil rights movement. If anything, BLM resembles much more the antilegal – or, at least, nonlegal – revolutionary movements of the traditional Marxist or socialist left, in strategy, if not in ideology.

Yet if two of the most important contemporary political and social movements would seem to illustrate quite clearly how mobilizations *for* justice – environmental, racial, or otherwise – can also be understood as a backlash *against* the incapacities of law and legal categories, a third and final example is more ambiguous. Like BLM, the #MeToo movement began in the United States through the organizing of small groups of activists who also used different digital platforms to promote awareness of the movement and its objectives. The #MeToo movement, for which the hashtag itself serves as both the symbol of the movement and statement of one of its organizational logics – the creation of solidarity through the acknowledgment of shared experiences of harm – fights against cultures of sexual abuse and harassment. Analogous to BLM, the #MeToo movement is animated by the principle that such cultures are pervasive, systemic, and reproduced in different forms around the world. And even more obviously than BLM, #MeToo is now a global movement, in which the translation of the English-language hashtag into dozens of languages becomes a vehicle for contextualizing the general global problem of sexual abuse and harassment into national, regional, and local cultural terms.

But *unlike* both Extinction Rebellion and BLM, the #MeToo movement engages deeply with law and legal categories, both in the way in which the movement frames its objectives, and in the way that legal mechanisms are key tools in the fight for justice. Beyond high-profile criminal prosecutions or civil procedures against powerful figures in business, entertainment, academia, and in many other sectors, #MeToo activists frame the movement as part of a wider struggle for women's rights (Vogelstein & Stone 2021). In this sense, the example of the #MeToo movement shows how juristocratic reckoning is never simple or uniform. At the same time that movements like Extinction Rebellion and BLM can be located as part of a backlash against the failures of law, the #MeToo movement maintains a partial anchorage in an earlier juristocratic history, the "Age of Human Rights," even as it also deploys methods of political activism well beyond the boundaries of law.

Although these examples of notable contemporary movements help to bring the themes of the volume into immediate focus, most of the chapters in *Reckoning with Law in Excess* examine the nuances of juristocratic reckoning through case studies that are less obvious or well known, yet nevertheless remain critical for reinforcing the scope of the volume's arguments and extending its explanatory reach.

I.3 Charting Taxonomies of Juristocratic Reckoning

Within the volume's broader framework around an expanded conception of juristocracy and what we argue are different forms of reckoning with the rise and fall of law, the chapters can be grouped into a number of taxonomic categories. It is important to recognize, however, that these groupings do not represent a comprehensive or complete taxonomy of juristocratic reckoning; instead, as open-ended taxonomies of reckoning, they offer an initial starting point, one that we hope other scholars will pick up and adapt to their own critical analyses of the lives and afterlives of law in the current conjuncture. In addition, the chapters in *Reckoning with Law* are not equally distributed among these groupings. Nevertheless, this imbalance should not be taken as a signal of relative importance, since the analytical distribution here is more a function of the kinds of practical exigences that characterize all such collective academic publications, especially those that have their origins in a workshop or conference. This is the reason we choose not to divide the volume's table of contents into parts that would – for these reasons – require an unequal distribution of chapters.

That said, and again, in our effort to use these initial groupings in part to point toward the fuller range of forms of juristocratic reckoning, we can identity three distinct categories that emerge from the richness and diversity of the volume's case studies. The first taxonomic grouping shines a light on the ways in which the state plays a critical role in the process through which law is freighted with importance and responsibility for social and political transformation as well as legitimization of the state itself, an overloading that often leads to backlash, resistance, and nonlegal mobilization. At least theoretically, one can imagine a spectrum of possible ways in which the state, any state, might be implicated in the different phases of juristocratic reckoning. The state itself might resist the demand for juristocracy; conversely, the state might be the main instrument for the apotheosis of law or the judicialization of politics. The latter may also slide into authoritarian forms of reckoning when the state captures legal doctrines and institutions in order to prevent their progressive usages against state abuses.

However, in all cases, the state will exercise a unique form of power in relation to juristocracy, including through its historic claim to monopolize the legitimate use of force. This is what several chapters in the volume demonstrate quite clearly: *states of juristocracy* are often profoundly shaped by the ways in which states attempt to manage the different phases of reckoning with law in excess for purposes that advance the interests of the state as much as the interests of social and political transformation. Of course, what these purposes are will vary widely by the kind of state involved: its history, its underlying political grounding, its changing fates, and so on. But the centrality of the state in states of juristocracy, in its dual meaning, remains the interconnecting taxonomic thread.

For example, Olaf Zenker's chapter takes up the iconically indexical case of South Africa, whose rainbow Constitution was used for decades as *the* primary example of juristocracy, the instrumentalization of law – especially constitutional law – as the privileged mechanism for social and political change and reparation for historical injustices. Yet as he shows, South Africa has been enveloped by a slow process of reckoning with the failures of "transformative constitutionalism," a process in which the South African state has played an important part in failing to deliver on its legal promises, in violently opposing popular protests, and in advancing a corrupt regime of state capture. His chapter examines contemporary debates over land reform, widely regarded as failing, and especially the proposal to amend the Constitution to allow for the expropriation of land without compensation.

Zenker's chapter explores more recent developments in the longer arc of post-apartheid South Africa, including the juristocratic reckoning of the South African state itself, which has been marked by the ambiguous and simultaneous rise of both constitutional *and* anti-constitutional populism, with uncertain implications for the country's post-iconic era. However, freeing South Africa from its iconic status of indexing law's allegedly messianic potential might clear the way for actors on all sides to engage collectively with hard-headed questions about how to best achieve redistributive justice through what Zenker calls "transformational triage."

Directly addressing state domination through law beyond the progressive promises of constitutionalism, the chapter by Julia Eckert and Kiri Santer uses a comparative approach to explore the ways in which states intervene amidst wider debates over the role of law to impose a more restrictive form of juristocracy from above. They describe a dynamic unfolding through authoritarian legalism restricting rights and remedies through law, the geopolitical dispersion of law in action, as well as the undermining of legal precedent through the singularizing logic of out-of-court settlements through the growing tribunalization of law. From legal pluralism in India to European migration law to the legal regulation of global capitalism, Eckert and Santer show how states (or supra-states, like the European Union) are able to use their positions of institutional power to impose (or deepen) hegemony *in the name of* juristocratic reckoning.

And finally, within this grouping of chapter themes, Nitzan Shoshan's study of housing activists and debates over housing law in Berlin likewise shows the ways in which states of juristocracy are both reshaped and reshaping within processes of juristocratic reckoning. In this case, like in Zenker's chapter, the conflict in question revolves around the relationship between land, property, and calls for social justice. However, *unlike* in the chapters by Zenker and by Eckert and Santer, here the demand for legal changes as an outflow of juristocratic reckoning takes place from below. In part as a critique of the German state's inability to use existing laws to promote housing equality, activists demand not less but *more* law as a response; in particular, a long-dormant provision of Germany's postwar Constitution, which would allow the state to "socialize" property currently owned by private multinational real estate companies. Shoshan's chapter reminds us that not all backlashes against juristocracy take the form of anti- or nonlegal political mobilization. For the housing activists in Berlin, the backlash against legal inaction or impotence might be seen as a strategy of social (or socialist) reckoning with the actually existing German state of juristocracy they find wanting.

A second taxonomic grouping of chapters is more heterogenous, in part because it involves a form of juristocratic reckoning that is itself necessarily more expansive. This is a form of reckoning in which the response to the elevation and then perceived failure of law and legal categories – usually those associated with state institutions – is not strictly anti- or nonlegal but rather what might be described as "alternatively legal." In such *alter-legal reckonings*, the dialectical backlash to juristocracy takes the form of alternative and creative reconceptualizations of law, some of which push the boundaries so far that it raises the question of whether what results should be considered legal claims or movements or mobilizations at all. Examples of reckoning with law in excess that seek to retain some semblance of legality or even, more broadly, normativity, can be explained as a strategic move, a way to harness some of the law's existing power while simultaneously reconfiguring its form and content. At the same time, reconceptualization-as-reckoning might also be understood as a reluctance to embrace fully anti- or nonlegal methods for social and political transformation, especially since some of these methods can easily give way to different kinds of violence.

A number of chapters in the volume illustrate the breadth of alter-legal reckonings as a distinct and important taxonomic category. As Lynette Chua puts it in her chapter, what we make of moments of law depends on where we look for legalities, which is a key insight that emerges from the different narratives she examines. The reconceptualizations of law she explores are diverse, from the use of human rights by Burmese activists as a form of what one of us has described as "connotative power" (Goodale 2007) to the Singaporean state's attempt to develop novel legal categories to regulate urban contagion. Under conditions of a recent authoritarian backlash in Myanmar, human rights practice as a way of life allows LGBT rights activists within and beyond Burmese territory to hold on to cyclical understandings of the temporal turns and transformative returns of juristocratic reckonings beyond formal law. By contrast, the *longue durée* of quarantine laws in Singapore has amalgamated a form of "governing through contagion" that fuses centralization and normalization in ways that produce fragmented temporal spaces of inter- and disconnections.

In Matthew Canfield's chapter, by contrast, the domains of reconceptualization are transnational. His case study builds on his long-term research with different movements for "food sovereignty" that have developed categories of rights, such as the right to food, beyond the boundaries of existing international human rights law. As Canfield argues, the articulation of the putative right to food represents a critique of the incapacities of international law to guarantee adequate food provision on a global scale while at the same time reaffirming the underlying value of rights themselves as a grammar of justice-seeking. This way, the counter-mobilization of the food sovereignty movement can be seen as a form of alter-legal reckoning, in which its critique of stakeholder capitalism pushes toward an expanded understanding, and lived reality, of postliberal democracy.

Mark Goodale's chapter moves from case studies of different instances of reconceptualization to a more theoretical and autocritical perspective. Returning to his recently published book, which examines the consequences of reinventing human rights for the future of social, political, and economic transformation, he extends his analysis to the question of juristocratic reckoning while also responding to initial questions about key concepts such as "translocality," rights pluralism, and dejuridification. Like the chapters of Chua and Canfield, Goodale's reflects on the ways in which reckoning with law in excess can – and, as he argues, *should* – take paralegal forms, given that more radical alternatives, often grounded in revolutionary methodologies, suffer from their own clear limitations, their own inadequacies and potential for failure.

In her chapter, Arzoo Osanloo examines the ways in which the practice of mercy-seeking within the Iranian criminal justice system has emerged as a surprising example of reckoning, not with the failures of law, but with its harsh rigor and entrenchment of the rule of an absolute sovereign. As she explains, Iran's legal system is shaped by a particular interpretation of Islamic law, which mandates a series of severe punishments for a wide range of infractions. In this sense, Iran's theocratic form of government is also a religious juristocracy, which reinforces the more general argument that juristocracy must be understood beyond either liberal legality or certain iconic examples. Yet if the practice of mercy in Iran represents a reconceptualization that pushes the boundaries of law, one in which victims can subvert criminal sentences by forgiving the perpetrators, it is also a practice that has ambiguous implications for social justice more generally. As Osanloo argues, similar dynamics are at play in unexpected places. Humanitarianism reveals itself to be rooted in similar appeals for mercy and care by distant others, thereby reproducing the very systems that modern human rights were intended to eradicate in favor of approaches ostensibly founded on principles of egalitarianism and respect for human dignity. In this way, the rise of mercy-seeking has the capacity to replace potential social and political transformation with supplication and, as she puts it, reduce everyone in society to a potential supplicant rather than a claimant.

Agathe Mora's chapter allows us to refine even further our understanding of the reconceptualization of law as one among many forms of juristocratic reckoning. However, unlike the different case studies in the volume in which the creative reimagining or reinvention of law is undertaken in order to increase the chances for social or political transformation, here it serves a quite different purpose: the technical fulfillment of an international mandate without concern for whether or not justice or reparation is actually achieved. Mora conducted research with the Kosovo Property Agency (KPA), a transitional justice mechanism established by the United Nations to supposedly resolve property disputes in the aftermath of the armed conflict in Kosovo in the late 1990s. As her chapters shows, the personnel responsible for enacting this mandate transformed the KPA into a bureaucratic instrument that "law-washed" complicated disputes in part as a critique of international law – especially human rights law – and its ability to truly resolve underlying social and political conflicts.

If reconceptualization-as-reckoning in Kosovo is a complicated response to the incapacities of law that reflects deep disenchantment combined with a kind of Weberian surrender to the imperatives of bureaucratic rationality, Kamari Clarke's chapter examines this category of juristocratic reckoning at its widest and, arguably, most ambitious scope. Her research explores different ways in which communities in Nigeria reckon with the failures and inadequacies of law, not only *as law*, but as both instrument and symbol of (neo-)colonial imposition. As she argues, the forces of international law, including the International Criminal Court (ICC), have had a particular impact within the political histories of contemporary postcolonial Africa. International criminal justice and human rights law have been promoted as universal – and thus ahistorical – tools for an equally abstracted conception of justice-seeking. Yet as Clarke's chapter demonstrates, the widespread resistance by communities in Nigeria to the mechanisms and power of international law is coupled with the development of a range of alternatives, including "moral vigilantism" anchored in religion and the use of forensic technologies by communities as form of local empowerment.

Finally, a smaller grouping of chapters in the volume illuminates yet another form of reckoning, one that does not reject the inadequacies of law in excess but, rather, seeks precisely to harness the power of juristocracy as an unconventional weapon of the weak, that is, as a strategy of resistance. These *juristocracies against the state* are similar to a wider phenomenon that Eckert et al. (2012) described as "law against the state," except that this taxonomic form of reckoning takes place in moments in which the state is in crisis, including crisis associated with the failure of state law itself. Such juristocratic reckonings thus often creatively engage with, resist, and transform those contemporaneous states of juristocracy that constitute the first taxonomic category (see above).

In her chapter, Penelope Anthias unpacks the complicated landscape of social and political mobilization in a region of Bolivia that is at the center of state-controlled hydrocarbon production. As she argues, the Bolivian state has failed to reconcile its ideological commitment to sustainability, as inscribed into its post-neoliberal plurinational Constitution of 2009, with its ever-expanding reliance on resource extractivism. Local communities respond to this failure – which is expressed in both legal and political terms – by mobilizing various forms of resistance, including a continued insistence on and claiming of rights. She demonstrates that community activists deploy law and rights not as construed by (neo-)liberal elites, but rather as part of a strategy of discursive and material struggle by those who have been affected most strongly by racialized dispossession. Without necessarily prioritizing legal processes over more disruptive forms of protest, Indigenous and peasant communities on extractive frontiers continue to reckon from below with the possibilities and limitations of law and rights. They do so, as Anthias shows, by reimagining themselves as guardians of the 2009 Constitution, guardians who must protect its vision even *against* the state. As custodians of a juristocratic settlement achieved through popular mobilization, they are able to denounce the state for violating the promises of the 2009 Constitution through its relations with transnational extractive corporations. Importantly, even if currently failing to bring about justice through the law, legal cases are still regarded as relevant in generating a legal record to be taken up again in the future under more ideal juristocratic conditions.

Finally, in her chapter on Indigenous legalities in Guatemala, Rachel Sieder examines yet another side of juristocracies against the state. As she explains, the development of Indigenous rights processes in the late twentieth century, especially in Latin America, can be understood as another case of iconic indexicality, in which the elevation of law was supposed to usher in a new era of postcolonial empowerment for Indigenous peoples who had suffered from centuries of colonial and neocolonial violence. However, Indigenous communities have realized that the promise of juristocratic justice is no match for a range of systemic barriers, including endemic racism, institutional bias, and economic and territorial dispossession. While Indigenous peoples successfully mobilized human rights during the first decades of the twenty-first century, the intensification of extractive industries accelerated state capture by corrupt elites and criminal networks, leading to a backlash of authoritarian regression, which stalled or reversed earlier legal victories.

Yet as the case study shows, Indigenous communities in Guatemala do not turn against the law. Instead, they mobilize along parallel tracks, including the use of state-sanctioned Indigenous rights law – however flawed – *and* local justice mechanisms "premised on alternative lifeworlds," as Sieder puts it. She urges us to view such persistent juristocracies against the state – continuously mobilizing the law amongst other horizons of justice even though the prospects of legal victory are bleak – in the *longue durée*. Within layered histories of repeated engagements with hegemonic forms of law since the colonial period, the current ebbs and flows in the dialectics of juristocratic reckoning are nothing new. As Sieder explains, the legal defense of Indigenous lands by Mayan activists still holds emancipatory potential, but only when viewed in the longer term, given that "legal engagements and framings form part of much wider and long-run processes of territorial defense, community organization, and subject formation."

I.4 (No) Conclusion: Moments, Momentums, and Mobilizations in the Living Archives of Law

The case studies assembled in this volume powerfully demonstrate, in all their complexity, diversity, and also divergence, that while the turn to law is never the only, and hardly ever an uncontested, option, the law does gain differential traction, comparatively speaking, in various places and within different contexts *over time*. This last point – the temporality of juristocracy – deserves more attention, since viewing the case studies through their various temporalities reinforces the wider point that dialectics of reckoning must be understood through their empirical and historical heterogeneities rather than as exemplars of an abstracted sociolegal category.

To begin with, and as several chapters illustrate quite clearly, in many settings there are, or have been, identifiable *moments* in which the law has been invested with unusual and peculiar weight and potentiality. Whether experienced more individually as a meaningful moment of powerful subject (re)formation, as with human rights as a way of life among Burmese LGBT activists, or celebrated and hailed more collectively as a new era of transformative constitutionalism or Indigenous rights, the phenomenology of legal times is nonlinear and multiple, subject to rhythms and flows, and at times shot through with memorable instances of iconic intensity and excessive significance (see also Chua 2021). While such moments of intensified juristocracy are often invested with popular hopes for transformative improvements through the law, various chapters in the volume demonstrate that such heightened and condensed legal times may also be closely tied to the authoritarian and repressive recourse to the law – in India, Guatemala, Bolivia, and beyond.

Demands and expectations of the law that overflow its more conventional and unremarkable carrying capacity may also envision its own time as one of duration. This can be seen in the enduring logic of mercy undergirding both humanitarianism and criminal prosecution in Iran, or as one of an "in-between," driven by a "logic of exception" animating the transitology of transitional justice (Anders & Zenker 2014), as in Kosovo. As the volume's chapters reveal in different ways, this sense of being right in the midst of intense legal time also gives way, at some point, to a sense of lagging behind, of being too late or after the fact, as the *kairos* – the right and opportune moment for legal engagements – has passed. This may be the case because the political climate changes when an authoritarian juristocratic backlash follows a phase of *right*-ful (or even *righteous*) hope, as in Myanmar, or because of growing popular disillusionment with law's unfulfilled promises, as in South Africa. This may also occur because the veneer of law's promises of equality, egalitarianism, and justice start to crumble, revealing (neo-)colonial forces that have been at work all along, as in Nigeria.

These descriptions of legal temporalities hint at a second observation, namely, that the timing of juristocratic reckoning is not simply sequential, a series of momentary snapshots confined to more or less momentous moments. Instead, drawing metaphorically on mechanics in physics, juristocratic moments also have differential *momentums*: they become plotted into different, and often conflicting, imaginations regarding the relative weight of rights and legal provisions and their varying capacities to *matter*, in the here and now, but also for the future. In this way, the times and timing of juristocratic dialectics must also be understood as a function of *directionality*.

Several contributions grapple directly with the different momentums of juristocratic reckoning and their complicated directions – future or otherwise. For example, Shoshan shows how housing activists in Berlin are fully aware that their movement takes shape long after the moment of constitutional "socialization" in Germany, yet they nevertheless attempt to give the afterlives of a less proprietary utopia new momentum. Canfield interrogates the practices of food activists who work toward maintaining the momentum for transformed understandings of food rights beyond the neoliberal imagination. Goodale invites us to reinvent human rights in the full awareness that the celebrated momentum of human rights, as we know them, has passed. Zenker sees potential for a more open and hard-headed "transformational triage" after the moment and momentum of South Africa's iconic indexicality. Clarke engages the potential end-times of law and its state form in asking what might lie beyond when people increasingly place their hopes in the more literal afterlives of religious belief, rather than engaging with the this-worldly afterlives of law.

Drawing on the physical imagery of momentum is helpful in highlighting the fact that the law differs, over time, in its capacity to carry the weight of heightened expectation and to signal the direction to which such legal movements become oriented, whether transitioning into or rather away from legal apotheosis. This physical imagery is also useful because it reminds us that how a specific momentum is perceived crucially depends on the frame of reference. This is where the analogy between physical momentum, at least in its classical-mechanic rendition, and juristocratic momentum, reaches its limits. While we assert that the notion of a dialectics of juristocratic reckoning is a useful analytic, the question of which moments and momentums prevail with regard to transformative practices, legal or otherwise, will always remain open and contestable. In other words, the subsumption of concrete empirical situations, practices, and events as viewed through a dialectics of reckoning will vary based on divergent perspectives, contextualizing narratives, and shifting scales of differing temporal horizons.

Whether the dormant provision of Germany's postwar Constitution for "socializing" property remains in post-juristocratic ruins as a paralyzing symbol of law's past failures, or whether it is the pre-juristocratic genie in the bottle that critics of private property regimes have been longing for all along, is a question with multiple possible answers and futures. And Chua's analysis of narratives of legalities and the fate of Burmese LGBT activists is also particularly pertinent here, as she compellingly mobilizes multiple temporalities in diverse and ongoing reckonings in an attempt to make sense of the contemporary moment of authoritarian backlash in Myanmar. In short, how the differing logics and stages of juristocratic reckoning come to play out in practice at different moments in time is profoundly shaped by the forms of *mobilizations* that are effectively put to work by various actors.

The two case studies from Bolivia and Guatemala discussed above under the taxonomy of juristocracies against the state explicitly highlight the various temporal horizons that Indigenous activists and lawyers mobilize in their current struggles over the protection of their lands. Apart from building their cases for potential litigation, these legal movements serve broader and longer-term goals. As Anthias and Sieder show, these juristocratic politics also help to translate alternative land ontologies and counter-hegemonic histories of land rights into the language of law so that they will be entered into the records of the state. In so doing, they actually work to *rebuild the record* of colonial and postcolonial racialized dispossession, which has consequences for future legal activism and offers at least the potential for some form of emancipation through the recrafted legal narratives that a rebuilt record affords.

More broadly, these processes of rebuilding the record speak to what Ann Stoler has analyzed as two distinct meanings of *the archive*, which are nevertheless blurred in practice: "the archive" as a concrete "body of documents and the institutions that house them"; and "the Archive" as "a metaphoric invocation for any corpus of selective collections and the longings that the acquisitive quests for the primary, originary, and untouched entail" (Stoler 2009: 45). The latter meaning is indebted to Michel Foucault's observation in *The Archaeology of Knowledge* that "the archive" – rather than primarily referring to a body of documents and the institutions that house them – "is the law of what can be said, the system that governs the appearance of statements as unique events" (Stoler 2002: 145), a historical a priori characterizing specific epistemes. Juristocratic reckonings in Latin America and beyond can thus be seen as simultaneously engaging with, and thereby seemingly succumbing to, the logics of the post/colonial archive, *while at the same time* challenging and reinscribing its "law of what can be said" with unruly meanings that redirect the historical a priori toward alternative futures.

If we take seriously the observation that how the dialectics of juristocratic reckoning become instantiated in concrete contexts, and are thus made socially consequential, is also profoundly shaped by the ways in which these settings are framed and *narrated* – that is, how social times become imbued with particular renditions of legal times (Beynon-Jones & Grabham 2019) – we also need to reflect on our own roles as scholars in creating and narrating moments of juristocratic reckoning. In other words, we must also reckon with "reckoning with law in excess" as a framing device for making sense of the comparative and relative rise and fall of law, in different settings and at various moments in time.

This brings us back to the starting point of both this Introduction and the volume itself: namely, our intuition that Hirschl's original framing of the early post-cold war order in terms of "juristocracy" did rightly identify an iconic moment and momentum that centered on the historic place of legal apotheosis, while missing (out on) its own indexicality in referencing a much broader transhistorical phenomenon. At the same time, current debates about the demise of the rule of law, debates that are themselves skewed by geopolitical and intellectual power inequalities, offers us yet another moment in which to think through the dialectics of juristocratic reckoning, yet this time in a way that acknowledges its own iconic indexicality.

In observing both the analytical utility of the framework of juristocratic reckoning and the fact that the search for empirical evidence of specific examples will often yield inconclusive or ambiguous results, we note that "reckoning with law in excess" may also function as a relational antidote against renditions of particular moments, momentums, and mobilizations in *any* archive of law that are too definitive, too self-assured. Instead, by conceiving of these archives as living and multiple, constantly in the making by multiple actors with different purposes, we acknowledge that both the many lives of law, and the framework developed in this volume, must also be understood as similarly inconclusive, similarly open to multiple interpretations, directions, and futures.

References Cited

Agathangelou, Anna M. 2017. Decolonial Theory and the Question of Palestine. *Journal of Holy Land and Palestine Studies* 16(1): 1–17.

2019. Border(ing) Work: Theorizing Border Work and the Syrian Refugee Crisis. *Geopolitics* 24 (3): 634–654.

Allen, Susan Hannah and Amy Yuen. 2022. *Bargaining in the UN Security Council: Setting the Global Agenda.* Oxford: Oxford University Press.

An-Na'im, Abdullahi Ahmed. 2016. The Spirit of Laws Is Not Universal: Alternatives to the Enforcement Paradigm for Human Rights. *Tilburg Law Review* 21 (2): 255–274.

Anders, Gerhard and Olaf Zenker. 2014. Transition and Justice: An Introduction. *Development and Change* 45 (3): 395–414.

Beynon-Jones, Siân M. and Emily Grabham, eds. 2019. *Law and Time.* Abingdon: Routledge.

Bishr, Mohamed and Werner Kuhn. 2007. Geospatial Information Bottom-Up: A Matter of Trust and Semantics. In S. I. Fabrikant and M. Wachowicz, eds., *The European Information Society*. Berlin: Springer-Verlag, 365–387.

Célestine, Audrey and Nicolas Martin-Breteau. 2016. “Un mouvement, pas un moment”: Black Lives Matter et la reconfiguration des luttes minoritaires à l’ère Obama. *Politique américaine* 28 (2): 15–39.

Chua, Lynette J. 2021. Interregna: Time, Law, and Resistance. *Law & Social Inquiry* 46 (1): 268–291.

Clarke, Kamari Maxine. 2017. Rethinking Sovereignty through Hashtag Publics: The New Body Politics. *Cultural Anthropology* 32 (3): 359–366.

D’Souza, Radha. 2018. *What’s Wrong with Rights?: Social Movements, Law and Liberal Imaginations*. London: Pluto.

Di Giminiani, Piergiorgio. 2018. *Sentient Lands: Indigeneity, Property, and Political Imagination in Neoliberal Chile*. Tucson: University of Arizona Press.

Eckert, Julia, Brian Donahoe, Christian Strümpell and Zerrin Özlem Biner, eds. 2012. *Law against the State: Ethnographic Forays into Law’s Transformations*. Cambridge: Cambridge University Press.

Extinction Rebellion. 2023. Our Values. https://rebellion.global/about-us/.

Foucault, Michel. 2002[1969]. *Archaeology of Knowledge*. London: Routledge.

Goodale, Mark. 2007. The Power of Right(s): Tracking Empires of Law and New Modes of Social Resistance in Bolivia (and Elsewhere). In M. Goodale and S. E. Merry, eds., *The Practice of Human Rights: Tracking Law Between the Global and the Local*. Cambridge: Cambridge University Press, 130–162.

2022. *Reinventing Human Rights*. Stanford: Stanford University Press.

Hirschl, Ran. 2004. *Towards Juristocracy: The Origins and Consequences of the New Constitutionalism*. Cambridge, MA: Harvard University Press.

Hopgood, Stephen. 2013. The Endtimes of Human Rights. Ithica, NY: Cornell University Press.

Jasanoff, Sheila. 2011. *Reframing Rights: Bioconstitutionalism in the Genetic Age*. Cambridge, MA: MIT.

Klug, Heinz. 2000. *Constituting Democracy: Law, Globalism and South Africa’s Political Reconstruction*. Cambridge: Cambridge University Press.

2018. Decolonisation, Compensation and Constitutionalism: Land, Wealth and the Sustainability of Constitutionalism in Post-Apartheid South Africa. *South African Journal on Human Rights* 34 (3): 469–491.

Koskenniemi, Martti. 2011. What Use for Sovereignty Today? *Asian Journal of International Law* 1 (1): 61–70.

Krygier, Martin, Adam Czarnota and Wojciech Sadurski, eds. 2022. *Anti-Constitutional Populism*. Cambridge: Cambridge University Press.

Loughlin, Martin. 2022. *Against Constitutionalism*. Cambridge, MA: Harvard University Press.

Mattei, Ugo and Laura Nader. 2008. *Plunder: When the Rule of Law Is Illegal.* Malden, MA: Blackwell.

McNeilly, Kathryn. 2017. *Human Rights and Radical Social Transformation: Futurity, Alterity, Power.* London: Routledge.

Meierhenrich, Jens and Martin Loughlin, eds. 2021. *The Cambridge Companion to the Rule of Law.* Cambridge: Cambridge University Press.

Morales, Leticia. 2017. The Discontent of Social and Economic Rights. *Res Publica: A Journal of Moral, Legal and Political Philosophy* 24 (2): 257–272.

Moyn, Samuel. 2018. *Not Enough: Human Rights in an Unequal World.* Cambridge, MA: Belknap Press of Harvard University Press.

Nichols, Robert. 2020. *Theft Is Property: Dispossession and Critical Theory.* Durham: Duke University Press.

Niezen, Ronald. 2020. *#Human Rights: The Technologies and Politics of Justice Claims in Practice.* Stanford: Stanford University Press.

Pirie, Fernanda. 2021. *The Rule of Laws: A 4,000-Year Quest to Order the World.* New York: Basic Books.

Posner, Eric. 2014. The Twilight of Human Rights Law. Oxford: Oxford University Press.

Postero, Nancy and Eli Elinoff. 2019. Introduction: A Return to Politics. *Anthropological Theory* 19 (1): 3–28.

Ristovska, Sandra. 2016. Strategic Witnessing in an Age of Video Activism. *Media, Culture & Society* 38 (7): 1034–1047.

Roberts, Christopher N. J. 2015. *The Contentious History of the International Bill of Human Rights.* New York: Cambridge University Press.

Rubin, Jonah S. 2020. Exhuming Dead Persons: Forensic Science and the Making of Post-fascist Publics in Spain. *Cultural Anthropology* 35 (3): 345–373.

Schwöbel, Christine E. J. 2010. Organic Global Constitutionalism. *Leiden Journal of International Law* 23 (3): 529–554.

Sikkink, Kathryn. 2017. *Evidence for Hope: Making Human Rights Work in the 21st Century.* Princeton: Princeton University Press.

Slaughter, Steven. 2015. The G20's Role in Legitimating Global Capitalism: Beyond Crisis Diplomacy? *Contemporary Politics* 21 (4): 384–398.

Stark, Barbara. 2015. How the Age of Rights Became the New Gilded Age: From International Antidiscrimination Law to Global Inequality. *Columbia Human Rights Law Review* 47 (1): 151–197.

Stoler, Ann Laura. 2002. Colonial Archives and the Arts of Governance. *Archival Science* 2: 87–109.

2009. *Along the Archival Grain: Epistemic Anxieties and Colonial Common Sense.* Princeton: Princeton University Press.

Terretta, Meredith. 2012. "We Had Been Fooled into Thinking that the UN Watches over the Entire World": Human Rights, UN Trust Territories, and Africa's Decolonization. *Human Rights Quarterly* 34 (2): 329–360.

Tushnet, Mark and Bojan Bugarič. 2021. *Power to the People: Constitutionalism in the Age of Populism*. Oxford: Oxford University Press.

Vogelstein, Rachel B. and Meighan Stone. 2021. *Awakening: #MeToo and the Global Fight for Women's Rights*. New York: PublicAffairs.

Weeks, Sindiso Mnisi. 2022. South African Legal Culture and its Dis/ Empowerment Paradox. In M.-C. Foblets, M. Goodale, M. Sapignoli and O. Zenker, eds., *The Oxford Handbook of Law and Anthropology*. Oxford: Oxford University Press, 56–72.

Wilson, Richard. 2001. *The Politics of Truth and Reconciliation in South Africa: Legitimizing the Post-apartheid State*. Cambridge: Cambridge University Press.

Zenker, Olaf, Cherryl Walker and Zsa-Zsa Boggenpoel, eds. 2024. *Beyond Expropriation Without Compensation: Law, Land Reform and Redistributive Justice in South Africa*. Cambridge: Cambridge University Press.

1

Reckoning with Transformative Constitutionalism

Land Reform, Expropriation Without Compensation, and the Iconic Indexicality of Post-apartheid South Africa

OLAF ZENKER

1.1 Introduction: "Hi Mzansi, Have We Seen Justice?"

On January 7, 2022 Lindiwe Sisulu, then South African minister of tourism and high-profile politician of the ruling African National Congress (ANC), published an article in several national newspapers, entitled "Hi Mzansi, Have We Seen Justice?" Using "Mzansi" as a colloquial expression for South Africa, she rhetorically asked whether the nation had experienced justice since the first democratic election in 1994 marking the end of apartheid. Insisting that economic justice had not been achieved – especially the redistribution of land – she argued that the law had done little to really change anything. To the contrary, South Africa's "beautiful constitution" and "the rule of law" had merely functioned as "a palliative." Constituting "foreign belief systems," they required "mentally colonized Africans" in leadership positions and as interpreters of the law who, as "House Negroes," acted as their own oppressors. This, Sisulu claimed, was particularly the case "in the high echelons of our justice system," which needed an overhaul. Drawing an explicit parallel to the January 6, 2021 attack on the US Capitol (exactly one year earlier), Sisulu claimed that the situation was not very different from that in South Africa, seemingly implying that many people on both sides of the Atlantic did not really care for the law and were willing, if necessary, to break it. She ended by forcefully arguing:

> If the law does not sufficiently address the issue of the food fight, the law will fail, and inevitably it will play out in the streets. We have a neo-liberal constitution with foreign inspiration, but who are the interpreters? And where is the African value system of this constitution and the rule of law?

> If the law does not work for Africans in Africa, then what is the use of the rule of law? (Sisulu 2022a)

Commentators were quick to point out that Lindiwe Sisulu – long-term anti-apartheid activist and daughter of ANC legends Walter and Albertina Sisulu – had been a member of parliament since 1994. A long-standing member of the National Executive Committee (NEC) of the ANC, Sisulu started in government as deputy minister of home affairs, successively serving as minister of intelligence, defense, public service and administration, human settlements, international relations and cooperation, human settlements, water and sanitation, and finally, tourism. Thus, Sisulu was effectively criticizing the government she had been actively serving for several decades (Msimang 2022). Others suggested that Sisulu was preparing, yet again, to run for party presidency at the ANC National Conference in December 2022 (she indeed tried subsequently, but failed), with an eye to the South African general elections in 2024. She was hence mobilizing support within ANC's "Radical Economic Transformation (RET)" faction, still loyal to the ousted former President Jacob Zuma, against the more moderate faction around current President Cyril Ramaphosa. This take was nicely captured, for instance, in a Zapiro cartoon depicting this exchange as a "Game of Thrones 2024" sacrificing "the Constitution," "black judges," as well as the Acting Chief Justice Raymond "Zondo" in the battle against President Ramaphosa (see Figure 1.1). Others regarded all this merely as Sisulu's cynical ploy to distract from the upcoming "State Capture Reports" of the Commission of Enquiry chaired by the Acting Chief Justice Zondo, detailing the perpetrators and their deeds in South Africa's massive wave of high-level corruption (and likely also compromising herself).

Irrespective of the ultimate motives behind the various moves in this public exchange, the latter is indicative of a recent sea change in South African public debates on "the Constitution": While South Africa emerged as the poster child for liberal constitutionalism during the 1990s, in recent years the Constitution is increasingly seen as part of the problem, rather than the solution, of persisting inequalities. How has this change come about and what are the consequences for actually existing transformative constitutionalism, if the latter has to operate within an era increasingly disenchanted and disillusioned with "law's potential" (Dyzenhaus 1992)? This chapter sets out to provide some answers to these crucial questions of our contemporary moment in South Africa and beyond.

Figure 1.1 "Game of Thrones 2024."
Cartoon by Zapiro, *Daily Maverick* (January 22, 2022).

In order to do so, the chapter first outlines in Section 1.2 the unlikely emergence of strong constitutionalism during the South African transition to democracy during the 1990s, turning South Africa into an iconic case of "juristocracy" (Hirschl 2004), indexically operating as a metonymic exemplar for the proclaimed transformative potential of law at large. This effected a marked shift in the landscape of hegemonic discourses and public perceptions from a rhetoric of revolution to rights talk, entailing a perceptible judicialization of politics. Section 1.3 demonstrates how this process has played itself out in the field of post-apartheid land reform, in which the constitutional duty for a tripartite reform as enshrined in the property clause (Section 25) of the Constitution has ostensibly been processed under the rule of law in contradistinction to the contemporaneous extralegal land occupations in neighboring Zimbabwe. Yet the tide of public perception regarding the effectiveness of constitutionalism slowly started to turn after the first democratic decade, as sketched in Section 1.4. A significant increase in popular insurgencies through disruptive protests, wildcat strikes, as well as xenophobic violence came to coalesce with state-sanctioned violence, epitomized in the Marikana massacre in 2012, an increasingly populist rhetoric, and the multi-sited breakdown of numerous state functions under President Zuma's corrupt regime of "state capture," all jointly revealing spreading discontent with the new constitutional order. It is within this broader context that recent debates about an amendment of the Constitution allowing for "expropriation without compensation" should be seen. Section 1.5 charts the dynamics of this latest turn in South Africa's "anti-constitutional populism" (Krygier et al. 2022), pointing toward contestations around the need and effectiveness of such a constitutional amendment: While public hearings revealed enormous support for such an amendment in the hope of fast-tracking economic redistribution and social justice, many experts working in the fields of law, land reform, and redistributive justice do not see the Constitution as the main problem (while differing in their alternative solutions to persisting inequalities). Section 1.6 concludes with a reflection of this complex South African dialectic of juristocratic reckoning, evaluating the potentials and pitfalls of a continued project of transformative constitutionalism in an era in which South Africa's moment of iconic indexicality is deeply contested, if not coming to an end.

1.2 Post-apartheid Juristocracy: Transitioning from Revolution to Rights

The "negotiated revolution" (Waldmeir 1997) in South Africa in the early 1990s inaugurated a marked shift toward strong constitutionalism that also came to characterize this period at a global scale (Klug 2000). After the minority government had lifted the ban on the ANC, white elites and representatives of the black majority engaged for the first time in public. However, the initial negotiations for a democratic transition at the Convention for a Democratic South Africa (CODESA) collapsed in mid-1992, leading to escalating violence and mass upheaval. Bilateral negotiations in 1993 brought about agreement for a transition to democracy in two phases: first, the drafting of the 1993 Interim Constitution, which came into force in April 1994 with the first democratic elections; and second, the drafting of the final 1996 Constitution by the Constitutional Assembly and its approval by the Constitutional Court (Hirschl 2004: 28). This final Constitution adopted in 1996 comprises an extensive Bill of Rights (Sections 7–39), including substantial socioeconomic rights and constitutional obligations for far-reaching redistributive measures, and established an independent judiciary (including a strong Constitutional Court) under the auspices of a new constitutional, rather than parliamentary, supremacy (Klug 2000).

However, at the time it was far from obvious that the South African transition to post-apartheid would lead to a strong constitutional regime. In the context of the armed struggle and mass mobilization of the anti-apartheid movement during the 1980s under conditions of repressive states of emergency since 1985, widespread expectations on both sides envisioned or feared a radical revolution entailing, among others, nationalization of existing land holdings in line with a commitment to the 1955 Freedom Charter emphasizing socialization and redistribution, while marginalizing private property (Klug 2018: 472–478).

Yet neither the white minority regime nor the liberation movement were in a position to bring their stalemate to a conclusive end: the apartheid regime found it increasingly difficult to legitimate its rule under conditions of mass mobilization and growing international isolation, while the armed struggle of the ANC's military wing – *Umkhonto we Sizwe* (MK) – was increasingly drained of military support by the dissolving Soviet Union and deprived of its last Southern African base in Angola as part of the United Nations (UN) brokered independence deal for Namibia in 1990 (Klug 2018: 472–473). Under these conditions, constitutionalism increasingly emerged as a necessary compromise; moreover, it offered a viable strategy for containing profound political differences through constitutionally enshrining and thereby postponing political conflict to be resolved by future legislation and, if needed, by an impartial judiciary.

However, while these pragmatic factors explain how the parties got to the negotiating table, they do not account for the fact that the transition to electoral democracy under a strong Constitution would prove durable in the coming years. As Jens Meierhenrich (2008) argues, this was made possible by a deeply entrenched common legal culture on *both* sides of the negotiation table. This South African legal culture of a "legality of law" entailed shared assumptions about how to act through legal procedures, facilitating "the gradual construction of trust among adversaries, thus accelerating regime formation and government formation" (Meierhenrich 2008: 55).

This was so, as various observers have noted, because the apartheid regime, whatever else it was, was a regime of laws (Abel 1995). Put differently, the apartheid regime gave tremendous importance to "the rule of law," even if it rather operated as a "rule *by* law" (Abel 1995). Since the apartheid state carried out its repression and discrimination through the mechanism of law and simultaneously outlawed most political action, this strong emphasis on legality and alleged respect for the rule of law made it promising for some of the anti-apartheid struggle, especially since the 1980s, to shift to the legal battlefield as a form of "politics by other means" (Abel 1995: 12–14). Such legal activism was substantially limited, however, because parliament under apartheid was expressly supreme, unconstrained by a Bill of Rights, and to a great extent exempted from independent judicial review (Abel 1995: 3, 489, 540). Nevertheless, this situation still helped to reproduce a long-standing legal culture in South Africa that – as Meierhenrich argues – opened up a window of opportunity for the emergence of a strong constitutional order.

Within this emergent new order, addressing the economic legacies of apartheid through directly dispossessing the *ancien régime* was precluded. Instead, the new democratically elected government made use of more indirect means. Besides development plans that became increasingly adjusted to globalized neoliberal capitalism, these means have prominently included affirmative action through preferential procurement policies and black economic empowerment (BEE) as well as land reform (Klug 2018: 470–471).

From early on, such measures operating through law and under the new rule of law were envisioned and discussed as offering great potential for progressive struggles beyond law's more conventional roles of (mere) regulation and conflict resolution. David Dyzenhaus (1992) expressed early hopes about "law's potential" if the right kind of legal culture with a strong emphasis on the important role of jurisprudence was put in place. Karl Klare famously defined "transformative constitutionalism" as

> a long-term project of constitutional enactment, interpretation, and enforcement committed (not in isolation, of course, but in a historical context of conducive political developments) to transforming a country's political and social institutions and power relationships in a democratic, participatory, and egalitarian direction. Transformative constitutionalism connotes an enterprise of inducing large-scale social change through nonviolent political processes grounded in law. (Klare 1998: 150)

Having in mind "a transformation vast enough to be inadequately captured by the phrase 'reform,' but something short of or different from 'revolution' in any traditional sense of the word" – as Klare (1998: 150) went on to explain – hopes for transformative constitutionalism to deliver progressive outcomes and, ultimately, social justice were evidently high. As Theunis Roux (2013) argues, the Constitutional Court indeed emerged as a key institution during the first democratic decade, developing a robust and distinctly South African progressive jurisprudence about the purposes and possibilities of liberal constitutionalism with the idea of a caring and capable state at its center (see also Roux 2022).

Drucilla Cornell (2014) goes even further: Rather than seeing the transitional shift "from revolution to rights" (Robins 2008) as a failure of the liberation movement entailing a narrowing down of revolutionary possibilities, Cornell argues that, to the contrary, the changes in the nature of the law made South Africa's transition a truly revolutionary achievement. Recoupling law with radical changes fought for during the struggle against apartheid, the new constitutional order has allowed post-apartheid citizens for the first time to go to court in order to seek civil, political, and socioeconomic justice. However, this legal revolution, Cornell insists, has not simply emerged *sui generis*. It has to be continuously fought for and connected to localized idioms of justice, as she shows with regard to the prominent emergence of *ubuntu* – "humanity (toward others)" in isiZulu – as a guide for ethical living within much of post-apartheid jurisprudence. This process evolves both *formally* through the official creation of law within a rights-based constitutional framework and *informally* through extralegal actions of insurgent citizens fighting for justice, thus jointly pushing for a truly revolutionary constitutional transformation.

The historical events of the transition to democracy in South Africa as well as the prominent reading of this new order in terms of the progressive possibilities of a transformative constitutionalism thus ushered in a new era of "juristocracy," as Ran Hirschl (2004) has called it. Juristocracy, in Hirschl's rendition, deviates from a vision of democracy as majority rule governed predominantly by the principle of parliamentary sovereignty, in that

> minorities possess legal protections in the form of a written constitution, which even a democratically elected assembly cannot change. Under this [juristocratic] vision of democracy, a bill of rights is part of fundamental law, and judges who are removed from the pressures of partisan politics are responsible for enforcing those rights. (Hirschl 2004: 2)

This constitutionalization of rights and fortification of judicial review led to a new regime of constitutional supremacy and an active judiciary that Hirschl (2004: 3) defined as the hallmarks of "juristocracy." This hegemonic model of liberal democracy came to dominate post-apartheid South Africa for years to come and turned it into "a model for other transitional democracies" (Smith 2017: 124).

Two observations are relevant in this context that move the analysis of juristocracy beyond Hirschl's more confined usage of the term. First, while Hirschl concentrated on the *substantive* specificities of this new model of juristocratic democracy (that is, its insistence on the protected rule of independent judges through inalienable rights), its *formal* peculiarities got somewhat lost: namely, the excessive, almost messianic expectations that came to be vested in "the law" as *the* master modality for all societal transformation. It is this juristocratic reckoning with law *in excess*, its affective investment with seemingly eschatological possibilities to achieve the hitherto impossible, that arguably made South African transformative constitutionalism so special. At the same time, and this leads over to a closely related second observation, transformative constitutionalism in South Africa came to be seen not only as exceptional, but also as exemplary: As noted in the previous paragraph, South Africa turned into "a model for other transitional democracies" as it was increasingly celebrated also internationally as a paradigmatic case – an *icon* – *indexing* a redemptive reckoning with law as *the* tool for social transformation *tout court*. One prominent and emotionally charged domain in which this post-apartheid juristocratic reckoning has been clearly brought to bear in its full iconic indexicality is the contested field of state-driven land reform.

1.3 "Putting Land Rights in the Right Hands under the Rule of Law": Land as a Shifting Terrain for Transformative Constitutionalism

Against the backdrop of the iconic indexicality of the new Constitution, "internationally celebrated" (Roux 2022: 100) and widely regarded as one of the most progressive in the world, the South African government immediately embarked upon a massive land reform program in order to address the persisting racial inequalities in access to, and control of, land as well as the historical injustices on which these inequities have been based.

Aimed at "putting land rights in the right hands under the rule of law," as then Minister for Agriculture and Land Affairs Ms Lulama Xingwana aptly put it in 2007,[1] South African land reform has exemplified an ostensive belief in transformative constitutionalism as the preferable way to address and redress persisting landed inequalities. This insistence on the rule of law also needs to be seen in the specific context of

[1] In her Foreword to the *Annual Report 2006/2007* of the Commission on Restitution of Land Rights (2007: 4).

contemporaneous land policies in neighboring Zimbabwe. Upon Zimbabwean independence in 1980, the Lancaster House Agreement had restricted land reform for ten years in such a way that the new government could only obtain land on the basis of the "willing buyer, willing seller" principle. While the Zimbabwean legislature removed this limitation from its Constitution in 1990, the government, in practice, still continued following this principle afterwards. However, in the late 1990s the ruling Zimbabwe African National Union Patriotic Front (ZANU-PF) adopted more aggressive land acquisition policies beyond the rule of law when confronted with a serious electoral challenge. The shadow of Zimbabwe, with its subsequently collapsing economy, has loomed large in South African land reform debates ever since, explaining the long-term emphasis in government assurances of reforming South African lands exclusively under the rule of law (Klug 2018: 488–489).

Given the overall dynamics behind the emergence of post-apartheid juristocracy discussed above, it is hardly surprising that the mandate for future land reform ultimately became enshrined in the property clause (Section 25) of the final Constitution: A balanced constitutional protection of both existing property rights and the right to redress for race-based violations of past property rights emerged as a strategic compromise during the constitutional negotiations (Klug 2000: 124–136, 2018: 477–488; Walker, 2008: 50–69). Thus, Sections 25(1)–(2) establish that property may only be expropriated for a public purpose or in the public interest in terms of a law of general application and subject to compensation agreed to by those affected or decided by a court. Subsection 25(3) specifies that compensation must be "just and equitable," reflecting an equitable balance between the public interest and the interests of those affected, and mentions an open list of factors for the determination of just and equitable compensation (such as current use, the history of acquisition, market value, the history of state subsidies, and the purpose of expropriation).

Moreover, Sections 25(4)–(9) define explicit constitutional duties to bring about equitable access to all South Africa's natural resources, including a tripartite land reform program allowing for the *restitution* of former land rights, a more equitable access to land through land *redistribution*, and legally secure land tenure through statutory *tenure reform*. Notably, Section 25(8) exempts the state from the protective provisions of this property clause for land, water, and related reforms redressing past racial discrimination, provided that such exemption is in accordance with the limitations clause (Section 36(1)). The latter requires that rights in the Bill of Rights may be limited only to the extent that such limitation is reasonable and justifiable in an open and democratic society based on human dignity, equality, and freedom.

The ultimate emergence of these constitutional provisions for both property protection and substantive land reform was to a considerable extent shaped by the work of land activists and lawyers. These activists had met and cooperated during apartheid within a land network incorporating NGOs such as the Surplus People Project or the Transvaal Rural Action Committee (TRAC), as well as human rights lawyers working, for instance, for the Legal Resources Centre (LRC) or the Centre for Applied Legal Studies (CALS) at the University of the Witwatersrand Law School (Klug 2000: 128–129; Walker 2008: 59–64). Having been heavily involved in the struggle against forced removals under apartheid, some members of this network formed a Land Claims Working Group in 1991. This group had close connections with members of the ANC Land Commission as well as the ANC Constitutional Committee, involved in the constitutional negotiations at the World Trade Centre in Kempton Park. Members of the group succeeded in influencing negotiations to such an extent that both the constitutional duties for land reform and nonmarket factors in the determination of compensation for existing landowners ultimately became enshrined in the constitutional provisions pertaining to property (Klug 2000: 129–136; Walker 2008: 61).

It is interesting to note that several of those legal and nonlegal land activists, who had first fought apartheid through litigation and then profoundly shaped constitutional and statutory arrangements for future land rights and the emerging land reform program, subsequently became civil servants during Mandela's presidency (1994–99). During this time, the Department of Land Affairs under its minister Derek Hanekom was strongly characterized by a rights-based approach (James 2007: 34–41). A tripartite land reform program, addressing the above-mentioned constitutional duties for *land redistribution*, *land restitution*, and *tenure reform*, was established with a strong welfarist emphasis on benefitting the poor and landless (Lodge 2002: 74).

After the second democratic elections in 1999, the new government under President Thabo Mbeki prompted a significant policy reappraisal regarding land reform. Derek Hanekom, the white Afrikaner farmer, was replaced by Thoko Didiza as the new minister with an African middle-class background – as were many of Hanekom's English-speaking, white, middle-class, left-liberal high-rank officials (Lodge 2002: 74–79; James 2007: 39). Hence, in 1999 and 2000 many of these legal land activists again left the civil service (Walker 2008: 14). Many of them subsequently reverted to using the law against the state. Yet under the new juristocratic regime, the situation had changed quite fundamentally:

> Before 1994, the LRC – alongside the land NGOs – had used its legal muscle to challenge the apartheid state on its intent to shift the African population around the countryside. Now, after 1999, some of its members would be using that muscle in contests with the post-apartheid state. They would be doing so, specifically, by holding that state to the laws they had passed whilst briefly occupying positions and portfolios within it. (James, 2007: 37)

In other words: During the transitional negotiations legal land activists who had fought the apartheid state were centrally positioned to shape foundational constitutional provisions for both protected property rights, including land rights, and the constitutional duty for a substantive land reform. After the first democratic elections in 1994, the "developmental" post-apartheid state made possible by these provisions then constituted an ideal environment for many of these activists to put into practice, now as civil servants, their rights-based and pro-poor agenda. The compulsory constitutional provisions for land reform they themselves had helped to institute could now be further elaborated through a cluster of statutes that explicitly recognized more extensive rights. However, after 1999 under President Mbeki the political tide turned away from a rights-based, pro-poor agenda toward neoliberal policies focusing instead on a new class of black commercial farmers as well as toward an "African Renaissance," re-empowering chiefs at the expense of rural citizens-as-subjects. Hence, since the 2000s, many legal land activists have engaged these shifts toward neoliberalism and neotraditionalism through various means provided by transformative constitutionalism, including consultancy and policy advice, parliamentary submissions, public statements (often based on research), as well as public interest litigation.

This can be briefly illustrated with regard to each of the three legs of land reform: Concerning *tenure reform*, legal land activists successfully worked toward a constitutional challenge of the Communal Land Rights Act (2004) which was struck down by the Constitutional Court in 2010. While the Act was declared invalid due to procedural mistakes, activists had additionally argued that the quasi-judicial rights of the minster to determine relevant "communities" as well as the discretion of traditional councils without downward accountability mechanisms put the tenure of communities at risk (Claassens & Cousins 2008; Zenker 2012). A new

Communal Land Tenure Bill (BX-2017) that was finally introduced in 2017 is still undergoing the legislative process.

Land restitution also witnessed a landmark case of cause lawyering: While the Restitution of Land Rights Act (1994) had originally provided only for the official lodgement of claims before December 31, 1998, President Zuma announced during his 2013 State of the Nation Address that the government would reopen the process of registering land claims. On June 29, 2014 he signed the Restitution of Land Rights Amendment Act (2014), which reopened the lodgement period and extended it until June 30, 2019. However, legal land activists were again crucial in supporting a constitutional challenge of the Restitution of Land Rights Amendment Act. On July 28, 2016 the Act was declared invalid by the Constitutional Court from the date of the judgment – (again) because of its improper procedural enactment (Zenker 2018).

Finally, with regard to *land redistribution* activists have mostly concentrated on policy advice, legal consultancy, and public statements – given that parliament, so far, has failed to enact comprehensive legislation enabling citizens to gain equitable access to land. This failure has led to the state relying on a discretionary, unclear, and haphazard application of policies, often producing contradictory outcomes. Prominent examples of such critical activist involvements include participation in the "High-Level Panel on the Assessment of Key Legislation and the Acceleration of Fundamental Change (HLP)," chaired by former President Kgalema Motlanthe, as well as the "Presidential Advisory Panel on Land Reform and Agriculture (PAPLRA)," appointed by President Cyril Ramaphosa, which published their reports with detailed recommendations for land reform improvements in 2017 and 2019, respectively.[2]

Looking back, what becomes evident in the field of post-apartheid land reform is the confident centrality that has been afforded to "the law" as the dominant modality through which to conceive, construct, criticize, or contest specific reform measures with the intention to profoundly transform South African society. However, over the past decade growing criticisms of the limited impact and slow pace of South African juristocracy in general and of law-based land reform in particular have

[2] See The High Level Panel on the Assessment of Key Legislation and the Acceleration of Fundamental Change (HLP) (2017) and The Presidential Advisory Panel on Land Reform and Agriculture (PAPLRA) (2019).

substantially altered public discourse, revealing more complex and ambiguous dialectics of juristocratic reckoning at play.

1.4 Insurgent Democracy: Transformative Constitutionalism and Its Discontents

Since the end of apartheid, transformative constitutionalism has evidently made some progress toward more social justice in general as well as toward land redistribution and more tenure security in particular. Nevertheless, popular expectations for substantive and meaningful transformation have clearly not been met (Seekings & Nattrass 2015; Leibbrandt & Pabón 2021). Thus, the combined progress of land restitution and redistribution in 2019 still amounted to under 10 percent of all commercial land, compared to the transfer target of 30 percent that the government had set itself (PAPLRA 2019: 12). Constant delays and shifting deadlines have also characterized the land restitution program (Zenker 2015). Moreover, despite some attempts at protecting informal land rights through various statutory measures, in the absence of an encompassing Communal Land Tenure Act secure rights to land are still the preserve of a small South African minority. Under conditions of land administration failures, corruption, and ineptitude, limited production and post-settlement support, lack of coordination between government departments, and only inadequate evidence on the livelihood impacts, land reform under transformative constitutionalism hardly seems a success story (PAPLRA 2019: 12–13).

Beyond land, the ANC government early on identified a range of plans and policies designed to address racialized inequalities and tackle widespread poverty. Various service delivery and infrastructural targets were set through development plans such as the 1994 Reconstruction and Development Programme (RDP) and its more neoliberal successor, the Growth, Employment, and Redistribution strategy (GEAR). These included a major rollout of low-income housing projects and the provision of free basic services (water, electricity) for households falling below certain income thresholds.[3] Affirmative action measures such as preferential state procurement and various black economic empowerment (BEE) policies have also shifted resources to (some sections of) the black majority. Moreover, social grants have been progressively offered to

[3] For a comprehensive discussion of service delivery, see Palmer, Moodley, and Parnell (2017).

vulnerable groups, including children, and extended during the recent COVID-19 pandemic. This has clearly helped in denting poverty. However, in light of the dramatic decrease of formal employment in the new millennium as well as the dwindling economy in the wake of the global recession of 2008, the extending system of social grants, more public services, and some ownership of assets have merely ameliorated the simultaneously growing inequality of earnings (Leibbrandt & Pabón 2021: 177, 179, 188). In other words: Despite state interventions and relative improvements the South African Gini coefficient measuring income inequalities has remained relatively stable at around 0.65–0.67 between 2006 and 2015 in the context of a worsening job-scarce economy, ensuring that "South Africa remains one of the most unequal societies in the world" (Leibbrandt & Pabón 2021: 175–176).

As Trevor Ngwane (2019) dryly observes, if we take apartheid society as the benchmark, then everything has improved; but if the aspirations and dreams of the liberation struggle are used as a touchstone, "then to say the ANC has failed is to speak truth to power" (Ngwane 2019: 238). Theunis Roux highlights how persistent inequalities have weakened "public attachment to the ideal of liberal constitutionalism in South Africa" (Roux 2022: 99). Joel Modiri aptly summarizes the conundrums of transformative constitutionalism that have become ever more present, and pressing, in recent years:

> Two decades since the enactment of the present constitution, problems of inequality, poverty, violence and social exclusion persist stubbornly along racial lines, and much of the optimism of the early 1990s concerning the promises of new legal and political order has dissipated . . . The durability and endurance of "past" inequalities and injustices illustrate that the "new South Africa" – lauded as a "miracle nation" with the "best constitution in the world" – can no longer be regarded as an unqualified success. (Modiri, 2018: 295)

Not that dissatisfaction with, and critique of, transformative constitutionalism is only a recent phenomenon: Critical accounts of the failure of the liberation struggle as a "revolution deferred" (Murray 1994) as well as of the economic and social consequences of the negotiated transition emerged early on, pointing to the "limits to change" within the political economy of transition (Marais 1998). Hirschl's own account of "juristocracy" was, of course, also intended as a critique of the constitutionalization of rights which he saw as a means through which threatened elites appropriate the political process and thereby prevent, rather than enable, more social justice (Hirschl 2004: 12, 218). Seen in this light, the

Figure 1.2 "A Strong Constitution,"
Cartoon by Dr Jack & Curtis, *Daily Maverick* (December 10, 2021).

globally increased "fetishism of the law" and the judicialization of formerly political protest, in the course of which "class struggles" metamorphosed into "class actions" (Comaroff & Comaroff 2006: 22, 27) appeared as worrying from early on.

Yet despite such ongoing critiques, transformative constitutionalism, as a discursive formation, still managed for quite some time to uphold its hegemonic status. Only in recent years have public references to the "Strong Constitution" in an ironic, if not cynical key become more frequent, highlighting its inefficacy in view of "all the challenges" confronting South Africa (see Figure 1.2).

In order to develop a deeper sense of the growing dissatisfaction and disillusionment with post-apartheid juristocracy, a closer look at various forms of insurgent expressions is instructive. To begin with, the rates of public protests have substantially increased over the past decades. As Carin Runciman and colleagues observe on the basis of police-recorded protests, between 2004 and 2012 protests classified as "peaceful" increased by 104 percent, whereas those classified as "unrest" increased by 329 percent (Runciman et al. 2016: 36). Thereafter, there has been a steady increase in the total number of crowd-related incidents, but the rise is far more marked with "unrest-related" than "peaceful" incidents (Runciman et al. 2016: 39). Between 1997 and 2013, labor protests were the most common (about 46 percent), followed by community protests with about 22 percent of the total (Runciman et al. 2016: 5). The latter – often also called "service delivery protests" – can be interpreted as a "rebellion of the poor" (Alexander 2010), expressing anger about the insufficient provision of public goods: for example, water, sanitation, waste collection, electricity, education, and public health.[4] Trevor Ngwane (2019: 230) refers to such practices as "insurgent democracy." Through often violently disrupting the normal functioning and ideological assumptions of the existing social order, such insurgency allows us, he argues, to "focus critically on the fundamental limitations of liberal democracy in South Africa from the point of view of the restless masses" (Ngwane 2019: 230).

Labor protests, even more common than community protests (see above), constitute another area where "insurgent citizens" (Brown 2015) have been fighting for their rights, especially in the context of wildcat strikes. South African trade unions had built their power during the anti-apartheid struggle, leading to the tripartite alliance between the ANC, the South African Communist Party (SACP), and the Congress of South African Trade Unions (COSATU) as a hegemonic bloc in post-apartheid times. Yet this intimate relationship has increasingly detached union leaders from their workers' constituency, seemingly focusing primarily on their own upward mobility and personal investment opportunities. Feeling disowned by their own unions, dissatisfied workers have resorted to wildcat strikes. These actions also lay behind the Marikana massacre in 2012, when workers struck over pay and living conditions at the Lonmin-owned platinum mine at Marikana in Northwest Province against the wishes of their union, the National Union of Mineworkers (NUM), a COSATU affiliate. On August 16, 2012 police fired live rounds into a crowd of striking mineworkers, killing thirty-six and injuring seventy-eight others. These killings immediately evoked comparisons to massacres committed by the apartheid state. However, this time violence was committed by a multiracial police force serving a democratic state,

[4] A prominent example of such protests consists in #FeesMustFall, a social movement of university students in 2015–16 campaigning for affordable university education for all (see Booysen 2016).

which immediately turned Marikana into a deeply troubling signal event of the post-apartheid order (Sinwell & Mbatha 2016).

While community protests and workers' strikes are amenable to a reading along the lines proposed by Drucilla Cornell (see Section 1.2), namely as insurgent, sometimes extralegal events progressively pushing the boundaries of the transformative revolution, the situation is more complicated with regard to the unprecedented wave of intense xenophobic violence in 2008; during two weeks in May more than 60 people were killed, 700 wounded, and 100,000 displaced, with foreign-owned shops and homes being demolished (Landau 2010: 213–214). Given that most victims were African noncitizens, officially categorized as such by the state, some have argued that "the state was implicated in xenophobic attitudes" (Brown 2015: 70); yet ordinary citizens were, of course, immediately involved, claiming that foreigners were "stealing 'our freedom'" (Klotz 2013: 213). Some argue that under conditions of dramatically increased unemployment and inequality, xenophobic violence – that returned in a second wave in 2015 – has functioned as a social commentary on the profound disjuncture between the expansive promise of constitutional rights and their highly uneven fulfilment in practice. Drawing an analogy to Grigory Potemkin who built real villages in the Crimea during the eighteenth century, but simultaneously papered over their highly unequal spread, Stuart Woolman and Michael Bishop thus speak of a "Potemkin Constitution":

> We have a Potemkin Constitution because ... many of our new institutions and new constitutional doctrines are very *real* and a marvel to behold. At the same time, the root causes of the [xenophobic] riots of 2008 can be traced to a failure ... to translate the promise of South Africa's liberation into a substantially better life for the majority of South Africans. (Woolman & Bishop, 2013: 2–3, original emphasis)

Another extralegal practice profoundly challenging and undermining the rule of law in South Africa for more than a decade has consisted in excessive corruption under the presidency of Jacob Zuma (2009–18). Commonly referred to by the label "state capture" – named after the highly critical report "State of Capture" published in October 2016 by the Office of the Public Protector Thuli Madonsela, marking the beginning of the end of Zuma's reign – it has comprised an extensive network of high-ranking politicians and related business partners engaged in "the manipulation of state organs for self-enrichment purposes" (Ngwane

2019: 229). An earlier report by the same public protector had already revealed the extent to which Zuma had used state funds to refurbish his rural homestead at Nkandla in KwaZulu-Natal Province. Brought before the Constitutional Court, the latter found both parliament and the president to be in breach of their constitutional obligations, condemned the president's behavior, and ordered repayment of all illegitimate expenditure (Roux 2022: 111).

Since the replacement of Jacob Zuma by Cyril Ramaphosa – first as president of the ANC at the party's National Conference in December 2017, and then in early 2018 as the president of South Africa – Ramaphosa has attempted to repair the numerous constitutional institutions incapacitated during Zuma's reign. However, with the Zuma faction powerfully reorganized under the banner of "Radical Economic Transformation (RET)" and still holding substantial power in the party's National Executive Committee (NEC), Ramaphosa has not had sufficient support within the ANC to do so effectively (Roux 2022: 108–112). However, in his attempt at undoing this "state of capture" Ramaphosa was supported by the work of the official Commission of Inquiry chaired by Judge Zondo which investigated between 2018 and 2022 the corruption detailed in the public protector's "State of Capture" report.[5]

In a way, the steadfast work of the public protector, the Constitutional Court, President Ramaphosa as well as the Zondo Commission can be seen as signs of a still functioning and resilient constitutional order, of juristocracy at work. Yet Ramaphosa's difficulties within his own party to effectively eradicate corruption may sound a note of caution, pointing toward a growing popular discontent with the law: When Zuma appeared reluctant to cooperate with the Zondo Commission throughout 2020–21 and repeatedly failed to appear before it despite court orders directing him to do so, the Constitutional Court sentenced him to fifteen months' imprisonment for contempt of court on June 29, 2021. However, the subsequent imprisonment of Zuma on July 7, 2021 sparked a massive wave of civil unrest, rioting, and looting within KwaZulu-Natal and Gauteng Provinces – the "Zuma unrest" – that lasted until July 18, 2021 (Hunter, Wicks & Singh 2021). Whether or not these violent forms of extralegal insurgency can still be seen as part of "the struggle for constitutional transformation" (Cornell 2014) remains an open question,

[5] For an analysis of how and why state capture happened, see Buthelezi and Vale (2023).

shimmering in and out of focus within an increasingly complex and ambiguous dynamic of juristocratic reckoning.

1.5 Expropriation Without Compensation: Within and beyond the Rule of Law

The most prominent, explicit, and pervasive expression in recent years of widespread perceptions that transformative constitutionalism in general, and land reform in particular, have fallen short of their promises to bring about substantive redistributive justice has consisted in extensive public controversies surrounding "expropriation without compensation." Dominating South African public discourse and the popular imagination since early 2018, the idea of expropriating land for redistributive purposes without paying any compensation first appeared as a serious option in December 2017. At the time, the ANC declared at its National Conference that "expropriation of land without compensation" should be one of the key mechanisms available to government, as long as it did not threaten agricultural production, food security, and economic investment (ANC 2017: 11). As mentioned before, this was the National Conference during which the Zuma faction lost against the more moderate faction around Cyril Ramaphosa, when the latter – rather than Nkosazana Dlamini-Zuma, the preferred candidate of the more "Radical Economic Transformation (RET)" faction – was elected with a narrow majority as the new ANC president. It was widely perceived at the time that the inclusion of "expropriation without compensation" into the conference resolutions served as a compromise and partial victory of the RET faction, with only lukewarm support from Ramaphosa himself.

In fact, the idea of expropriation without compensation had already been fervently advanced by the left-populist party Economic Freedom Fighters (EFF) founded in 2013 by Julius Malema – the charismatic but highly controversial former president of the ANC Youth League (ANCYL) who had been expelled from the ANC in 2012 because of repeated insubordination. Increasing its support base at every election, the EFF established already in 2014 that "[e]xpropriation of South Africa's land without compensation for equal redistribution in use" is one of the "seven non-negotiable cardinal pillars" of its party program (EFF 2019: 9). Thereafter, the EFF continuously but unsuccessfully pressed for expropriation without compensation (Roux 2022: 112–118).

Against the backdrop of the 2017 ANC resolution, the EFF tabled a motion in parliament to review the need to amend the property clause

(Section 25) of the Constitution to allow for expropriation of land without compensation.[6] On February 27, 2018 the National Assembly passed a significantly softened version by including the ANC caveats of not threatening agricultural production, food security, and economic investment, and established a parliamentary "Constitutional Review Committee (CRC)" to investigate the matter. This committee spent much of 2018 in a public consultation process that garnered a huge response. At a series of countrywide public hearings, the vast majority of people in attendance expressed support for a constitutional amendment. In addition, the committee received over 600,000 written submissions, a response that was exceeded only by the public consultations organized by the Constitutional Assembly in 1995 (Hall 2024: 144). In contrast to the public meetings, the overwhelming majority of written submissions rejected amending the Constitution. To a large extent, this split in public opinion reflected South Africa's racial divisions, with those on the side of change overwhelmingly black, and white South Africans in favor of retaining the status quo. However, black public opinion on the matter was not monolithic, with class differences playing a significant role (Hall 2024).

When the Constitutional Review Committee reported to the National Assembly in November 2018, it supported an amendment to the Constitution that would "make explicit that which is implicit," namely, that expropriation without compensation is permissible within the existing constitutional order. On December 4, 2018 the National Assembly concurred (by a vote of 209 for and 91 against) and accordingly framed a mandate for an "Ad Hoc Committee" to develop the relevant legislation. This committee was established in February 2019 but, because of the magnitude of the task, compounded by the outbreak of the COVID-19 pandemic and the associated national lockdown shortly thereafter, it only tabled its final report in September 2021. This report officially introduced the Constitution Eighteenth Amendment Bill to parliament. The preamble to the bill identified two main purposes: "to provide that where land and any improvements . . . are expropriated for the purposes of land reform, the amount of compensation payable may be nil," and to provide "the circumstances where the amount of compensation is nil." A related purpose was to "enable state custodianship of certain land in order for citizens to gain access to land on an equitable basis."

[6] See Zenker and Walker (2024) for a detailed reconstruction of the expropriation without compensation process.

The development of this bill dominated proceedings after 2019. Most opposition parties, such as the Democratic Alliance (DA), the mostly KwaZulu-based Inkatha Freedom Party, the Freedom Front Plus, as well as the African Christian Democratic Party, regarded expropriation without compensation as unconstitutional and opposed the amendment. The EFF rejected the bill's framing, arguing for a more radical amendment that would permit a broad-based program of expropriation leading to permanent state custodianship of all land – effectively nationalization. Its differences with the ANC crystallized around this issue. While the EFF saw state custodianship as the prize, the ANC envisioned it as a temporary stage between the acquisition and redistribution of land (*Daily Maverick*, May 31, 2021). Riddled with factional infighting, the latter did not espouse a coherent position, instead combining some "constitution-blaming with investor-reassuring" in a way that Ruth Hall (2024: 146) aptly describes as "talk EFF, walk DA." Ultimately, its official position was to limit expropriation without compensation to specific circumstances, without abandoning the principle of private land ownership.

When attempts to reach a compromise around this issue failed in July 2021, the EFF withdrew its support for the Amendment Bill, effectively condemning it to fall short of the constitutional threshold of a two-thirds majority in parliament. On December 7, 2021 the final vote in the National Assembly was 204 votes in favor of the amendment and 145 against, meaning that it was not carried and the status quo, with all its different interpretations, remained (*Daily Maverick*, December 7, 2021). However, given that the new Expropriation Bill (B23D-2020) – which was recently passed by both the National Assembly and the National Council of Provinces and sent to the president for assent on March 27, 2024 – also explicitly engages the specific circumstances in which "nil compensation" may be just and equitable, these heated constitutional debates are far from over.

A cross-section of divergent positions on these matters also became apparent among those experts that President Cyril Ramaphosa appointed to the above-mentioned "Presidential Advisory Panel on Land Reform and Agriculture (PAPLRA)" in September 2018. The panel brought together ten South Africans as "a feat of political engineering," as Ruth Hall (herself a member), observes: "five women, five men; seven black, three white; two lawyers; two presidents of national farmer associations; two individual leading farmers (one young black woman and one older white man); two agricultural economists (both men); and two interdisciplinary social scientists (both women)" (Hall 2024: 154). Running in parallel to the legislative process, this panel was mandated to provide a unified policy perspective on land reform (restitution, redistribution, and tenure reform) and also to consider the circumstances, procedures, and institutions related to a future policy of expropriation without compensation. Its report published on May 4, 2019 while the amendment process was still ongoing tellingly reflects disagreement on the issue of expropriation without compensation: whereas the majority of the panel supported amending the constitution, the (white) president of the national farmer association AgriSA as well as the older white farmer opposed this policy and any amendment (PAPLRA 2019: 103). While emphasizing that the current property clause (Section 25) of the Constitution already allowed for "just and equitable compensation" below market value (see Section 1.3 above for the factors in Section 25(3) determining such compensation), the panel expressed divergent opinions regarding the question of whether or not the state could already expropriate land without compensation under the current constitutional framework (PAPLRA 2019: 72).

Broadening the focus on public(ized) opinions by legal and land reform experts beyond the Presidential Advisory Panel, several observations are worth mentioning. First, although the panel seemed divided regarding the existing possibilities under the current constitutional framework to expropriate land for reform purposes without compensation, many legal experts have insisted that such a constitutional amendment is, in fact, not legally necessary. Thus, Advocate Tembeka Ngcukaitobi argues that "properly interpreted, the Constitution does not prohibit the expropriation of land without compensation" (Ngcukaitobi 2021: 173); while Roux equally regards an amendment as "legally unnecessary" (Roux 2022: 99; similarly Klug 2018: 490–491). Much technical discussions seemed to center on the question whether the peculiar wording "*without* compensation" contradicted the constitutional obligation to *always* provide "just and equitable compensation." Therefore, proposals for the constitutional amendment as well as the new Expropriation Bill shifted toward speaking about "nil" or "zero" compensation in order to suggest that there can be "just and equitable" circumstances in which the amount of compensation is actually zero. This can also be seen as one of the main reasons behind the peculiar wording used by the CRC for its proposal to amend the Constitution in order "to make explicit that which is implicit" (see above).

Second, the specific circumstances under which the state could carry out expropriation with zero compensation have dominated much of the technical discussions. The new Expropriation Bill in Section 12(3) offers an open list of circumstances potentially allowing for "nil compensation" – such as unused private or state-owned land, abandoned land, and land worth less than direct state investment.

Third, while many experts support, in principle, the possibility of zero compensation in circumscribed circumstances (irrespective of whether they regard a prior constitutional amendment as necessary), there is broad agreement that the actual number of such cases will be very small and that the transformative potential of expropriation without compensation is thus limited (e.g., PAPLRA 2019: 74; Ngcukaitobi 2021: xii). This is so because Section 25(3) of the property clause, and the limitations clause (Section 36) of the Constitution require striking an equitable balance between the public interest and the interests of current landowners, without imposing undue hardships and thereby disproportionately individualizing the costs for societal transformation. For this reason, many legal experts agree that while zero compensation will be very rare, many more cases of expropriation with partial compensation are, and always have been, possible. But these already existing constitutional possibilities have not yet been tested, let alone reached. For this reason, the presidential panel recommended a "compensation spectrum," ranging from "zero compensation" via "minimal compensation" and "substantial compensation" to "market-related compensation," against the backdrop of a typology of situations indicating how compensation should be approached in each case (PAPLRA 2019: 94).

Fourth, in light of the enormous public attention that expropriation without compensation has attracted over the past years and the emotional, intellectual, and financial investments that went into the project of the ultimately failed constitutional amendment, Ngcukaitobi rightly asks: "was the exercise worth it?" (Ngcukaitobi 2021: 212). He answers both in the positive and negative: to him, the debate was worthwhile because it "brought home the reality that land reform must be anchored in the rule of law," and, he claims, "many now accept this as true" (Ngcukaitobi 2021: 212). In another sense, however, Ngcukaitobi sees the true challenges of land reform as actually sidelined and occluded by the extensive and exclusive focus on "expropriation without compensation," namely:

> the structural flaws of the system, weak and dysfunctional institutional structures, corrupt officials, greedy landowners, the absence of people-centred ethics in the political class, and failures of the legislature to translate the Constitution into tangible laws. (Ngcukaitobi, 2021: 212–213)

Put more strongly, he argues that "the Constitution is the wrong target. Post-liberation politics and the adoption of market-friendly policies have failed the Constitution's ambitious socially redistributive and inclusive goals" (Ngcukaitobi 2021: 206). This aptly summarizes a widespread perception. Hence, hardly any expert working in the field of land reform sees the constitutional property clause, as it stands, as the primary obstacle for South Africa's urgently needed radical transformation.

This leads to a last concern that was also the main driving force behind the conference "Compensation through *Expropriation Without Compensation*? Constitutional Amendment, Land Reform, and the Future of Redistributive Justice in South Africa" that I co-organized with Cherryl Walker in February 2022 at the Stellenbosch Institute for Advanced Study (STIAS), South Africa, namely the attempt to recenter the expropriation without compensation debate within a broader conception of redistributive justice, which includes but is not defined by land reform (Zenker & Walker 2024: 22–27). Assembling leading experts from law, sociology, anthropology, and agrarian studies, the workshop brought debates around transformative property law, the challenges of land reform, and how to advance redistributive justice into conversation with each other, charting different pathways toward a substantively more just society.[7]

As this brief sketch indicates, many legal experts and land activists empirically studying, theoretically reflecting, and politically intervening into land reform and the transformation of property relations in South Africa have supported an extensive expropriation of land with just and equitable compensation below market value (including zero compensation), while insisting that a much more radical transformation can still thrive – and could have thrived all along – under the rule of law. In other words, following Ngcukaitobi's dictum that "the Constitution is the wrong target," a more radical decolonization of South Africa's massively skewed rights landscape can still be achieved, so it seems, under the banner of transformative constitutionalism. However, while this might be a plausible analysis with regard to the legal technicalities of expropriation without compensation and land reform more generally, such a stance has to reckon with the fact that South African public culture has increasingly become disenchanted with the transformative potentials of "the law" as such.

[7] The results of this exchange were published in an open access volume – see Zenker, Walker and Boggenpoel (2024).

1.6 Conclusion: Reckoning with Transformative Constitutionalism after Iconic Indexicality

How to make sense of the rapid rise and fall of South Africa's enchantment with the law, of the complexities of its dialectics of juristocratic reckoning as exemplified in recent debates of expropriation without compensation, and of a temporal consciousness, in which South Africa's moment of iconic indexicality seems to be withering away?

According to Hall, the insistence on a constitutional amendment and blaming the Constitution for the failures of land reform runs deeper than a literal reading of the law, constituting instead a political act of criticizing the state for its failure to actually achieve substantial land redistribution (Hall 2024: 161). In other words, this has been a "call for the decolonisation of landed property relations" (Hall 2024: 161) rather than for abandoning transformative constitutionalism as such. In an important sense, this is indeed the case. After all, the entire expropriation without compensation debate has been about the legal – *juristocratic* – process of amending the Constitution toward a more progressive framing, making explicit that which has so far been only implicit in law.

Yet, in another sense, Ngcukaitobi seems right in pointing out an evident weakness of such juristocratic reasoning: "[i]f the Constitution allows, implicitly, for the compulsory expropriation of land without compensation, then why amend it rather than enforce it?" (Ngcukaitobi 2021: 207). In other words, *amending* transformative constitutionalism appears, once again, only strong on yet another round of progressive legal promises, but remains weak on finally delivering on them. And the fact that not even the constitutional amendment process itself was ultimately successful surely has not increased popular support for the juristocratic order either. Thus, it remains an open question whether Ngcukaitobi's positive reading of the expropriation without compensation debate as at least making many accept that "land reform must be anchored in the rule of law" (see Section 1.5) is ultimately not too optimistic. Whether or not oneself believes – *normatively* – in the compatibility between decolonization and transformative constitutionalism, it seems increasingly evident – *descriptively* – that more and more people in South Africa no longer do. Many are deeply skeptical that post-1994 constitutionalism has adequately responded to the fundamental contradictions generated by colonization and apartheid (Modiri 2018: 295). This is the reason "[w]hy decolonisation and not transformative constitutionalism" (Sindane 2021) – increasingly construed as mutually exclusively alternatives – seems to be gaining popular support.

And yet, as an act of mobilization, confrontation, and refusal, it is important to recall the discussion above, differentiating between Hirschl's *substantive* notion of juristocracy, defined in terms of the constitutionalization of rights and the fortification of judicial review, and a *formal* notion of juristocracy, entailing a redemptive reckoning with law *in excess* as *the* master modality for all societal transformation. It is precisely because South Africa's (substantive) shift toward constitutional supremacy with a strong judiciary was simultaneously (formally) vested with strong messianic expectations regarding law's potentials for realizing radical change that South Africa could become an icon indexing (also internationally) law's alleged eschatological possibilities at large. In other words: post-apartheid South Africa not only shifted toward a new juristocratic model of transformative constitutionalism – the latter was simultaneously freighted with unrealistic juristocratic demands and expectations overflowing law's normal carrying capacity, and was thereby set up for (relative) failure that is more and more becoming evident. Law in general, *as law*, arguably has the ironic, if not paradoxical potential, to increase intrinsically the probability of revealing its own failures *by itself*, of inviting having its bluff called given the stark contrast between its explicit promise and usually wanting practice. This general tendency of the law toward exhibitionist self-debasement becomes massively aggravated, however, when simultaneously coupled with exalted juristocratic expectations regarding law's allegedly infallible centrality.

Seen in this light, the current passing of South Africa's moment of iconic indexicality, understood as a growing disenchantment with law's proclaimed excessive potentials, might actually be a good thing. It may allow apprehending transformative constitutionalism more realistically as only one possible means, besides others (political, social, economic, religious, cultural etc.), for achieving more transformational change in all its multidimensional complexity. Reckoning with transformative constitutionalism after iconic indexicality may, therefore, make possible a more sober, nuanced, and contextual analysis of the relative potentials and pitfalls of concrete legal measures, as compared to other transformative modalities, than was previously possible under conditions of exalted legal apotheosis. By transcending a false binary of, in principle, either defending or opposing transformative constitutionalism, such a move possibly facilitates engaging in a much-needed process of what could be called a "transformational triage."

Taking inspiration from medicine, where triage refers to a process of determining the order of priority for treating multiple sufferers under conditions of limited supplies, transformational triage equally highlights, under conditions of severely limited resources, the necessity for a political process of balancing and weighing, on the basis of evidence, various concerns and interests in the management of transformational change through contested forms of relative prioritization: What, in terms of urgency, efficacy, and efficiency, needs to be done, in which order, in which time scale, by whom and – importantly – through which transformative modality? Given that a large arsenal of political, legal, social, economic, and other measures for promoting transformative justice is readily available and that a plethora of public goods simultaneously clamor for attention, this requires making and justifying strategic choices as well as negotiating the attendant trade-offs, and managing the political fallout that can be expected to follow such setting of priorities. Conceptualizing these necessary negotiations in terms of a transformational triage has the benefit of keeping the obvious in focus – namely, that under conditions of limited resources not everything can be done at the same time and that sequence, the order of priority, does make a difference.

Reckoning with transformative constitutionalism in terms of a transformational triage also has the added benefit of allowing the evaluation of the potentials and pitfalls of a continued project of transformative constitutionalism both *internally*, with regard to how actually existing legal practices have fared vis-à-vis their actual potentials, and *externally*, when compared to alternative modalities at hand. In light of the above discussions of South African land reform in general and the expropriation without compensation debate in particular, it seems as if, after all, transformative constitutionalism in South Africa has not yet fully exhausted its possibilities. Generally speaking, transformative constitutionalism has been rightly criticized because its practice, rather than its potential, has been found wanting: an increasingly inactive and corrupt executive has not sufficiently implemented and enforced the law as it stands; the legislative has failed to pass consistent and constitutionally required transformative legislation (e.g., on land redistribution, tenure security, or expropriation); and the judiciary could equally have been more transformative and less conservative, in terms of its jurisprudence, contributing to what Sindiso Mnisi Weeks (2022) calls the "dis/empowerment paradox" of South African legal culture.

More specifically, refocusing the expropriation without compensation debate in terms of a transformational triage, three issues deserve highlighting with regard to their contribution toward more redistributive justice. First, given the profoundly transformed economy and ecology of land in contemporary South Africa, future land reform needs to venture substantially beyond a narrow focus on land redistribution for agriculture (see Walker 2024). Second, rather than trying to reduce state expenditure piecemeal through cumbersome and excessively litigation-based expropriation without compensation and thereby make only some contemporary landowners pay, it might be more efficient as well as more just to expand substantially the revenue for radical transformation through a transformational tax (in the form of a capital levy) that progressively spreads the costs across South African society at large, thereby also charging colonial beneficiaries across the scale who happen not to own land today (see Klug 2024). Third, given that land and agriculture is no longer the motor of the nation's wealth, it might be more productive to first and foremost effect radical transformation through direct cash payments – for instance, through a Basic Income Grant (BIC) – rather than locking capital into increasingly unproductive land for the relatively few (see Ferguson 2024). These are all measures – faster, more effective, and more radical in profoundly affecting far more people than currently the case in land reform – that, based on a transformational triage, can still become operative within the framework of transformative constitutionalism.

This is so even though, thirty years into its new democratic dispensation, South Africa's earlier excitement with its own iconic status indexing the proclaimed transformative potential of law at large, has increasingly given way to substantial disillusionment with law's actual possibilities. As has become clear, South Africa too (like any other place) is subject to the ebbs and flows of juristocratic reckoning. However, this has evidently not led to an unambiguous move into post-legality, once and for all. In her article discussed at the beginning of this chapter, Lindiwe Sisulu dismissed the rule of law *tout court* as a foreign belief system and fundamentally questioned its use, if the law did not work for Africans in Africa. Yet less than a week later, after stirring a hot debate, Sisulu somewhat backtracked in another article (Sisulu 2022b), putting again stronger emphasis on the need to truly deliver on the rights promised *in the Constitution*. It is this ambiguous oscillation back and forth, into and beyond the rule of law, that increasingly characterizes, and complicates, the dialectics of juristocratic reckoning in South Africa today.

References

Abel, Richard L. 1995. *Politics by Other Means: Law in the Struggle against Apartheid, 1980–1994.* New York: Routledge.

African National Congress (ANC). 2017. *54th National Conference: Report and Resolutions*. Johannesburg: ANC.

Alexander, Peter. 2010. Rebellion of the Poor: South Africa's Service Delivery Protests – a Preliminary Analysis. *Review of African Political Economy* 37 (123): 25–40.

Booysen, Susan, ed. 2016. *Fees Must Fall: Student Revolt, Decolonisation and Governance in South Africa*. Johannesburg: Wits University Press.

Brown, Julian. 2015. *South Africa's Insurgent Citizens: On Dissent and the Possibility of Politics*. Auckland: Jacana.

Buthelezi, Mbongiseni and Peter C. J. Vale. 2023. *State Capture in South Africa: How and Why it Happened*. Johannesburg: Wits University Press.

Claassens, Aninka and Ben Cousins, eds. 2008. *Land, Power & Custom: Controversies Generated by South Africa's Communal Land Rights Act*. Cape Town: Legal Resources Centre.

Comaroff, John L. and Jean Comaroff. 2006. Law and Disorder in the Postcolony: An Introduction. In Jean Comaroff and John L. Comaroff, eds., *Law and Disorder in the Postcolony*. Chicago: University of Chicago Press, 1–56.

Commission on Restitution of Land Rights. 2007. *Annual Report 2006/07*. Pretoria: Department of Land Affairs.

Cornell, Drucilla. 2014. *Law and Revolution in South Africa: Ubunto, Dignity, and the Struggle for Constitutional Transformation*. New York: Fordham University Press.

Dyzenhaus, David. 1992. Law's Potential. *Canadian Journal of Law and Society* 7 (2): 237–251.

Economic Freedom Fighters (EFF). 2019. *Economic Freedom Fights Constitution, as Amended and Adopted in December 2019 by the Economic Freedom Fighters' Second National People's Assembly in Johannesburg Nasrec*. Johannesburg: EFF.

Ferguson, James. 2024. Redistribution of What? Beyond Land in the Moral Politics of Distribution. In Olaf Zenker, Cherryl Walker and Zsa-Zsa Boggenpoel, eds., *Beyond Expropriation Without Compensation: Law, Land Reform and Redistributive Justice in South Africa*. Cambridge: Cambridge University Press, 288–297.

Hall, Ruth. 2024. The Constitution's Mandate for Transformation: From "Expropriation without Compensation" to "Equitable Access to Land." In Olaf Zenker, Cherryl Walker and Zsa-Zsa Boggenpoel, eds., *Beyond Expropriation Without Compensation: Law, Land Reform and Redistributive Justice in South Africa*. Cambridge: Cambridge University Press, 143–164.

The High Level Panel on the Assessment of Key Legislation and the Acceleration of Fundamental Change (HLP). 2017. *Report of the High Level Panel on the Assessment of Key Legislation and the Acceleration of Fundamental Change*. Pretoria. Government Printer.

Hirschl, Ran. 2004. *Towards Juristocracy: The Origins and Consequences of the New Constitutionalism*. Cambridge, MA: Harvard University Press.

Hunter, Qaanitah, Jeff Wicks and Kaveel Singh. 2021. *Eight Days in July: Inside the Zuma Unrest that Set South Africa Alight*. Cape Town: Tafelberg.

James, Deborah. 2007. *Gaining Ground? "Rights" and "Property" in South African Land Reform*. Abingdon: Routledge.

Klare, Karl E. 1998. Legal Culture and Transformative Constitutionalism. *South African Journal on Human Rights* 14 (1): 146–188.

Klotz, Audie. 2013. *Migration and National Identity in South Africa, 1860–2010*. New York: Cambridge University Press.

Klug, Heinz. 2000. *Constituting Democracy: Law, Globalism, and South Africa's Political Reconstruction*. Cambridge: Cambridge University Press.

2018. Decolonisation, Compensation and Constitutionalism: Land, Wealth and the Sustainability of Constitutionalism in Post-apartheid South Africa. *South African Journal on Human Rights* 34 (3): 469–491.

2024. Redistributive Justice, Transformational Taxes and the Legacies of Apartheid. In Olaf Zenker, Cherryl Walker and Zsa-Zsa Boggenpoel, eds., *Beyond Expropriation Without Compensation: Law, Land Reform and Redistributive Justice in South Africa*. Cambridge: Cambridge University Press: 268–287.

Krygier, Martin, Adam W. Czarnota and Wojciech Sadurski, eds. 2022. *Anti-constitutional Populism*. Cambridge: Cambridge University Press.

Landau, Loren B. 2010. Loving the Alien? Citizenship, Law, and the Future in South Africa's Demonic Society. *African Affairs* 109 (435): 213–230.

Leibbrandt, Murray and Fabio Abdrés Díaz Pabón. 2021. Inequality in South Africa. In Arkebe Oqubay, Fiona Tregenna and Imraan Valodia, eds., *The Oxford Handbook of the South African Economy*. Oxford: Oxford University Press, 175–191.

Lodge, Tom. 2002. *Politics in South Africa: From Mandela to Mbeki*. Cape Town: David Philip.

Marais, Hein. 1998. *South Africa, Limits to Change: The Political Economy of Transformation*. Cape Town: University of Cape Town Press.

Meierhenrich, Jens. 2008. *The Legacies of Law: Long-Run Consequences of Legal Development in South Africa, 1652–2000*. Cambridge: Cambridge University Press.

Mnisi Weeks, Sindiso. 2022. South African Legal Culture and its Dis/empowerment Paradox. In Marie-Claire Foblets, Mark Goodale, Maria Sapignoli and Olaf Zenker, eds., *Oxford Handbook of Law and Anthropology*. Oxford: Oxford University Press, 56–72.

Modiri, Joel M. 2018. Introduction to Special Issue: Conquest, Constitutionalism and Democratic Contestations. *South African Journal on Human Rights* 34 (3): 295–299.

Msimang, Mavuso. 2022. Lindiwe Sisulu's Extraordinary Attack on South Africa's Constitution. *Daily Maverick*, January 9, 2022, at www.dailymaverick.co.za/article/2022-01-09-lindiwe-sisulus-extraordinary-attack-on-south-africas-constitution.

Murray, Martin J. 1994. *Revolution Deferred: The Painful Birth of Post-apartheid South Africa*. London: Verso.

Ngcukaitobi, Tembeka. 2021. *Land Matters: South Africa's Failed Land Reforms and the Road Ahead*. Cape Town: Penguin.

Ngwane, Trevor. 2019. "Insurgent Democracy": Post-apartheid South Africa's Freedom Fighters. *Journal of Southern African Studies* 45 (1): 229–245.

Palmer, Ian, Nishendra Moodley and Sue Parnell. 2017. *Building a Capable State: Service Delivery in Post-apartheid South Africa*. London: Zed Books.

The Presidential Advisory Panel on Land Reform and Agriculture (PAPLRA). 2019. *Final Report of the Presidential Advisory Panel on Land Reform and Agriculture*. Pretoria: Presidency.

Robins, Steven. 2008. *From Revolution to Rights in South Africa: Social Movements, NGOs & Popular Politics after Apartheid*. Woodbridge: James Currey.

Roux, Theunis. 2013. *The Politics of Principle: The First South African Constitutional Court, 1995–2005*. Cambridge: Cambridge University Press.

2022. Constitutional Populism in South Africa. In Martin Krygier, Adam W. Czarnota and Wojciech Sadurski, eds., *Anti-constitutional Populism*. Cambridge: Cambridge University Press, 99–137.

Runciman, Carin, Peter Alexander, Mahlatse Rampedi et al. 2016. *Counting Police-Recorded Protests: Based on South African Police Service Data*. Johannesburg: University of Johannesburg Social Change Research Unit.

Seekings, Jeremy and Nicoli Nattrass. 2015. *Policy, Politics and Poverty in South Africa*. New York: UNRISD/Palgrave Macmillan.

Sindane, Ntando. 2021. Why Decolonisation and Not Transformative Constitutionalism. *Pretoria Student Law Review* 15 (1): 236–254.

Sinwell, Luke and Siphiwe Mbatha. 2016. *The Spirit of Marikana: The Rise of Insurgent Trade Unionism in South Africa*. London: Pluto.

Sisulu, Lindiwe. 2022a. Hi Mzanzi, Have We Seen Justice? IOL Independent Online, January 7, 2022, at www.iol.co.za/dailynews/opinion/lindiwe-sisulu-hi-mzansi-have-we-seen-justice-d9b151e5-e5db-4293-aa21-dcccd52a36d3.

2022b. Lindiwe Sisulu Responds to Criticism of Her Opinion Piece Titled, "Hi Mzansi, Have We Seen Justice?" IOL Independent Online, January 12, 2022, at www.iol.co.za/dailynews/opinion/lindiwe-sisulu-responds-to-criticism-of-her-opinion-piece-titled-hi-mzansi-have-we-seen-justice-4e817611-4027-4c32-8eef-1a8416e8fd67.

Smith, Nicholas Rush. 2017. The Rule of Rights: Comparative Lessons from Twenty Years of South African Democracy. *Comparative Politics* 50 (1): 123–141.

Waldmeir, Patti. 1997. *Anatomy of a Miracle: The End of Apartheid and the Birth of the New South Africa*. London: Viking.

Walker, Cherryl. 2008. *Landmarked: Land Claims and Land Restitution in South Africa*. Athens: Ohio University Press.

2024. Land Reform and Beyond in Times of Social–Ecological Change: Perspectives from the Karoo. In Olaf Zenker, Cherryl Walker and Zsa-Zsa Boggenpoel, eds., *Beyond Expropriation Without Compensation: Law, Land Reform and Redistributive Justice in South Africa*. Cambridge: Cambridge University Press, 214–237.

Woolman, Stuart and Michael Bishop. 2013. *Constitutional Law of South Africa*, 2nd edn, Revision Service 5. Cape Town: Juta.

Zenker, Olaf. 2012. The Juridification of Political Protest and the Politicisation of Legalism in South African Land Restitution. In Julia Eckert, Brian Donahoe, Christian Strümpell and Zerrin Özlem Biner, eds., *Law against the State: Ethnographic Forays Into Law's Transformations*. Cambridge: Cambridge University Press, 118–146.

2015. Failure by the Numbers? Settlement Statistics as Indicators of State Performance in South African Land Restitution. In Richard Rottenburg, Sally Engle Merry, Sung-Joon Park and Johanna Mugler, eds., *A World of Indicators: The Making of Governmental Knowledge through Quantification*. Cambridge: Cambridge University Press, 102–126.

2018. Land Restitution (Old and New), Neo-traditionalism, and the Contested Values of Land Justice in South Africa. In Jessica Johnson and George H. Karekwaivanane, eds., *Pursuing Justice in Africa: Competing Imaginaries and Contested Practices*. Athens: Ohio University Press, 243–263.

Zenker, Olaf and Cherryl Walker. 2024. Beyond Expropriation Without Compensation: Law, Land Reform and the Future of Redistributive Justice in South Africa. In Olaf Zenker, Cherryl Walker and Zsa-Zsa Boggenpoel, eds., *Beyond Expropriation Without Compensation: Law, Land Reform and Redistributive Justice in South Africa*. Cambridge: Cambridge University Press, 3–32.

Zenker, Olaf, Cherryl Walker and Zsa-Zsa Boggenpoel, eds. 2024. *Beyond Expropriation Without Compensation: Law, Land Reform and Redistributive Justice in South Africa*. Cambridge: Cambridge University Press.

2

Beyond Here Lies Somethin'

Juristocratic Reckonings in Two Narratives of Legalities

LYNETTE J. CHUA

In this chapter I present two narratives of legalities: how the state deploys law and how people interact with and experience law. The volume editors' treatment of juristocratic reckoning, especially the language of first and second phases, suggests a linear worldview in which legalities and law travel and develop linearly along with human societies, moving from one phase of reckoning to the next, perhaps eventually into utopia or dystopia. The two narratives in this chapter illustrate a different worldview, one in which human societies, law, legalities, and thus juristocratic reckonings develop cyclically as well as chronologically.

The two narratives are based on my research projects, one recently completed and the other still ongoing. The first narrative concerns a "human rights practice as a way of life," a legality flowing with connotative power (Goodale 2007). Instead of relying on the direct, instrumental power of human rights, a group of Burmese activists draws upon the capacity of rights to change the way they feel about themselves and generate the momentum to inspire, encourage, and rally others to take up collective political action. Although their country has once more descended into widespread insurrections, some of these activists still carry hope for human rights as they fight back and flee into exile again. The second narrative is about "governing through contagion," a legality afflicting state centralization over strategies of control of infectious

Inspired by the title of Bob Dylan's song, "Beyond Here Lies Nothin". I am grateful to my research assistants who contributed to the two projects discussed in this chapter, and Elizabeth Lan Lan Ko for her help with the copy editing of this chapter. Funding for the writing and research of the Governing through Contagion project is provided by the Singapore Ministry of Education Academic Research Fund Tier 1 (WBS: A-8000923-00-00). I presented a modified version of this chapter as my keynote speech at the 2023 Law and Society Association of Australia and New Zealand Annual Conference at the Faculty of Law, University of Technology Sydney, Sydney, Australia, on December 6, 2023.

diseases, and processes of normalization-moralization and inter/dysconnectedness. The Singaporean state's strategies to regulate contagion grew out of earlier epidemics and global circulations of capital, violence, and ideas and mutated according to the entanglements of relationships among humans, animals, microorganisms, and technologies. As humans comply with, resist, or otherwise interact with strategies of control, these relationships produce dysconnectedness that exposes, perhaps exacerbates, existing injustices.

Although the two narratives depict divergent contexts, they capture distinctive profiles of juristocratic reckoning. In the narrative about human rights practice as a way of life, I identify three coexisting perspectives that transcend the volume editors' suggestions of different phases of juristocratic reckoning; in the story about governing through contagion, I show that a more expansive chronology and cast of actors can shape the way we understand moments of law as juristocratic reckoning. What we make of a moment of law depends on where we look for legalities, where we situate them, and how we appreciate their highs and lows.[1]

2.1 Narrative One: Human Rights Practice as a Way of Life

> Our people know human rights from their suffering. The human rights concept comes from their lives. It comes from their real life, real suffering.
>
> (Chua 2019: 68)[2]

From 2012 to 2019 I conducted ethnography on a self-described LGBT (lesbian, gay, bisexual, and transgender) rights movement that emerged in Myanmar in the 2000s and flourished in the 2010s, during the relatively more liberal period of ostensibly semicivilian rule. I was drawn to this movement because I was curious about how a group of people gained access to human rights despite being additionally marginalized due to their sexuality/gender within a general population already oppressed under military rule. I wanted to understand how they found the means and courage to organize collectively and how they reinterpreted the international discourse of human rights in light of their religious beliefs and local understandings of sexual and gender roles.

[1] My treatment of the relationship between law and temporalities draws upon an earlier essay, "Interregna: Time, Law, and Resistance" (Chua 2021).

[2] Unless otherwise indicated, the contents of Narrative One are based on *The Politics of Love in Myanmar* (Chua 2019).

The quote above came from the movement founder whom I called Tun Tun, when I asked how he would answer skeptics who thought human rights were alien to him and his compatriots. His answer fundamentally shaped my thinking about the movement's human rights practice, that is, how they interpreted, adapted, and used human rights. To Tun Tun and his fellow activists, to know human rights is to feel them. Tun Tun and fellow activists appreciated human rights by feeling what it is like to live in their absence – to feel the pangs of suffering – and what living in their presence augurs– to experience feelings the opposite of anguish, fear, and shame.

When living in exile in Thailand in the early 2000s, Tun Tun and other dissidents from earlier uprisings against the military, such as the 1988 protests, were drawn together by their disaffection for the military regime. Pioneers of the LGBT rights movement like Tun Tun additionally shared the pain of being discriminated as sexual and gender minorities, even within the dissident and exile community, a feeling that resonated with newcomers whom they invited to join the nascent movement. As this small group learned about human rights from one another, they drew from this deep well of personal emotions to help them merge the international discourse of human rights with the norms, beliefs, and understandings of power and hierarchy in their society. Through practicing human rights they changed their feelings about themselves, their approach to relationships with family, friends, and strangers and thus their relationally constituted selfhood. They also altered their perceptions of their own suffering – not as the consequences of bad karma or moral demerits due to transgressions in past lives but as human rights violations for whom somebody or something, such as the police or unjust laws, should be blamed. Also, by practicing human rights together as part of the movement, these activists built a community united by their emotional fealty toward human rights and their affection for one another as friends and confidantes.

Hence, in this first narrative, people enact legality through an emotional practice that animates human rights, giving them meaning and consequence. In this legality, emotions do not merely serve instrumental purposes for human rights activists to deploy as conduits or strategies. Emotions embody *all* aspects of practicing human rights, including the meaning making, circulation, implementation, and production of their outcomes. In *The Politics of Love in Myanmar* (Chua 2019), I named this legality, "human rights practice as a way of life."

2.1.1 *A Legality of Connotative Power*

Despite two decades of practicing human rights the Burmese LGBT rights movement did not succeed in reforming state law; for example, removing the penal provision that criminalizes same-sex relations or amending the provisions on police powers misused by officers to extort and threaten transgender women. Although lawyers allied with the movement have defended queer Burmese prosecuted in court under the above-mentioned provisions, movement activists had little expectation that they could change the law through the judiciary, known for its ineptitude, corruption, and abuse of power.[3] They placed slightly more hope in the legislature, having met on multiple occasions with National League for Democracy (NLD) parliamentarians and NLD leader Aung San Suu Kyi. However, movement leaders are realistic that sexual and gender minorities sit among a long list of other social groups also in need of legal redress, such as political dissidents, women, children, and ethnic and religious minorities.

Yet remarkably, human rights practice as a way of life is capable of achieving social change and empowerment. It is a legality brimming with connotative power (Goodale 2007) – as opposed to its more direct, instrumental capacity – to transform the ways people perceive and respond to their problems. Contrary to advocacy via formal legal channels, such as lobbying the legislature and litigating in the courts, the capacity of this legality to achieve social change starts with the self.

"I want after their training, they can come up with their idea . . . and what they want to do in the future for their community, for their society" (Chua 2019: 73). Shared feelings of pain, fear, and despair drew old and new activists together, but suffering in and of itself was insufficient to motivate them to understand and mobilize human rights collectively. Movement leaders took newcomers through a social process of grievance transformation to elicit, remake, and produce emotions that made sense of human rights for them. The process started with changing one's

[3] Only in one instance did a group of activist lawyers file a constitutional challenge questioning the trial court's findings of fact and accusing the police of unduly pressuring a transwoman in their custody to plead guilty by withholding access to antiretroviral medication meant for suppressing the progression of the HIV virus. They appealed the case to the Supreme Court but were unsuccessful. After the final court decision, when I asked movement leaders for the Supreme Court judgment, they could not remember where they had stored the document physically or electronically and showed little interest in it.

feelings about oneself – from negative feelings such as self-hatred, shame, and fear to positive feelings of confidence, optimism, and belief that they did not deserve to be mistreated because of their sexuality or gender. Then, as indicated by the quote above, movement leaders built on these positive feelings among newcomers to encourage them to join their movement and take up its collective practice of human rights.

The self-transformation occurred as LGBT rights activists imbued human rights with familiar cultural schemas and resources, such as their common experiences of suffering, Buddhist karmic beliefs, and social norms that regulate behavior, roles, and obligations to produce three core meanings of human rights: *dignity, social belonging, and responsibility* (of the rights bearer). Even though they drew the concept of dignity from international human rights discourse, they infused it with local notions that stress the importance of social belonging. To be accepted, to feel that one belongs in one's family or larger community, is to have dignity. In addition, they associated dignity with LGBT identities, which are usually linked to human rights discourse. They interpreted LGBT identities to signal respect for their selfhood, compared to their experiences of being insulted with derogatory words in the local language.[4] The term LGBT also signalled belonging to a new community of LGBT rights activists bound by their particular practice of human rights. Although "LGBT" does not encompass all local sexual and gender subjectivities, movement leaders intended the terminology to be a "necessary fiction" (Weeks 1995) to coalesce a force of political opposition. To unleash this force to achieve their dignity and social belonging, they further believed that the rights-bearer bore the responsibility to act by participating in collective action. Taken together, the three meanings of human rights indexed a social and collective self, rather than an individuated, autonomous person, and rendered human rights a collective good that ought to be collectively achieved.

Thus, the legality of human rights practice as a way of life sets off the momentum for social change from within the self. Following personal transformation, LGBT rights activists resisted the precarity of their lives and created a community united by their emotional fealty to human rights and affective ties to one another. As a collective, they mounted political action to challenge social norms and state laws.

[4] Of course, not everyone in the movement considered the use of local terms to be derogatory. In addition, outside the movement, activists did use these words among themselves and among other friends as terms of endearment.

That human rights could be made meaningful in village corners, shophouses, and dingy hotel rooms, far away from the great halls of the United Nations and the state capital, shows us their malleability to be changed and to change. This malleability threads the self, the group, and the social and state together. By tracing this legality, paying close attention to emotions, I analyzed and detailed how personal, grassroots and formal institutional dimensions of change are interrelated.

2.1.2 Multiple Temporalities, Multiple Reckonings

Human rights practice as a way of life, the legality continuously enacted by a group of Burmese activists, does not completely exemplify the volume editors' notion of juristocratic reckoning of the "first phase." According to the editors, the *loci classicus* of the first phase is the South African case examined in Chapter 1, where activists or state actors amplify law as a mechanism to address injustices. However, in the case of the Burmese LGBT movement, human rights did not become juridified in the sense of being formalized by the state institutions of Myanmar.

Instead, I suggest three alternative perspectives to understand the practice of human rights as a way of life. One is to treat the practice as a pre-first phase, taking place *prior to* the first stage of juristocratic reckoning described by the editors. Arguably, law was never juridified in Myanmar, much less human rights. Some Myanmar scholars argue that law, more than anything else, is a violent weapon of the state, a tool to crush dissent and make people bend to a political and social order desired by those in control (Cheesman 2015). Therefore, the activists in my narrative are attempting to mobilize human rights collectively to reach the first phase where the state would formalize human rights in legal instruments and through other official actions, and these laws and legal procedures would become the privileged mechanism for the state, activists, and other parties to address injustices.

Another perspective is to regard human rights practice as a way of life as *post*-second phase. According to the editors, the second phase of juristocratic reckoning involves coming to terms with the ineffectiveness of juristocracy. Confronted with a long list of criticisms I do not need to reiterate here, human rights are arguably undergoing the second phase. Nonetheless, the Burmese LGBT movement's practice is not merely a response to the failure of human rights around the world. In the midst of human rights failures and atrocities by Myanmar's state actors, these activists imbue the discourse with hope as they mobilize it *beyond* the boundaries of law (or formal law, at the very least).

The "pre-first" and "post-second" perspectives on human rights practice as a way of life can coexist. The first perspective is situated in the temporality of Myanmar, whereas the second sits within the global temporality of international human rights. The temporality of Myanmar overlaps with those of other societies, all of which are embedded within the global temporality of the second perspective. Since February 2021, these observations are even more poignant and bring to light a third perspective on juristocratic reckoning by the Burmese LGBT movement's human rights practice.

2.1.3 *Aftermath*

On February 1, 2021 Myanmar's military, the *Tatmadaw,* blocked roads in the capital city, Nay Pyi Taw, and the largest city, Yangon. The *Tatmadaw* detained Aung San Suu Kyi and other leaders of NLD, which won a landslide victory in the November 2020 elections. They proclaimed a year-long state of emergency and transferred government power to the military commander-in-chief. Burmese citizens have since staged protests and civil disobedience campaigns, and the *Tatmadaw* has retaliated with intensifying violence.[5] At the time of writing, the post-coup military junta is estimated to have killed about 1,900 people.[6] Shortly after the coup, ousted parliamentarians set up a government in exile, the National Unity Government.[7]

"I have a commitment. I believe in human rights. I will never give up. I believe in doing the right thing, and the right thing will win" (Chua 2019: 143). Tun Tun, who uttered these words, and his fellow activists were filled with hope and dreams only a few years ago. The 2021 coup and its aftermath seem to have smashed them into smithereens.

Perhaps we feel as though human rights have failed. Again. The legality of human rights practice as a way of life has turned into yet another story consigned to the human rights library of failures. We might say, the malleability of human rights, their connotative capacity to enable and encourage Tun Tun and his compatriots to envision a more egalitarian, more loving society, led adherents down a dead-end street. Ardent

[5] www.bbc.com/news/world-asia-55902070 (last visited on May 23, 2022).

[6] https://aappb.org/?p=21537 (last visited on May 23, 2022).

[7] www.nugmyanmar.org/en/ (last visited on May 23, 2022).

belief in human rights might have made things worse. Burmese who insisted on their basic rights to elect their leader and then called upon the results to be honored might have precipitated their own deaths, when state operatives put them down with bullets, batons, and worse. We might say, human rights themselves are over, their intimations trampled upon by soldiers and crushed by tanks.

Or have they? Since the coup, it has been difficult to stay in touch with activists in Myanmar, partly due to technological challenges and partly out of concern for surveillance. Any online conversations have been brief and mundane: "How are you?"; "I'm okay"; and deliberately so. But movement leaders have not stayed quiet.

In the early days of the coup, I occasionally caught glimpses on social media of some activists in my study. One night, they were banging pots and pans in protest. On another day, in broad daylight, they were marching on the streets with banners identifying themselves as "LGBT" who rebuff the military's latest deposition of Aung San Suu Kyi. From timid youths, the younger activists in my study have transformed into leaders and, in the wake of the 2021 coup, participants of civil disobedience and organizers of demonstrations against the resurgence of dictatorship. By early 2022, some LGBT rights activists had fled to Thailand and returned to their old bases, where the movement started in the 2000s among exiles of earlier military regimes. They did not turn away from human rights. They are intent on continuing their human rights practice, by reestablishing their presence in exile and providing support to those who stayed behind in their homeland. Participating in the legality of human rights as a way of life connected LGBT rights activists to larger resistance against the coup and to the government in exile. It enabled some of them to escape the immediate trauma and terror of the current regime, find reprieve, and try to restore their hopes. As a human rights organization in exile, they continue to obtain international funding to sustain their operations and live without the fear of imminent mortal danger. Maybe one day they could also stop jumping up, startled every time they hear a sudden loud noise outside the window.

After the 2021 coup, everybody in Myanmar was exposed to the military dictatorship's brute force. However, state violence had always existed, even in the relatively freer days of the 2010s. Maybe it was more compartmentalized, exerted more explicitly against and felt more acutely among minorities, women, the poor, and others in lower stations of Burmese social hierarchy. Before the coup, the LGBT rights movement's human rights practice contained faults and fault lines that reflected such inequalities and injustice. Bamar Buddhists dominated the leadership, and the movement privileged the majority ethnic and religious group over minorities in their outreach; transgender women and gay men – who enjoy male privilege, despite their sexuality or gender, on the basis of their assigned sex at birth – occupied the leadership ranks to the detriment of transgender men and lesbians; urban movement leaders with better formal education and English language ability controlled the purse strings and, consequently, tried to influence the agenda of grassroots organizers; and, for the price of gaining social belonging, movement leaders promoted homonormativity, by disciplining the behavior of their constituents to make them more palatable to mainstream society and drawing distinctions between "good"' and "bad" queers (Moran 2004). In the attempt to rise from the ashes in exile, to be reborn at their place of birth, where and how will old faults and fault lines reemerge?

> "Do you feel that you have just gone full circle, back to what it used to be, working in exile?"

> "No. The situation has changed. We accomplished a lot in ten years (the length of time that the movement was based inside Myanmar)."

Speaking almost twenty months after the coup, this activist felt that he and his compatriots had raised greater awareness about LGBT rights and that sexual and gender minorities had gained greater acceptance in Myanmar. During the anti-military protests, he did not believe that LGBT rights activists experienced discrimination from fellow protestors. In fact, he added, the then NLD-led government was going to repeal within five years the penal provision that criminalizes same-sex sexual relations.[8]

In the aftermath of the 2021 coup, human rights practice as a way of life is presenting one more type of juristocratic reckoning. If we situate it within the temporality of Myanmar, it is a reckoning of the previous pre-first phase, that is, the failed attempts at juridifying human rights in their country and therefore not reaching the first phase. This reckoning is not the same as the second phase, when already institutionalized laws and rights fail to live up to the goals and aspirations of social justice – because this Burmese legality had never undergone the first phase of formal juridification. If we situate the aftermath within the global

[8] In the interest of their safety, I withhold certain details about these activists and their activities following the 2021 coup.

temporality of human rights, then it is a continuation of the "post-second phase," a persistent mobilization beyond (formal) law. From either perspective, the legality of human rights practice as a way of life moves cyclically, but it does not trace the same circular patterns nor return to exactly the same spot, as it simultaneously traverses linearity and changes with chronological time, from the pre-2010 era of military reign through the relatively freer days of the 2010s to the current period following the 2021 coup.

2.2 Narrative Two: Governing through Contagion

> #iGotMyShot. With vaccination, you are protecting yourself and your loved ones. Let's continue to be socially responsible and mask up. Thank you for doing your part! – VACCiNATION SG.[9]

Since April 2020, a colleague and I have been conducting ethnography on strategies of control against contagious diseases in Singapore.[10] At the beginning of our research, Singapore – where I live and work – had just entered a two-month "circuit breaker," a term the government used in place of "lockdown." The government prohibited gatherings: it closed schools, recreational facilities, businesses and most workplaces; mandated physical distancing; and permitted only "essential" activities such as outdoor exercise, urgent medical visits, and the purchase and delivery of food and household necessities. We were inspired by the imposition of COVID-19 restrictions, their rapidly shifting nature in response to the evolution of the virus as well as the variations of such restrictions around the world. However, we were not merely interested in COVID-19. We wanted to analyze the interactions of state institutions, ordinary citizens, and contagious diseases across time and space and understand how strategies of control – variously aimed at prevention, containment, enforcement, and education – grew out of earlier episodes of contagion and were disseminated through capitalism, colonialism, and international bodies like the World Health Organization.

[9] Packaging of reusable mask distributed at a vaccination center inSingapore, May 11, 2021.

[10] Narrative Two is based on an ongoing project and the writings that my colleague and I have produced from the project so far (Chua & Lee 2021; Lee & Chua 2023; Chua & Lee 2024). We collect and analyze colonial and media archives, contemporary print media, internet and publicly accessible social media materials, observational data, and interviews with public health personnel, social workers, and ordinary residents.

Using Singapore as our case study, we argue that as governments and their populations engage with strategies of control in response to contagious diseases, they recursively produce "governing through contagion." The controls prescribe behavior, discipline subject morality, and ultimately strive to ensure that a population avoids incurring medical costs and stays productive so as to achieve the economic aims of the political order and secure its legitimacy. Governing through contagion may coexist with, enhance, or undermine other forms of governance and regimes of control unrelated to the primary aim of managing infectious diseases.

To formulate the theoretical framework of governing through contagion, we draw from postmodernist theories on security but intersect them with the interdisciplinary field of science and technology studies (STS) to foreground nonhuman agency alongside that of humans. The nonhuman includes creatures such as mammals and microorganisms, and the nonliving such as technologies of law and medicine. The contents of strategies of control, including its modes of power, depend on the relationships among humans, other living beings, and the nonliving. Therefore, the influence of governing through contagion expands and diminishes as strategies of controls produce, emerge from, and shift to a web of human/nonhuman/nonliving relationships.

Hence, in this second narrative, humans enact legality alongside their co-species, all with the capacity to transform their interrelated fates. The state usually possesses great but not total control. Strategies of control imposed by the state are susceptible to the failings and inconsistencies of human actors and the machinations of government, the activities of nonhuman species, and the quirks and shortcomings of nonliving things. They are also momentarily pregnable by human resistance.

2.2.1 Legalities of Centralization, Normalization, and Inter/Dysconnectedness

Governing through contagion contains three features: centralization and technology of law; normalization and technologies of moralization; and inter/dysconnectedness and the rearticulation of difference. The three features morph with strategies of control, and the phenomenon of human resistance threads through all three. I illustrate these features with my collaborative study on Singapore and draw examples from three temporal contexts – the colonial era of 1868–1915, the 2003 Severe Acute Respiratory Syndrome (SARS) outbreak, and the COVID-19 pandemic.

Centralization and technology of law: The more centralized state infrastructures are, the more quickly the state can deploy and probably the more efficiently it can implement strategies of control. In Singapore, where the legislature and executive are functionally fused, the government is able to roll out strategies of control quickly. After the legislature enacts primary legislation, the executive expeditiously issues orders and directives and nimbly mobilizes personnel for enforcement.

The colonial years of 1868–1915 laid the foundation for fast, coordinated responses to contagious diseases. The British designated Singapore as a trading post in 1819 and as part of the Straits Settlements Crown Colony in 1867. The governor of the Straits Settlements effectively controlled the Legislative Council (LegCo) and dominated law-making. The Quarantine Ordinance, passed in 1868, was the first to empower the governor to regulate outbreaks on land and incoming vessels carrying diseased persons or animals. In 1886, LegCo replaced the 1868 ordinance with the Quarantine and Prevention of Disease Ordinance (QPDO), which increased executive powers to isolate and remove infected humans, such as Chinese immigrants bearing the bubonic plague, and creatures such as dogs with rabies arriving on European ships. Developed in response to the recursive relationships among humans, critters, and germs, by 1915 the QPDO would become the infrastructural scaffolding for a centralized approach to contagious threats.

After decolonization, Singapore's postcolonial government used the Westminster parliamentary infrastructure to retain and embolden the colonial scaffolding. The QPDO, renamed the Quarantine and Prevention of Disease Act (QPDA), served as the legislative basis for postcolonial Singapore's governance of contagion until 1976. To better address the conditions of international trade and travel connected to the spread of malaria and typhoid, the government replaced the QPDA with the 1976 Infectious Diseases Act (IDA). The IDA reinforced the colonial strategies of control and stayed essentially unchanged for twenty-seven years.

The 2003 SARS outbreak marked the next formative phase of governing through contagion, when Singapore reported 238 probable cases and 33 deaths. The deadliness of the virus triggered two rounds of legislative amendments that enhanced state infrastructures. The amendments concentrated medical-related functions of investigation, prevention, and containment of outbreaks (previously shared with environmental agencies) to the Ministry of Health (MOH); expanded the definition of "health officers" to enable the deployment of more enforcement personnel; widened the scope of quarantine from hospitals and other "suitable" locations to "home quarantine"; allowed MOH to restrict the entry of persons and goods into public or private premises; and penalized anyone who knew or suspected they were suffering from an infectious disease for being out in public and exposing others (save for going to medical treatment).

The SARS amendments set the stage for another critical phase of governing through contagion in Singapore: COVID-19. In the two months leading up to the circuit breaker in April 2020, MOH issued regulations under the IDA to prescribe physical distancing requirements, crowd sizes, and telecommuting. Ninety-six hours after the prime minister announced the circuit breaker, parliament passed the COVID-19 (Temporary Measures) Act (CTMA), and the government issued the first of many CMTA regulations the same evening. The CMTA increased executive powers already found in the IDA and extended them to economic activities: for example, protecting businesses and individuals from the inability to perform contractual obligations, or to pay damages, rent, or loans as a result of pandemic-related difficulties.

It may seem as though governing through contagion expanded progressively from the colonial period to COVID-19. However, highly centralized infrastructures merely supply the legal technology. Whether governing through contagion will expand chronologically depends on the relationships among humans, contagion, and the state. In addition, different strategies of control toward the same contagion may entangle dissimilar relationships. For example, the colonial government was more hesitant about implementing vaccination laws compared to laws on quarantine and movement restrictions. Although it was already concerned about the spread of smallpox in the 1850s, especially among children, it waited until 1868 to pass laws requiring vaccination for children and until 1915 for adults. A key reason for this hesitancy was technological deficiency. The colonial government did not know how to procure sufficient vaccine matter, which was originally humanized lymph, or how to transport it across long distances. It was only in the 1890s that the government managed to increase the vaccination rate faster, when it learned to switch to, and obtain, calf lymph.

But my collaborator and I also surmise that the government implemented smallpox vaccination measures more cautiously because it involved boundary-crossing from the nonhuman (the vaccine matter) to the human. Colonial elites made rhetorical noise about consent, and officials constantly discussed the religious objections of "natives." Although consent was probably nominal, these issues suggest that the government was somehow uncomfortable about imposing vaccination on the colonized. By comparison, it gave little to no consideration to their wishes when implementing control measures such as those on quarantine and protective gear.

Like smallpox vaccination, COVID-19 vaccination involves crossing the boundary from nonhuman into human by introducing into the human body biological matter taken from the COVID-19 virus (in different forms depending on the type of vaccine). The Singaporean government did not make COVID-19 vaccination compulsory. Instead, it encouraged vaccination through legal technologies already in place to implement other strategies of controls, to the point that choosing not to vaccinate became highly inconvenient and troublesome. For instance, it revised containment regulations to require "vaccination differentiation," such that unvaccinated persons were banned from dining out at restaurants and cafes or entering shopping malls. When it launched child vaccination, children whose parents did not agree to vaccination were allowed to attend class but barred from after-school activities. The government also stopped covering the COVID-19 medical expenses of people who chose not to vaccinate.

Normalization and technologies of moralization: Governing through contagion in its most powerful form can achieve normalization, a deep form of dominance that shapes the discourse and norms lying behind conduct regulated by strategies of control to the point of moralization. In the most "normalized" state, the government would not need to explicitly enforce the law to compel behavior. People would obey the strategies of control without question and perhaps with full acceptance and participation in its enforcement, such as surveilling, reporting on, and demanding other subjects to comply.

Governing through contagion achieves normalization-moralization by employing law and other technological means such as vaccines, thermometers, test kits, contact-tracing apps, and quarantine facilities. The opening lines taken from the packaging of a reusable mask, which I received as I entered the thirty-minute observation area after getting my first Pfizer shot, epitomizes the combination of law and other technologies to achieve normalization-moralization. The message portrayed mask-wearing not as a legal requirement (except under limited circumstances)[11] but as a moral act – something that a responsible person would

[11] At the time of my vaccination, it was compulsory to wear masks at all times in public spaces unless engaging in strenuous exercises. At the time of writing, the government had removed the requirement except for visiting medical facilities.

do. Moreover, by signing off as "VACCiNATION SG," a play on the word, "vaccination," the government campaign depicted getting vaccinated as doing one's part for the nation.

The degree and contents of normalization-moralization vary across contagious episodes and sociolegal contexts, corresponding to the contagion's nature, human perceptions of the contagion, and their experiences with state logics of security and technologies. In the Straits Settlements, governing through contagion sought to safeguard the colony's public health to ensure the British Empire's economic and political hierarchy. The normalization-moralization contents of governing through contagion aimed to "civilize" "native" subjects, whom colonial officers were afraid would induce contagious spread with their culturally inferior habits. For instance, sanitary officials used chemicals to disinfect "native" dwellings and replaced "Asian" sewage disposals with Westernized sanitation systems; inspectors patrolled neighbourhoods to monitor habits such as hand washing and spitting; and officials characterized vaccination as an act of beneficence aimed at overcoming "native" prejudice.

In the postcolonial era, governing through contagion's normalization-moralization contents focused on constructing resilient, productive subjects who are united under a "Singaporean" identity and contribute to the nation's prosperity. SARS and COVID-19, respectively, established and reaffirmed the "socially responsible" subject. When the legislature passed the IDA amendments in response to the SARS outbreak, parliamentarians emphasized the critical role of law in enforcing socially responsible conduct. Politicians publicly shamed the "socially irresponsible," such as an infected family who roamed around town against doctor's orders. State-controlled media constantly reminded the population to wash their hands with soap and monitor their temperature, and ordinary citizens joined in, writing letters to newspapers to berate fellow subjects to be responsible and practice "good" hygiene. By the time of COVID-19, the "socially responsible" subject had been arguably formed. Children, parents, and teachers had cultivated the habit of temperature-taking, a requirement for students since the SARS days. Landlords put up flyers reminding people to sanitize their hands, wear masks, and maintain physical distances. Retailers and restaurants required customers to scan a QR code with their smart phones or government-issued tokens for contact-tracing purposes. Enforcement personnel dubbed "safe-distancing ambassadors" roved about shopping malls, markets, and parks, officers surveilled the quarantined by their smart phones, and zealous Singaporeans exposed lawbreakers by tracking social media postings and filming illicit actions. Government vaccination campaigns drummed the beat of "social responsibility," as we saw with the package wrapping, and the experience of getting vaccinated became part of everyday conversation.

Of the three periods, COVID-19's reach of normalization-moralization is probably the most extensive. However, similar to centralization, normalization-moralization does not necessarily progress chronologically. It fluctuates according to human relationships with technologies and contagions of the day. In colonial Singapore, Chinese coolies associated early facilities of quarantine with poor treatment and death and refused to cooperate. During the SARS and COVID-19 era, there were people – for comfort or whatever reason – who refused to comply with quarantine orders or wear masks.

Resistance toward vaccination especially complicates the course of normalization-moralization. During the COVID-19 pandemic, people who refused vaccination cited their own moral or religious reasons, concerns with their bodily reactions, or doubts about the vaccine technology. In the colonial period, the resistance against smallpox vaccination among one segment of Malay Muslims was also on religious grounds, alternative moral beliefs that vaccination went against providence. However, some Malay Muslims also resisted vaccination because of technological inadequacies. About 30 percent of child smallpox vaccinations in the earlier period failed to produce the required bodily response, partly due to the incompetence of government-appointed vaccinators' and partly due to the poor quality of lymphs. Consequently, angry parents refused to subject their children to "revaccination." This act of resistance had broad implications, because the supply of smallpox vaccines relied on extracting lymph from the vesicles of recently, successfully vaccinated persons for use in vaccinations on other people (Lee & Chua 2023).

Inter/dysconnectedness and rearticulation of difference: The third theme of governing through contagion flows from the first two. Interconnectedness refers to the physical, spiritual, and economic linkages via technology among humans and between humans and contagion. Dysconnectedness refers to inequitable divisions among humans which are the result of technology and often exacerbations of existing differences.

To begin, contagion relies on interconnectedness with and among people by way of technologies such as food and land exploitation, transportation, and dense urban architectures. Meanwhile, strategies of control deploy technology to separate contagion from humans and the (possibly) infected humans from the uninfected, such as by quarantine, masks, and vaccines. These interconnections and (attempts at) disconnections lead to dysconnectedness. For example, the ability or willingness to establish disconnections from fellow humans and nonhumans to curb the spread of contagion varies across individuals due to race, class, legal status, or other attributes associated with social stratification. Such dysconnectedness highlights and at times worsens existing differences. In colonial Singapore, epidemics disproportionately affected Chinese coolies and brothel workers and were aggravated by the government's differentiated enforcement and quarantine facilities, which separated Europeans from "natives," and upper-class Asians from Chinese coolies. During the SARS period, "unskilled" foreign laborers were forced into quarantine upon entry, but "professional" foreigners could self-quarantine. During the COVID-19 pandemic, the government also applied border controls differently between Singaporeans and foreigners and between "professional" foreigners and "migrant" workers. Moreover, migrant workers could not adopt distancing measures to protect themselves in crammed living quarters rented by their employers.

Furthermore, the theme of inter/dysconnectedness brings out the equivocal effects of resistance. Although resistance can disrupt governing through contagion, it can also produce more dysconnectedness. In colonial Singapore, when Chinese coolies ran away from squalid quarantine facilities, they were prosecuted and punished. By comparison, when Chetties – a South Asian mercantile community – complained about their smallpox quarantine conditions, the colonial government responded by constructing differently classed wards for Europeans and Asian elites. In addition, as mentioned above, when Malay Muslim parents refused "revaccination" for their children, colonial officials conveniently attributed their resistance to "native" prejudices and brushed aside their concerns about the deficiencies of vaccine technology that had caused the unsuccessful, initial attempts. During the COVID-19 pandemic, some Singaporeans cast people who resisted mask-wearing or physical distancing measures as "socially irresponsible." If the offenders were not Singaporean, especially if they were migrant workers, the ostracization often contained underlying tones of classism, racism, or xenophobia already present in society.

2.2.2 *Multiple Agents, Multiple Reckonings*

Because of the COVID-19 pandemic a greater number of scholars started to pay attention to public health laws regulating human conduct and movement. During the pandemic, public health laws also seemed to have exceeded the public health mission by having to carry the additional weight of politics: In some societies COVID-19 regulations were swiftly politicized by rivalling factions to serve their positions and advantages. As a result the politicized regulations, their implementations, and the resistance against them produced inter/dysconnectedness. If we concentrate on COVID-19, we might surmise that COVID-19 was an iconic moment of indexing for juristocratic reckoning and ask which phase the interactions with COVID-19 regulations represented.

However, our analysis of governing through contagion shows that public health laws develop in a recursive, gradual manner in relation to nonhuman beings and the nonliving. Governing through contagion retreated when no imminently deadly contagion lurked, whereas law did not necessarily prevail in times of heightened danger. Governing through contagion sometimes failed to expand when it was tempered by resistance of the human variety or uncontrollable or unpredictable behaviors of contagions and technologies.

Even if we accept COVID-19 as a moment of reckoning for public health laws, the legality of governing through contagion nevertheless offers another perspective on juristocratic reckoning by casting attention on a longer span of chronological time and a broader range of actors. In the narrative about the legality of governing through contagion in the Straits Settlements and Singapore, while significant and extraordinary, COVID-19 is not the only moment of juristocratic reckoning nor the genesis for harnessing legal power to subdue contagious diseases. Rather, COVID-19 is merely one of many moments in the relationship among humans, the nonliving, and the nonhuman. Like human rights practice as a way of life in my first narrative, governing through contagion is a legality that simultaneously moves chronologically and cyclically, informed by but learning from and evolving from the past.

2.2.3 *After Contagion?*

Many contagious diseases are now distant memories. Some of them, like smallpox, are no more than a checkbox on a child's vaccination record in Singapore and other societies. As the COVID-19 virus mutated, becoming more contagious but less lethal, people's perceptions of danger dropped. My students half-joked about catching the virus to "get it over with." At the time of writing this essay, governments around the world have drastically eased or removed COVID-19 restrictions.

What should we make of the lessons from governing through contagion thus far, including COVID-19 and especially the strategies of control that rely on legal power? Perhaps we cannot draw a single conclusion. After all, governing through contagion depends on the ever-changing configuration of human and nonhuman connections. We do not know which new contagions lie await and which may return. However, I speculate that governments and human actors will most probably call upon law, in collaboration with other technologies, to fight the next contagion. Whether or not future phases of governing through contagion will display juristocratic reckonings worthy of iconic indexicality – as the volume editors have in mind in Chapter 1 – will depend on human–nonhuman interactions. The legality of governing through contagion will probably endure, lying endemic, and like contagion will break out with the next shift in this complex set of relationships. And so we shall participate in governing through contagion, willingly or reluctantly, our fates conjoined.

2.3 Beyond Reckoning Lies Reckoning

The two narratives offering different profiles of juristocratic reckonings tender an ambivalent answer about the limits of law. In the first story, human rights practice appears to have failed after almost two decades, confronted with a recalcitrant regime that deploys law to abuse and terrorize. In the second narrative law is preoccupied with economic security and embattled with disease, perhaps inadvertently worsening injustices. Moreover, legal mobilization and resistance could be held back by law's connections to other normative orders, nonhuman beings, and things.

Nonetheless, the two stories do offer hope. In the aftermath of the 2021 coup, Burmese LGBT activists are reviving their human rights practice. Their leaders are back in exile in a neighboring country, once again informed by their recent struggles and fuelled by more memories of rage and suffering. Maybe their practice will still embody old faults and fault lines of ethnicity, religion, and gender, but maybe not in the same variation. Maybe they will learn from the past and do better this time. Around the world, the scale of COVID-19-related tragedies and strategies of controls drew our attention to wrongful treatments of marginalized human populations, as well as those of humankind's co-species and of the environment. After this bout of contagion, burdened with tragic remembrances and informed by new possibilities of technology, maybe we can hope that humans and their governments will be more willing and able to address injustices that were exposed during the pandemic and find creative ways for law and other technologies to aid them.

Legalities move to and through chronological time, but they may not develop linearly. Legalities may carry forward old habits and problems, but they can also turn well-worn formulas into new permutations, changing them bit by bit. Because law connects to people, state and social institutions, creatures, and objects, legalities may assume multidimensional shapes traversing in plural directions and trajectories. Along these journeys in times of juristocratic reckoning, whatever the phase or name we give them, law may embody the potential to wreck harm, stay indifferent to suffering, or propel the currents of social justice.

References

Cheesman, Nick. 2015. *Opposing the Rule of Law: How Myanmar's Courts Make Law and Order*. New York: Cambridge University Press.

Chua, Lynette J. 2019. *The Politics of Love in Myanmar: LGBT Mobilization and Human Rights as a Way of Life*. Stanford: Stanford University Press.

2021. Interregna: Time, Law, and Resistance. *Law & Social Inquiry* 46 (1): 268–291.

Chua, Lynette J. and Lee, Jack Jin Gary. 2021. Governing through Contagion. In Victor V. Ramraj, ed., *Covid-19 in Asia: Law and Policy Contexts*. Oxford: Oxford University Press, 116–132.

Chua, Lynette J. and Jack Jin Gary Lee, eds. 2024. *Contagion, Technology, and Law at the Limits*. Hart.

Goodale, Mark. 2007. The Power of Right(s): Tracking Empires of Law and New Modes of Social Resistance in Bolivia (and Elsewhere). In M. Goodale and S. E. Merry, eds., *The Practice of Human Rights: Tracking Law Between the Global and the Local*. Cambridge: Cambridge University Press, 130–162.

Lee, Jack Jin Gary and Chua, Lynette J. 2023. Smallpox Vaccination and the Limits of Governing through Contagion in the Straits Settlements, 1868–1926. *Law & Policy* 45 (3): 331–352.

Moran, Leslie J. 2004. Sexuality in Law and Society Scholarship. In Austin Sarat, ed., *The Blackwell Companion to Law and Society*. Oxford: Blackwell, 487–505.

Weeks, Jeffrey. 1995. Necessary Fictions: Sexual Identities and the Politics of Diversity. In Jeffrey Weeks, ed., *Invented Moralities: Sexual Values in an Age of Uncertainty*. New York: Columbia University Press, 82–101.

3

After Constitutionalism

Current Pathways of Legal Domination

JULIA ECKERT AND KIRI SANTER

3.1 Introduction

In this chapter we flip the perspective of juristocratic reckoning, which the editors of this volume see as a process taking place "from below," on its head. We argue that if there is reckoning to be observed, it is a reckoning from above, a return not to the "conventional roles" of law but a return to a different idea of the state, and of limits to its contestability through law. The expectation overload toward law that we observed in the last decades were, in many cases, expectations toward the state, as a caring state, one that would ensure the well-being of all its citizens (see e.g., Eckert 2011, 2020). In that sense, demands expressed through law, and responded to by states through law, were part of struggles over governmental regulation, then carrying within them the notion that government should have social justice at its core.

We write this chapter shortly after the overruling of *Roe vs. Wade* which ended fifty years of abortion rights in the United States. In the same week the Supreme Court ruled against restrictions on carrying guns in public space. Both decisions were sharp reminders that rights are fragile and liberal constitutions insufficient to enduringly protect non-hegemonic groups in an age of democratic decline. They point toward law's sociality, its nonfixity, and the possibility for it to be shaped in favor of and strategically utilized by repressive government, all the while maintaining the outward appearance of liberalism and the possibilities of democratic participation. Rather than speaking of such moments as

We would like to thank the participants in a retreat in Kleinfrendenwalde Germany in the summer of 2022, for their precious comments on this paper: Matthieu Bolay, Johanna Mugler, Sharib Ali, Lucien Schönenberg, Paule Pastre, Devhuti Shaw, and Fazil Moradi.

"processes of reckoning *against* the law" (Goodale and Zenker, this volume), we would rather assert that law has no "normal" or "conventional" character independent of historical figurations of rule; what law is considered normal or conventional is always the outcome of historical struggles, including struggles through law. In these, law is redefined (Eckert et al. 2012). So, it is with the uneasy uncertainty of what yet another set of worrisome legal developments will bring, that we assert the necessity to think the manifold manifestation of current forms of legal domination. Thus, unlike the editors of this volume, we cannot observe a return to law's "normal" or "conventional" role in "conflict resolution, government regulation, and the social response to wrongdoing." Rather, what we see is a (re-)turn to a particular convention of state governance through law as a means of rule. This mode of governing decidedly repudiates encompassing visions of social protection and substantive equality.

Furthermore, we see little evidence for the claim of the juridification of protest contributing to its depoliticization.[1] We also argue thus, that the lessening significance of legal mobilization is not necessarily a result of the frustrations with the limited possibilities of law. Far from it. These limited possibilities of law were always perceived, particularly by organized collective struggles. We assume that there were only rare cases of social struggles in which hopes for caring polities were located entirely in the mobilization of "law against the state"; mostly, law was but one instrument among many in struggles for social justice. This was so also in cases where there had been encompassing promises by a developmentalist vision of the state and an activist judiciary advocating for a proactive interpretation of the constitution and holding governments to it, like in pre- and post-emergency India. There, too, collective struggles for social justice never confined themselves to the mobilization of law but combined legal with more overtly political means of struggle, ranging from demonstrations, negotiations with political representatives and state agencies, to forming parties.

Thus, what we observe instead is an *active diminishment of the already limited possibilities of law to be mobilized for social justice*. This is what

[1] In contrast, judicialization, that is the transfer of decisions from parliaments and governments to courts, has produced specific forms of depoliticization. Mostly, the critics of judicialization have deplored that authority is transferred from more representative instances such as parliaments or elected governments to an unrepresentative and unaccountable judiciary. This can lead to political concerns being shifted to "surveillance and judgement" away from questions of "legitimacy, participation and representation" (Randeria 2007: 39).

this text is about. We do not say that the active diminishment of legal possibilities is always a direct response to legal mobilization "from below." We consider it a wider trend that abandons not law's promises, but state promises, or limits them to newly restricted constituencies, often precisely to those that have not mobilized law against the state because they have been well served by the legal order as it stood.

We focus on three current trajectories of legal development: namely, authoritarian legalism, as a blunt mode of limiting the possibilities of law; the sophisticated mode of the dispersion of jurisdiction that fragments states' legal responsibilities, recalibrates the hierarchies between different bodies of law, and diminishes the reach and accessibility of specific protective bodies of law; and the benevolent mode of the tribunalization of conflict resolution, which introduces a logic of law that is not oriented toward general norms that are applied to particular cases, but confines itself to individual cases, thereby diminishing the possibilities of precedent and the wider alliances that mobilize around precedent. We observe authoritarian legalism in its incremental implementation in India, where systematically, legal measures have been introduced in recent years to "legalize" a dual-law situation long in the making that limits access to law to specific population groups. This can be observed in many other places. We observe the dispersion of jurisdiction in relation to the borders of Europe, where the access to the laws that would nominally regulate these borders (e.g., asylum law) is thwarted by the creation of new legal zones and jurisdictional responsibilities. We observe the tribunalization of conflict resolution with relation to the regulation of global capitalism, where seemingly egalitarian procedures increase asymmetries and "singularize" injuries.

These examples are not part of one governance assembly; they are not connected, and in many aspects they are incomparable. While differing from each other to the degree that they cannot be compared, and without being part of an integrated strategy or governance modality, they all share the characteristic of constructing legal impediments to access to law, either in procedural or material legal innovations. Moreover, they all constitute (albeit in very different forms and contexts) a response to the constitutional state, and, more specifically, to an order which aspires to an equality of treatment under the law. These three modalities selectively respond to that project, and in doing so produce legal modes of exclusion and pathways out of constitutionalism.

Such impediments to claim-making through law have always existed. What is of interest to us here is to understand current developments of obstacles to access law, which themselves take place through legal operations. The various sidelinings of constitutionalism each have their own historical specificity; they respond to specific historical situations. Looking at these different examples of the ways in which governments create alternatives to constitutionalism, we can take a broader view that is not limited to authoritarian legalism and illiberal democracies. It is not our intention here, however, to belittle the latter's modes of leaving constitutionalism behind, or to compare the three modes in terms of resulting misery. Rather, our aim is to point to these contemporary modes with the thesis in mind that there is a more general trend to curtail the role of law as a means of the struggle for social justice. These pathways, despite their differences, each evade, abolish, and replace the norms that many social struggles set their hopes in and the legal procedures that they have been able to enter into. Moreover, one could say, this trend in effect curtails a central tenet of liberal law, namely, its very liberalism.

We consider it the particular possibility of an anthropological perspective on law to leave behind the perspective on "law's" essential limits (in the language of critical legal studies), or an ahistorical notion of law's "normal" or "conventional" role, to consider law as having characteristics but not essences, and therefore to be (re-)made in social interactions. It seems important to us to move away from the rather general discussion of law's limits – however conceived – or of the related "law-versus-politics" arguments, to take a close look at how and what specific type of law prevents some social change and initiates another kind, and how forms of politics articulate with law in specific ways in different historical figurations. This is what we want to examine here. We outline the effects of these three modalities and argue that taken together, they are not putting an end to constitutionalism but rather, contributing to a new constitutional order in which political injunctions are authoritatively institutionalized through law but cannot be contested through it anymore. The conventional role of constitutional law to provide for the possibility to address governments and state authorities through law is increasingly diminished, and law is reduced to a one-sided instrument of rule. Thus, rather than speaking generally about the limits of law for social transformation, we want to look more precisely at the diverse but specific contemporary limits that are actively erected – possibly precisely because law's possibilities for social transformation were recently used and expanded by much "legalism from below."

3.2 The Blunt Mode: Authoritarian/Fascist Legality in Current India

India is a good example to discuss what in the Introduction to this volume is referred to by Goodale and Zenker as a context in which "*law, broadly conceived, is freighted with demands and expectations that overflow its normal institutional, instrumental, and normative carrying capacity.*" India's postindependence leaders succeeded in establishing the state at the core of India's society, both through its constitutional promises and its institutional presence. The state, as the distributor of rights and entitlements and the preserver of order "was transformed from a distant, alien object into one that aspired to infiltrate the everyday lives of Indians, proclaiming itself responsible for everything they could desire" (Khilnani 1999: 41). This idea of the Indian state has shaped political negotiations even beyond its heyday and despite the fact that it neither fulfilled its promises, nor avoided the excesses of its modernist projects. Such negotiations increasingly also involved the mobilization of law, especially since India's higher judiciary sought to remedy its utter failure during the emergency of 1975–7 to safeguard civil rights by taking an activist stance to hold successive Indian governments accountable to the rights enshrined in the Indian constitution.

The reorientation of the state in the course of the neoliberal transition in India has, like in many other countries, taken the route of recalibrating the boundaries of the legitimate body politic. Hindu nationalism[2] has had the role of ideologically orienting this shift in the idea of the polity. With the ever-increasing role of Hindu nationalist political organizations in the national and state-level legislatives and their "march through all institutions," this including the higher judiciary, a differentiation of membership rights has been increasingly pursued through law,

[2] Hindu nationalism, or Hindutva, is first and foremost a unifying project that considers the threat to the community to lie in disunity, internal dissent, or contestations of the social order. It is not the denial of difference as such, since difference is institutionalized (e.g., in the caste system), but the denial of conflict between those who are considered different, especially when it concerns contestations of the social order. Thus, notions of threat relate intrinsically to the way that "order" is understood, that is, to the factors presumed to be existential for social peace. The idea of a body politic shaped by harmonious "internal" relations – that is, the organic vision of the nation held by Hindu nationalism and the denial of conflict entailed in it – has been conflated with the neoliberal approach of the quasi-automatic regulation of social inequality through market-form interactions. This confluence has led to a more fundamental delegitimization of conflict, especially when it concerns contestations of the social (or national) order.

adjudication, and legislation. While citizenship was in India, as elsewhere, always far from equal (e.g., Jayal 2001: 249), the differentiation of membership rights has gained a new degree of legitimacy.

The development of dual law in India began in the field of security laws, namely, the country's successive anti-terrorism laws. Anti-terror laws and special security legislations have a long history in India; independent India incorporated several colonial preventive laws into its criminal law and enacted successive anti-terrorist legislation. In recent years these laws have been used to target particularly Muslims, lower caste, and tribal communities. At the same time, there has been a shift of perceiving what is classified as terrorism from an "internal" problem of dissatisfied minorities, to an "external" threat: Terrorism, and in particular, Muslims accused of terrorism, have been constructed as alien others.

Divergent group-related perceptions of militancy were entered into anti-terrorism law when POTA (the Prevention of Terrorist Activities Act) was enacted. POTA confined the definition of terrorist violence to violence that (a) operates clandestinely and (b) shows clear evidence of premeditation. Clandestinity is frequently referred to as proof of planning and of malevolent intent; premeditation and planning are proof of intent, distinguishing premeditated violence from an affective one that does not fall under anti-terrorism laws. Considering the partisan position of the state agencies, the "need" to operate clandestinely is very unequally distributed between majority and minority organizations; hence, both clandestinity and premeditation are characteristic more often of minority violence. For majority organizations, clandestinity is not necessary, because they can most often ensure the cooperation or nonintervention by the local police. Majority violence by Hindus, moreover, has frequently been considered spontaneous, often irrational, and affective; it is thereby removed from the purview of anti-terrorism law. Muslim violence, however, owing to the fact that it is perceived as both clandestine and premeditated, falls under the definition of terrorism (Eckert et al. 2012). Differentiated legal treatment of the same deeds according to the ascriptive identity of the suspect or accused initiated a system of dual law. In effect, while preventive laws have been used against many forms of social and political protest, and also against protesters nominally Hindu, protest by Muslims, Dalits, and tribals entails extreme risks to be dealt with under security laws with its lack of protective safeguards.

This system of dual law was dramatically expanded beyond the regulation of protest and unrest, when in December 2019 the government under Prime Minister Modi enacted the Citizenship Amendment Act

(CAA) and, simultaneously, updated the National Register of Citizens. The two measures complemented each other: The Citizenship Amendment Act was revised to grant refugees from neighbouring countries immediate access to Indian citizenship if they were Hindus, Jains, Sikhs, Parsees, or Christian. Muslim refugees were not included and had no right to obtain citizenship when fleeing these neighbouring countries. Thereby, religion was for the first time in independent India's history the decisive criterion for the right to citizenship. At the same time, the Indian government launched the updating of the National Population Register (NPR) which registers all people residing in India, both citizens and noncitizens. The NPR made it possible to identify clearly noncitizens within India. This would enable authorities to deport people who were residing "illegally" in India. Anyone who could not prove their citizenship – which millions do not, lacking documents such as birth certificates or even ration cards that would prove their long-term legally recognized residency, for example – might be denied Indian citizenship and rendered stateless. While Hindus and other religious groups mentioned in the CAA would obtain citizenship anew via the CAA, Muslims without proof of citizenship would lose any legal status in India and be threatened with deportation. Detention centers were and are being built in several states to hold "illegal" residents before deportation, above all in Assam, where 1.9 million people are threatened to be stripped of their citizenship.

These developments that establish a dual law system beyond criminal justice, and also in citizenship laws, are further complemented by laws of several Indian states that Mayur Suresh has termed "social segregation laws" (Suresh 2021). These include the "disturbed areas act" as well as the laws of several Indian states such as Uttar Pradesh, Karnataka, Madhya Pradesh, and Kerala against a so-called love jihad, criminalizing interfaith marriages between Hindus and Muslims, and, more particularly, between Hindu women and Muslim men. The ban on cow slaughter in several states has led to a wave of so-called cow vigilantism that Muslims suspected of transporting cows for the purpose of slaughter have fallen victim to. There is rarely any state sanction against these vigilante murders.

These Indian examples of enacting special laws for a specific part of the population is not unprecedented at all – far from it. In the context of electoral democracies, much attention has been given to constitutional reform such as that of Hungary,[3] or the changes in the rules governing

[3] See: https://verfassungsblog.de/category/debates/restoring-constitutionalism/.

the judiciary such as in Poland (e.g., Pech & Scheppele 2017). Both are defining for illiberal democracies, in as much as they rearrange the division of powers by expanding executive powers while limiting civil liberties. What we first want to point to here is that there have been numerous efforts in other legal fields such as criminal law, civil law, or citizenship laws that similarly transform the relation between citizens and the state, often specific groups of citizens and the state,[4] which have been less discussed and have not been identified as forms of authoritarian legalism.

Moreover, the delineation of a Hindu polity does not stop at these legislative innovations. Rather, juristocratic reckoning in Modi's India has meant a thorough sidelining of law. "Law has been rendered impotent," felt a prominent lawyer. To not an insignificant degree such sidelining of law is achieved through judicial delay, that is, courts not taking up claims and petitions, so that victims of abuses are faced with a fait accompli that the courts are unwilling to reverse; or that promotions of oppositional candidates within the judiciary are simply never appointed, rendering courts dysfunctional (and further contributing to the tremendous backlog of cases at all judicial levels). Thereby the collegiate is encouraged to suggest candidates for promotion they know will be approved by the government.

For these strategies of influencing adjudication and judicial appointments to proceed systematically, all institutions of the state have by now been manned with members of, or people subservient to, the Sangh Parivar (the "family" of Hindu nationalist organizations, this including the ruling party, the BJP, as the political wind of the Sangh Parivar) in numbers significant enough to undo judicial independence. The Hindu nationalist forces have excelled in a systematic and long-term march through the institutions that all other illiberal democracies can be envious of.

The second tentative observation we want to make with this example is that these legal restrictions on the (legal) participation of some, as well as the systematic undermining of judicial independence, with which law is rendered partisan, announce globally resurfacing notions of nonconflictive polities; they potentially delegitimize more generally the employment

[4] The denationalization of "suspect subjects" (Schiffauer 2006) has now arrived also in liberal democracies, such as Britain (Hong 2021). In Germany, religious freedoms, and in particular: symbols of religious identity in public, have been interpreted differently for members of established Christian churches, than for the less centrally organized adherents to the various denominations of Islam.

of law as a means of expressing alternative understandings of polities. The derecognition of the Muslims in India as legitimate members of the body politic, and their increasing social and legal definition as alien others in law, commencing with the treatment of Muslim collective violence under anti-terrorism laws, and culminating in the potential denationalization of Muslim citizens without state documents, has recently been increasingly expanded to the collective action of other groups with ascriptive identity markers, such as tribals and Dalits. Over the decades there has been a transition from role to ascriptive identity in the categories that underlie state constructions of threat. However, the organicist ideas of the Hindu nation that have informed these exclusions have more generally delegitimated antagonistic political stances: antagonistic collective action is increasingly treated as a matter of preventive and security laws (Eckert 2014). Thus, possibilities for access to the (liberal) protections of law become ever more conditional on both a majoritarian identification of legitimate belonging and nonantagonistic political positions.

3.3 The Sophisticated Mode: Dispersing Jurisdiction

Our second example concerns the use of law in international and transnational governance. Under globalization, it has been argued that "cunning states" (Randeria 2003) are able to selectively mobilize the language of sovereignty to avoid international interventions in some domains such as human rights whilst willing to yield to or apply the rules of others (such as in international trade). The issue of selectivity often relates to the scalar politics of law. In "statist visions of law and the spatiality of the state" (Basaran 2020: 28), boundaries between the national and the international are considered to be clear, with the state defined as the central locus of politics and of the predominant unit of the international order. In fact, whilst law might be rendered visible through the principle of sovereignty over territory (Basaran 2020: 34), law in international governance often operates in much more invisible ways, weaving together and thus blurring different scales of jurisdiction. This, in turn, makes selective exclusions from mechanisms of accountability possible because state and territory have been fragmented by governance processes. Hence, accountability mechanisms, which include provisions for fundamental rights protections, are rendered ineffective by shifting boundaries of jurisdiction enabled by governance through/with law. This is the case in much of migration governance arrangements which mix formal and informal structures of cooperation to "manage" unwanted migration (Lavenex 2016: 457).

At the external borders of the European Union different types of law are layered and employed to achieve cooperative interdiction of migrants fleeing by sea. Cooperative interdiction is the coordinated and unequal collaboration between European authorities (the maritime coordination centers of nation states but also EU agencies and ministries) and Libyan officials, to bar migrant sea-crossers from accessing European territory and jurisdiction. Cooperative interdiction has a complex legal architecture, which has evolved through the dynamic interplay between border externalization policies such as Integrated Border Management and litigation efforts to ensure that noncitizen's access to law (here: rights and protection) is maintained in the face of these multileveled processes of bordering.

The 2012 *Hirsi Jamaa* v. *Italy* case at the European Court of Human Rights was a landmark case that rendered unlawful Italy's handing over of migrants to the Libyan coastguard on the high seas. It extended the extraterritorial reach of the court, reviewing the actions of agents of states, party to the convention, even when they find themselves outside of the territorial boundaries of the state. However, this case has seemingly also instructed European states on how to continue to conduct policies with similar outcomes to the one condemned in *Hirsi*, only in a way that makes them more impermeable to judicial review. Jessica Greenberg (2021) has called this phenomenon "counterpedagogy."

The consequences of this "instruction" are twofold. On a practical level, the implementation of interdiction policies which aim to bar migrants from accessing EU territory have taken on a "contactless" (Moreno-Lax & Giuffré 2017) quality in terms of the law. Legal distance is put between the enablers of a policy (the EU and member states such as Italy) and the subjects targeted by these policies. The implementors (the Libyan coastguard) act as a buffer. To achieve this controversial outcome which is both material (interdiction) and legal (reduction of accountability mechanisms) the dispersion of law across varying levels of governance (which respond to different logics of review and serve different purposes) plays an important role. The European Emergency Trust Fund for Africa (EUTF), for example, acts as a key resource to train the Libyan coastguard, to equip and monitor them. The fund is thus technically dispersed across diverse development and humanitarian policy objectives, as well as directorate-generals and implementation partners responsible for them. Contributing to the fund are states, but a large majority of the funds also stem from the EU Development Fund (EDF) which is managed outside the EU budget and therefore retains a strong intergovernmental character.[5] Moreover, through a logic of crisis exception, the very regulation of emergency trust funds exempts them from EU public procurement rules (Spijkerboer & Steyger 2019). The EUTF is instrumental in the achievement of cooperative interdiction, built out of European regulations. It is an instrument of governance that seeks to control the movement of nonEU citizens and participates simultaneously in various ways to their exclusion from law.

At sea, international maritime law contains both the injunction for migrant lives to be preserved *and* the footing for justifications by the EU authorities to delegate responsibility to their Libyan counterparts. Indeed, since the notification of the Libyan Search and Rescue Region (SRR) in June 2018, Libya has become formally responsible for coordinating rescues across a vast area of international waters. The Libyan SRR then provides a veil, a legal "cut" (Strathern 1996) in a network of interrelations making it harder for migrants to address the European Court of Human Rights since the actors that effectively violate their rights do not fall under its jurisdiction. Migrants cannot, therefore, sue European actors for violations of European human rights law, such as the prohibition of collective expulsions, rights to an effective remedy and the nonrefoulement principle.

Distance is created between the EU member states and their policies, which are carried out by others, and funded through programs that appear tangential to the ongoings in the Libyan Search and Rescue Region in the Southern Mediterranean. This, once more, leads to accountability being diffused to the degree of being well-nigh intractable. In relation to denying access to law for those concerned, the assemblage of policies and practices outsourcing migration control operate in multifarious ways that are not coordinated but in effect produce a hermetic sealing off of the European legal sphere for migrants: they cannot access asylum law because they never reach the shores on which they can claim asylum. The question is further complicated by the fact that law comes with distinct kinds of authority that can be amplified when different "types" of law are combined in strategic ways. For example, in the Mediterranean the criminalization of rescue which takes place through domestic channels combined with international law used to justify and enable certain kinds of governance makes for a kind of "empowered" law.

[5] It is approved intergovernmentally but administered by the EU Commission.

The force of law is amplified because of its duality: it is the legal architecture that enables bordering processes, but law itself also becomes a mobile border.

The "dialectics of transnationalism" (Mann 2013) which push *both* the policies and their judicial review into the transnational realm enable the skilful reorganization not just of material law but its sphere of validity and applicability. In the end, state responsibility disappears in the dynamic assemblages of international governance in today's world.

3.4 The Seemingly Benevolent Mode: The Tribunalization of Conflicts

Our third example is more subtle, ambiguous in its implications, and benign in its legitimation. It comes from the broad field of regulation of contemporary global capitalism and focuses on the settlement of disputes between multinational corporations and the states that host their activities, and the people who are negatively affected by their activities and sue the multinational corporations. Legal battles against multinational corporations are usually settled out of court if they are not dismissed beforehand. Procedures such as out-of-court settlements and alternative dispute resolution appear to be a broader trend in dispute resolution. They aim to reach agreement between the parties, focusing on the particular circumstances of an individual case and the unique constellation of the parties involved. It is generally argued that such alternative forms of dispute resolution primarily benefit plaintiffs who cannot afford lengthy and expensive litigation. Settlements reduce litigation costs, make reparations more accessible to victims, and can alleviate suffering more effectively by avoiding the need to deal with apportioning blame.

While the procedural norms governing these practices are becoming more and more convergent, and the forms of conciliation and mediation are becoming standardized and subject to increasing professionalization (see Bolay 2021[6]), cases are treated in their uniqueness, or what I have called elsewhere: "singularization" (Eckert 2021). Instead of finding solutions according to a general norm and seeing the general norm in the individual case, individual solutions are sought for a particular dispute. Settlements do not focus on the specifics of a case and how those specifics can be related to a general norm. Rather, cases are treated as singular

[6] M. Bolay, 2021. Arbitraging Extraction (Arbitrex): Arbitral Reasoning and New Legal Topographies of Extraction. Manuscript on file with the author.

because they involve a unique relationship between the parties involved; they need not have aspects comparable to others, and if they do, they need not be addressed in the negotiations that lead to a settlement.

For many claimants, justice is closely linked to the attribution of "fault" (see Lindt 2020; Loher 2020). It is the public verdict and its condemnation of a wrong that is central to the understanding of justice of many claimants. However, the settlements, which often take the place of litigation in transnational corporate responsibility disputes, usually do not result in a judgment; they do not assign fault. Such settlements do not require a judgment of fact, a verdict of fault, or an adjudication of guilt. They usually dispense with judgment and substitute both judgment and punishment with conflict resolution.

Because the settlement makes unnecessary a decision on whether a company is actually at fault and thus legally responsible, it cannot be used as precedent in similar cases (see also Robinson & Lazarus 2008). This prevention of precedent is aided by the fact that settlements are made *in camera* and under private contract law. The parties are free to agree on which standards apply to the settlement. If the parties involved are obliged to keep the outcome secret, settlements and the norms activated in them are completely removed from public view. Even if it is learned under what conditions the settlement was reached, that is, what arguments about duties and responsibilities went into it, it has no relevance to other cases because it is a private agreement that applies only to that specific constellation of actors and their claims against each other. The "case" in question is therefore unrepeatable, that is *singular*. Thus, claims are no longer treated as "cases" but as singular "incidents," and references to standards applicable in similar cases that might be relevant become irrelevant.

Such "singularization" thus occurs in several ways: by avoiding a judgment of fault that associates the case with a general norm, by private agreement between the parties involved, and by secrecy. All of this prevents the case from becoming a precedent or simply an example or model for others. Because the absence of a judgment assigning guilt also prevents the establishment of precedent, the two central concerns of plaintiffs in litigation – justice and the prevention of future harm – remain unfulfilled.

Singularization decouples cases from the systematic nature of law and directs hopes once directed toward "justice" toward individual remedies. This new logic affects the very idea of law. Law no longer functions by subsuming specific cases under a general principle that is valid beyond the specific parties to a dispute; rather, it becomes an instrument of mediation. A different logic emerges that develops neither systematics nor forms of dealing with normative pluralism, but leads to a radical singularization in which commonalities can at best be found in procedural norms. Singularization proceeds by rendering comparability irrelevant and relationality obsolete; the idea of normative coherence that drives aspirations in law is circumvented, and cases claimed to be equal to others are dissolved in the singular relations between the parties to the individual agreement. This diminishes access to law in a complex manner, not only by eliminating precedent and thus also potential alliances across cases; it thereby also forecloses the entangled hopes in law (Eckert 2021; Krisch 2021) that create what Susanne Baer (1998) has called "legal trouble," that is, the multitudinous engagements of legal norms that incrementally reshape their meaning, opening up the possibility to claim what does not – yet – exist in dominant legal discourse and hence think and speak it into being.[7]

3.5 Effects: A Conclusion

These three processes can be seen as ways to limit what Schwöbel (2010) has called "organic global constitutionalism," and which Santos and Rodrigues-Garavito have described as "Law and Globalization from below" (Santos & Rodriguez-Garavito 2006; see also Eckert et al. 2012). Such "organic" constitutionalism "from below" puts the definitional emphasis on the participative practice that constitutionalism must embody: Santos & Rodriguez-Garavito (2005: 11) assert that [S]ubaltern actors are a critical part of processes whereby global legal rules are defined." Forefronting processuality rather than stabilization, the participative and political reappropriations and usages of legal equality are always *striving* toward the normative "better," which is still to come. In that way, constitutionalism is a tool for change, for transforming the limitations of the current social order (Schwöbel 2010; Eckert 2018, 2021). It allows for plurality, both in terms of representation through the recognition of cultural difference within the national body

[7] See the arguments of Maksymilian del Mar (2017: 51) on how legal imagination in legal fictions and other forms of legal reasoning provide new possibilities of interpretation "hinting at the possibility, perhaps even desirability . . . of introducing, more explicitly, a new rule in the future."

politic, and in terms of forms of participation through the use of formal and informal political processes.[8]

The modalities of law outlined above foreclose such openness of "organic" constitutionality. They do not put an end to constitutionalism, or turn away from law, not even as an instrument of politics, but rather limit and shape it in specific ways.

This becomes visible if we are to trace the effects of the different processes of legal domination described in this text. In the first example, the amendment brought to citizenship law in India is a further step in the exclusion of some citizens from the body politic and the solidification of majority rule announcing a more fundamental denial of the legitimacy of political conflict. The derecognition of minority groups as legitimate members of the body politic, and their increasing social and legal definition as alien others, with no political rights in and to the body politic, is, in the case of India, easily expanded to other collective action, in particular that of groups with ascriptive identity markers such as tribals and Dalits. Thus, possibilities for participation in the national body politic becomes ever more conditional on the majoritarian identification of legitimate belonging. This is also the case for access to the protections of the law: restrictions on law being used as an expression of antagonistic claims on the state are increasingly treated as a matter of security laws.

In the "sophisticated mode" the "cutting" of noncitizens' links to European jurisdiction – even though they are subjected to it – heavily skews European supranational constitutionalism in favor of European subjects. In the benevolent mode, law is no longer a claims-making instrument and becomes a way to avoid the staging of antagonistic relations of power in the public sphere, thus limiting the possibilities of attaining justice through the public attribution of fault. Law becomes in this way an instrument of rule, since the possibilities of appeal are ruled out by the written procedures of arbitration themselves.

States and international institutions of governance, as well as powerful economic actors, rely on law to carry out their activities of governing or of accumulation. Law provides them with a language for the justification of operations. The idea of law as a form of global architecture that should guarantee some forms of participation has to simultaneously be

[8] Organic global constitutionalism recognizes that the division between the public and private spheres of action have historically favored "'masculine' ethical orientations" through the division between justice and rights as "public" issues and care and responsibility as constricted to the private sphere (Schwöbel 2010: 536).

downplayed (e.g., with out-of-court settlement which are supposedly better for the victims, or when law is dispersed to create zones of nonjurisdiction) whilst being upheld at the same time (governance through legal means and emphasis on repressive processes having taken place through democratic means, the language of rights being used by states to legitimate their operations).

The emerging constitutional order we have sketched out is marked by "dual governance." Matters continue to be subject to law both national and international but can be turned into matters of governance measures by various actors at their expediency. Worryingly, these developments could be seen to thereby complete (and transform) what neoliberalism could not entirely accomplish despite its diminishment of human rights to a notion of sufficiency (Moyn 2018). Neoliberal reason did not eclipse *Homo politicus* as Wendy Brown (2015) would have it. The rationale of *Homo economicus* has not erased citizenship's "distinctly political morphology" (Brown 2015: 109). Instead, when faced with the effectiveness of organic constitutionalism, repressive governments and powerful economic actors are redoubling their efforts to reshape law as a tool of political participation and moving it toward an instrument of rule alone.

Law as a space, institution, but especially as a field of participation seems to pose specific threats to current political and economic orders, not as demand overload, but as – not necessarily effective, but nevertheless visible and audible – critique, in which visions of alternatives are expressed in a language that is intelligible to the powers that be. The three pathways clarify in different ways the fact that in the current globalized world, democratic participation in legal struggles poses a real threat to different kinds of power. Empirically, it would be difficult to trace the causal trigger of the juristocratic reckoning from above that we describe; to argue that juristocratic reckoning systematically happens in direct reaction to organic constitutionalism would be untenable. There are fundamental differences between the pathways we outline in terms of the dialectics of reckoning at play; still, we make the following propositions to consider how the relation between the mobilization of law against the powers that be, and the reckoning from above, unfolds. Out-of-court settlements are perhaps the clearest response to social movements mobilizing law to defend their rights. Corporate actors are concerned by the reputational damage that a conviction against their activities would create. In this example, the targeted "doer of harm" is not a state, hence the stakes of maintaining the outward promise of legal participation are lower. Corporate actors are more concerned about reputational damage than they are about maintaining legitimacy in a situation of rule. In the Central Mediterranean, the relation between legal interventions that have sought to constrain executive power and the subsequent reaction of states is more ambiguous, if only from the perspective of time; almost ten years separate the state behavior condemned in the *Hirsi* judgement and the development of the Libyan SRR. In between, an international NATO-led intervention participated in the ousting of the Libyan leader Muammar Gaddafi, which affected the geopolitical stability of the region, prompting new challenges for the control of the external border from the perspective of European authorities. Arguably though, the jurisprudence of the ECHR shapes the possibilities for the types of extraterritorial policies that the EU and its member states develop in terms of border control. The relation between litigation "from below" and state behavior in this case is sinuous and not a causal reaction. However, the fact that governments feel it necessary to ever-diminish the legal possibilities of migrants classified as noneligible by limiting Asylum law, by proliferating classificatory distinctions between groups of migrants in law, and by sharpening regulation for all classes of migrants, is evidence of its influence. In India there is considerable evidence that laws have been reformulated in a way that expands the possibilities of quenching litigation against state agencies (Eckert et al. 2012). Security laws, in particular, have been regularly employed to punish protest, both protest that employs law and that which employs more overtly political tactics. Thereby, the possibilities for the traditionally prolific mobilization of law by Indian citizens are effectively limited.

The advent of juristocracy has seen struggles for and through law. In today's world though, the pushback against these struggles appears to manifest in several ingenious ways in which new obstacles are erected to limit the participative potentiality of law. If a waning of juristocracy is taking place, it seems not to be shaped by less law. Rather, emerging limitations to constitutionalism are achieved by way of and at the same time with the aim of preserving (legal) privilege. Although the three dynamics that we have described operate in vastly different manners and transform law and legality in seemingly divergent ways, they all in effect diminish the legal remedies available to "the have nots" (Galanter 1974), and particular the legal remedies they can muster to contest government rule.

Taken together, the three cases point toward the emergence of a constitutional order that is averse to political conflict being carried out through law; political orders are authoritatively institutionalized through law, but cannot be contested through it anymore.

References

Baer, S. 1998. Inexcitable Speech: Zum Rechtsverständnis postmoderner feministischer Positionen am Beispiel Judith Butler. In A. Hornscheidt, G. Jähnert and A. Schlichter, eds., *Kritische Differenzen: geteilte Perspektiven*. Opladen: Westdeutscher Verlag, 229–243.

Basaran, T. 2020. A Journey through Law's Landscapes: Close Encounters of the Scalar Kind. In C. J. Greenhouse and C. L. Davis, eds., *Landscapes of Law: Practicing Sovereignty in Transnational Terrain*. Philadelphia, PA: University of Pennsylvania Press, 23–36.

Brown, W. 2015. *Undoing the Demos: Neoliberalism's Stealth Revolution*. Cambridge, MA: MIT.

Del Mar, M. 2017. Legal Reasoning in Pluralist Jurisprudence. In N. Roughan and A. Halpin, eds., *In Pursuit of Pluralist Jurisprudence*. Cambridge: Cambridge University Press, 40–63.

Eckert, J. 2011. Introduction: Subjects of Citizenship. *Citizenship Studies* 15 (3-4): 309–317.

2014. Preventive Laws and the Policing of the Urban Poor. In N. Gooptu and J. Parry, eds., *The Persistence of Poverty in India*. New Delhi: Social Science Press, 291–316.

2018. The Morals of Liability: Some Thoughts on "Humanitarians in Court." *Journal of Legal Pluralism and Unofficial Law* 50 (3): 375–378.

2020. Neglect and the Imaginations of Care: Some Brief Thoughts Inspired by Monique Nuijten's Work. In E. D. Rasch, O. Salemink, B. Büscher and M. Köhne, eds., *Engaged Encounters: Thinking about Forces, Fields and Friendship with Monique Nuijten*. Wageningen: Wageningen Academic, 45–48.

2021. Entangled Hopes. Towards Relational Coherence. In N. Krisch, ed., *Entangled legalities beyond the State*. Global Law Series. Cambridge: Cambridge University Press, 399–423.

Eckert, J., B. Donahoe, C. Strümpell and Z.-Ö. Biner. 2012. Introduction: Laws, Travels and Transformations. In J. Eckert, B. Donahoe, C. Strümpell and Z. Ö. Biner, eds., *Law against the State: Ethnographic Forays into Law's Transformations*. Cambridge Studies in Law and Society. Cambridge: Cambridge University Press, 1–22.

Galanter, M. 1974. Why the "Haves" Come Out Ahead: Speculations on the Limits of Legal Change. *Law & Society Review* 9: 95–160.

Greenberg, J. 2021. Counterpedagogy, Sovereignty, and Migration at the European Court of Human Rights. *Law & Social Inquiry* 46 (2): 518–539.

Hong, C. 2021. The Citizen as Mere Human: Litigating Denationalization in Post 9/11 UK. *Anthropological Theory* 21 (2): 154–79.

Jayal, Niraja Gopal. *Citizenship and Its Discontents: An Indian History*, Cambridge, MA: Harvard University Press, 2013.

Khilnani, S. 1999. *The Idea of India.* New York: Farrar, Straus & Giroux.

Krisch, N. 2021. Framing Entangled Legalities beyond the State. In N, Krisch, ed., *Entangled Legalities beyond the State.* Global Law Series. Cambridge: Cambridge University Press, 1–32.

Lavenex, S. 2016. Regional Migration Governance. In T. Risse and T. A. Börzel, eds., *Oxford Handbook of Comparative Regionalism.* Oxford: Oxford University Press, 457–485.

Lindt, A. 2020. Transnational Human Rights Litigation: A Way of Obtaining Effective Remedy Abroad? *Journal of Legal Anthropology* 4 (2): 57–77.

Loher, D. 2020. Everyday Suffering and the Abstract Time-Reckoning of Law: Reflections on the Allocation of Responsibility for an Asbestos Disaster in Italy. *Journal of Legal Anthropology* 4 (2): 17–38.

Mann, I. 2013. Dialectic of Transnationalism: Unauthorized Migration and Human Rights, 1993–2013. *Harvard International Law Journal* 54 (2): 315–392.

Moreno-Lax, V. and Giuffré M. 2017. The Rise of Consensual Containment: From "Contactless Control" to "Contactless Responsibility" for Forced Migration Flows. In S. Singh Juss, ed., *Research Handbook on International Refugee Law.* Cheltenham: Edward Elgar, 82–108.

Moyn, S. 2018. *Not Enough: Human Rights in an Unequal World.* Cambridge, MA: Harvard University Press.

Pech, L. and K. L. Scheppele. 2017. *Poland and the European Commission, Parts I–III: Requiem for the Rule of Law*, VerfBlog, 2017/3/03, https://verfassungsblog.de/poland-and-the-european-commission-part-iii-requiem-for-the-rule-of-law/, DOI: 10.17176/20170303-131734.

Randeria, S. 2007. De-politicization of Democracy and Judicialization of Politics. *Theory, Culture & Society* 24 (4): 38–44.

2003. Glocalization of Law: Environmental Justice, World Bank, NGOs and the Cunning State in India. *Current Sociology* 51 (3–4): 205–328.

Robinson, J. and L. Lazarus. 2008. *Report for the UN Special Rapporteur on Business and Human Rights: Obstacles for Victims of Corporate Human Rights Violations.* Oxford: Oxford Pro Bono Publico.

Schiffauer, W. 2006. Suspect Subjects: Muslim Migrants and the Security Agencies in Germany. In J. Eckert, ed., *The Social Life of Anti-Terrorism Laws.* Bielefeld: Transcript Verlag, 55–78.

Schwöbel, C. E. J. 2010. Organic Global Constitutionalism. *Leiden Journal of International Law* 23 (3): 529–554.

de Sousa Santos, B. and C. A. Rodríguez-Garavito. 2005. Law, Politics, and the Subaltern in Counter-Hegemonic Globalization. In B. de Sousa Santos and C. A. Rodríguez-Garavito, eds., *Law and Globalization from below: Towards a Cosmopolitan Legality.* Cambridge: Cambridge University Press, 1–26.

Spijkerboer, T. and E. Steyger. 2019. European External Migration Funds and Public Procurement Law. *European Papers* 4 (2): 493–521.

Strathern, M. 1996. Cutting the Network. *Journal of the Royal Anthropological Institute* 2 (3): 517–535.

Suresh, M. 2021. The Social Life of Law in Authoritarian Contexts. www.soas.ac.uk/research/social-life-law-authoritarian-contexts.

4

Re-presenting Rights

Food Sovereignty and the Struggle for Postliberal Democratic Governance

MATTHEW C. CANFIELD

In July 2021, activists gathered to voice their opposition to the UN Food Systems Summit. At a time when the global pandemic kept people from leaving their homes, activists from around the world nonetheless virtually convened for a four-day virtual "counter-mobilization" to elaborate their criticisms of the summit, share their grievances, and imagine alternative people-centered food systems. During the opening plenary of the "People's Counter-Mobilization to Transform Food Systems" one activist – a peasant farmer living in Germany and member of the European Coordination of the international peasant movement, *La Vía Campesina* (LVC) – offered an elegant summary of activists' critique of the summit:

> Although the Summit propagates itself as inclusive – that anyone can participate – from the beginning, the process of organizing the Summit was opaque ... sidelining the existing human rights-based United Nations institutions as well the legitimate platforms of organized civil society and indigenous peoples. The "multistakeholderism" propagated by the Summit is a very dangerous threat for democratic food systems. On one hand, it ignores the enormous asymmetries of power, resources, and evident conflict of interests. On the other hand, it bypasses responsibilities of governments.

For many of the activists engaged in the counter-mobilization, the UN Food Systems Summit brought into view a fundamental shift in the organization and exercise of global power. Although multistakeholder forms of governance have been proliferating across international institutions for decades (Bäckstrand 2006; Gleckman 2018), this form of governance had never before been adopted so expressly as the format of a UN global summit. Activists saw the multistakeholder organization of the summit as a reflection of the influence of the World Economic Forum (WEF), which had for years been promoting a global redesign of international institutions to conform to its vision of "stakeholder capitalism" (World Economic Forum 2010a). Just prior to the summit, it had signed a memorandum of understanding with the UN secretary-general (Canfield, Anderson & McMichael 2021). At the counter-mobilization, the German activist described multistakeholderism as a supreme threat to small-scale food producers and workers. She explained that it not only enabled corporations to exercise significant influence, but also that it fundamentally undermined the ability of social movements to challenge this influence by representing all food system actors as "stakeholders."

For the movements engaged in the counter-mobilization, the expansion of multistakeholder forms of governance raised a difficult strategic dilemma. For decades, movements such as LVC had demanded to be included in global policymaking, arguing that nation-states alone did not adequately represent their interests. In the 1990s, they articulated the claim of "food sovereignty" to oppose the liberalization of food systems and demand that those most marginalized by industrialized food systems – peasants, small-scale food producers, food-chain workers, and indigenous peoples – be directly involved in decision-making about food and agriculture (Desmarais 2007; Desmarais, Wiebe & Wittman 2011). At a time when human rights were ascending as the dominant claim and vision of social justice, these movements purposefully sought to frame their claims in terms of *sovereignty* because they saw human rights as too individualistic, state-centered, and technocratic (Claeys 2015). Indeed, they sought to challenge the liberal political and legal systems that had consistently failed to address food insecurity and construct a new democratic vision for social, economic, and ecological ordering (Trauger 2014). But now that they were actively being invited to participate in the summit's multistakeholder process – a form of post-liberal network governance – they had to confront new questions about the forms of participation and governance that they were demanding.

In distinguishing their vision of governance from the multistakeholder framework promoted by the WEF, activists returned to using the language of human rights. During one of the lead-up meetings to the counter-mobilization, an indigenous peasant leader from Mexico told civil society organizations that the main problem was that "the Summit is not focusing on human rights and the right to food." He explained, "We are not necessarily asking for us to be included, we do not want to legitimize a process that we don't agree with. We are asking for it not to be a corporate food summit." In the ensuing weeks and months, movements took up this activists' approach arguing that they were not stakeholders, but *rights*-holders. In mobilizing rights, movements sought to remind states of their role as duty-bearers under international law.

In this chapter I examine how food sovereignty movements are deploying the language of human rights to confront the contemporary mutations of neoliberalism. Numerous scholars have insisted that neoliberalism is not dying, but reinventing itself in new authoritarian forms (Callison & Manfredi 2019; Hendrikse 2021). This has led many legal scholars to understandably criticize human rights as a powerless discourse that may in fact serve to facilitate neoliberalism rather than offer a bulwark against it (Moyn 2018; Linarelli, Salomon & Sornarajah 2018; Whyte 2019). However, observers of food sovereignty movements argue that these movements have always mobilized human rights "transgressively" (Patel 2009), combining their visions of food sovereignty with the language with the right to food in strategic ways (Claeys 2015). In mobilizing human rights, food sovereignty activists do not seek to rebuild the liberal legal order. Rather, I argue that as they confront the institutionalization and legitimation of neoliberal inequalities through multistakeholderism, they mobilize rights to construct new forms of democratic postliberal governance.

My argument builds on anthropological and sociolegal scholarship that has emphasized the ways that movements often use human rights language creatively by investing rights claims with local meanings and different visions of social justice (Rajagopal 2003; Goodale & Merry 2007; Merry et al. 2010). However, such scholarship has focused less on economic rights claims in the context of neoliberal forms of governance. In this shifting set of political and legal arrangements, rights play a key role in shaping regulatory values and structures (Morgan 2007; Darian-Smith & Scott 2009). Drawing on my ethnographic observation of food sovereignty networks engaged in Rome-based UN processes, I argue that food sovereignty activists mobilize the right to food as what political theorist Michael Saward calls a "representative claim" – a performative and constitutive claim that challenges "who, and what, may count as representative politically" (Saward 2006: 299). Saward argues that representative claims are performative, aesthetic, and cultural practices through which new constituencies are constituted. Food sovereignty movements have been principally concerned with just that – constructing constituencies of peasants, food-chain workers, small-scale farmers, indigenous peoples, poor urban consumers, and others across borders to construct collective identities and shared demands for social and political change. By investing these practices into their rights claims, they constitute new democratic constituencies that seek to hold powerful actors and institutions to account.

In elaborating this argument, I begin by describing the articulation and elaboration of food sovereignty as a postliberal social justice claim. I then consider how activists have mobilized food sovereignty with the human right to food in an effort to shape the structure and practice of governance in the UN Committee on World Food Security (CFS), which has served as a key arena of global governance that food sovereignty activists have been successful in significantly influencing. In the face of constant threats to transform the structure and practice of governance in the CFS or to shift decision-making out of the CFS altogether – culminating in the UN Food Systems Summit – food sovereignty movements have drawn on the language of human rights. In concluding, I consider how the food sovereignty movement's mobilization of rights as representative claims offers a radical vision for postliberal governance.

4.1 The Postliberal Politics of Food Sovereignty

The term "food sovereignty" has contested origins (Edelman 2014), but the most common narrative of food sovereignty traces its articulation to LVC in 1996. Activists framed food sovereignty as an alternative to the language of "food security," which then dominated global policy debates about hunger and malnutrition. Activists saw the language of food security as legitimating the liberalization of food and agricultural markets and, more broadly, the commodification of food. By contrast, food *sovereignty* emphasized the political dimensions of food as a common good and demanded greater democratic control over food systems. In its 1996 Tlaxcala Declaration, LVC first articulated the claim of food sovereignty, proclaiming "We are united in our rejection of the economic and political conditions which destroy our livelihoods, our communities, our cultures and our natural environment. We are determined to create a rural economy which is based on respect for ourselves and the earth, on food sovereignty, and on fair trade."[1]

When activists initially developed the claim of food sovereignty, they understood it as a demand for states to be able to determine their own food and agricultural policy. Yet they quickly refined the meaning of food

[1] "Tlaxaca Declaration of Vía Campesina." International Conference of the Via Campesina Tlaxcala, Mexico, April 18–21, 1996. Available at https://viacampesina.org/en/ii-international-conference-of-the-via-campesina-tlaxcala-mexico-april-18-21/.

sovereignty as different groups began to claim "food sovereignty" at local and regional levels. Indigenous peoples and peasant farmers claimed food sovereignty at sub- and supranational levels, while small-scale food producers in the global North began to claim food sovereignty to demand more local food systems. By 2007, when food sovereignty activists convened in Mali for the Nyèléni Conference, they articulated a broad and inclusive vision of food sovereignty as "the right of peoples, communities, and countries to define their own agricultural, labor, fishing, food and land policies which are ecologically, socially, economically and culturally appropriate to their unique circumstances."[2]

The transformation of the meaning of food sovereignty from a claim for state sovereignty to a more diffuse claim about peoples' rights to control their food systems reflected changing global understandings of the operation and exercise of sovereignty. Saskia Sassen (2008) describes how neoliberal globalization transformed the relationship between national territory, authority, and rights through changing global forces of power. To be clear, sovereignty has never been monopolized by the Westphalian nation-state, and even this vision of sovereignty was constructed in the shadow of colonialism and unequal integration into global law and politics (Anghie 2007; Getachew 2020). Nevertheless, national sovereignty was effectively diminished, both through human rights, which effectively recognized limits to national sovereignty as well as through the expansion of private international law, which vested power in private actors. Neoliberalism further empowered transnational private actors (Cutler 2020). By the 1990s and 2000s, political scientists began recognizing that sovereignty had become effectively embedded in relational, networked relations that included both state and nonstate actors (Slaughter 2005; Grewal 2009). This networking of sovereignty undermined the liberal "walls of separation" that were established to police the boundaries of the political and establish spheres of liberty (Walzer 1984). As private power pushed the boundaries of the private–public distinction, new technologies of "governance" emerged – including soft law, certifications, and other voluntary forms of regulation – that transformed the form, operation, and exercise of power (Davis, Kingsbury & Merry 2012).

In the face of what Sassen (2008) describes as changing "geographies of power," movements of peasants, small-scale food producers, and food chain-workers began to articulate new horizons of justice. In claiming food

[2] "Food Sovereignty: A Right for All." Political Statement of the NGO/CSO Forum for Food Sovereignty. 2002. Available at https://nyeleni.org/spip.php?article125.

sovereignty, they sought to transcend the state-centered focus of dominant social justice such as human rights. In doing so, food sovereignty activism became exemplary of what Nancy Fraser describes as the changing grammar of justice claims in the context of neoliberal globalization. Fraser argues that the dominance of the "Keynesian–Westphalian" frame of most social justice claims came to operate as "a powerful instrument of injustice" because it misrepresented political boundaries through which power operates and thereby excluded marginalized peoples from pursuing their justice claims. Building on her scholarship on recognition and redistribution – two axes of justice within the nation-state (Fraser & Honneth 2003) – Fraser adds the third axis of representation. "Representation is always already inherent in all claims for redistribution and recognition," she writes. "The political dimension is implicit in, indeed required by, the grammar of the concept of justice. Thus, no redistribution or recognition without representation" (Fraser 2009: 21).

Building on peasant struggles throughout the twentieth century (Wolf 1969), contemporary food sovereignty activists seek *redistribution* through the trade rules and public investment that support local and territorial markets over global markets as well as *recognition* of peasants and small-scale food producers to determine how they wish to produce food and earn their livelihoods. But food sovereignty movements also seek *representation* within local, regional, and transnational arenas of governance that regulate food systems in order to hold the transnational actors involved in food systems accountable. Indeed, this is what makes food sovereignty such a noveljustice claims.

As food sovereignty emerged as the dominant collective action frame of LVC and allied movements, it sometimes caused friction with human rights. Though human rights have emerged as the dominant grammar of international justice claims (Moyn 2012), food sovereignty sought to transcend what they saw as multiple limits of human rights – the individualist framing, their state-centered focus, and their technocratic legal framing (Claeys 2015). Food sovereignty activists seek to overcome these representational limits of human rights in two ways. First, in articulating food sovereignty as a collective claim that is focused at local, regional, and global levels, they challenge dominant liberal meanings of rights. As both a good on which people depend for their livelihoods and a public good, food does not easily fit into the liberal schemas of social and economic organization. Thus, as food sovereignty activists seek to build democratic, decentralized, and diverse food systems, they are reenvisioning justice around the relational networks through which food is produced and provisioned.

Second, food sovereignty activists seek to democratize these networks through new forms and practices of representation that empower grassroots movements and hold powerful actors accountable. Indeed, a key principle of food sovereignty movements is their commitment to the autonomy of movements that mobilize food sovereignty and the self-representation of marginalized peoples. These practices have been critical in enabling them to develop solidarity among a diverse set of constituencies (small and mid-size farmers, peasants, pastoralists, food-chain workers, the urban poor, fisherfolk, etc.) across uneven relations of global power. They also offer a sharp contrast to what had operated undemocratically in human rights institutions as an implicit delegation of representation to international NGOs that often claim to represent victims of human rights violations. This caused tensions between international NGOs and food sovereignty movements in the 1990s. For example, in 1996, LVC refused to be part of a statement of the NGO Forum to the World Food Summit even though NGOs had inserted language on food sovereignty into the statement for fear of cooptation (Desmarais 2002).

In seeking to overcome the representational limits of human rights, food sovereignty activists have effectively assembled a postliberal justice claim. Yet what distinguishes food sovereignty movements from reactionary right-wing calls for popular sovereignty is their ongoing assertion and engagement with human rights. Indeed, although food sovereignty activists have sought to transcend what they see as the representational limits of human rights, they have not abandoned claims for the right to food altogether; activists continually emphasize the right to food as a cornerstone of food sovereignty. Their strategic mobilization of these two claims thus reveals critical dynamics between emerging postliberal legal formations and their relationship to existing discourses and grammars of social entitlement and justice.

4.2 Claiming Food Sovereignty and Mobilizing Rights in Global Governance

Since the very first articulation of food sovereignty in the 1990s, activists have fixed their eyes on transforming global legal structures to promote decentralized and democratic governance over food systems. Yet their vision of democratic global governance has consistently been threatened by alternative participatory structures proposed by hegemonic actors. In the mid-1990s, LVC's demands were focused largely on an institution that was intransigent to civil society participation: the World Trade

Organization. LVC therefore sought out other institutions they could influence to oppose trade liberalization. Early after activists had first articulated the concept of food sovereignty, LVC convened in Rome outside of the World Food Summit. There they further elaborated a series of principles – including human rights, agrarian reform, protecting natural resources, reorganizing the food trade, social peace, and democratic control – and became increasingly focused on the Food and Agriculture Organization (FAO) as a potential site of strategic influence. After all, FAO's mission to end hunger and promote rural livelihoods not only fit more closely with LVC's goals, it was also more welcoming to civil society.

A few years after the summit, when the FAO began preparing for the "World Food Summit: five years later" (WFS:fyl), LVC intensified their efforts to influence the process. LVC joined together with like-minded social movements and NGOs to form the International Planning Committee for Food Sovereignty (IPC) to help build a new framework for engaging food sovereignty movements and other civil society organizations in the process. As the IPC began developing new mechanisms to facilitate civil society engagement in the WFS:fyl process, a new participatory ethos was emerging across the United Nations. The 1992 Earth Summit in Rio de Janeiro is generally cited as the "beginning of the participatory turn of global environmental governance" (Bäckstrand 2006). In the period between the 1992 Earth Summit and the follow up, ten years later in Johannesburg, the UN Commission on Sustainable Development became a locus for developing what was termed a "multistakeholder" approach to governance that identified "major groups" and sought to integrate them into global governance. At the same time, however, global justice or "anti-corporate globalization" movements were experimenting with new organizational forms and repertoires of contention in which participatory democracy was key (Juris 2008; Maeckelbergh 2009). The 2001 World Social Forum, held in Porto Alegre, Brazil, centered participatory and deliberative democracy as the key practice of movement building and demand for global transformation (Smith 2004). In contrast to the top-down framework of assembling "stakeholders" to participate in global processes – a process that effectively sought to institutionalize the practice in liberal democracy of providing equal opportunities to all affected persons and groups to influence political decisions – food sovereignty activists pursued a more substantive vision of democracy in which those *most* marginalized and most affected would be at the center of decision-making processes.

The tensions between these two formulations of democracy were faced directly by the IPC in their preparation for the WFS:fyl. The IPC was preparing for what would become the NGO/CSO Forum for Food Sovereignty in 2001 just as the World Summit for Sustainable Development in Johannesburg was also being organized. The IPC's approach to participation was drawn from the practices of the food sovereignty movement and rooted in activists' commitment to autonomy and self-representation. The IPC defined its role as providing a platform for organizations to represent themselves, not to facilitate consensus or represent peoples' movements. This approach "contrasted sharply" with the approach of the multistakeholder dialogues of the Commission on Sustainable Development (CSD). As Nora McKeon explains, "the Major Groups had been predefined by an intergovernmental forum, whereas the IPC emerged from an on-going civil society process of self-definition" (McKeon 2009: 56). A key difference was that the IPC excluded the private sector, whereas the major groups included the private sector in multistakeholder dialogues. Indeed, as one of the key organizers of the IPC would later put it, "The task for the IPC is . . . to open the political space within the FAO for all popular organizations and movements. The aim is to increase effective democracy, not only bringing new groups into the UN's charmed circle, but also their concerns, methodologies and militancy" (Colombo & Onorati 2013: 67). The differences between the IPC and the multistakeholder processes of the CSD would be a point of enduring tension.

By all accounts, the success of the NGO/CSO forum of WFS:fyl led the FAO to pursue a more formal relationship with the IPC. In 2002, the IPC and the director-general of the FAO and the IPC engaged in an "exchange of letters" in which they spelled out their relationship, recognizing the IPC as the FAO's "principal global civil society interlocutor on the initiatives and themes emerging from the WFS:fyl" (McKeon 2009: 72). In his letter, Director-General Jacques Diouf recognized IPC's approach to participation, explaining "both parties concur with the need to distinguish between the interests of social movements/non-profit NGOs and those of private sector associations, and to make separate interface arrangements for those categories of organizations" (McKeon 2009: 72). The director-general specified that the four major themes of the NGO/CSO summit – "the right to food and to food sovereignty; local population's access to management of, and control over, local resources; small-scale, family-based agro-ecological methods of food production; and trade and food sovereignty" – would form the basis for their relationship (Colombo & Onorati 2013: 67). The exchange of letters not only played a key role in legitimating the IPC's vision of participation with its separation of civil society and the private sector and autonomous organization, it also explicitly recognized their claim of food sovereignty.

In the ensuing two years, the IPC worked to create opportunities for social movements to participate in the FAO by promoting a rights-based approach. One of the key outcomes of the WFS:fyl was the formation of an Intersessional Working Group to develop a set of voluntary guidelines on the right to food. The formation of the working group and the eventual guidelines were significant in two respects. First, the "Voluntary Guidelines to Support the Progressive Realization of the Right to Adequate Food in the Context of National Food Security" was the first time that a human right had been negotiated outside of the Geneva-based United Nations human rights institutions. Although it contained multiple compromises, which even the name of the document implied, it nonetheless reaffirmed the normative significance of human rights in driving food and agricultural policy. Second, the working group included the participation of the IPC. Several NGOs from the Right to Food Working Group of the IPC participated in the negotiation of the guidelines. As a result, the guidelines clearly specified that participation by stakeholders – including the private sector and civil society – was a key component of a rights-based approach to food and nutrition. The guidelines, which were adopted by the UN Food and Agriculture Organization in 2004, became the foundation for further civil society engagement in the FAO.

Indeed, three years later, when the world faced a global food and financial crisis, LVC, the IPC, and other food sovereignty activists mobilized to push governments to address the structural drivers of the crisis through the rights-based approach elaborated through the voluntary guidelines. While multiple institutions, including the G8, the World Bank, and the UN Secretariat all vied to respond to the crisis, civil society organizations successfully argued to reform the (CFS), a previously technical body in the FAO (Duncan 2015). The reform of the CFS was oriented around two values: evidenced-based decision-making, and inclusivity. To address the former, the CFS established a High-Level Panel of Experts (HLPE) to provide expert guidance on policy issues. In terms of the latter, there was significant debate. The IPC argued for an autonomous civil society mechanism based on the model of the IPC to facilitate the participation of civil society organizations in the CFS. Meanwhile, although the private sector had neither been involved in the negotiations of the guidelines on the right to food, nor the reform of the CFS, the United States lobbied vigorously for their inclusion.

The final structure of the reformed CFS in many ways reflected the vision of participation that the IPC had promoted. Food sovereignty movements succeeded in advocating for the establishment of two autonomously organized mechanisms – The Civil Society and Indigenous Peoples Mechanisms (CSIPM)[3] and the Private Sector Mechanism (PSM) – that distinguished between the private sector and civil society. The former would include not only transnational corporations, trade associations, and philanthropies, but also organizations that represented large-scale commercial farmers. The latter included NGOs and social movements with "particular attention to organizations representing smallholder family farmers, artisanal fisherfolk, herders/pastoralists, landless, urban poor, agricultural and food workers, women, youth, consumers, Indigenous Peoples, and International NGOs whose mandates and activities are concentrated in the areas of concern to the Committee" (Reform of the Committee on World Food Security Final Version 2009). Both the PSM and CSIPM were included as "stakeholders" of the CFS.

The CSIPM's structure, which was established based on a proposal developed by the international NGO Oxfam International, the IPC, and Action Aid International was particularly important because it helped to institutionalize the food sovereignty movement's practices of self-representation and autonomy (Gaarde 2017). The initial proposal emphasized that the CSIPM "will respect pluralism, autonomy, and self-organization. It will ensure a balance of gender, regions, constituencies, and genders."[4] The CSIPM established eleven different constituencies and seventeen subregions. Importantly, only one of the constituencies was allocated for international NGOs, the other ten were all allocated to groups including smallholder farmers, fisherfolks, pastoralists, indigenous peoples, landless peoples, women, youth, consumers, urban food insecure, and food and agricultural workers. The CSIPM emphasized that it did not represent

[3] At the time of the reform, the name of the mechanism was the Civil Society Mechanism. In 2018, it changed its name to the Civil Society and Indigenous People's Mechanism, and in 2022 it began using the abbreviation "CSIPM." To avoid confusion, I use this abbreviation throughout the text.

[4] "Proposal for an International Food Security and Nutrition Civil Society Mechanism for Relations with the CFS." 2009. Available at www.csm4cfs.org/wp-content/uploads/2016/03/Proposal-for-an-international-civil-society-mechanism.pdf.

the voices of these constituencies but served to facilitate their participation in the CFS. Through a creative system of quotas and constituencies for participation, the CSIPM created its own system of prefigurative democratic governance (Claeys & Duncan 2019).

Though the CFS included "stakeholders" in the policy-making process of the CFS, it also maintained states as the only voting "members" of the committee. The innovative inclusive structure of the reformed CFS not only enabled it to claim greater legitimacy, but also authority over global food and agricultural issues. Indeed, the CFS rebranded itself as "the foremost inclusive international and intergovernmental platform for all stakeholders to work together to ensure food security and nutrition for all." Food sovereignty activists hailed this structure as an example of democratic global governance (McKeon 2015). Yet as social movements would come to find, it would be a fragile victory. For just as the CFS was reformed, the World Economic Forum (WEF) embarked on what it called the "Global Redesign Initiative" that endeavored to transform global political and legal organization and expand "the geometry of cooperation to capitalize on the wider availability of non-state expertise and resources" (World Economic Forum 2010b). Through this initiative, the WEF would seek to dismantle the structure that the CSIPM had carefully worked to build through the reform.

4.3 Countering the Threat of Stakeholder Capitalism

I started ethnographic fieldwork in the UN Committee on World Food Security in 2013, just three years after the reform. I had not planned to do fieldwork in the CFS, but at several gatherings of food sovereignty movements, I heard repeatedly about the CFS and its importance for movements worldwide. Activists were using the CSIPM as a convergence space for food sovereignty globally. Moreover, their experiences in the CSIPM were also shaping their broader approach to global and transnational governance. That year also turned out to be a good year to begin attending the CFS: 2013 was a year of renewal for the CSIPM. Many of the designated "focal points" for subregions and constituencies started new terms. This included the North American focal point, which switched from an American activist to a Canadian NGO-worker focused on biodiversity and seeds. Because there were many new people attending the CSIPM, those who had been participating in the CSIPM and CFS made the extra effort to orient other civil society members to these forums.

In the period between 2009 and 2013, the CSIPM had been involved in negotiating several different "policy recommendations" and "voluntary guidelines" – all forms of soft law that the CFS develops in an effort to promote policy convergence and international cooperation on food and agricultural issues. Activists in the CSIPM saw some of these instruments as major successes. For example, the CSIPM celebrated the Voluntary Guidelines on the Responsible Governance of Tenure (VGGTs) as a major victory because they offered an alternative to the dominant model of privatization that has been a hallmark of neoliberal land policy. But other policy recommendations, such as those on "Food Price Volatility and Food Security" were extremely contentious. Members of the CSIPM walked out of the negotiations because some governments refused to recognize the underlying drivers of food price volatility.

During my first year attending the CFS, I couldn't help but notice the ubiquity of the term "multistakeholder." Even though civil society in the CFS were opposed to describing themselves as stakeholders, they nonetheless leveraged this term in seeking to strengthen their voices in negotiations. In negotiations and strategy sessions, I heard activists constantly emphasizing that as a stakeholder of the process their comments should be equally considered in decision-making processes. At the same time, I also heard governments using the term to support their own positions and interests when they had the support of whatever stakeholder they were referring to, either civil society or the private sector.

By 2014, however, some of the activists most deeply involved in the CSIPM were growing disenchanted with CFS. I observed members of the CSIPM negotiate the CFS Principles for Responsible Investment in Agriculture and Food Systems, which were especially contentious because of their potential role in regulating land grabs and other forms of investment. During the negotiations, the chair of process continuously ignored the suggestions of the CSIPM. Throughout the process it was clear that some "stakeholders" had more power than others. Although the language of multistakeholderism may have served as a strategic discourse for civil society members, activists became increasingly concerned about it. One activist – the leader of an NGO based in South Asia – who served as a facilitator in the negotiation of the principles to other civil society activists in a strategy meeting after a long day of negotiations that multistakeholderism was a fundamental problem. Although it had enabled the participation of civil society, she said that multistakeholderism "does not recognize asymmetries of power." She said she was worried that the voices of social movements were being coopted. "How do we justify our being here with the work that is being done in the regions?" she asked the room. She, like others, were worried that if they participated in negotiations of principles that would later be used to dispossess peasants and small-scale producers, they would legitimize the very instruments they sought to resist.

In the three consecutive years I attended the CFS, it became increasingly clear that multistakeholderism was not simply a format of participation, it was also a way for governments to evade duties and obligations. Governments and the private sector were often happy to include language within negotiated documents about "multistakeholder" inclusion, but they were much less willing to include language that demanded fidelity to human rights. For example, in negotiations over policy recommendations on biofuels in 2013, for example, a Canadian delegate brazenly vetoed the incorporation of language related to human rights. This led the CSIPM to once again face the question of whether they should walk out. Prior to the negotiations, they had identified the inclusion of human rights as a "redline" – something they would not give up – because they insisted that food production, rather than using food for fuel, was critical to the fulfillment of the right to food. Similarly, in 2014, many governments continuously pushed back against the CSIPM's attempt to frame investment in terms of human rights (Canfield 2018).

The CSIPM's determination to include human rights language in policy documents was based on two objectives. First, the CSIPM saw human rights as an antidote to the "voluntary" nature of the policy recommendations and guidelines produced by the CFS. Human rights were protected by international treaties and laws. Therefore, anchoring policy recommendations in binding legal obligations was thought to strengthen the work of the CFS. Second, insisting on a rights-based approach, the CFS sought to assert that those who were *most affected* by rights violations as rights-holders should have a stronger voice than simply *all affected* stakeholders.

By contrast, the private sector sought to reaffirm their own vision of multistakeholderism and push back against civil society's attempt to imbue their own voice with greater legitimacy. Over the seven annual, week-long CFS meetings I have attended, I have watched participants from the Private Sector Mechanism (PSM) constantly try to dismantle the boundary between the "private sector" and "civil society" that the IPC had labored to maintain. For years, this attempt has centered around the definition of farmers. Participants from the PSM – a rotating cast of farmers and small-business owners flown in from different parts of the world – have read impassioned speeches about how all farmers are entrepreneurs and that the distinction between small-scale and large-scale farmers makes little sense. Through these statements the PSM seeks to undermine the CSIPM's legitimacy and suggest that the boundary between civil society and the private sector is arbitrary.

In recent years, the PSM has grown more emboldened in challenging the CSIPM. In 2016 and 2017, one member of the PSM, a global organization that represents commercial farmers, began advocating for the creation of a new "farmer's mechanism." They argued that "farmers are not adequately represented by the CS[IP]M," because it represents social movements. They also argued that farmers were not adequately represented in the PSM because "they represent agri-business and not farmers."[5] The PSM was not ultimately successful in creating this new farmer's mechanism, but its ongoing efforts illustrates how transnational private actors continually try to undermine the symbolic authority and claims to representation of the CSIPM.

At the same time that the private sector was launching its attack on the CSIPM, governments around the world were becoming increasingly right-wing and more hostile to civil society and human rights. I watched as the United States government, which had long promoted agri-business, became increasingly hostile to the deliberative process. It worked with illiberal governments, such as Russia, to undermine negotiations in the CFS. At the same time, governments that had once been supporters of the CSIPM, such as Brazil, became increasingly hostile as their governments turned right-wing.

In 2017, at the annual Civil Society Forum before the CFS, social movement activists warned of an increasingly hostile environment. One activist from a network of food-chain workers described "seeing a dangerous form of multistakeholderism, for those who are willing to engage, there is a growing space for them. Corporations enter these multistakeholder spaces and they show a kind and friendly face for themselves." In the same forum, an indigenous activist told the audience that "We need to be rebels. We need to continue on our efforts in relation to the CFS because it's the first international instrument that we have created like it." He described how "increasingly we've seen that [the CSIPM is] losing human rights in documents." A longtime participant from LVC explained that "There are governments that think we need to maintain

[5] Evaluation of the Committee on World Food Security. 2017. Available at www.csm4cfs.org/wp-content/uploads/2017/03/CFS-Evaluation-Final-Report-14-April-2017.pdf.

the spirit of this reform, where civil society participates on an equal level with governments that draw up right to food policy and there are other countries that seek to the destroy this process and reform the reform." That same year, an evaluation of the CFS revealed criticism of the CSIPM. Some "CFS members and stakeholders," the report explained, "were critical of the manner in which the CSM functions. The mechanism is seen to dominate discussions and overshadow the contributions of others. They were also critical of the CSM's use of language that appears confrontational to others, and felt that the CSM pushed the 'rights agenda' too aggressively."

Nonetheless, CSIPM members continued to mobilize human rights as one of few resources at their disposal. In a declaration entitled "It's Time to Recommit," the CSIPM sought to reaffirm the CFS' commitment to human rights. The report proclaimed "We, the people, are the most important agents for change. We are the organizations of the rights-holders, while governments and intergovernmental institutions are the duty-bearers. We are the most important producers, processors, and providers of food and nutrition worldwide ... our voices ... most be heard more strongly in the future." Their statement offered several proposals to strengthen the CFS to address food insecurity and malnutrition. Throughout the statement they sought to affirm human rights duties and their voices at the center of the process.

Despite their effort to promote human rights, it was clear that within the CFS there was little support for the CSIPM. In 2019, the chair of the CFS drew on the language of inclusivity to argue that the CFS was not being inclusive *enough*. "We need to keep the inclusiveness as the first guiding principle of the reform," he told the plenary of the CFS. In order to keep the CFS relevant, they needed to create new stakeholders. I learned from members of the CSIPM that the chair sought to somehow reform the CFS in a way that gave into the ongoing pressure from various governments and the private sector to dilute the voice of the CSIPM. It was clear that the chair knew something that activists didn't about the political pressures on the CFS. That year, I sat in the back of the Plenary Hall with members of the CSIPM when the UN secretary-general appeared by video link announcing a surprise "UN Food Systems Summit." Activists were immediately suspicious. Who had called for this summit?

Along with activists in the CSIPM, I would later learn that the UN Food Systems Summit was planned only after the UN Secretariat had signed a strategic partnership with the WEF. As described earlier, the

WEF had been promoting the multistakeholderization of multilateral governance since 2007 through what it called the Global Redesign Initiative. In 2020, the WEF released a new program called the "Great Reset." This more ambitious vision of the Global Redesign Initiative was focused on creating a "new social contract" modeled on what Executive Chairman Klaus Schwab calls "stakeholder capitalism." As Schwab explains, "'Stakeholder capitalism'... positions private corporations as trustees of society, and is clearly the best response to today's social and environmental challenges" (Schwab 2019). This vision of stakeholder capitalism was embedded within the structure of the UN Food Systems Summit. Unlike past global food summits, which had been organized as multilateral summits, this summit was organized as a multistakeholder summit – drawing on all relevant and affected stakeholders in an effort to transform the food system. Not only was it organized outside of the CFS, its leadership was drawn from a mix of powerful philanthropies such as the Bill and Melinda Gates Foundation and the World Economic Forum. It developed a complicated multistakeholder process that confused even governments (Canfield, Anderson & McMichael 2021).

After a few months of trying to understand how they might engage in the summit, the CSIPM decided to boycott it. Through their mobilization, food sovereignty activists developed a robust critique of multistakeholderism. They released a series of infographics about multistakeholderism that illustrated their critiques with headlines like "illusions of equality" and "privatizing public life." In a report they published, entitled "Exposing Corporate Capture of the UNFSS through Multistakeholderism," they described multistakeholder governance as a structure that "allows powerful transnational corporations, their platforms and associations to direct international and national policy making, financing, narratives and governance while promoting corporate friendly, false solutions to food systems in crisis" (Chandrasekaran et al. 2021). In their report, they traced the connections between the overlapping networks of philanthropic, corporate, and intergovernmental actors that promote multistakeholder initiatives at local and global levels. In doing so, they illuminated the acceleration of multistakeholderization as part of a concerted strategy of the World Economic Forum, the Bill and Melinda Gates Foundation, and others.

In their statement "No to Corporate Food Systems! Yes to Food Sovereignty!" the CSIPM framed their challenge to multistakeholderism in the language of human rights. "Instead of being grounded in human rights, the UNFSS is a multistakeholder forum in which all actors, whether governments, individuals, regional/international agencies, or business/corporation representatives are portrayed as equal participants. But stakeholders are not necessarily rights-holders: people's and communities' rights and sovereignty should not be confused with private-sector business interests."

4.4 Conclusions: Rights as Representational Claims

Through the claim of food sovereignty, movements have sought to overcome the limits of liberal legalism and respond to the changing political and legal landscape. Like scholars, they recognize that the nation-state no longer serves as the sole site of economic and normative organization. Food sovereignty movements therefore seek to democratize the networks through which sovereignty and power now operate. In doing so, they offer an expansive and radical justice claim. Yet as they seek to institutionalize the representative practices they have developed, they face strong opposition from powerful governments and transnational private actors that are offering their own vision of a postliberal global order. This vision is increasingly cohering around "multistakeholderism" – a vision of governance that Wendy Brown (2015) convincingly argues economizes democratic rationalities.

Multistakeholderism has the trappings of liberal democracy because it emphasizes "*equivalent opportunities* for all affected persons to participate in and exercise control over societal regulatory processes" (Scholte 2014: 11), but it does so at the expense of entrenching inequalities. Indeed, numerous analyses have critiqued multistakeholderism's fiction of formal equality as a mode through which power asymmetries are reproduced (McKeon 2017; Gleckman 2018; MSI Integrity 2020). Not only are transnational corporations, philanthropies, and powerful states often able to invest greater energy and resources in these arenas, but they are also able to leverage their economic power to exert influence outside of these arenas. Jonathan Davies suggests that by relegating hierarchy to the shadows, "the coercive modalities of governing thus tend to disappear from view" (Davies 2012: 2687). It is for this reason that food sovereignty movements identify multistakeholderism as the greatest threat to the democratic order they wish to build (Manahan & Kumar 2022).

In challenging multistakeholderism, food sovereignty movements have turned to the language of human rights. In mobilizing rights, however, they do not seek to simply reconstruct a state-centered form of global governance. Indeed, as Raj Patel (2009) has argued, food sovereignty movements mobilize the right to food *transgressively* as a democratic claim. He likens food sovereignty movements' use of human rights to what Hannah Arendt described as "the right to have rights." By mobilizing the right to food, they demand that those most affected by food systems or *rights-holders* should be at the center of decision-making. In other words, they seek to construct a more democratic form of governance grounded in the voices, visions, and needs of those marginalized by industrial food systems.

Food sovereignty movements thus mobilize the right to food as what Michael Saward calls a "representative claim" – a political, performative, and cultural process that constitutes new constituencies that demand accountability. Saward argues that representative claims cannot be conjured out of thin air – they are constrained by those discourses that remain salient. He explains: "Representative claims that are compelling, or which resonate among relevant audiences, will be made from 'ready mades', existing terms and understandings which the would-be audience will recognize . . . Claims must repeat the familiar as well as (indeed, in order to) create something new; must iterate features of political culture to cross a threshold of potential acceptability" (Saward 2006: 303). In the context of international institutions, human rights remain the dominant discourse – a language of social justice that potentially comes with constraints. In her study of human rights and gender violence, for example, Sally Merry (2008) points out that human rights remain rooted in a liberal framework that emphasizes individuality and autonomy – frameworks of liberal rights that may not always be resonant in local contexts. Food sovereignty movements too may face this constraint, particularly when the right to food is construed through an individualistic lens. But as food sovereignty movements articulate the right to food through a collective framework, they reconstruct it as a representative claim. Indeed, in mobilizing the right to food, they demand not only to be included in decision-making, but also demand that institutions, arenas, and processes of governance be accountable to them.

As they mobilize this claim in the context of stakeholder arenas of governance, they offer a new vision of democratic governance. They are not alone in seeing radical possibilities in this postliberal context. Political theorist Eva Sørensen argues that "the emergence of a system of network governance does not endanger the image of liberal democracy. It rather can be seen as a step toward its radicalization" (Sørensen 2002: 716). She contends that the blurring of boundaries between public and private makes it possible to make egalitarian claims for democracy beyond the formal political sphere to the market. Moreover, as it blurs the boundaries between states, it allows new constituencies to emerge beyond the nation-state. Instead of democracy being grounded in accountability to the "people," the imagined community of the nation-state (Anderson 2006), networked processes necessitate a constant struggle for the "legitimate right to construct the identity of the represented, and make political decisions with reference to this identity" (Sørenson 2002: 698). Through representative claims, she argues, new "peoples" are brought into being and institutions are made accountable (see also Knappe & Schmidt 2021). These peoples may be those excluded by the imagined publics of nation-states, but they can also be new alliances that seek to democratize the material, judicial, and communicative networks through which global capitalism has spread. Such an approach requires attending to the micropolitical, cultural processes through which representative claims constitute constituencies or "peoples" in whose name democracy is grounded.

Still, while food sovereignty movements may be reconstructing human rights to build decentralized and democratic food systems through postliberal forms of governance, they face significant challenges. On the one hand, their claims for human rights are easily co-opted and reinterpreted through an individualistic framework that legitimates the liberalization of food and agriculture. Indeed, this was why food sovereignty activists initially eschewed framing their social justice claims through the language of human rights. On the other hand, their claims for democratic postliberal governance are often reinterpreted simply as a claim for "inclusivity," thereby legitimating the expansion of multistakeholder forms of governance that reproduce the status quo. As powerful actors and institutions seek to incorporate, contain, and co-opt the democratic claims of food sovereignty movements, they face difficult dilemmas over how to resist theses forces while maintaining their autonomy and radical visions of transformation.

References

Anderson, Benedict R. O'G. 2006. *Imagined Communities: Reflections on the Origin and Spread of Nationalism*. New York: Verso.

Anghie, Antony. 2007. *Imperialism, Sovereignty and the Making of International Law*. Cambridge: Cambridge University Press.

Bäckstrand, Karin. 2006. Democratizing Global Environmental Governance? Stakeholder Democracy after the World Summit on Sustainable Development. *European Journal of International Relations* 12 (4): 467–498.

Brown, Wendy. 2015. *Undoing the Demos: Neoliberalism's Stealth Revolution.* Cambridge, MA: MIT.

Callison, William and Zachary Manfredi. 2019. *Mutant Neoliberalism: Market Rule and Political Rupture.* New York Fordham University Press.

Canfield, Matthew C. 2018. Disputing the Global Land Grab: Claiming Rights and Making Markets through Collaborative Governance. *Law & Society Review* 52 (4): 994–1025.

Canfield, Matthew C., Molly D. Anderson and Philip McMichael. 2021. UN Food Systems Summit 2021: Dismantling Democracy and Resetting Corporate Control of Food Systems. *Frontiers in Sustainable Food Systems* 5. https://doi .org/10.3389/fsufs.2021.661552.

Chandrasekaran, Kirtana, Shalmali Guttal, Madhuresh Kumar, Laura Langner and Mary Ann Manahan. 2021. Exposing Corporate Capture of the UNFSS through Multistakeholderism. www.foodsystems4people.org/wp-content/ uploads/2021/11/UNFSSreport2021-pdf.pdf.

Claeys, Priscilla. 2015. *Human Rights and the Food Sovereignty Movement: Reclaiming Control.* New York: Routledge.

Claeys, Priscilla and Jessica Duncan. 2019. Do We Need to Categorize It? Reflections on Constituencies and Quotas as Tools for Negotiating Difference in the Global Food Sovereignty Convergence Space. *Journal of Peasant Studies* 46 (7): 1477–1498.

Colombo, Luca and Antonio Ononorati. 2013. *Food: Riots and Rights.* London: IIED. www.iied.org/sites/default/files/pdfs/migrate/14626IIED.pdf.

Cutler, A. Claire. 2020. Locating Private Transnational Authority in the Global Political Economy. In Peer Zumbansen, ed., *The Many Lives of Transnational Law: Critical Engagements with Jessup's Bold Proposal.* Cambridge: Cambridge University Press, 321–347.

Darian-Smith, Eve and Colin Scott. 2009. Regulation and Human Rights in Socio-Legal Scholarship. *Law & Policy* 31 (3): 271–281.

Davies, Jonathan S. 2012. Network Governance Theory: A Gramscian Critique. *Environment and Planning A: Economy and Space* 44 (11): 2687–2704.

Davis, Kevin E., Benedict Kingsbury and Sally Engle Merry. 2012. Indicators as a Technology of Global Governance. *Law & Society Review* 46 (1): 71–104.

Desmarais, Annette Aurelie. 2002. Peasants Speak: The Vía Campesina – Consolidating an International Peasant and Farm Movement. *Journal of Peasant Studies* 29 (2): 91–124. https://doi.org/10.1080/714003943.

2007. *La Via Campesina: Globalization and the Power of Peasants.* London: Pluto.

Desmarais, Annette Aurélie, Nettie Wiebe and Hannah Wittman. 2011. *Food Sovereignty: Reconnecting Food, Nature and Community.* Wantage: Pambazuka.

Duncan, Jessica. 2015. *Global Food Security Governance: Civil Society Engagement in the Reformed Committee on World Food Security.* New York: Routledge.

Edelman, Marc. 2014. Food Sovereignty: Forgotten Genealogies and Future Regulatory Challenges. *Journal of Peasant Studies* 41 (6): 959–978.

Fraser, Nancy. 2009. *Scales of Justice: Reimagining Political Space in a Globalizing World.* New York: Columbia University Press.

Fraser, Nancy and Axel Honneth. 2003. *Redistribution or Recognition?: A Political-Philosophical Exchange.* New York: Verso.

Gaarde, Ingeborg. 2017. *Peasants Negotiating a Global Policy Space: La Vía Campesina in the Committee on World Food Security.* Abingdon: Taylor & Francis.

Getachew, Adom. 2020. *Worldmaking after Empire: The Rise and Fall of Self-Determination.* Princeton: Princeton University Press.

Gleckman, Harris. 2018. *Multistakeholder Governance and Democracy: A Global Challenge.* New York: Routledge.

Goodale, Mark and Sally Engle Merry. 2007. *The Practice of Human Rights: Tracking Law between the Global and the Local.* Cambridge: Cambridge University Press.

Grewal, David Singh. 2009. *Network Power: The Social Dynamics of Globalization.* New Haven: Yale University Press.

Hardt, Michael and Antonio Negri. 2001. *Empire.* Cambridge, MA: Harvard University Press.

Hendrikse, Reijer. 2021. The Rise of Neo-Illiberalism. *Krisis* 41 (1): 65.

Juris, Jeffrey S. 2008. *Networking Futures: The Movements against Corporate Globalization.* Durham, NC: Duke University Press.

Knappe, Henrike and Oscar Schmidt. 2021. Making Representations: The SDG Process and Major Groups' Images of the Future. *Global Environmental Politics* 21 (2): 23–43.

Linarelli, John, Margot E. Salomon and Muthucumaraswamy Sornarajah. 2018. *The Misery of International Law: Confrontations with Injustice in the Global Economy.* New York: Oxford University Press.

Maeckelbergh, Marianne. 2009. *The Will of the Many: How the Alterglobalisation Movement Is Changing the Face of Democracy.* London: Pluto.

Manahan, Mary Ann and Madhuresh Kumar. 2022. The Great Takeover: Mapping of Multistakeholderism in Global Governance. Amsterdam, Netherlands: Transnational Institute. www.tni.org/files/publication-downloads/the_great_takeover_-_updated_14_april_2022.pdf.

McKeon, Nora. 2009. *The United Nations and Civil Society: Legitimating Global Governance – Whose Voice?* London: Zed.

2015. *Food Security Governance: Empowering Communities, Regulating Corporations.* New York: Routledge.

2017. Are Equity and Sustainability a Likely Outcome When Foxes and Chickens Share the Same Coop? Critiquing the Concept of Multistakeholder Governance of Food Security. *Globalizations* 14 (3): 379–398.

Merry, Sally Engle. 2008. Transnational Human Rights and Local Activism: Mapping the Middle. *American Anthropologist* 108 (1): 38–51.

Merry, Sally Engle, Peggy Levitt, Mihaela Şerban Rosen and Diana H. Yoon. 2010. Law From Below: Women's Human Rights and Social Movements in New York City. *Law & Society Review* 44 (1): 101–128.

Morgan, Bronwen. 2007. *The Intersection of Rights and Regulation: New Directions in Sociolegal Scholarship*. Farnham: Ashgate.

Moyn, Samuel. 2012. *The Last Utopia*. Cambridge, MA: Harvard University Press.

2018. *Not Enough: Human Rights in an Unequal World*. Cambridge, MA: Harvard University Press.

MSI Integrity. 2020. Not Fit-for-Purpose: The Grand Experiment of Multi-Stakeholder Initiatives in Corporate Accountability, Human Rights and Global Governance. www.msi-integrity.org/wp-content/uploads/2020/07/MSI_Not_Fit_For_Purpose_FORWEBSITE.FINAL_.pdf.

Patel, Raj. 2009. Food Sovereignty. *Journal of Peasant Studies* 36 (3): 663–706.

Rajagopal, Balakrishnan. 2003. *International Law from below: Development, Social Movements, and Third World Resistance*. New York: Cambridge University Press.

Reform of the Committee on World Food Security Final Version. 2009. CFS:2009/2 Rev.2. Committee on World Food Security. www.fao.org/tempref/docrep/fao/meeting/018/k7197e.pdf.

Sassen, Saskia. 2008. *Territory, Authority, Rights: From Medieval to Global Assemblages*. Princeton University Press.

Saward, Michael. 2006. The Representative Claim. *Contemporary Political Theory* 5 (3): 297–318.

Scholte, Jan Aart. 2014. Reinventing Global Democracy. *European Journal of International Relations* 20 (1): 3–28.

Schwab, Klaus. 2019. What Kind of Capitalism Do We Want? | by Klaus Schwab. Project Syndicate. December 2, 2019. www.project-syndicate.org/commentary/stakeholder-capitalism-new-metrics-by-klaus-schwab-2019-11.

Slaughter, Anne-Marie. 2005. *A New World Order*. Princeton: Princeton University Press.

Smith, Jackie, 2004. The World Social Forum and the Challenges of Global Democracy. *Global Networks* 4: 413–421.

Sørensen, Eva. 2002. Democratic Theory and Network Governance. *Administrative Theory & Praxis* 24 (4): 693–720.

Trauger, Amy. 2014. Toward a Political Geography of Food Sovereignty: Transforming Territory, Exchange and Power in the Liberal Sovereign State. *Journal of Peasant Studies* 41 (6): 1131–1152.

Walzer, Michael. 1984. Liberalism and the Art of Separation. *Political Theory* 12 (3): 315–330.

Whyte, Jessica. 2019. *The Morals of the Market: Human Rights and the Rise of Neoliberalism*. New York: Verso.

Wolf, Eric R. 1969. *Peasant Wars of the Twentieth Century*. University of Oklahoma Press.

World Economic Forum. 2010a. Everybody's Business: Strengthening International Cooperation in a More Interdependent World. www.weforum.org/reports/everybodys-business-strengthening-international-cooperation-more-interdependent-world.

2010b. Everybody's Business: Strengthening International Cooperation in a More Interdependent World. Geneva, Switzerland: World Economic Forum.

5

Translocal Dilemmas

Social Mobilization and Justice-Seeking beyond the Boundaries of Law

MARK GOODALE

5.1 Introduction

For those of us who came of age – intellectually, politically, ethically – from the late-1980s through the 1990s, the current conjuncture can appear bewildering and unmoored in very particular if no less destabilizing ways. Trained as a Marxist political scientist and budding "Sovietologist" – yes, that was actually a thing – I spent most of my undergraduate years absorbing in the deepest possible ways I could manage the ways and means of historical materialism, the enduring centrality of class conflict, and the patent injustice in the way surplus value became the corrupting means through which accumulated wealth and power were intertwined, hardwired into institutions of all kinds, and made the basis for multigenerational inequalities. Far from the analytical subtleties of today's intersectional theory, which rightly views social violence and marginalization as the subject- and context-specific result of microhistories of exclusion and categorical denial, the universalizing scope of Marxist political and social analysis was a blunt instrument. We were taught to sort factors from the outset into either the base (political economic variables) or superstructure (religion, ethnicity, nationality, race, etc.). Those factors assigned to the base deserved our greatest attention – either as scholars or activists – while those in the superstructure were treated as carefully forged ideological distractions meant to keep those who were actually allies in a common historical materialist struggle divided, at odds with each other, and forever alienated from what Marx had described as their/our true "species-being."

At the same time, if the Marxist diagnosis of the problem – and, in the end, there really was only *one* problem – was crystal clear in its globalizing simplicity and self-imposed theoretical myopia (base, base, base, base), so too was its framework for action, its solution to the injustices of global capitalism. Although the dialectical rotation of history was inevitable – synthesis bifurcating into antagonistic conflict, only to be resolved through a new synthesis, itself to give way to a new antagonism, and so on – it was possible, with enough determination, willingness to sacrifice, and, of course, knowledge of political economy, to end class conflict and its manifold and devastating consequences. With a laser focus on the ever-unfolding tragedy of what Thomas Piketty (2014) would later reaffirm as the "central contradiction of capitalism," political action was supposed to be concentrated on overturning the thing itself. In this great task, intellectuals were given an important position as truth-tellers, as deniers of false consciousness, and as arbiters of which factors in the struggle merited our attention and which factors should be unmasked as false idols.

And yet, with the end of the cold war and the rapid collapse of global socialism, the power of Marxism as a social and political theory, a theory whose influence had been profound across a vast swath of academic, institutional, and associational life, likewise collapsed – albeit more gradually and with less intentionality. Geopolitically, despite the presence of isolated Marxist-Leninist states like North Korea or Cuba, the most important and consequential remainder – the People's Republic of China – was already well on the way to being restructured into the authoritarian capitalist juggernaut it would eventually become. In less than twenty-five years, as Evan Osnos (2014) has chronicled, China produced more capitalist wealth than was created globally during the entire period of the Industrial Revolution. And not surprisingly, during this same span of hyper-capitalist growth that is euphemistically described as "socialism with Chinese characteristics," economic and social inequality exploded in China, reaching levels of stratification that are equivalent to those of the "mature" capitalist economies like the United States.

But if Marxist politics largely disappeared even while the processes it claimed to uncover became dramatically and calamitously more inescapable in the coming years and decades, what, if anything, replaced it as a logic of mobilization for the suddenly bereft and rudderless political left? As is well known and rehearsed by now, the vacuum created by the implosion of socialism was quickly filled by a radically different framework for understanding and responding to injustice – a framework that was shaped, in one way or another, by human rights, which is to say, shaped by a category of international and national law. Although some left-wing theorists-in-mourning like Nancy Fraser (1995) were soon worrying about the long-term consequences of a transformation in which the struggle for rights-based recognition became the new framework for "postsocialist" politics, these prescient voices were largely drowned out amidst the millenarian fervor associated with the "power of human rights" (Risse, Ropp & Sikkink 1999). Although this fervor found expression in landmark international gatherings like the 1993 Vienna Conference and the 1995 Fourth World Conference on Women (in which Hilary Rodham Clinton declared that "human rights are women's rights, and women's rights are human rights"), it was a sea-change shift that nevertheless seemed completely oblivious to the ways in which the new "moral grammar of social conflicts" (Honneth 1996) was actually incompatible with the political economic grammar of historical conflict that it supplanted.

What happened next in this condensed intellectual and political history is also becoming equally well rehearsed: The global human rights revolution would prove to be no match for either the deep-seated structures of global, regional, and national economic inequality that became increasingly naturalized during the "Age of Human Rights" (Annan 2000), or the vast spectrum of demands for justice, demands that were rooted in particular places, particular histories (not *History*), and particular legacies of social suffering. If Marxism was a blunt instrument that claimed universal validity for class conflict and the purifying necessity for anti-capitalist revolution, the rights-based struggle for recognition would prove to be equally and problematically blunt. Although the Preamble to the Universal Declaration of Human Rights projected a world in which legally recognized and protected inclusion in the fictive kinship category of "the human family" would form the foundation for "freedom, justice, and peace in the world," the multifarious realities of injustice would give the lie to the power of supposedly ontologically transversal moral values like "dignity" or "social progress." Despite the valiant efforts by scholars such as Sikkink (2017) and Howard-Hassmann (2018) to defend human rights notwithstanding the overwhelming incapacities of rights-based politics within the swirling "maelstroms" of an "unequal world" (Moyn 2018), in the end, the fusion of a more recent critique from the disenchanted postsocialist left (Hopgood 2013) with an older and more historically embedded postcolonial critique of human rights and international law (Mutua 2001; Anghie 2005; Clarke 2009) signaled the final unraveling of the juridified future imagined in Vienna and Beijing.

This chapter gives me the opportunity to expand on a series of recent interventions about the consequences of this unraveling – for critical scholarship (both disciplinary and interdisciplinary), for the state of (mostly Euro-American) progressive politics, and for the urgent need to develop alternative approaches through which the most pressing and intractable problems might be confronted. In the next section, I pick up the intellectual historical narrative by examining what has happened in the wake of the "endtimes" (Hopgood 2013) of human rights and other categories of law that were invested with the weight of social, political, and, to a lesser extent, economic transformation. Although, as the Introduction to this volume explains, the use of juristocracy to describe the elevation of law during certain historical moments is meant to be transhistorical, my own contribution focuses on one of these extended moments, one that transcends specific national or regional case studies. After tracing the trajectory of this historically significant moment of juristocracy up to the present, I then introduce my own proposition for what might be thought of as the "futurelives" of human rights, one that recognizes the force of the recent critical fusion described above, but which is not, in the end, circumscribed by it.

Although my argument for "reinventing human rights" (Goodale 2022) was meant to examine fairly comprehensively the ways in which a radically reformulated account of human rights was still possible, an account, moreover, that might yet prove capable of galvanizing new and more sustainable forms of translocal social and political action, this intervention nevertheless left certain key concepts rather underdeveloped. In both this and the following section, the chapter returns to these key concepts in order to thicken the argument for a reinvented human rights as a framework for multiscalar social mobilization and justice-seeking. Yet as will be seen, this framework does not return "human rights" to its grounding in law – national, regional, or international. As I argue, the case for detaching human rights – conceptually and institutionally – from law seems to me as compelling as ever, perhaps even more so in light of the violent impotence of the international system writ large in the face of crises such as the global COVID-19 pandemic and Russia's invasion of Ukraine.

The chapter ends by reflecting more generally on the dilemmas and potential limitations of reimagining progressive politics beyond the rule of law. With a number of historical and contemporary examples of both ideological and political overreach in view, I argue that a reinvented human rights – or any other alternative proposal – must grapple with the imperatives of pluralism and the need to temper the fiery struggle for change of whatever kind with the cooling values of tolerance and solidarity, even if this means letting go of the chimera of revolution once and for all.

5.2 The Rise and Fall of Post-Cold War Juristocracy and Its Consequences

In 2004, the political theorist Ran Hirschl published an influential study of the ways in which specific forms of law had become increasingly more important, even hegemonic, over the first decade of the post-cold war. In particular, he focuses on what he describes as "constitutionalization and the judicialization of mega-politics," that is, the absorption by the mechanisms of constitution-making and national legal reform of long-standing political, social, and economic demands, including demands for different forms of justice during times of transition. For example, he invokes as a sort of paradigmatic case of the "judicialization of mega-politics" the "widely celebrated South African constitutional revolution," in which the ubiquitous and deeply-rooted consequences of the "notorious apartheid regime" were supposedly rectified through post-apartheid South Africa's rights-based process of reconciliation and political change (see Zenker's chapter in this volume; see also Zenker, Walker & Boggenpoel 2024).[1]

Yet as others observed both during this same period, and after, the hegemonization of particular categories of law went well beyond consti tutionalization (Couso, Huneeus & Sieder 2010; Kirsch 2012; Ramstedt 2012). In fact, what Hirschl describes as post-cold war juristocracy came to characterize a much wider range of processes, from the transformation of international development into a mode of human rights activism (Goodale 2008) to the juridification of post-conflict ideology and practice through the formation of a global "transitional justice" regime (Hinton 2018; Clarke 2019). Regardless of the differences and gaps in the ways in which this particular instantiation of juristocracy came to shape the post-

[1] Again, this section must be read in relation to the Introduction to the volume, which develops in much more detail a theoretical argument about juristocracy and the dialectics of reckoning with law in excess that is meant to be transhistorical. For purposes of my own chapter, I focus on a particular moment of juristocracy, one that has itself become a key marker of what the Introduction describes as "iconic indexicality." In other words, notable instances of iconically indexical juristocracy can be associated with global, rather than national or regional, histories.

cold war world, it is important to acknowledge the extent to which the apotheosis of a number of consequential categories of law was viewed as a major advance, as a way of giving new institutional and normative form to a wide range of longstanding social, political, and economic claims.

But it is also important to be quite clear about the ways in which a post-cold war and globalizing juristocracy related to both "the law" more generally and the rule of law as a logic of social ordering and institutional justification. Clarity about the contours of post-cold war juristocracy also helps to sharpen the historical and theoretical understanding of its emergence and, even more, to guide a consideration of the eventual fall of post-cold war juristocracy, which was a form of reckoning that follows inevitably whenever the law has been elevated beyond its intrinsic capacities. First, to return to my condensed intellectual history above, the rise of post-cold war juristocracy and the collapse of socialism were closely connected. In other words, the juridification of social and political life in different parts of the world was an effect of the fall from global legitimacy of a long tradition of revolutionary leftist politics and ideology, which had obviously taken a wide range of forms over the preceding decades, but which shared to greater or lesser degrees a commitment to a Marxist analysis of conflict, capitalism, "accumulation by dispossession" (Harvey 2003), and the drivers of historical change. In the absence of either the Marxist historical vision or its blueprint (however modified) for revolution, something else was needed.

It was in this context, as we have also seen above, that institutions, activists, and intellectuals alike turned to particular forms of law, most of them based in one form or another around rights, that is, entitlements that are derived from ontological inclusion in any number of interrelated – but not always perfectly consistent – categories of identity: human, women, children, cultural minority, Indigenous, and so on. The underlying logic of the post-cold war juridification of politics through rights went something like the following: The enduring inequalities and claims that had been the basis for Marxist/socialist revolutionary mobilization throughout most of the twentieth century would now be addressed through the legal recognition of social value and belonging.

Beyond the centrality of rights, however, post-cold war juristocracy was also expressed in another important domain – that of "transitional justice." Yet here too juridification is linked to the widespread collapse of Marxist revolutionary models and state projects. Instead of the use, for example, of the infamous "dictatorship of the proletariat" (Lenin 1975

[1919]), "post-conflict" (not post-*revolutionary*)[2] processes were dominated by the imposition – usually by international institutions – of different legal or quasi-legal mechanisms through which the post-conflict order was defined and set in motion. As with human rights, here too law was meant to take the place of nonlegal forms of social and political change, not a few of which had been associated with some of the preceding century's worst mass atrocities.

So this is the first part of the clarification around post-cold war juristocracy: it was a historically bounded yet globalizing instance of a wider transhistorical phenomenon that involved the rise of particular categories of law. These categories of law were intended to stand in for earlier frameworks that offered vastly different solutions for the same set of social, political, and economic problems, solutions that had (fairly suddenly) become illegitimate. And, to refer to the theoretical arguments made in the volume's Introduction, the post-cold war rise of law can be taken as a first stage in a longer process of dialectical reckoning, in this case with the failure of Marxist and socialist politics to usher in the anticipated global overthrow of capitalism.

The second part of the clarification follows from the first: If post-cold war juristocracy, the apotheosis of rights and narrowly framed regimes of justice-seeking, took place in terms of a limited number of categories of law, this means, importantly, that much – perhaps most – of law regardless of scale or region was excluded from this highly consequential process of globalizing – *not* global – dialectical reckoning. In other words, the "judicialization" or "juridification" of politics had nothing to do with the immense spectrum of laws and legal processes that regulate everything from criminal procedures to intellectual property. This is not to say, of course, that "the law" remained static in different places and times while rights-based forms were amplified in importance and scope during these same years, a spectrum of diversity that is demonstrated across the different chapters in this volume.

But the difference is that unlike the legal categories at the center of a globalizing post-cold war juristocracy, the many other categories of law –

[2] Given that the current volume features a chapter by Arzoo Osanloo, one of the leading scholars of justice processes and culture in Iran (see, e.g., Osanloo 2009, 2020), it is important to note that by "revolution" I am referring to Marxist or socialist revolution and its variants. This doesn't take account of other forms of revolution, for example, the Iranian Islamic revolution of 1979, or, of course, the late-eighteenth-century "rights of man" revolutions of France or the US.

again, national, regional, international – evolved, were reformed, or remained in the grip of the "dead hand," based on factors that had nothing to do with the ways in which the "politics of recognition" came to replace the "politics of redistribution," to return to Nancy Fraser's argument.

And if this two-part clarification helps us understand the rise of post-cold war juristocracy as a critical reckoning with the failures of revolutionary politics during a particular historical moment, it also allows us to better understand the shape and implications of what followed, that is, what happened when these categories of law themselves failed to serve their transformative purposes. Again, to speak of the fall of post-cold war juristocracy is not to make a claim about the global waning of law *as such*. If the expansion of certain categories law during the early post-cold war was the result of variations on the juridification of politics, as we have seen, the corresponding reckoning with the failures of juridification gave way to something like the "dejuridification" of politics, that is, the increasing marginalization of human rights norms and legal institutions as privileged instruments for social and political change.

However, from around 2008 onward something else took place: this multifaceted and diverse process of "dejuridification" overlapped with a more widespread and diffuse sidelining of the rule of law itself – both internationally and nationally. If post-cold war juristocracy was a globalizing instance of a wider phenomenon, so too has been the corresponding backlash-as-reckoning and its expression in various forms of anti-legal populism.

As I have argued (Goodale 2022), I put significant stock in the implications of the response by the leading global economic powers – the G20 – to the upheavals of the financial crisis of 2007–8, in which the contradictions of global capitalism yet again created system instability. The shock to the global capitalist system opened a trapdoor on regional and national markets and led to the loss of at least $2 trillion from the global economy. Beginning in November 2008, the G20 began meeting at least once every year in order to ensure that international collaboration around global capitalist markets would become the overriding logic of international relations and global governance.

Despite the widely diverse range of political, ideological, regional, historical, and cultural differences among the elite body of G20 states (which even includes at least one nominally Marxist-Leninist state – China), the goal was to reaffirm allegiance, despite these vast differences, to the monopoly of capitalism as the world's only legitimate political economy. Even in the face of any number of high-profile confrontations over the intervening years, most notably a series of cold war-like standoffs between the US and China (whose combined nominal GDPs are more than 50 percent of global GDP itself),[3] the inevitability and centrality of global capitalism were never in dispute.

Despite the fact that the postwar international system – itself a repackaging of a much older Westphalian international order of formally autonomous nation-states organized around the principle of sovereignty – had remained relatively powerless across more than six decades of decolonization, neocolonial wars, insurgency, repression, resource crisis, and genocide, from the killing fields of Cambodia to ethnic cleansing in the former Yugoslavia, the UN and its various bodies had managed to maintain at least a semblance of significance, at least a symbolic presence as the institutional embodiment of postwar internationalism and an icon for the Kantian fantasy of "perpetual peace." But even though it was – perhaps intentionally – unremarked upon at the time, I would date the G20's dramatic declaration of global capitalist solidarity as the moment when the rule of law-based international system, with its august tribunals and cadres of "post-conflict justice junkies" (Baylis 2008), a system that had been on life support for decades, was definitively replaced as both the ideological and practical locus of global power.[4]

Beyond the institutions and aspirations of international law, the fall of post-cold war juristocracy also coincided with the marginalization of the rule of law at more national and local levels during this same post-2008 period. This second development has usually been associated with the

[3] A comparison of the enormous differences *among* the members of the G20 is also illustrative. For example, the size of the Chinese economy is much closer to that of the US than it is to the third largest economy by nominal GDP (Japan). If the US economy is $5 trillion larger than China's, China's is *$15 trillion* larger than Japan's. Even more stunning, the Chinese economy is larger than the *combined* economies of the next six largest (Japan, Germany, India, UK, France, Canada). Leaving aside China, the US economy is larger by nominal GDP than the next nine countries combined (Japan, Germany, India, UK, France, Canada, Italy, Brazil, and Russia).

[4] In reference to the ongoing (as of May 2024) Russian invasion of Ukraine, an act of military aggression that can be understood in part as a move by Russia to expand control over economic resources and improve its supply routes, it is telling that other members of the G20 club moved first to harness the power of the market to punish Russia for its transgression, rather than mobilize the international legal system. Despite the sound and fury around, for example, the fact that Russia was eventually removed from the UN Human Rights Council, this was entirely symbolic, a form of internationalist nostalgia, which ultimately signified nothing.

amorphous (re-)emergence of populism as a loose description for resistance to elite control of political parties, economic wealth, and social capital. However, at the national level, the impact of populism on the rule of law has been ambiguous. If the two terms of Donald Trump in the US were examples of a right-wing populist head of state seeking to undermine the rule of law from *within* the corridors of political power, the cases of ideologically similar leaders like Viktor Orbán of Hungry, or the Tory leadership that oversaw the UK's populist withdrawal from the European Union, are less clear cut. Has Orbán sought to undermine the rule of law in Hungary or, instead, to harness the rule of law as one among several instruments of populist power? Did the 2016 vote and follow-on parliamentary processes through which a succession of populist Tory governments oversaw Brexit undermine the rule of law, or, as in Hungary, demonstrate that state-populism and the rule of law are perfectly compatible under the right (or wrong . . .) conditions?

Yet it is at the level of social and political movements – the level that concerns me most directly in this chapter and elsewhere – where the overlap between the fall of post-cold war juristocracy and the broader marginalization of the rule of law itself is most striking. On the one hand, contemporary right-wing (broadly conceived) movements organized around ethno-nationalism, racial (white, or otherwise) supremacy, religious nationalism (as in Modi's India), neofascism, and so on, are largely contemptuous of the rule of law, especially when such movements see state institutions as allies of the cultural, ethnic, or religious forces that right-wing movements seek to destroy. In particular, the logic and methods of right-wing mobilization emphasize the purifying necessity for violence and the importance of sacrificial performance, both of which take place outside of, and often against, state institutions, including legal institutions.[5] But on the other hand, because right wing social and political movements *rarely* turned toward human rights or other categories of law during the post-cold war period in the first place, their contempt for the rule of law during the current period of reckoning with the failures of law is of little interest.

With contemporary left-wing social and political movements (again, broadly conceived), however, the situation is quite different. Here, the

[5] Although not a central theme of my research, I had the occasion to track these dynamics ethnographically in the course of an extended study of the "cultural and democratic" revolution in Bolivia (see Goodale 2019, 2020).

trajectory is more complicated, beginning with the fact that many left-wing movements played a central role in the shift to human rights and other law-based forms of activism during the first decade or so of the post-cold war. As we have seen, this was also the period in which human rights activism led to the push for new treaties, new tribunals, and the judicialization of political demands in the form of human rights prosecutions and rights-based claims-making. In other words, during the rise of post-cold war juristocracy, the remnants of the former traditional revolutionary left found themselves tightly bound to the rule of law and its institutional mechanisms.

But the eventual reckoning with the failures of post-cold war juristocracy by the erstwhile left led to a corresponding reckoning with the commitment by what would later be described as "progressive" movements to the law as an instrument of social and political change. In fact, the turn away from human rights activism as a privileged mode of mobilization by a range of generally left-wing movements was a key factor in precipitating the "endtimes" of human rights and other juridified expressions of the politics of recognition. Yet these politics not only remained, even as they were "dejuridified"; they deepened and became more urgent. The difference, which continues to have major implications for the potential for lasting transformative change and the possibilities for social and political mobilization at larger scales, is that the turn away from human rights has coincided with – or, perhaps, has led to – a turn away from the rule of law as a boundary-setting social value. And in this – that is, in methodology, if not in ideology – much contemporary progressive politics resembles the traditional revolutionary left it ultimately replaced.

But instead of accumulation by dispossession or the "central contradiction of capitalism," the struggle continues to be waged – as it was during the period of post-cold war juristocracy – over questions of recognition, of collective identity, and other "moral grammars" of social conflict. So now we can begin to narrow the problematic, the likely consequences of reckoning with law in excess by and through contemporary progressive politics. In relation to social and political movements that constitute much of the afterlives – through a series of historical twists and turns – of the traditional Marxist and socialist left, we must consider the fact that nonjuridified and revolutionary approaches are being put to use at the service of a maturing politics of recognition. What kinds of new possibilities are suggested by this synthesis? And, perhaps even more important, what kinds of limitations?

5.3 Reinventing Human Rights: An Autocritique

It was in part as a way of responding to these and similar questions that I framed a recent intervention (Goodale 2022). The extended argument for "reinventing human rights" is also a multidimensional critique of the structural, historical, and conceptual failures of the existing international human rights system, a critique that helps explain *why* progressive movements have turned away from the promises of post-cold war juristocracy. Nevertheless, this is not to say that what I propose as an alternative to existing human rights is always congruent with the shape and vision of many highly visible contemporary social and political movements. Indeed, in the chapter's Conclusion, I return to the broader problem of how progressive movements might or might not express the values of a reinvented human rights.

However, what I want to do at this point is to engage in a reflexive exercise in autocritique, that is, to restate the main argument of the intervention and then acknowledge those dimensions of the argument that remained admittedly underdeveloped. In the next section, I then respond to these ambiguities by thickening the presentation of the argument and then pushing several of its main concepts further. This will allow me to both provide a point of contrast with emerging features of various contemporary social and political movements and to recognize the dilemmas that remain – despite this thickening – with the proposal itself.

The proposal begins with a reexamination of different approaches to the ontological status of human rights, from the naturalist (Howard-Hassmann 2018) to the political (Goodhart 2013) to the historical (Hunt 2007). In the end, I find Hunt's orientation the most fruitful: that existing human rights, those codified in the major international documents and prevailing discourse, were "invented" over the course of centuries, with certain turning points proving foundational: the French Revolution and the promulgation of the "Declaration of the Rights of Man and of the Citizen"; the ultimately failed attempt to make human rights a part of the response to the catastrophe of World War I through the League and Nations and the so-called Minority Treaties; and, of course, the ratification of the Universal Declaration of Human Rights (UDHR) in 1948.

There are two aspects of Hunt's approach that influence my own: First, the clear recognition that existing human rights should not be understood, as the naturalist tradition has it, as "universal," that is, as moral-ontological entitlements that somehow have inhered in all human beings for all time just waiting to be revealed for the first time in the late eighteenth century in France and Britain's North American colonies; and second, and relatedly, that this particular normative heritage, which would eventually come to have much wider scope and influence, was, on the contrary, the result of a long, contested, and dynamic process of social construction. Although the prospect – or, rather, the specter – of social constructivism has loomed over the history of existing human rights since the beginning, as an idea that – if accepted – threatens to render human rights into a framework that is subject to social and political manipulation and thereby denude human rights of their apparent existential power, my argument is that we have no choice but to embrace the reality of social constructivism and learn to harness its transformative potential.

Thus, the argument continues, if existing human rights were invented, they can be reinvented. I then take up the next question: In light of everything we know about the history and practice of existing human rights, and in the face of a daunting range of the world's most pressing problems, *should* human rights be reinvented, even if what emerges is radically different than what exists today? My response to this question is *yes*. But given the way in which I attempt to outline what a such a reinvention might look like, why describe such an alternative vision as "human rights"? This is the first ambiguity, to which I will return in the chapter's next section.

Having taken the position that only a profoundly reformulated approach to human rights can serve as a viable replacement framework for the existing system of laws and political institutions, I then go on to examine critically the different key dimensions of the international human rights system, including its relationship with global capitalism, the centrality of the nation-state, the relationship between human rights and national and international law, and the historical and cultural problems with human rights universalism, among others. This wide-ranging reconsideration leads me to argue that a reinvented human rights must be conceived not only beyond the control of state institutions and even the principle of sovereignty itself, but also beyond the boundaries of law. Regarding the latter, I take something that was implicit in Samuel Moyn's (2018) dismantling of existing human rights – in which he frequently alludes to the sad spectacle of celebrating isolated human rights prosecutions while the world burns – to its logical conclusion: that in order to reimagine human rights in ways that might prove truly efficacious and transformative, they must be detached from their juridical roots.

Yet this is not, by extension, an argument against law or legal systems or against the rule of law itself, despite the fact that the rule of law as a political ideology and logic of governance has been linked at times with various forms of "plunder" (Mattei & Nader 2008). Rather, it was intended to clear the way for a completely different grounding for a reinvented human rights, a grounding that also recovers and retains a number of valuable aspects of the existing model. But if a reinvented human rights is neither a system of international/national law, nor a set of norms under the control of nation-states, then what is it? This is a second ambiguity with the proposition, also to be addressed with more clarity below.

The abandonment of the "universal" in universal human rights has a number of important implications for the proposition. On the one hand, the rejection of the natural rights underpinning of existing international human rights opens the door for what turns out to be a striking alternative: instead of human rights universalism, the argument is that a reinvented human rights should be built around *pluralism*. But rather than a limitless and ungrounded approach to diversity that resembles extreme forms of relativism, I adopt instead an account shaped by the late writings of Isaiah Berlin, who used the concept "human values" to describe a still somewhat vague but nevertheless finite range of values and practices – and, we can add, "rights" – that would pass muster under the following test: that they are values and practices, however disparate, that are, even with much effort and education, mutually recognizable, and thus might at least *potentially* form the basis for collaboration across the many boundaries that divide us. Yet, as I acknowledge, the actual shape and content of such an approach to human rights based on pluralism would seem to raise as many questions as it purports to resolve.

And on the other hand, the abandonment of human rights universalism in favor of human rights pluralism points to the need to clarify the bases for collective mobilization. Universal human rights was/is predicated on the assumption that our supposed common humanity, which is meant to take priority over, and serve as a check on, all the existing categories that otherwise reflect our vast diversity, would ultimately animate social and political action on all levels. If we would just recognize that we were all, in fact, members of the same "human family," we would treat each other as we are supposed to treat members of our real families – with respect, support, and a willingness to work together to solve family problems. But human rights pluralism gives up this fraught kinship metaphor; we are not, and nor should we think about ourselves, as members of a single "human family," even in the face of global problems that affect people and communities at a global scale.

Yet if human rights pluralism centers the value of diversity, of difference of opinion and history, even of conflict over visions for the future, what is its basis for social and political mobilization? In other words, when a "spirit of brotherhood," as the Preamble to the UDHR puts it, is rejected as the basis for social and political action, what new "spirit" might take its place? My response is to propose an alternative logic of mobilization, a logic that I describe as "translocality." By translocality I mean an ongoing imperative for people to form alliances across the sharp boundaries of our plural lives; that alliance-building, in this sense, is the necessary precondition for being able to confront the most serious crises; and that the imperative to form wider alliances directed toward meaningful social, political, and economic change should be given priority over other approaches to change or justice – no matter how necessary or valuable in their own terms – that do not equally privilege translocal solidarity, tolerance, and the capacity to forge collective "life projects" (Blaser 2004) amidst social, ideological, and ethical multiplicity.

But – and here I come to the final ambiguity to be taken up below – beyond the seemingly obvious fact that translocality has a certain utilitarian value, that is, assuming that the broader goal of ameliorating global problems is sufficiently convincing *across* place, time, and belief, what are its more specific parameters? If translocality suggests a going beyond the local, what, in this sense, does the local mean, especially given the problematic place of "the local" as an ordering device within everything from international development to human rights treaty monitoring? And from the other side, what kinds of alliances can and should be the outcome of translocality? Is every diverse social and political movement, one that is directed toward transformative change, an expression of translocality as I understand it – in other words, an expression of a "reinvented human rights"?

5.4 Thickening the Argument, Pushing Outward

In light of the preceding summary of the main arguments behind the proposal to reinvent human rights, and the recognition of several ambiguities and dilemmas around these arguments, let me now attempt to clarify several problems by way of leading into the more reflective discussion in the chapter's final section. First, if the framework is deeply anti-institutionalist, if it requires human rights to be detached from its existing anchorages in both legal and political systems (at different levels), if it instead reimagines human rights as an ongoing imperative to form – and act upon – new social and political movements, then why describe this vision as "human rights" at all, especially given the fact that both "human" (as a constructed category of belonging) and "rights" (as an imagined set of immanent entitlements) are meant to be left behind in the process of reformulation?

The response to this question is both pragmatic (or, neopragmatic) and conceptual. For the first, what I mean is that even this radically different vision for the future of human rights recovers from the past, and preserves from the present, as much as it "reinvents." In particular, the existing human rights system – despite its manifold flaws and structural weaknesses – was viewed by many as a framework for action that became instrumental through what the neopragmatist philosopher Richard Rorty – implicitly gesturing toward Flaubert? – described as "sentimental education" (Rorty 1993). As he explained, the world would be a better, more peaceful, more egalitarian place if more people learned about the suffering of others and came to see such suffering as the urgent concern of the whole.

To the extent to which enough people around the world – whether post-1948 or post-cold war – actually came to embrace what Rorty calls a "human rights culture" of mutual empathy, I would want to hold on to this advance, something the feminist moral philosopher Annette Baier (1991) would have described as a "progress of sentiments." The category "human rights," in this sense, functions as a signifier of everything of enduring value in that which was "invented," including the "ability to see the similarities between ourselves and people very unlike us as outweighing the differences" (Rorty 1993: 129).

The conceptual response to the question "Why human rights?" is also related to a key dimension of the existing system. Much more than a signifier, the proposition retains – or, even more, depends upon – what might be thought of as the "cosmopolitan imperative," that is, the obligation to construct and live categories of identity *maximally* rather than minimally. Although the orthodox cosmopolitanism of existing human rights – one in which the "global community" was the privileged outermost ring in a set of nested concentric circles, from which we were expected to "draw the circles somehow toward the center" (Nussbaum 1996: 9) – turned out to be a completely "misbegotten" (Goodale 2020) ideal toward which the postwar human rights system was supposedly directed, the demand to conceive of collective belonging as both *emergent* and *projective* seems to me to be absolutely necessary. To the extent to which this approach to identity forms a bridge between that which was invented and that which remains to be reinvented, it is yet another reason to retain the use of "human rights."

The second ambiguity to be clarified is how to understand a reinvented human rights that has been "dejuridified," that is, detached from its close association with legal instruments, tribunals, and monitoring mechanisms. Here the clarification also underscores an unresolved dilemma in the proposition. If "human rights" is to be reconceived as a means through which new movements might coalesce beyond the boundaries of law, a means, moreover, that puts great weight on the transformative potential of translocal alliance-building and social praxis, something important is necessarily sacrificed: the regulating effects of the rule of law itself.

Although I still believe that the "logics of law . . . are particularly ill-suited to the broader tasks of economic and social transformation toward which a reinvented human rights must be directed" (Goodale 2022: 78), "dejuridification" is a move that is nevertheless made with much trepidation, especially given that the violence of "arbitrary extra-legal power" (Thompson 1977: 265) has been associated historically with *both* right-wing and left-wing (now "progressive") politics. Although I will return to the problem of "arbitrary extra-legal power" in the Conclusion, it is enough to acknowledge here that power, in this sense, can and does take many forms, including new forms of digital erasure and bullying, which coexist with other online activist movements that mobilize in ways that otherwise capture much of the spirit of a reinvented human rights (see Niezen 2020).

Attempting to clarify the final ambiguity also allows me to affix a more prescriptive scaffolding onto the proposal. As I have argued, translocality is the logic of mobilization at the center of a reinvented human rights, a logic that demands the formation of alliances *across* the many categories of difference that continue to divide us. But in order to have any meaning in practice, translocality must also function as a limiting device, that is, as a way of sorting the entire universe of social and political movements into those that express the values and objectives of a reinvented human rights from those that do not. The first limitation relates to an important distinction between *inclusionary* and *exclusionary* categories of difference. In order for a particular movement to express the values of translocal alliance-building within the meaning of a reinvented human rights, both the problem toward which the mobilization is directed, and the basis on which the new alliance is justified, must be inclusionary.

Although perspectives will differ regarding which kinds of problems meet this criterion – economic and social inequality, climate change, resource conflicts, ethno-nationalism, for example – the problem (or problems) must be viewed from within the translocal alliance itself as one of inclusionary scope and importance. At the same time, translocality must lead to alliances that involve the mobilization of people from different identity categories; put otherwise, mobilizations based around essentialized categories of identity that tend to exclude, deny, or demand various kinds of erasure, would not express the values of a reinvented human rights.

Nevertheless, translocality *would be* consistent with much of the contemporary politics of recognition/identity, *but only* to the extent to which recognition was understood to be a means unto an end – for example, the creation of more just economic and social systems – rather than an end itself. In other words, from the perspective of a reinvented human rights, a mutual appreciation for cultural, historical, religious, and other categories of difference is valuable, but only as a basis for deepening solidarity as a transversal moral value, or "sentiment" (Baier 1991). Otherwise, difference in the absence of solidarity, empathy, and tolerance, remains much too volatile, a value that is all too easily weaponized in the service of ideologies and movements that run directly counter to the vision of a reinvented human rights.

5.5 Conclusion: Tolerance and Multiplicity at the Limits of Post-ideological Change

> However, . . . tolerance cannot be indiscriminate and equal with respect to the contents of expression, neither in word nor in deed; it cannot protect false words and wrong deeds which demonstrate that they contradict and counteract the possibilities of liberation. Such indiscriminate tolerance is justified in harmless debates, in conversation, in academic discussion; it is indispensable in the scientific enterprise, in private religion. But society cannot be indiscriminate where the pacification of existence, where freedom and happiness themselves are at stake: here, certain things cannot be said, certain ideas cannot be expressed, certain policies cannot be proposed, certain behavior cannot be permitted without making tolerance an instrument for the continuation of servitude.
>
> Herbert Marcuse, "Repressive Tolerance."

In late 2010, Rhoda Howard-Hassmann, a distinguished Canadian scholar, responded to a request to write an essay that explicitly took up what she considered the most critical dilemmas confronting the maturing post-cold war human rights project. Howard-Hassmann, like others who wrote essays as part of a volume (Howard-Hassmann 2013), was encouraged to examine these dilemmas freely, without overly due regard to broader disciplinary or other sensibilities. The point was to give key thinkers the chance to express themselves in ways that they might have otherwise resisted – because of institutional pressure, or lingering personal doubts, or worry about the uncertain implications of their analyses.

The main thrust of Howard-Hassmann's (2013) essay was to reject the various critiques of universal human rights, which she associated with the ideological and intellectual abuses of postmodern social theory and its dependence on what Benedict Anderson described as "homogeneous empty time" (Anderson 1991: 24). According to Howard-Hassmann, this prevailing postmodern temporality tends to simplify, essentialize, or elide the complex lessons of history. But leaving aside her rejection of postmodern and postcolonial critiques of human rights, what struck me then (as now) is an anecdote she relates by way of explaining her own trajectory as a human rights scholar and activist.

Howard-Hassmann, whose father immigrated to Canada as a refugee from Nazi Germany, was a student at McGill University in Montreal from the mid-1960s to the mid-1970s. During this time, the university was a hotbed of student activism against the war in Vietnam, colonialism, and racial injustice, among other forms of structural and historical violence. Yet what affected Howard-Hassmann at the time was not the righteousness of the struggles being waged by her fellow student-activists, but the chilling extremism of their methods and visions for change.

As she explains, in a passage that will always shape my own thinking, "many of my acquaintances worried about being too 'bourgeois': I remember debates about whether we would be willing to kill our own parents in the name of the Revolution" (Howard-Hassmann 2013: 174). In other words, the radical politics of the era were such that a young student like Howard-Hassmann actually seriously considered the question of whether she would be willing to kill her own father, a Jewish refugee from Nazi Germany, if the cause of justice demanded it of her.

In May 2022, I found myself engaged in a lively debate of my own with a colleague from the US, an anthropologist whose critical perspectives on a range of questions over the years have always resonated with me. Given that I had left the US in 2014 to take up a chair at the University of Lausanne, my institutional and political experiences during the intervening years had been quite different than hers. She explained the ways in which university life had profoundly changed for both students and faculty alike; among other things, she worried about the cleavages that had opened up between students and professors. Yet she hastened to add that she – like many of her colleagues, within anthropology and beyond – wanted (or, perhaps, *needed*) to be seen as allies of students, many of whom were vigorously engaged in different political and social movements for justice.

But then she added something that I found as chilling, in its own way, as Howard-Hassmann's anecdote. When I asked her how she navigated this cleavage, one in which an increasingly revolutionary progressive politics was transforming the landscape of American academia, she replied that she and her colleagues had no choice but to engage with the prevailing ethos, which she described as "absolutist." This was offered both as an empirical description and justification for the fact that what Herbert Marcuse had called (in 1965) "repressive tolerance" had returned with a vengeance. The struggle for justice – within and beyond academia – had come to mean yet again that "certain things cannot be said, certain ideas cannot be expressed, certain policies cannot be proposed, certain behavior cannot be permitted."

I begin this concluding section in this way in order to make sure that the wider stakes are crystal clear and to leave no doubt about the fact that the consequences of social mobilization and justice-seeking beyond the boundaries of law also entail costs. It is also a way to draw a distinction between a number of models: the Marxist revolutionary politics of Howard-Hassmann's youth; the revolutionary – but "postsocialist" – progressive politics of our time; and the vision for a reinvented human rights that I have described above and elsewhere, which shares elements in common with the first two in certain respects, but diverges sharply in others. A relatively straightforward application of the prescriptive criteria from the preceding section would explain much of this divergence, but not all.

If a reinvented human rights imagines new forms of social and political mobilization that depend upon translocal alliances and the value of pluralism, it will always be in tension with other approaches to justice and change that depend upon ideological or other forms of "absolutism," whether these approaches demand the reeducation or "smashing" (Hinton 2016: 59) of counter-revolutionaries or the no-platforming of people who cannot be allowed to speak, the banning of ideas that cannot be expressed, and the interdiction of policies that cannot be proposed. It could be, given the way in which Marcuse's manifesto captures the *zeitgeist* almost perfectly for both the late 1960s and today, that is, across vastly different political landscapes, that the real problem is the methodology of revolution itself, which necessarily relies on ideological and other dichotomies to which a reinvented human rights must remain opposed.

To abandon, once and for all, revolutionary change as the vague endpoint toward which all our labors and sacrifices should be directed is to let go of the idea that once *the* truth is known, even to only an enlightened few, its realization justifies any means. As Marcuse (1965: 90) put it, the "telos of [repressive] tolerance is truth." But I disagree. If we reject, as we should, the grotesque contradiction of tolerance as a form of righteous *intolerance*, and return it to its place as a marker of acceptance, forbearance, and freedom from bigotry, then the end goal of tolerance is not truth, but solidarity. And if solidarity, in this sense, is the underlying value that animates the proposition for a reinvented human rights, it is a value that contains within itself a recognition of its own limits, limits that cannot be overcome.

Even in the face of the great crises, which seem to cry out for revolutionary upheaval, the replacement of "absolutism" with the kinds of inclusionary praxis that must be at the heart of a reinvented human rights will necessarily create barriers to at least the promise of rapid social, political, and economic transformation. In other words, to return to Isaiah Berlin's final essay, written in the last year of his long life, the problem is that most revolutionaries – of whatever stripe – believe that "in order to create the ideal world eggs must be broken, otherwise one cannot obtain an omelette" (Berlin 2000: 14). Yet history reveals a long record of broken eggs and very few, if any, omelettes. Indeed, most revolutionary/progressive movements, according to Berlin, become vast exercises in egg-breaking as an end unto itself, in which violent strategies of dehumanization come to doom the politics of the left as much as they more obviously do the politics of the right.

It is in light of these dilemmas and limitations that the proposition to reinvent human rights must, in the end, be understood. Pluralism, tolerance, solidarity, humility, irresolution – these are not the values that align with either the dominant model for revolutionary change of the decades before the rise of certain categories of law during the period of post-cold war juristocracy, or with the "absolutist" politics of recognition that came to replace this model during the current period of reckoning with the failures of law in excess. They are, instead, the values of a global politics that might very well remain, despite it all, too radical (in its alterity, not methods), too late, and thus forever "otherwise-than-actual" (Bryant & Knight 2019).

References Cited

Anderson, Benedict. 1991. *Imagined Communities: Reflections on the Origin and Spread of Nationalism*. London: Verso.

Anghie, Antony. 2005. *Imperialism, Sovereignty and the Making of International Law*. Cambridge: Cambridge University Press.

Annan, Kofi. 2000. The Age of Human Rights. In Project Syndicate. www.project-syndicate.org/commentary/the-age-of-human-rights?barrier=true.

Baier, Annette. 1991. *A Progress of Sentiments: Reflections on Hume's Treatise*. Cambridge, MA: Harvard University Press.

Baylis, Elena. 2008. Tribunal-Hopping with the Post-conflict Justice Junkies. *Oregon Review of International Law* 10: 361–390.

Berlin, Isaiah. 2000. The Power of Ideas. Princeton: Princeton University Press.

Blaser, Mario. 2004. Life Projects: Indigenous Peoples' Agency and Development. In M. Blaser, H. A. Feit and G. McRae, eds., *In the Way of Development: Indigenous Peoples, Life Projects and Globalization*. London: Zed, 52–71.

Bryant, Rebecca and Daniel M. Knight. 2019. The Anthropology of the Future. Cambridge: Cambridge University Press.

Clarke, Kamari Maxine. 2009. *Fictions of Justice: The International Criminal Court and the Challenge of Legal Pluralism in Sub-Saharan Africa*. Cambridge: Cambridge University Press.

2019. *Affective Justice: The International Criminal Court and the Pan-Africanist Pushback*. Durham: Duke University Press.

Couso, Javier, Alexandra Huneeus and Rachel Sieder. 2010. *Cultures of Legality: Judicialization and Political Activism in Latin America*. Cambridge: Cambridge University Press.

Fraser, Nancy. 1995. From Redistribution to Recognition? Dilemma of Justice in a "Postsocialist" Age. *New Left Review* 212 (June–August): 68–93.

Goodale, Mark. 2008. *Dilemmas of Modernity: Bolivian Encounters with Law and Liberalism*. Stanford: Stanford University Press.

2019. *A Revolution in Fragments: Traversing Scales of Justice, Ideology, and Practice in Bolivia*. Durham: Duke University Press.

2020. The Misbegotten Monad: Anthropology, Human Rights, Belonging. In D. Celermajer and A. Lefebvre, eds., *The Subject of Human Rights*. Stanford: Stanford University Press, 48–63.

2022. *Reinventing Human Rights*. Stanford: Stanford University Press.

Goodhart, Michael. 2013. Human Rights and the Politics of Contestation. In M. Goodale, ed., *Human Rights at the Crossroads*. New York: Oxford University Press, 31–44.

Harvey, David. 2003. *The New Imperialism*. Oxford: Oxford University Press.

Hinton, Alexander. 2016. *Man or Monster? The Trial of a Khmer Rouge Torturer*. Durham: Duke University Press.

2018. *The Justice Facade: Trials of Transition in Cambodia*. New York: Oxford University Press.

Hirschl, Ran. 2004. *Towards Juristocracy: The Origins and Consequences of the New Constitutionalism*. Cambridge, MA: Harvard University Press.

Honneth, Axel. 1996. *The Struggle for Recognition: The Moral Grammar of Social Conflicts*. Cambridge, MA: MIT.

Hopgood, Stephen. 2013. *The Endtimes of Human Rights*. Ithaca: Cornell University Press.

Howard-Hassmann, Rhoda E. 2013. Historical Amnesia, Genocide, and the Rejection of Universal Human Rights. In M. Goodale, ed., *Human Rights at the Crossroads*. Oxford: Oxford University Press, 172–182.

2018. *In Defense of Universal Human Rights*. Cambridge: Polity.

Hunt, Lynn. 2007. *Inventing Human Rights: A History*. New York: W. W. Norton.

Kirsch, Stuart. 2012. Juridification of Indigenous Politics. In J. Eckert, B. Donahoe, C. Strümpell and Z. Ö. Biner, eds., *Law against the State: Ethnographic Forays into Law's Transformations*. Cambridge: Cambridge University Press, 23–43.

Lenin, Vladimir. 1975[1919]. The Dictatorship of the Proletariat. In R. C. Tucker, ed., *The Lenin Anthology*. New York: W. W. Norton, 489–491.

Marcuse, Herbert. 1965. Repressive Tolerance. In R. P. Wolff, B. Moore, Jr. and H. Marcuse, eds., *A Critique of Pure Tolerance*. Boston: Beacon, 81–123.

Mattei, Ugo and Laura Nader. 2008. *Plunder: When the Rule of Law Is Illegal*. Malden, MA: Blackwell.

Meierhenrich, Jens. 2018. *The Remnants of the Rechtsstaat: An Ethnography of Nazi Law*. Oxford: Oxford University Press.

Moyn, Samuel. 2018. *Not Enough: Human Rights in an Unequal World*. Cambridge, MA: Belknap Press of Harvard University Press.

Mutua, Makau. 2001. Savages, Victims, and Saviors: The Metaphor of Human Rights. *Harvard International Law Journal* 42 (1): 201–245.

Niezen, Ronald. 2020. *#Human Rights: The Technologies and Politics of Justice Claims in Practice*. Stanford: Stanford University Press.

Nussbaum, Martha. 1996. Patriotism and Cosmopolitanism. In J. Cohen, ed., *For Love of Country*. Boston: Beacon, 3–20.

Osanloo, Arzoo. 2009. *The Politics of Women's Rights in Iran*. Princeton: Princeton University Press.

2020. *Forgiveness Work: Mercy, Law, and Victims' Rights in Iran*. Princeton: Princeton University Press.

Osnos, Evan. 2014. *Age of Ambition: Chasing Fortune, Faith, and Truth in the New China*. New York: Farrar, Straus & Giroux.

Piketty, Thomas. 2014. *Capital in the Twenty-First Century*. Cambridge, MA: Belknap Press of Harvard University Press.

Ramstedt, Martin. 2012. Processes of Dis-embedding and Displacement: Anomie and the Juridification of Religio-ethnic Identity in Post-new Order Bali. In M. Ramstedt and F. I. Thufail, eds., *Asian Ethnicity: Law and Religio-ethnic Identity in Post-new Order Indonesia*. Abingdon: Routledge.

Risse, Thomas, Stephen C. Ropp and Kathryn Sikkink. 1999. *The Power of Human Rights: International Norms and Domestic Change*. Cambridge: Cambridge University Press.

Rorty, Richard. 1993. Human Rights, Rationality, and Sentimentality. In S. Shute and S. Hurley, eds., *On Human Rights: Oxford Amnesty Lectures 1993*. New York: Basic Books.

Sikkink, Kathryn. 2017. *Evidence for Hope: Making Human Rights Work in the 21st Century*. Princeton: Princeton University Press.

Thompson, E. P. 1977. *Whigs and Hunters: The Origin of the Black Act*. London: Penguin.

Zenker, Olaf, Cherryl Walker and Zsa-Zsa Boggenpoel, eds. 2024. *Beyond Expropriation Without Compensation: Law, Land Reform and Redistributive Justice in South Africa*. Cambridge: Cambridge University Press.

6

The Enduring Logic of Mercy

Humanitarianism and the Eclipse of Human Rights

ARZOO OSANLOO

6.1 Introduction

In this chapter I explore the persistence of the logic of mercy as a contemporary global *zeitgeist*. I do so through two seemingly divergent, yet overlapping and co-constituting prisms, criminal sanctioning and humanitarianism, and show how, together, they construe mercy as an enduring ideology of our time. Drawing on research I have conducted in Iran's criminal justice system, I explore the linkages between mercy in criminal justice and the increasingly global turn away from social justice movements based on human rights and toward care-based appeals, such as humanitarianism. The latter is just one major arena of increased reliance on and appeals to care or "care work" over claims to inherent rights; others include charity, aid, and philanthropy.

In Iran's "victim-centered" criminal justice system, in homicide and other major crimes, the victims' families possess a right of "exact" retribution, quite literally (Osanloo 2020: 3). That is, victims' immediate family members may exercise their right to have a perpetrator executed. In these cases, however, victims' family members may also forgo retributive sentencing and forgive the perpetrator. A variety of interests – legal, social, religious, and even economic – shape the concerns of victims' families as they consider whether to exercise the right of retribution by forgoing rather than executing it.

To help to bring about forbearance, Iran's criminal codes compel individuals, especially those working in the judiciary, to pursue reconciliation between parties to the extent possible. However, another dimension of this system is that the entire negotiation or reconciliation process is extrajudicial, ad hoc, unregulated, and therefore, discretionary.

Thus, this legal and moral duty to seek reconciliation, on the one hand, while lacking formal guidelines for how to do that, on the other, has generated a veritable cottage industry of "forgiveness work" throughout Iran. Diverse actors, from actual actors and celebrities to religious scholars, defense lawyers and social workers, to anti-death penalty activists, fill in or populate this cottage industry to promote and persuade victims' families to forgo retribution in favor of some sort of settlement and reconciliation.

This work, while immediate and interpersonal, is also part of a broader attempt, perhaps even a movement, aimed at changing the culture on the ground, endeavoring to do what the activists call the "cultural work," to make people in society at large feel more forgiving, merciful, compassionate, and more caring toward one another. They try to replace the initial emotional and perhaps historically inscribed urge toward revenge, of which retribution is already a diminution, to one of mercy and compassion based on many practices grounded in local traditions and rituals as well as faith.

While being merciful or seeking mercy may possess qualities associated with a "seasoning" of justice (Derrida 2001), the inclination toward mercy and merciful grants, such as granting pardons to persons convicted of crimes, is both a legitimation and entrenchment of the rule of an absolute sovereign over the judiciary or the legislative branch, as in Iran. This normalization of the resort to mercy has its critics, especially among Iranian defense lawyers, who eschew the criminal justice system's capacity to reduce everyone in society to a potential supplicant.

These criticisms echo the concerns of forced migrants, whose own increased reliance on aid, charity, and mercy, including the granting of discretionary relief to refugees, reduces us all to potential supplicants. And today, beyond Iran and refugee camps, the increased recourse to aid, charity, and philanthropy, as with mercy, further entrenches state power through the standardization of states' discretionary powers, such as the granting of pardons by presidents from Iran to the United States. This state of affairs, I argue, is not simply emerging from "pre-modern" laws, as critics of Iran might suggest, nor is it due to the neoliberal maelstrom that Samuel Moyn (2018) offers. Rather, I suggest, the contemporary embrace of "care work," with its increasing recourse to humanitarianism, draws from the same reasoning as that of Iran's victim-centered criminal justice system. To make sense of this claim, I turn to Arendt's critical work on human rights and her finding that the failure of nation-states to protect minorities would lead to the certain diminution of all rights (the rights of man) (Arendt 1951).

Arendt's findings are reinforced by the more recent work of historian Mark Mazower, who has shown that the ascendance of human rights in the postwar era was a "strange triumph" – having grown from a compromise intended to privilege individual rights over the rights of collectivities, to one aimed at maintaining the status quo, in other words, the authority of the state and its sovereign power (Mazower 2004).

Indeed mercy is always-already tied to much of the presumptive international laws that aim to protect minority groups from the majority, even those in the name of human rights. And this is not by accident. International criminal laws and laws of war are, themselves, derived from domestic criminal legal systems that privilege the state's sovereign powers. Thus, far from being based on democratic principles and the rights of individuals through an inherent personhood, humanitarianism reason takes as its very source the often faith-based foundation of mercy or some other version of it.

Thus, in the under-examined foundations of humanitarianism – domestic criminal law – through which ordinary appeals for mercy and care for (distant) others emerge, we unwittingly reproduce the very systems that modern human rights were intended to eradicate in favor of approaches to humanity that are, ostensibly, founded on principles of egalitarianism and respect for human dignity. From here we can perceive how we, even in the global North, have never been modern.

6.2 Mercy's Room for Forgiveness

To begin this exploration, I turn to a case that drew me to study Iran's victim-centered approach to criminal justice (Osanloo 2020). I was sitting in on a murder case in Tehran's Provincial Criminal Court. The three-judge panel had just rendered its ruling in a murder case. They held that the prisoners had intentionally killed their victim. The sentence was in-kind retribution and it was up to the victim's family members to decide if they wanted it to be carried out.

In Iran's justice system, in homicide and other major crimes, the family of the victim possesses the right of retribution. That is, victims' family members may exercise the right to have the perpetrator executed. However, they may also forgo retributive sentencing and forgive the perpetrator. In fact, victims' families often enter into negotiations to agree to some punitive measures short of execution.

Another dimension of this system is that the negotiation or reconciliation process, if you will, is extrajudicial, ad hoc, and by and large unregulated – but that does not mean that judiciary officials are not involved. Judicial officials are implicated at every step of the process. In fact, Iran's code of criminal procedure imposes an imperfect duty on all government officials to bring the parties to *solh* (reconciliation).

Moments after the chief judge issued the ruling, he added, "But there is room for forgiveness in this case." With a wave of his hand, he cleared the courtroom, leaving the two sides, several journalists, social workers, and me. To assure the propriety of what was about to take place, the chief judge reiterated the end of the hearing, "Everything is over. This is the start of the reconciliation and settlement meeting."

As though taking those words as a cue to step away from the role of impartial trier of fact to sage adviser, one the associate judges stepped off the judge's dais and walked over to the parties holding his arms out as he reiterated "There is room for forgiveness in this case."

The parties had no dispute over the facts: two daughters and a mother had murdered their father/husband. The defendants while not denying the killing, attempted to mitigate the sentence by revealing their father/husband's years of abuse – verbally, emotionally, and physically.

The judges who spoke about the "room for forgiveness" had been apprised of the abuse in statements the defendants had written and submitted to the court, but as hearsay, the statements carried little weight. There were no witnesses, police reports, or physical evidence to substantiate the claims of abuse. Thus, while judges were aware of the mitigating circumstances, the strict interpretation of intentional murder left them with no possible ruling other than intentional murder, for which there is no other sanction besides *qisas* (retribution-in-kind).

So the judges and social workers all crowded around the victims' family members, who were the plaintiffs, and each in their own way cajoled, persuaded, and chastised the victims' family members to forgo their right of retribution. Some focused on faith-based appeals; some on the essence of justice; some merged the two; others attended to the psychological relief the family members of the victim would feel once they let go of their grief and anger. Still others focused on what the victim would have wanted, while some emphasized the serious mitigating factors in the case.

Upon listening to these mounting entreaties, first the uncle, the victim's brother, cried out, "I am not ready to execute them, but right now I am exploding with grief. So many times, I told them, 'If something is wrong, come tell me . . .' but they never did. The last time, I said, 'If you don't like my brother, then divorce.' All these people are getting divorced."

Not wanting to retry the facts of case, the chief judge, now as principal mediator, spoke, "We don't want to hear this now." Then more softly, he added, "Our duty in all our cases is to arrive at reconciliation. I want to ask this of you, that you try to come to a solution between you."

One of the aunt's responded, "They don't pray," in an effort to undercut the womens' character and credibility. Looking directly at her two nieces across the aisle, she added, "If my brother was so bad, then why didn't you tell me."

The young women were shepherded by the social workers and prison guards toward their aunts and uncle. The social workers, the guards, and others admonished the young women, "Plead with them. Go!" As the women hesitantly approached, their aunts began castigating them anew. The guards stood closely by to protect them from physical harm, while the journalists hung back, hurriedly documenting the situation on their notepads.

Then girls then fell to their knees and begged for their lives and through their tears repeatedly begged, "Forgive us. Please. Please, forgive us." The aunts looked away, their arms folded at their chests. Instead, they looked up at the crowd of mostly women gathered around them.

"Why should we forgive? Why should we be merciful when they were not?"

As though playing the part of the chorus in a Greek tragedy, the observers, including the prison guards and journalists, were advocating emphatically to spare the lives of the women. Different women spoke with varying degrees of rapidity.

"They did wrong, but you do right!"

"I won't forgo retribution."

"By killing them, you won't receive God's mercy."

From the far end of the room, the chief judge was tidying his desk and packing his briefcase. He spoke over the others in a more authoritative plea, "With your mercy, you will be helping them to become better people."

"They said those things about our brother!

No, I will not agree."

After some time of this very intense pressure, in the end the victims' family members each signed a document stating that they had forgone their right to retribution "without any doubt or uncertainty." The mood in the room shifted to a lighter and indeed festive one. The social workers began planning a celebratory party to praise the act of forbearance. The prison guards declined to shackle the defendants, who would return to prison to await formal sentencing, which would include a sentence of between three and ten years for the state harm of public disturbance.

I filed out with the judges and asked about their intensive efforts during the mediation. The chief judge stated that in all of the cases before him, he had both a legal and moral duty to seek a settlement short of death. When I further inquired about their motivations, the judges in these cases frequently responded with some variation of their legal and moral duty to seek forgiveness.

It is this legal and moral duty to seek reconciliation, without any formal guidelines for how to do that, I have argued, has generated a cottage industry of forgiveness work. Throughout Iran, diverse actors, including celebrities, religious scholars, defense lawyers, social workers, and anti-death penalty activists, inhabit and even produce this cottage industry.

In my research for this project which spanned thirteen years (2007–20), I studied the legal, social, religious, and even economic conditions through which families gain this right of retribution and exercise it by forgoing rather than implementing it. In simple terms, I was interested in exploring who forgives in these cases where victims' family members possess an unfettered right, at least legally, to seek retributive sanctioning.

Now, the work of these activists is very delicate as it can, and sometimes does, backfire. While forgiveness work is intensely proximate, the activists I spoke to also intended their efforts to have wider impacts, the culmination of which was a social movement emphasizing compassion and mercy. These strategies, which they referred to as the cultural work, included artistic expression in the form of theater, poetry, and prose, and drew heavily from local traditions, rituals, and faith-based practices. They emphasized the indigenous nature of the values of compassion and mercy over those of revenge and retribution, and they set about to change the values that their society prioritizes.

My interlocutors' engagement with a kind of social work that extends directly from Iran's justice system and, ostensibly, the faith of the vast majority of its people, publicly underscores the state's power. Yet the broader goal of many of these actors is to change the laws on the books. Short of that, because retribution is said to be immutably enshrined in the Qur'an, they seek to change the cultural palate to one in which forbearance is the norm and retribution the exception. And there have been some slight changes to these laws, substantively and procedurally, that help bring about this "feeling of forgiveness," as my interlocutors refer to it, across broad sectors of society. Their strategies and increasingly their expertise, include their knowledge of the Quran, their eloquence, empathy, and even an embodied performativity, work together to change the possibilities on the ground – that is, to get the family members of the victim to imagine what it means to forgive rather than seek retribution.

In this context, my interlocutors insisted, the victims' families were not simply relinquishing the right of retribution, they were also giving themselves permission to renounce their pain and sorrow. For this reason, some social workers acknowledged, the forgiveness work in which they engaged took years before achieving its goal of forbearance. For in order to forgo retribution, victims' families had to be able to put aside their grief. In this sense, forgiveness work also involves cultivating a new affect and a new way of being. It is slow work that is generously nurtured by numerous social actors.

To be sure, the forgiveness work that I explore takes place through the state's legal apparatus even as it extends to, includes, and implicates its citizens such that we can say that the state corrals, and in some ways even constrains the field of possibility. At the same time, social workers draw from a broad lexicon of cultural resources that include rituals, piety, and reason to appeal to the victim's family members and attempt to cultivate this feeling of forgiveness.

Rather than chiding state agents on rights-based concerns or appealing to human rights discourses that hold little interest to aggrieved families, these activists work through intersubjective ethical dialogues based on mercy and compassion, which, in Shi'ism, are connected to the higher principles (*maqasid*) of justice.

6.3 What Do Appeals to Mercy Conceal about Justice?

My scholarship on Iran's victim-centered criminal justice system by and large explores how these "forgiveness workers" work – labor – to make this room for forgiveness. While many different kinds of actors are engaged in this practice, some, almost exclusively defense lawyers, rebuked and detested it. One lawyer derided the whole system: "Look what they make us do! Do you see how they make people beg? We want law, rights; Why should they have to beg for forgiveness? [My client] doesn't need mercy; she needs justice; she needs law."

Having laid some of the social context for forgiveness work I introduced, I now want to turn to the lawyers and consider the reasoning behind the disdainful attitude that almost every lawyer with whom I spoke had about this forgiveness work. That is, I want to explore just what it is about forgiveness work that the vast majority of rule of law advocates found so troubling. In other words, why do legal actors object to the Iranian state's capture of legal pluralism?

The lawyers I interviewed were critical of the fact that in Iran, murder is treated as a private tort versus a criminal case prosecuted by the state. And of course, looking at the case of Iran, a rogue state often in the crosshairs of Western rule of law standards, facilitates a critical assessment that reveals the faults and flaws of a logic of mercy that requires one party to become a supplicant to a party who has the power over the life and death of another.

Criminal laws are adjudicated by state actors and institutions and the measure of mercy requires sovereign state power, which can take many forms – pardons, reprieves, or clemency, to name a few. That mercy allows for a curbing of a due punishment is significant given that it may also comprise a justice response to structural inequality (Meyer 2010).[1]

At its core, this description is a humane response in the face of very real mitigating circumstances, but it is one that is weighed and carried out by those in positions of power, through their broad discretionary authority. Pardons are subject to unequal application, subject to the whims of the sovereign or, in contemporary times, well-resourced public campaigns, often requiring entrenched support or at times, celebrities shining a light on injustice. In most jurisdictions, state officials make the determination that the person who caused the harm is deserving of this lessening of a due punishment.

Mercy in such contexts may also possess the quality of translocal justice that is the subject of this volume. Yet, even as a translocal corrective to injustice, mercy is inimical to a modern understanding of human rights, another translocal signifier of justice, precisely because mercy hangs on the sole discretion of a ruling authority – a higher power (Osanloo 2006). The sovereign confers mercy, while through a human rights approach to justice, the question of the *deservingness* of the lessening of a punishment is connected to a human's inherent worth

[1] Derrida (2001) refers to this as "mercy seasoning justice," an approach that suggests mercy enhances the very "taste" of justice.

and dignity and is never envisioned to be at the mercy of another's whims and caprices, politics, or vengefulness.

Human rights organizations and Iranian human rights lawyers have said as much about Iran's system. And even when Iran's judiciary announced changes to the penal codes, such organizations and lawyers still roundly criticized Iran's practices, particularly with respect to human rights, dignity, and the right to life, and urged Iran to change its laws even further. To be sure, international human rights organizations, alongside Iranian human rights lawyers, have objected to the Iranian justice system, particularly with respect to human rights, dignity, and the right to life. They have diligently urged Iran to further amend and revise its laws to bring them into conformity with international human rights conventions which the country has ratified.

Yet many human rights groups and individuals who support these conventions in the global North applaud, seek, and encourage mercy, compassion, and other "humane" responses to tragic circumstances, even as they are critical of how Iran's victim-centered justice system mobilizes mercy. In what follows, I seek to tease out this tension surrounding mercy and unpack what I observe as its enduring logic in our contemporary times. In so doing, I consider the relationship that contemporary "justice" responses to other kinds of tragic events have to theories of criminal justice like that of Iran's, which is premised on extending mercy. I suggest that in contemporary and even aspirational appeals to human rights, this logic of mercy persists, albeit unwittingly. The impulsive or unconsidered intrusion of mercy in ostensible human rights concerns inadvertently upends the very core values and considerations of justice upon which human rights are premised.

6.3.1 Juristocracy's Hidden Peculiarities

In 1941 legal anthropologist Robert Redfield gave an address in which he distinguished state law in contemporary societies from what he referred to as "primitive law" (Redfield 1964). This use of the term "primitive" was both a common term for the times and also the very thing Redfield was arguing against. That is, Redfield's address was responding to Bronislaw Malinowski's contention that law can be found in all societies as rules that individuals follow for "personal and social reasons" (Redfield 1964: 2). Redfield considered this definition of law to be overly broad and argued that it failed to capture the "special peculiarities of law" in state-centric legal systems. Redfield began by noting that:

> to us, who live under a developed system of law, law appears as something very different from the personal and cultural considerations which motivate our day-to-day choices of action. It appears as a system of principles and restraints of action with the accompanying paraphernalia of enforcement. The law is felt to be outside, independent, and coercive of us. Within its labyrinths we find our way as best we can. (Redfield 1964: 2–3)

Thus, Redfield points to a critical feature of statist legal systems: that courts "are powerless to recognize obligations" that societies based on custom were able to account for (Redfield 1964: 3). Redfield's understanding of what we might refer to as "prejuristocratic" societies found that such obligations derive from social relations and socially diffuse but commonly held beliefs about compensation for loss and conflict avoidance, which are structured through moral codes of honor.

Of course, today in many contexts that draw from multiple temporalities of justice and possess nostalgic investments about them, ideas about such obligations remain, but they are often beyond the capacities of juristocratic institutions to address. Thus, in contemporary societies, actions that are based on social duties often appear anomalous and are unaccounted for by legal institutions. As Redfield notes, "The highly developed state with its powerful law looms so large that perhaps we do not always see that within it are many little societies, each in some ways a little primitive society, enforcing its own special regulations with a little primitive law of its own" (Redfield 1964: 4).

Redfield goes on to point out that a key feature that distinguishes statist legal systems is that they treat harmful actions, such as murder or theft, as violations of impersonal law – as crimes – rather than as first and foremost harms to specific persons or groups. This contrasts with their treatment in nonstate societies as harms that are suffered by the victim's family. While poring over a number of ethnographic examples, Redfield shows that legal institutions and proceedings in nonstate societies are concerned with mediating the quest for redress by the victim's next of kin, whether by facilitating compensation or regulating retaliation. They thereby address the concern with social obligations, which in these cases amounts to the victims acquiring some kind of settlement or retribution.

In contemporary legal systems, however, the state, in a sense, assumes the victim's right to attain redress: it seizes the harmful action as an injury to the whole of society, treating it primarily as a violation of state-enacted criminal law, and only secondarily as a harm to the victim or the victim's family. That the legal system attributes greater importance to the crime against the state than the harm to the victim is reflected in the harsher punishment it metes out, as severe as incarceration and death, while victims, if they choose to pursue redress at all, may seek only monetary damages. Thus, what such societies often leave unaddressed is the damage to the underlying relationship between the victim and perpetrator and the need for repair.

As Redfield, among others, points out, the shift in murder from a tort (private action) to a state prosecution is a defining moment for the modern state and its legal institutions because it is at this point in which the state takes the reins of determining who lives and who dies and it is further a defining moment of sovereign power.[2] And yet, a continued element of the state's calculus in deciding who lives and who dies is its pardon power.

From a human rights standpoint, it is possible to discern how the logic of mercy, embedded in the pardon power, is troubling. Appeals to compassion, such as those in the case I describe above, are pleas to powerful authorities to grant mercy; they are based on the potential of benevolence as opposed to the necessity of equality. They rely on and reentrench social, class, race, and gender hierarchies – rather than egalitarianism, a cornerstone of human rights. And while mercy or the power of pardon can be used as a corrective in justice-seeking, those decisions are often emotional, sometimes irrational, and the resulting system is deeply unequal and arbitrary.

To shed light on some of the concealed effects of the state's continued authority in pardon power, I return to Redfield, who suggested that "modern" law emerges when the state distinguishes criminal law from tort (or personal injury) law, with the former addressing harms to state and society and the latter concerned with harms to individuals. Thus, as disputing became more juristocratic, states privileged punishment for transgressions against society over the restorative aim of mediating between two sides of a conflict (Braithwaite 2002: 7).

That is to say, our contemporary understanding of law emerged from "the development of systems of compensation or of forms of socially approved retaliation in ... what might be called a rudimentary law of torts" (Redfield 1964: 12). This rudimentary tort law included formal (legal) process and specific sanctions. The overall goal of this incipient

[2] See also, Foucault 1996.

law, Redfield found, was to contain "unlimited revenge" between families or tribes. He saw this process of standardization and systematization of retaliative sanctions as developing into a "modern" justice system at the point when the laws of a society began to be more concerned with punishing the harm committed against society as a whole, rather than just the injury to victims and their next of kin. "The beginning of law may . . . be sought," Redfield wrote, both "in the extent to which there is formal process" and in the extent to which offenses are "thought to be also, or only, wrongful acts committed against the society," but it is only with this last transformation that formally imposed sanctions become "the impersonal application of force – that we are likely to think of as criminal law" (Redfield 1964: 12).

While Redfield examines the missing social elements of harm, I turn to what persists after the juristocratic takeover of states adjudicating personal harms. The transformation elides the residue and remainder of what is an affective appeal to power, not in the name of or for the purposes of effectuating justice, but rather for seeking that authority's benevolence.

And here is where I want to draw attention to the logic of mercy as one that is not simply evident in prejuristocratic, so to speak, disputing processes. Rather, the pardon power with its attendant logic is present in contemporary justice systems throughout the global North. Indeed, humanitarian laws, otherwise known as the laws of war, that have emerged over the last four hundred years to protect civilians during times of conflict derive from these very processes.

I suggest that the same logic guides much of the humanitarian approaches to major social problems in our world today, with special consideration for the current refugee crisis. The refugee crisis exceeds the conditions of possibility of statist, juristocratic problem-solving, not only due to its vastly larger scale, but also because of the inability of its analytic to address the idea of social obligations, to which Redfield was attuned. And yet, as we live through an era of myriad, protracted humanitarian crises: multiple war zones, as well as climate, economic, and global health disaster zones, hundreds of millions of people have fallen into need – of aid, charity, or relief, and have been relegated to performing the role of supplicants in order to obtain such services. The bottom line is that "modern" lawfare seeks responses to these problems in juristocratic remedies, when, in fact, these are better thought of as social problems in need of remedies that are attuned to the wider moral obligations that underlie the substantive laws.

6.4 The Cruel Logic of Mercy

The cruel logic of mercy or its cruel irony is evident in its contemporary codified forms starting with the Universal Declaration of Human Rights (UDHR), Article 14, that provides that those fleeing their places of residence owing to a well-founded fear of persecution have a right to seek asylum. This language is reminiscent of a criminal seeking a federal pardon. They have the right to ask – to beg.

And as with the pardon, the grant of relief to a person with a well-founded fear of persecution, a refugee by definition, is considered humanitarian and thus also a discretionary grant. Legal scholars, jurists, and political leaders made this deliberate decision in the wake of the horrors of World War II. With the rise of nation-states and their greater affinities for imagined homogenous communities, the rights-claims of individuals who fell outside of the states' normative Constitution would be cast aside and left to the mercy of those states. Writing in the wake of the postwar international system, Hannah Arendt saw the effects on refugees clearly and noted, "the prolongation of their lives is due to charity and not rights" (Arendt 1951: 296).

As many are aware, we are currently seeing the worst refugee crisis since World War II. This is an interesting correlation because our laws protecting refugees derive from the crisis in World War II. The *1951 Convention Relating to the Status of Refugees* is the primary legal treaty that guides nation-states' approaches to refugees and asylum seekers who reach their borders.

There is no right to asylum. There is only the right to seek asylum, just as a person indicted of legal transgressions has a right to procedure in the form of a fair trial. Technically, asylum seekers do not even have that, a point which Arendt also noted (Arendt 1951). Only once the refugees reach the borders or specific zones for processing them into such nation-states, can refugees or stateless persons seek legal relief. In point of fact, these remedies are increasingly diminishing as a result of constraints that the states themselves create.

The refugee must ask the sovereign for asylum, often as a supplicant, and the more supplicating the better for their cases. These are people who have committed no crime, particularly as asylum seekers with criminal convictions are ineligible under the Convention (as are persons convicted of war crimes, crimes against humanity, serious nonpolitical crimes, and other politically inscribed views, such as, in the US, being a member of the Communist Party). Nation-states adopting the Convention, moreover, often define criminal activity even more broadly for purposes of evaluating applications for asylum.

The 1951 Convention placed specific temporal and geographic parameters on refugees seeking relief. Only refugees from postwar Europe were eligible to apply for asylum. And even then, asylum was a discretionary grant – from the sovereign. While the 1967 Protocol Relating to the Status of Refugees removed the temporal and geographic constraints on asylum applicants, the entire international system for refugee protection emerged to protect European refugees during and after World War II.

The raced/ist legacy of this system is still intact in important ways. This is evident in the treatment of refugees from the global South, to whom these treaties, arguably, were never intended to apply. Palestinians, many of whom were made refugees after the British mandate over Palestine ended, and the conflict began, were specifically excluded from both treaties and these exclusions continue until today. For Palestinians, a separate but unequal system of temporary aid exists through the creation of a United Nations agency, the United Nations Relief and Works Agency (UNRWA). After more than seventy years of UNRWA activities, it beggars belief that the humanitarian crisis to which it is responding is provisional. UNRWA, nonetheless, is funded at a small fraction of the UN's other relief agency, the United Nations High Commissioner for Refugees.[3] It is significant that UNRWA's mandate is to "manage" rather than solely to provide temporary relief, as humanitarian aid is otherwise intended.

Overall, this refugee relief system is not one based on the inherent dignity of the human. Rather, it is intended as temporary and discretionary humanitarian aid by a conglomeration of sovereigns, while the ultimate grant of asylum, which can be both temporary and revocable, is conferred by the sovereign authority who has the power to decide who

[3] UNRWA, created in December 1949, is a relief and development agency originally intended to provide jobs for public works projects and direct relief to Arab Palestinians who fled or were expelled from their homes during the fighting that followed the end of the British mandate over the region of Palestine, managing 5 million refugees from the 1948 and 1967 wars. UNRWA is the only agency dedicated to helping refugees from a specific region or conflict and is separate from UNHCR. UNHCR was formed in 1950 and is the main refugee agency and helps refugees from all over the world with the exception of Palestinian refugees. It has a specific mandate to aid refugees by eliminating their refugee status through three durable solutions: local integration, resettlement, or repatriation whenever possible. In contrast, UNRWA does not try to eliminate the problem. It manages it.

lives and who dies. Refugees' claims of their suffering are often denuded of politics in order to trade on the compassion of those with power.

Thus, the rights-based critique of the Iranian criminal justice system, particularly the condemnation that relief is bestowed through the discretionary grant from a merciful sovereign, is also one that applies to the international system to protect refugees and other forced migrants. And, to be honest, beyond the humanitarian approach to the treatment of refugees and stateless populations, we can today observe numerous other social issues whose recourse to redress are to avail themselves of the "care economies" that are emerging and flooding our contemporary moment. This is evident not only with the elderly or the sick (consider the now ubiquitous GoFundMe crowdfunding campaigns) but also the calls for governments to "forgive" student debt. Now, with the overturning of *Roe v. Wade* in the United States, even reproductive rights are being contained through prohibitions that increasingly require women to supplicate for care, aid, and even worse, for permission, rather than to exercise their inherent right to bodily autonomy.

These are grave and seemingly intractable problems, to be sure. Right now, it seems that compassion is the key driver for relief, humanitarian forms of relief, but we might ask what it would look like to have compassion and human dignity be the drivers of justice, of an egalitarian and secular system of rights based on the rule of law.

To be clear, law and politics have always been co-constituting. For this issue with regard to human rights, Mark Mazower made that clear when arguing that the individuated nature of the claims alongside of their unenforceability was always intended as a political compromise to give some features of rights-claims to individuals as opposed to presenting minority populations with group rights (Mazower 2004). Indeed, as Mazower shows, judicialization was never the intention of the UDHR. What it was, however, was a means of strengthening the sovereignty of new post–World War II nation-states from precisely those minority groups.

Similarly, the humanitarian laws that undergird much of the activities around the suffering of distant others are born of law – laws of war. Their intent was always to provide temporary relief in much the same way as the 1951 Convention. This, I suggest, is the discontent of our contemporary (and widening) humanitarian world system. It is not just a way to make war more humane, as Samuel Moyn (2021) has claimed: it is more than that. If the camp is the biopolitical nomos of our time, as philosopher Giorgio Agamben has noted (Agamben 1998), then humanitarianism, I contend, has become our *zeitgeist,* our very way of life,[4] the moral, intellectual, and cultural climate of our current era. Charity, mercy, pardon, relief, aid, and benevolence have become powerful signifiers of life and life-giving today. And as such, they are slowly undermining rights-claims, exactly as the Iranian cause lawyer put it to me, and precisely what Arendt wrote about some seventy years ago.

To use the term of salience to this volume, this juristocratic reckoning that we are seeing today in outsized humanitarianism is what Arendt presaged long ago when she wrote:

> insofar as the establishment of nation-states coincided with the establishment of constitutional government, they always had represented and been based upon the rule of law as against the rule of arbitrary administration and despotism. So when the precarious balance between nation and state, between national interest and legal institutions broke down, the disintegration of this form of government and of organization of peoples came about with terrifying swiftness. (Arendt 1951: 275)

Notably, Arendt aligns this fallout with "precisely the moment when the right to national self-determination was recognized for all of Europe and when its essential conviction, the supremacy of the will of the nation over all legal and 'abstract' institutions, was universally accepted" (Arendt 1951: 275).

For Arendt, the breakdown of interests and institutions was more than merely administrative. It also laid bare the contingent nature of the core principle of human rights: their inalienability. As it turns out, those rights are only enjoyed by citizens (Arendt 1951: 284).[5] The stateless are left to the "mercy" of the state (Arendt 1951: 283).

[4] In Part III, section 7, "The Camp as the 'Nomos' of the Modern," Agamben (1998) evokes the concentration camps of World War II: "The camp is the space that is opened when the state of exception begins to become the rule." Agamben continues, "What happened in the camps so exceeds (is outside of) the juridical concept of crime that the specific juridico-political structure in which those events took place is often simply omitted from consideration." The conditions in the camps were "conditio inhumana," and the incarcerated somehow defined outside the boundaries of humanity, under the exception laws of Schutzhaft. Where law is based on vague, unspecific concepts such as "race" or "good morals," law and the personal subjectivity of the judicial agent are no longer distinct.

[5] Later, Arendt continues, "The Rights of Man, after all, had been defined as 'inalienable' because they were supposed to be independent of all governments; but it turned out that the moment human beings lacked their own government and had to fall back upon their minimum rights, no authority was left to protect them and no institution was willing to guarantee them" (Arendt 1951: 292).

Thus, the international laws that aim to protect minority groups including refugees and stateless persons provide no recourse but to mercy. And this is not by accident. International criminal laws and laws of war are themselves derived from theories of crime and punishment that aim to preserve the power of the sovereign. Far from being based on democratic principles and the rights of individuals through inherent personhood, humanitarian logics have as their very source the faith-based foundations of mercy, often reprocessed through the contemporary frames of law, including the laws of war.

Again, to draw from Arendt, the consequences for the deprivation of rights is the denial of a political community. This loss of a polity, Arendt argues, is akin to being expelled from all of humanity – to being "nothing but human" (Arendt 1951: 297). Despite the contemporary resort to relief in the form of charity and aid, the loss of a political community for hundreds of millions of people who are today subjects of aid is a subtle if glaring residue of the failure of rights and of the judicialization of wider social and political problems. This includes the judicialization of the plight of refugees (Behrman 2014). Here, we are reminded of Redfield's concern with wider social obligations which are denied to persons lacking political community. This lack of political community is further observable in the rise of neoliberalism, which is also attributed to destroying the polity – or *demos* – for other populations (Brown 2015).

As with other reactionary backlashes, the hostility to refugee rights today is a form of neoconservatism that manifests from the same kind of power as neoliberalism (Farvardin 2020: 28). As state authorities render forced migrants to zones outside of the polity, they prefigure refugees and others who are similarly situated as subjects-in-need rather than as subject of rights (or as rights-bearing subjects).

Thus, a reckoning with juristocracy requires us to address key problems that arise from the judicialization of social and political crises – from the underlying conditions that lead to social injury to those of forced migration. These problems have their roots in the political exclusion and subjugation of large swaths of humanity, whom the laws render lawless and without legal redress, and hence only as subjects of aid.

6.5 Conclusion

I have drawn from research on the Iranian criminal justice system as well as international laws of war to explore the tension between humanitarianism and human rights, examining how discourses of care mask, seep into, and overtake endeavors that seek justice through human rights. In doing so, I have sought to demonstrate that logics of mercy pervade and cross nations, cultures, and legal systems even as they offer wholly different notions of citizenship, belonging, and democracy. Ultimately, I have sought to draw attention to the effects of logics of mercy, care, aid, and relief on the meanings and qualities of justice.

And this is the contradictory logic of espousing human rights through humanitarian care: the latter are based on benevolence and while they can be used for good deeds, they are also arbitrary, discretionary, and of course, unequal. Human rights, however, call for exactly the opposite. This is how humanitarianism comes to eclipse human rights. For, as long as humanitarian care is our *zeitgeist*, or the lens through which we make sense of and address persisting social and global problems, inequalities will persist and even be exacerbated.

How could we start to rethink refugee rights given the contemporary political conditions? Drawing from the works discussed here, we might start by taking into account the conditions that have fostered the refugee crisis. We might, moreover, consider that where or with which nation-states or political entities, social obligations should lie. Perhaps countries that invade or support invasions, even or especially if they do so on humanitarian grounds, should have the responsibility of taking in refugee populations that their incursions create.

References

Agamben, Giorgio. 1998. *Homo Sacer: Sovereign Power and Bare Life*. Trans. Daniel Heller-Roazen. Stanford: Stanford University Press.

Arendt, Hannah. 1951. The Decline of the Nation-State and the End of the Rights of Man. In *The Origins of Totalitarianism*. New York: Schocken, 267–302.

Behrman, Simon. 2014. Legal Subjectivity and the Refugee. *International Journal of Refugee Law* 26 (1): 1–21.

Braithwaite, John. 2002. *Restorative Justice and Responsive Regulation*. New York: Oxford University Press.

Brown, Wendy. 2015. *Undoing the Demos: Neoliberalism's Stealth Revolution*. London: Zone.

Derrida, Jacques. 2001. What Is a "Relevant" Translation? Trans. Lawrence Venuti. *Critical Inquiry* 27 (2): 174–200.

Farvardin, Firoozeh. 2020. Reproductive Politics in Iran: State, Family, and Women's Practices in Postrevolutionary Iran. *Frontiers: A Journal of Women Studies* 41 (2): 26–56.

Foucault, Michel. 1996. Truth and Juridical Forms. Trans. L. Williams with C. Merlen. *Social Identities* 2 (3): 327–341.

Mazower, Mark. 2004. The Strange Triumph of Human Rights, 1933–1950. *Historical Journal* 47 (2): 379–398.

Meyer, Linda Ross. 2010. *The Justice of Mercy*. Ann Arbor: University of Michigan Press.

Moyn, Samuel. 2018. *Not Enough: Human Rights in an Unequal World*. Cambridge, MA: Harvard University Press.

2021. *Humane: How the United States Abandoned Peace and Reinvented War*. New York: Farrer, Strauss, & Giroux.

Osanloo, Arzoo. 2020. *Forgiveness Work: Mercy, Law, and Victims' Rights in Iran*. Princeton: Princeton University Press.

2006. The Measure of Mercy: Islamic Justice, Sovereign Power, and Human Rights in Iran. *Cultural Anthropology* 21 (4): 570–602.

Redfield, Robert. 1964. Primitive Law. *University of Cincinnati Law Review* 33 (1): 1–22.

7

Law and the Afterlives of Utopia

Reckoning with Pasts and Futures in Berlin's Housing Movement

NITZAN SHOSHAN

7.1 Introduction

That the legal code depends for its operation on histories of interpretation and application as well as on frameworks of meaning that bear upon its textual corpus is surely a commonplace in legal scholarship, perhaps especially in anthropology. Yet much like the human DNA, the legal code too may include silent messages, inactive sections whose effective significance, for lack of usage, has remained opaque. Such silent codes may register the political interests or moral compasses of bygone times (e.g., Thompson 1975). They may also remain in the legal code as traces of lost worlds, as the afterlives of defunct futurities inscribed with a measure of permanence yet uncannily at odds with the social life that surrounds them. But what happens when, against all expectations, they become reanimated in a present with which they appear so out of sync? How, and with what effects, do they become reactivated and conjured out of oblivion to finally find their significance in the service of contemporary projects? How do they shift from their silent oblivion into the center of political controversy in juristocratic moments of resurgent investment in law as a site of struggle and a promise of justice?

Such is precisely the case of a constitutional article that in recent years has become a point of contention in the struggle for affordable housing in

For their helpful suggestions and constructive critiques, I'd like to thank the participants in the After Law workshop at the University of Lausanne, and particularly Mark Goodale and Olaf Zenker for their generous invitation; as well as the participants in the Interinstitutional Ethnography Workshop in Mexico City. I'm grateful to Carlos Arroyo, my research assistant, for his invaluable help in the preparation of this text.

Berlin. Article 15 of the German Basic Law (henceforth, the German Constitution) authorizes the state to "socialize"[1] privately owned land, industries, and natural resources. Despite its clear and explicit wording, however, it has never been used in the history of the Federal Republic. To be sure, it stands as a historical relic from an era in which notions of collective ownership and the public good seemed, for many, to represent legitimate claims on and limits to the sanctity of private property. It is doubtful that any similar formulation could find its way into law nowadays. And yet, here it is, a clear, straightforward proclamation of the constitutionally backed authority of the state to socialize private property and hand it over to the public, independently of the usual allowance that legal codes generally grant for expropriation by eminent domain.

In this chapter, I examine the struggle of a grassroots initiative to expropriate and "socialize" hundreds of thousands of apartments in Berlin from real-estate conglomerates by appealing, without precedent, to the German Constitution. In the face of legal loopholes in existing rent control legislation, unbridled financial speculation, and spiraling rents in the German capital, the *Deutsche Wohnen & Co. Enteignen* (Expropriate Deutsche Wohnen & Co.,[2] henceforth DWE for its German initials) campaign has in recent years fought to force the uncooperative governing coalitions of Berlin to transfer massive privately owned housing stock to collective, public ownership. It did so by taking recourse to law at multiple scales, from the Federal Constitution's socialization article to the Berlin state Constitution's instrument of popular referendum and its statutory law, where the expropriation would need to be legislated. Meanwhile, opposition to the campaign has come in the form of its ridicule as utopian and naive, of juridical delegitimization, of political lobbying, and of generous funding to counter-campaigns in the media. But it has also appeared as the advancement of less-radical – and arguably less effective – legal measures of rent control that have sought to defuse the movement's rising momentum. Hence, the DWE initiative has from its beginnings been forced to reckon with and invest its resources in a complicated juridical struggle in which, building on the

[1] The German word is *Vergesellschaftung*, or socialization, which carries somewhat different associations than *Nationalisierung*, or nationalization. While the official English translation of the Basic Law uses "nationalization," here I use socialization, which remains more faithful to the original and, in my opinion, better transmits the utopian dimension of the Article.

[2] *Deutsche Wohnen* was one of the major private real-estate holders in Berlin, and yet the campaign targets all real-estate conglomerates with massive investments in the city.

relatively recently codified instrument of popular democratic participation of the referendum, which in Berlin sets extremely high standards for success, and navigating a complex yet leaky regime of rent legislation, it aimed to reanimate the constitutional afterlives of past futures of mass utopia in the neoliberal present.

My discussion draws on a year of active participation in the movement from 2019 to 2020, during which I was a member of two workgroups, I canvassed neighborhoods, organized tenant groups, helped out with direct actions and demonstrations, plastered the city with posters, remained attentive to several email lists and chat groups, and had the opportunity for numerous informal conversations with activists and volunteers, as well as on follow-up interviews and ongoing review of developments and materials since then. The chapter proceeds in four sections. I first look at the relationship between law and futurity, particularly the shift toward the future-oriented prescriptivism of modern western law and its relationship with utopian thinking. Next, I describe the legal frameworks that in Germany define the juridical context, the possibilities, and the limits for the expropriation campaign, including not only the Federal Constitution but also Berlin's referendum law and the different rent-control legal mechanisms that have already been implemented. I then turn to consider housing as an arena for mass utopian imaginaries and the political mobilizations that have emerged around it, both globally and, more specifically, in Germany. Finally, I examine the DWE movement and its campaign to reanimate the utopian potentialities of law through the referendum on the expropriation of real-estate multinationals.

7.2 Law, Future, Utopia

European legal codes and praxes begin to genuinely orient themselves toward the future only in the modern period, whereas previously they were generally concerned with regulating the resolution of conflicts and disputes within existing social orders and political regimes. It is with the rise of modernity as an ideological force and an aspirational horizon that law turns to earnestly busy itself with laying out blueprints for what should be, rather than what is. Like other projects and imaginaries of modernity, it thus acquires a temporalized, future-oriented, utopian dimension. The US Constitution and the Declaration of the Rights of Man are perhaps the two most well-known examples of the inscription into legal documents of visions of utopian futures that mark a radical break with the past and the present, even if they reflect and emerge from prior historical developments of western imperialism and their attendant ramifications for legal and philosophical thinking.

The increased investment in codifying futurities into law went hand in hand with the important place that utopian thinking has come to occupy in modernity, which temporalized the previously spatial distance that marked the difference between utopia and the here-and-now and projected it onto a future horizon (Jameson 2004; Levitas 2010). While specific imaginaries of the future and their associated political agendas have varied greatly, they have all in one way or another relied upon and mobilized notions of historical progress – human, scientific, technological, and political. Of special importance to the present discussion, hope as a collective form of temporal attachment has found particular expression in the class-struggle social movements of the nineteenth and early twentieth centuries and in the idioms of the political parties that purported to represent, within liberal-bourgeois juridical frameworks, the interests of the workers and the oppressed; not least by pushing forward agendas that called for the rethinking of property rights or the abolition of those very frameworks within which they operated.

In more recent decades, scholars have written about a crisis of the utopian thinking that had accompanied modernist political projects. Fredric Jameson, for example, has argued that utopian thinking has turned unsustainable in an increasingly polarized world and that its postmodernist weakening has obstructed the imagination of historical difference and, with it, of alternatives to the present (Jameson 2004). According to Susan Buck-Morss, the fall of the Iron Curtain brought into sharp relief the emptiness of the utopian promises of mass prosperity that both capitalism and communism have proclaimed yet equally failed to deliver (Buck-Morss 2000). Other authors have similarly written about the difficulty of imagining meaningful futurities in the post-Fordist, post-cold war, neoliberal historical moment (Lomnitz 2003; Berlant 2007; Guyer 2007; see also Hartog 2017). With the notable exception of Samuel Moyn, however, few of these farewells to utopian imaginaries have reflected upon the juridical implications of the shifts they have described. For Moyn, human rights discourses, institutions, and legal framework have become the globally dominant utopian project starting in the 1970s as a displacement of earlier dominant utopian imaginaries that were centered on prosperity and equality (Moyn 2018, 2012). Their rise, then, has accompanied the demise of socioeconomic redistribution and class struggle as the defining registers of political aspirations.

To be sure, DWE activists emphatically insist that decent housing is a basic human right. Here, however, I use the concept of utopia to refer precisely to those once-prevailing, Marxist-inspired ideologies of collective ownership over the means of production that promised a future free of exploitation and to which the socialization article of the German Constitution owes its existence. The invocation of the constitutional article, which has never been used, by a grassroots movement in the contemporary context accordingly amounts to the reanimation of specific legal figurations of utopian attachments that have since become effectively defunct.

Looking at the DWE movement's legal strategy through this lens contrasts with two common approaches to the law in the social sciences. The first, dating at least as far back as Karl Marx's critique of liberalism but today strongly inspired by Foucault and Bourdieu, understands law as an instrument of control and domination in the service of power, for example as part of neoliberalism's punitive turn (Loic Wacquant 2001, 2012; see also Harcourt 2010; Kalb 2012), as the ethopolitical management of risk and control (Rose 2000), as racial criminalization (Feldman 2001) or as a regime of recognition of indigenous rights (Povinelli 2002; see also Greenhouse 2022). A second approach considers law as offering at least some protection from the excesses of power, whether in the efforts of Christian congregations to push back against what they perceive as encroachments upon their religious freedoms (McIvor 2020), in postconflict struggles for restitution for war-related damages (Lyons 2018), or in indigenous claims to juridical autonomy within state-sanctioned frameworks of "customary law" (Wright 1988; Jackson & Warren 2005; Hale 2006).

Of course, much anthropological literature has subscribed to neither of these two approaches entirely, instead underlining the contradictory and ambivalent potentialities and limits of legal regimes (Goodale 2017). And indeed, such ambivalences are palpable in the case of housing activism in Berlin, where law guarantees certain protections while also enabling wild real-estate speculation in the first place. But the approach taken here is different, inviting us to consider law as an archive of past futures and to look at how and to what effect such afterlives are reanimated and brought back into the limelight of political struggles in moments of juristocratic insurgency. The questions that arise, then, are how the seemingly outdated utopian aspirations that are reflected in Article 15 of the Constitution resonate with and become mobilized for a grassroots agenda that appears similarly at odds with contemporary understandings of property and rights; how they enter into friction with broader legal frameworks that govern property and real estate; how they challenge dominant political ideologies and present-day futurities in postreunification Berlin; and what transpires if and when their limits and their failures force a reckoning with the broken promises of law.

7.3 The Legal Frame(s)

In order to consider these questions, a few words about the legal frameworks that shape the juridical terrain within which the DWE campaign has proceeded are necessary. The document to which I have straightforwardly referred as the German Constitution is, in fact, anything but a straightforward constitution. Composed by reluctant German representatives as demanded by the occupying Allies and under the latter's watchful gaze, it was conceived and designed from the start to provide a provisional, temporary legal basis for the Federal Republic until such day as a united, unoccupied Germany could freely deliberate and sovereignly decide upon a lasting constitution. Hence its baptism as "The Basic Law" (*Grundgesetz*) rather than "The Constitution" (*Verfassung*). The Basic Law accordingly determined that it would expire when the German people freely adopt a constitution (Art. 146), a condition broadly understood to refer to an eventual reunification and an end to the occupation. However, in 1990, rather than becoming entangled in a drawn-out constitutional process that, furthermore, would have entailed the integration of the voices of former East Germans, viewed with suspicion by West Germans after four decades of communism, reunification was instead rushed through using a much speedier and simpler article that merely stipulated the right of German territories to join the Federal Republic and adopt its Basic Law (Art. 23). Thus, with minor modifications to articles that concerned German reunification and the sovereignty of the occupying powers, the Basic Law, born under division and occupation as a temporary placeholder, transitioned mostly untouched into the permanent constitutional law that was expected some day to replace it, without the country ever going through a free and sovereign constituent process.

Like most other parts of the Basic Law, then, reunification left Article 15 untouched. At the time of its writing, it represented a provisional political compromise between the Social Democratic opposition, still committed – at least officially – to the Marxist ideas of workers' ownership over the means of production and the eventual establishment of a socialist order, and the ruling conservatives. But its roots reach at least as far back as the 1918 November revolution, when workers' and soldiers' councils demanded the expropriation of German industry and forced a similar compromise in the 1919 Weimar Constitution, which also protected private property while leaving the possibility of socialization open (Hoffrogge 2021b). Following 1945, socialist political commitments were reinforced by a profound and broad distrust of heavy industry for its complicity with the Nazi regime, a sentiment shared by many conservatives. The general skepticism with which the private property-based free market economy was received in the immediate postwar years in the Federal Republic manifested itself plainly, for example, in the 72 percent who supported the inclusion of a socialization article in the Hessen state Constitution in 1946 or in the ten million-strong general strike for price controls in 1948 (Hoffrogge 2021a).

To be sure, Marxist-inspired ideas of collective ownership of the means of production had continued to resonate with certain sectors of West German society – especially labor unions – well into the early 1980s, as the powerful metal workers' union's (IG Metall) failed 1983 campaign to socialize the struggling steel industry using Article 15 demonstrates (Hoffrogge 2021c). Yet it is unlikely that a similar article would have found its way into a new German Constitution in 1990, some three decades after the Social Democrats officially left Marxism behind. At the same time, if it appears out of sync with today's hegemonic ideas of the sanctity of private property rights, at the time of its ratification the article was already a testament to a lost utopian horizon. Conceived under the shadow of the Iron Curtain and the triumphant domination of American capitalism in Western Europe, the Basic Law gave birth to a Federal Republic that would remain under conservative political reign and in the economic grip of ordoliberal orthodoxy for two decades before the recession of the mid-1960s paved the way for a thoroughly reformed, welfarist Social Democratic Party to power. Article 15 was, in this sense, from the very start already the afterlife of a past future. The present struggle to reanimate it is therefore doubly resurrectionist in nature.

A helpful way of explaining the peculiarity of Article 15 is to contrast it with the immediately preceding Article 14, which guarantees the rights of private property and its inheritance as well as the possibility of taking by eminent domain. Before the launch of the DWE campaign, housing activists had already raised the possibility of expropriation, especially with reference to Article 14's second paragraph, which proclaimed that "Property entails obligations. Its use shall also serve the public good," a condition which, in their view, the financial speculation-based profit maximization strategies of the real-estate multinationals clearly contravened (see, e.g., Villinger 2016). But Article 14 opens with the primacy of private property and only subsequently allows for expropriation by eminent domain with fair compensation. This has two important implications: first, expropriation may target only particular properties, not entire industries, and only with due justification; and second, it consists of a transaction of exchange at market value between the state and private owners.

By contrast, Article 15 implies a fundamental questioning of private property rights. Rather than proceeding from the sanctity of private property to then condition the possibility of its expropriation on proper justification and adequate compensation, it simply allows the transfer of "[l]and, natural resources, and means of production" to public hands for the sake of socialization. While the difference may appear minor, according to constitutional experts its implications are – or could be, since the article has never been put to the test – far reaching. The formulation suggests an understanding of private property not as a primary right but rather as an affordance of the sovereign state that may, accordingly, also be withdrawn. It is not only that entire economic sectors can be socialized, but also that justification is beside the point and that adequate compensation, in this reading, would accordingly consist not in the market value of the property but rather in whatever the state deems a fair and affordable restitution. In the case of Berlin, this means that the extremely low rates at which investors massively bought properties at a time when real estate in the German capital was dirt cheap, and the nearly bankrupt government desperately sold off many of its assets at bargain prices, could serve as the ground for calculating compensation, rather than today's skyrocketing real-estate values. The entire financial viability of the DWE campaign, in other words, rests on this constitutional residue of past ideologies of collectively owned property.

Although, at least hypothetically, the Constitution offered a legal path for the campaign, given that the expropriation would need to proceed through statutory measures the question remained of how to bring the Berlin legislature to enact the appropriate laws. This problem has been especially challenging given the absolute hostility of the ruling Social Democratic Party (SPD) and later Christian Democratic Union (CDU) (not to mention the liberals in the opposition) to the initiative, even while polls have shown broad support for it among voters across the political spectrum. In part as a bulwark against the return of populism and totalitarianism, Germany's federal law makes no allowances for referendums, and yet, for the very same reason, it grants the federal states relatively broad autonomy to do so. While Berlin's state law does permit referendums, it sets considerable obstacles for pursuing them successfully.

The rules are rather complicated and depend on the type of decision that is to be put for referendum, but for the purposes of the present discussion the process consists of three phases. First, a request for a consultation of popular interest in the referendum must be filed, accompanied by 20,000 signatures of residents with voting rights. Following a review of the legality of the proposed referendum by the government, popular interest must be substantiated by demonstrating, again with signatures, the support of at least 7 percent of eligible voters – some 170,000 people at present. The government must then proceed to administer the referendum within a legally binding time limit, either as part of a general election or independently. Winning the referendum requires a simple majority and the turnout of at least a quarter of eligible voters. The proposal itself can include either a bill, which if approved automatically becomes law, or alternatively a demand, which if passed obliges parliament and the government to act upon it.

The possibility of forcing an unwilling political elite to use Article 15 to expropriate large real-estate investors through the legal instrument of the referendum therefore implied that the initiative needed to become a broad-based, grassroots movement capable of mobilizing the necessary signatures, turnout, and votes. I will return soon to describe how – and how successfully – DWE confronted this challenge. For now, I want to note that this required of the movement to publicly engage another legal regime, namely housing and rent laws in Germany in general and Berlin specifically, and make a compelling case about their inadequacy – the very reason that, as far as the activists were concerned, the campaign had kicked off in the first place. In order to counter steep rent rises across urban areas in Germany, the federal parliament passed a law authorizing individual states to apply rent hike limits (*Mietpreisbremse*) to specific housing markets, restricting increases according to average rates in the immediate vicinity as determined by an index produced and published by the federal government. In Berlin, the regulation applies throughout the city, yet it excludes both new buildings and significantly renovated apartments. Another legal mechanism, based on the Federal Construction Law, allows municipalities to declare certain neighborhoods as "milieu-protected areas" (*Milieuschutzgebiet*, officially *soziale Erhaltungssatzung* or social conservation statutes), activating a number of regulatory restrictions – for example, prohibitions on converting rented to ownership-based housing and on luxury renovations or a municipal right of first refusal for buildings on sale – that aim to preserve the social structure of the area and constrain rapid demographic shifts. Finally, as the DWE campaign gathered pace and, in a move that many interpreted as seeking to sabotage its growing appeal, the Berlin parliament approved a five-year rent freeze, which, however, was struck down a year later when the Federal Constitutional Court determined that the state lacked the legal jurisdiction to do so. The success of the DWE campaign depended significantly on the effectiveness with which it could expose to a broad public the various loopholes that allowed real-estate speculators – and particularly large multinationals – to bypass such legal and regulatory restrictions. Before turning to discuss how the initiative achieved this goal, in what follows I briefly consider the relationship between housing, utopia, and social movements more broadly.

7.4 Housing and Mass Utopia

The right of every person to decent housing has long stood at the center of utopian imaginaries and political agendas in different historical contexts and under different ideological regimes. In Germany, the right to housing was codified in the Weimar Constitution, which was heavily influenced by socialist ideas and hence remarkably progressive for its time. After World War II, the Constitution of the German Democratic Republic (GDR), which, in many ways, preserved the constitutional principles of the Weimar Republic, similarly recognized the right to proper housing. In the Federal Republic, meanwhile, neither the Basic Law nor any other legal instrument has guaranteed the right to housing, and yet the right is acknowledged in several international charters to which the FRG was a signatory or a participant, including, for example, the United Nations Universal Declaration of Human Rights and the European Social Charter.

The human right to adequate housing, of course, implied as its correlate the obligation of states to provide housing to their citizens. Across the Iron Curtain, housing became an important index of the relative merit of contrasting economic and political regimes as well as a crucial sphere for producing the legitimacy of nation-states. In Germany, with its housing stock critically depleted due to the destruction of the war and with the arrival of many millions of ethnic Germans expelled from Eastern Europe, the provision of housing represented a particularly grave challenge for the two nascent states. While the strategies for confronting the housing crisis in East and West were different and reflected contrasting approaches to the relation between the market and the state, the provision of housing itself constituted in both cases a crucial component of the promise of mass utopia upon which both socialism and capitalism had built their claims to legitimacy. Nor were these promises limited only to the national scale. East German engineers, machines, and materials, for example, were sent in the 1970s to Vietnam as part of internationalist socialist solidarity to assist in the postwar reconstruction and particularly in the building of residential complexes (Schwenkel 2020).

If, throughout the twentieth century, adequate housing emerged as both a right and a utopian horizon or promise that oriented state-building projects, the urban housing movements that have proliferated throughout the globe, and which have operated in the interstitial space between this promise and its failure, in turn have articulated their own futurities and their own critiques of the present. Looking at locations as geographically far apart as Mumbai, New York, or Barcelona, researchers have argued that housing activists have created new forms of democratization, giving rise to utopian hopes (Appadurai 2002; Parés 2019; Mathers 2021). The sorts of grassroots democratic participation that such movements have developed, according to scholars, have generated novel imaginaries and configurations of citizenship, at times achieving a degree of autonomy from the constraining territorial scale of the nation-state (Holston 2001; Murphy 2016; Pérez 2022). In San Francisco, São Paulo, Mexico City, and elsewhere, studies have described how housing activism and other urban movements have consolidated communities and strengthened solidarities in contexts of deep social inequalities and marginalization, signaling potentialities for hope and emancipation (Howard 2014; Stavrides 2019; Kopper 2021; Law 2022). One need not necessarily subscribe to the deeply optimistic appraisal that much of this literature makes of the potentialities of housing activisms – much less agree with it on the actual effects that such urban mobilizations have had – to note the unmistakable air of utopian futurities that frequently enough offer inspiration for their struggles and that mark, as well, their scholarly understandings.

As in many other cities, Berlin housing activism has come in many colors, some uncompromisingly militant and profoundly radical in their commitment to alternative forms of social relations, others seeking redress for grievances formulated and pursued within existing legal, administrative, and political institutions and idioms. At the same time, like much else in Berlin, housing activism has reflected as well the unique position of the city within the (geo)political history of Germany, Europe, and the world at large. Long before reunification, the western part of the former capital, which had remained officially under the sovereignty of the occupying Allies, had become a refuge for young Germans in search of alternative lifestyles who found in it a cosmopolitan respite from what they experienced as a suffocating and provincial German culture, a tax-free haven where one could thrive with relatively modest resources, and a much-desired exemption from compulsory military service. While squatter communities were already well established in West Berlin, the fall of the wall ushered in a period of massive squatting of vacant, run-down residential buildings in former GDR central districts, which suffered from severe underpopulation because of East Germany's cost-effective prioritizing of new construction on the city's peripheries over the far more expensive renovation and conservation of older housing stock built to outdated standards and equipped with aging infrastructure. Apart from the sheer number of empty buildings available, the squatters benefitted as well from the People's Police's helpless confusion under a collapsing political regime and from the legal uncertainty about the private ownership of state properties throughout the former GDR. In many cases, squatters aspired to create autonomous, anarchist communities. As the city consolidated its unified police force and questions of ownership had largely been resolved, and notwithstanding sometimes violent resistance by squatters, throughout the 1990s the buildings had mostly been evicted.

In more recent years, however, while housing activism in Berlin has continued to reflect the geopolitical division of the city, it has largely emerged as local responses to the impact of processes of rapid gentrification, financialization, and speculation. In the decade after reunification, Berlin's population stagnated and rents remained low. As I mentioned above, it is during those years – starting in the late 1990s but especially following the meltdown of the Berlin state bank (Bankgesellschaft Berlin) in 2001 – that the insolvent, heavily indebted Berlin government sold off many state properties throughout the city, including some 200,000 apartments as well as land designated for residential construction, to investors and developers at bargain prices. The 2008 global financial crisis precipitated a further massive injection of capital into Berlin's housing market by publicly traded multinationals looking for safe investments (Hoffrogge 2019). The combined effect has been an extensive financialization of the city's housing market.

The arrival of the federal government to the new capital from its previous headquarters in Bonn, the national economic recovery from a long stagnation, major investments in urban infrastructure, and massive renovations of residential buildings funded with EU and Federal subsidies all contributed to Berlin's renaissance as a lucrative real-estate market. Within two decades, previously frontier western districts that had once straddled the Berlin wall and had become home to many immigrants and low-earning residents because of their lack of appeal to well-to-do West Germans had rapidly metamorphosed into coveted central areas. In the former east, where the better-off had relocated to newly constructed buildings on the city's periphery that offered additional space and modern facilities such as central heating or private bathrooms and kitchens, central neighborhoods that suffered from structural deterioration, aging infrastructure, and outdated living conditions and that, as a result, housed mostly working-class and less well-off residents, had turned into fashionable, cream-colored attractions for baby-stroller gentrifiers.

It is against this background of swift and drastic urban transformations and multinational financial speculation that many tenants' initiatives have come to life in the past two decades. Yet by and large they have remained focused on resisting changes in particular neighborhoods or even in particular buildings slated for eviction or major renovations, which allow landowners to bypass legal limits on rent hikes. One notable exception was the abortive 2015 campaign launched by a tenant association for a city-wide referendum on a bill that would have introduced better regulations on Berlin's remaining publicly owned housing companies. After the proposed legislation was shown to be legally unsound and certain to suffer defeat at the courts, the city government and the activists reached a compromise that granted some of the campaign's demands and the referendum was abandoned.

Finally, we cannot hope to understand the nature of housing activism in Berlin without considering the special place of rent in the city. With an unparalleled 85 percent of residents living in rented housing, Berlin towers far above any other major European urban area as a renters' city. This has meant, first, that the city's inhabitants are relatively well informed about their legal protections and benefit from the active and competent advocacy and support of tenant associations, on which they can count for free legal counseling and representation (Kusiak 2021). Second, it has also meant that for the overwhelming majority of its inhabitants the steep rise in real-estate values did not translate into a similar increase in the values of their properties but rather into a sharp climb in rent prices, which has far outpaced the increase in incomes and has created a strong incentive for landowners to evict older residents. The rent squeeze has affected not only residents but equally small retail businesses, many of which have not been able to compete with large chains and high-end shops. As a result, mobilizations with a focus on rent issues have taken on a critical contemporary problem and, potentially at least, could compellingly address very wide publics.

7.5 Socialize It!

This was precisely what the DWE initiative set out to do. Convinced that existing rent-control laws have proven utterly inadequate for responding to the escalating housing crisis, throughout 2017 activists deliberated on campaigning for a radical, unprecedented goal. They would use the legal instrument of the referendum to force the government to invoke Article 15 of the Constitution in order to socialize the properties of all private companies holding 3,000 or more apartments in the city. In this way, the campaign would leave unaffected (and unthreatened) both small property owners and the large housing collectives (*Wohnungsgenossenschaften*) that own and rent almost 200,000 apartments throughout the city. More radically still, the proposal would require the government not only to expropriate the multinationals that have been heavily speculating in Berlin's lucrative real-estate market but also to hand over the socialized apartments to their tenants, who would self-administer the buildings collectively. In the opinion of lawyers who have participated in the initiative as well as of constitutional experts with whom the campaign has consulted over the years, Article 15 would provide a solid constitutional basis for establishing the jurisdiction of the Berlin government to undertake the unilateral expropriation and, as importantly, would grant the state, rather than investors, the authority to determine the rate of fair compensation. This, in turn, would guarantee a viable and affordable financial plan for the socialization that would see the Berlin treasury recover its costs through rent in the medium term. Informed by the experience of the failed 2015 referendum campaign, this time around activists opted to put forward not a statutory bill but rather a resolution, which would require Berlin's parliament to subsequently formulate and approve the corresponding legislation.

With its agenda sufficiently hammered out, by 2018 the campaign was ready to go public. It won immediate and broad – though not always favorable – attention from the media and from political figures, in no small part thanks to the apparent outlandishness of its proposal. The many activists who joined the initiative composed a heterogeneous assemblage. Some were experienced, long-time organizers and members of leftist groups who identified in the campaign the potential for advancing anti-capitalist social agendas; others were disaffected tenants of multinational-owned properties or of buildings slated for sale to real-estate investors who sought assistance and solidarity with their local struggles and found the campaign's platform especially appealing; some were veterans of the 2015 referendum campaign or other housing activist groups; a few were active in labor unions or affiliated with political parties, especially the socialist *Die Linke*, which announced its support for the campaign early on; several were academics whose research interests focused on urban problems. Generally speaking, they included a broad generational spectrum and a balanced gender composition as well as a wide mix of class and educational backgrounds, with a marked underrepresentation of residents of outer districts and, especially given that many of the regular activities took place in a central neighborhood with a high ratio of Middle-Eastern immigrants, a certain scarcity of ethnic diversity.

While the initiative proved appealing for many and grew rapidly, its relationships with other institutions, groups, and organizations have been uneven. Whereas the electoral base of each of the ruling coalition parties has shown majority support for the initiative in poll after poll, their leadership, as I have already noted, has been divided, with the Social Democrats, the Conservatives, and the Liberals consistently opposing and struggling to smother it, the Greens remaining undecided and arguing for pursuing other, less radical solutions for the spiraling rents, and only the Socialists fully endorsing the campaign. Similarly, while some labor unions have come out in favor of the initiative, others have not. Meanwhile, the city's housing collectives have opposed it, despite their own adversarial relationship with real-estate multinationals, evidently out of concern for protecting their own properties (Hoffrogge 2021a). Finally, DWE's relationship with other housing movements and tenant associations was also complicated. On the one hand, the initiative practiced solidarity by offering organizational know-how and hands-on assistance to other groups, running activism workshops, moderating tenant assemblies, facilitating city-wide networking of local struggles, and mobilizing massive turnouts and staging spectacular, eye-catching performances in marches and demonstrations. On the other hand, activists reported resentment from members of other groups who felt that DWE had monopolized the attention of the media and had marginalized their own campaigns.

Strategically, DWE kept a clear focus on winning the referendum and on confronting the challenging hurdles that had to be overcome in order to do so. This overarching objective defined the strategies and the activities of all the different teams: the "start-help" workgroup reached out to budding tenants' groups throughout the city, provided organizing know-how, and canvassed neighborhoods; the "action" workgroup produced demonstrations, marches, and postering campaigns, designed and distributed propaganda materials, and offered logistical support; the "socialization" workgroup hammered out the juridical, budgetary, and institutional frameworks of the proposal so that it would be both compelling and viable; the "collection" workgroup dedicated its efforts to guaranteeing the successful collecting of sufficient signatures in support of the referendum, building and coordinating local neighborhood teams throughout the city; the public relations workgroup handled all external requests for information about the campaign; while the coordinating committee served as a supervisory board where representatives of the different workgroups and others directly elected by the plenary assembly came together to guarantee the smooth operation of the campaign as a whole. The general plenary assembly held weekly meetings to discuss campaign-wide issues, vote on decisions and proposals, and receive updates from the different workgroups, where much of the concrete labor took place.

The utopian impulse that stood at the center of the campaign, both in its conjuring of the constitutional afterlife of past hopes and in its imagining of a radically different future, brought with it ambivalent, contradictory effects. On the one hand, DWE has been ridiculed as peddling naïve fantasies. Detractors, often speaking on behalf of real-estate investors, as representatives of political parties, or in their role as reporters and commentators in the public sphere, have argued that DWE's proposal is, in fact, anti-constitutional, and, even if accepted, would therefore collapse before the legal challenges that would surely follow it; that its financial plan is unrealistic, underestimating the compensation that the state would need to pay private companies and overestimating its capacity to recuperate the expense with rents, and would end up driving Berlin into bankruptcy; that it would be politically impossible to find a majority that would support the necessary legislation, much less implement it, within any plausible electoral scenario in

Berlin; and, finally, that it represents populist demagoguery that would hinder an effective response to the rent crisis by deterring investments in construction and development rather than a feasible, serious solution to the problem. In brief, the unprecedented ambition and scope of the campaign have allowed its critics to dismiss it as utopian in a derogative sense.

On the other hand, the undeniable success that DWE has had in recruiting and motivating activists as well as in winning broad enthusiasm among Berlin's inhabitants and, indeed, far beyond it can hardly be understood without considering the extraordinarily daring, seemingly fantastical, in other words, utopian goal that it has introduced into the debate about housing and rents in the city. The absolute radicalism of a horizon that promised to rethink entirely the status and legitimacy of private property, when viewed both in relation to existing instruments for regulating the real-estate market and in relation to more general ideological presuppositions on which such instruments have been based, marked the campaign from the start as uniquely attractive for many who have lost faith in more-of-the-same solutions. The campaign's membership expanded rapidly and with it, too, its capacity for action and communication.

By summer of 2019, about a year after its public inauguration, the initiative collected within three months some 77,000 signatures (of which about 50,000 were eventually certified), handily completing the first phase of the referendum, the request for consultation of popular interest, which granted up to six months for gathering a minimum of 20,000 signatures of eligible voters. The Berlin government blocked its review of the proposed consultation for as long as it could but, after more than a year and following massive protests and the launch of a legal procedure against it, was eventually forced to concede that the text appeared legitimate and approve it, at which point the parliament received the proposal and had four months to deliberate and respond to it. Given that, as expected, the legislators failed to accept the proposal by turning it into law, in February 2021 the initiative proceeded to the next phase, which required the campaign to collect some 175,000 signatures, corresponding to 7 percent of eligible voters in the city, within four months. By the end of that period, DWE submitted some 350,000 signatures, far above the required minimum. The referendum was accordingly included in the Berlin state ballots during the federal elections of September 2021 and won the astounding support of 59 percent of the electorate.

The celebrations that followed the success of several years of intense work that set its sight on the referendum, however, were dampened by the results of the elections, in which the socialist *Die Linke*, the only political party that has consistently and unambiguously expressed its support for the initiative, suffered losses and entered the three-way governing coalition as the smallest party together with the socialization-skeptic Greens and Social Democrats, limiting its capacity of negotiation. Procedural electoral irregularities in 2021 eventually triggered a new election in 2023, bringing the CDU to power with the SPD as a junior coalition partner and killing any remaining hope that the government might follow the results of the referendum. The current conjuncture in Berlin has been marked by a clear lack of political will in both the executive and the legislative and in both the coalition and the opposition to move forward with an agenda evidently supported by a significant majority of the electorate. The period since the referendum has witnessed repeated delays and, in the view of activists, bad-faith tactics in discussions over how to implement the referendum.

In early 2022, these discussions culminated in the appointment of a committee with a mandate to recommend in favor or against the resolution as well as to review a draft socialization bill that DWE submitted. The initiative and the coalition parties each nominated delegates to the committee, almost all of whom were legal experts. Some DWE activists expressed little faith in the procedure and viewed it as a cynical ploy for delaying and evading implementation, citing the committee chair's known anti-socialization position, the decision to deliberate behind closed doors, and the yearlong mandate granted to it for issuing its verdict. Others showed cautious optimism, describing the majority of the committee's members as well respected, independent specialists and assessing the probability that most would endorse the referendum resolution as high. But, even with a favorable resolution, activists' expectations that the government would follow through the committee's work with appropriate legislation remained very low.

In spring of 2023, the committee concluded its work and ruled almost unanimously in favor of the constitutionality of DWE's proposal as well as for the legal soundness of the draft bill that the initiative had prepared. As activists had expected, the government, whose leadership had meanwhile changed from Social Democrats to Conservatives, remained uncooperative despite the results of the review process. Having exhausted all avenues and possibilities of negotiation, the DWE responded by launching a new campaign for a second referendum. This time around, voters will decide on an actual socialization bill, which, if approved, will automatically become statutory law in the state of Berlin. At the same time, all my interlocutors agree that even if socialization becomes law and regardless of how this happens, it will immediately face multiple legal challenges for alleged unconstitutionality as well as for a range of other juridical grounds, such as its compatibility with EU law or with the international trade agreements of the single market.

7.6 Conclusion

At the time of writing, then, the DWE initiative remains very much open-ended, with a wide range of possible outcomes. Its supporters, once again, embark upon the straining and uncertain path of securing enough signatures to hold a referendum and winning enough votes to approve the proposed bill. Many are skeptical about the prospects that the bill would withstand the onslaught of the multiple legal challenges that it is certain to face. Even if the initiative overcomes these hurdles, how the implementation of the law by an unwilling executive would proceed remains unclear. Yet, these great uncertainties notwithstanding, the activists with whom I have spoken recently feel strongly emboldened and vindicated by their triumphs, motivated to carry on their fight.

But the very success of the campaign might prove difficult to assess. Even if, for whichever of the reasons above, socialization as proposed by DWE fails, the effects of the campaign may very well prove consequential in at least four different ways. First, the massive mobilization that DWE achieved and the way in which its message resonated with such broad sectors of Berlin's inhabitants have placed the problem of affordable housing at the center of the city's politics, testifying palpably to the profound dissatisfaction of tenants with the government's policies. Although eventually struck down by the Constitutional Court, Berlin's rent-freeze law clearly emerged out of such preoccupations and the pressure on its government to address the crisis by other means – legal or administrative – is likely to continue, regardless of the fate of socialization. Second, Berlin's DWE campaign has already inspired socialization initiatives in Hamburg and Bremen, the Federal Republic's two other city-states, where the voting population's urban character raises the possibility of similar support. Interest in launching socialization campaigns has arrived from other federal states as well, though higher proportions of rural and small-town constituencies and higher rates of homeownership would no doubt present different and more challenging hurdles for such initiatives. Another, third aspect in which the DWE campaign may prove significant is its influence on other housing struggles, both in Germany and beyond it, even in contexts where socialization is not a legal option or a political objective. Housing initiatives from other parts of Germany and from many foreign countries have been keen to learn from DWE's experience and its effective organizing and campaigning strategy and have reached out to it for dialogue and exchange. Finally, the socialization campaign may serve as inspiration for struggles in fields other than housing, especially in Germany. Thus, for example, environmental activists could take up its example to campaign for the socialization of the entire energy sector or mining industry.

For all of the above, to speak of a moment of reckoning with juristocratic investments would seem premature for the case of DWE, where, despite setbacks, disappointments, and innumerable obstacles, the law – both constitutional and statutory – continues to stand at the core of the political struggle. That it continues to do so, and with such powerful traction, owes in great part to how it codifies, mediates, and permits the awakening of presumably moot utopian horizons of collective ownership that appear dated and out of place in the neoliberal present and yet, at the same time, seem once again extraordinarily compelling for so many. This utopian past, sedimented in the legal code as a silent message, a never-used constitutional article, suddenly appears ready to hand, available for redeeming the future, for galvanizing not only radical political imaginaries but equally the commitments to take to the streets in pursuit of their realization.

References

Appadurai, Arjun. 2002. Deep Democracy: Urban Governmentality and the Horizon of Politics. *Public Culture* 14 (January): 21–47. https://doi.org/10.1215/08992363-14-1-21.

Berlant, Lauren. 2007. Nearly Utopian, Nearly Normal: Post-Fordist Affect in La Promesse and Rosetta. *Public Culture* 19 (April): 273–301. https://doi.org/10.1215/08992363-2006-036.

Buck-Morss, Susan. 2000. *Dreamworld and Catastrophe: The Passing of Mass Utopia in East and West*. Cambridge, MA: MIT.

Feldman, Allen. 2001. White Public Space and the Political Geography of Public Safety. *Social Text* 19 (3): 57–89.

Goodale, Mark. 2017. *Anthropology and Law: A Critical Introduction*. New York: New York University Press.

Greenhouse, Carol J. 2022. Social Control through Law: Critical Afterlives. In Marie-Claire Foblets, Mark Goodale and Olaf Zenker, eds., *The Oxford Handbook of Law and Anthropology*. Oxford: Oxford University Press, 19–35.

Guyer, Jane I. 2007. Prophecy and the Near Future: Thoughts on Macroeconomic, Evangelical, and Punctuated Time. *American Ethnologist* 34 (3): 409–421. https://doi.org/10.1525/ae.2007.34.3.409.

Hale, Charles R. 2006. Activist Research v. Cultural Critique: Indigenous Land Rights and the Contradictions of Politically Engaged Anthropology. *Cultural Anthropology* 21 (1): 96–120. https://doi.org/10.1525/can.2006.21.1.96.

Harcourt, Bernard E. 2010. Neoliberal Penality. *Theoretical Criminology* 14 (February): 74–92. https://doi.org/10.1177/1362480609352785.

Hartog, François. 2017. *Regimes of Historicity: Presentism and Experiences of Time.* Trans. Saskia Brown. Paperback edn. European Perspectives: A Series in Social Thought and Cultural Criticism. New York: Columbia University Press.

Hoffrogge, Ralf. 2019. Housing for the People. *Jacobin*, 2019. https://jacobin.com/2019/04/berlin-housing-referendum-tenant-organizing.

2021a. Der Volksentscheid Hat Gewonnen – Und Geht Jetzt Erst Richtig Los. *Jacobin*, 2021. https://jacobin.de/artikel/der-volksentscheid-hat-gewonnen-und-geht-jetzt-erst-richtig-los-deutsche-wohnen-enteignen-volksentscheid-berlin-spd-giffey/.

2021b. Kapitalismuskritik Am Wohnungsmarkt: "Das Problem an Der Wurzel Packen". *Taz.De*, 2021. https://taz.de/Kapitalismuskritik-am-Wohnungsmarkt/!5760422/.

2021c. Stahlwerk Jetzt! *Analyse & Kritik*, 2021. www.akweb.de/gesellschaft/wie-die-ig-metall-1983-die-stahlindustrie-vergesellschaften-wollte/.

Holston, James. 2001. Urban Citizenship and Globalization. In Allen J. Scott, ed., *Global City-Regions: Trends, Theory, Politics*. Oxford: Oxford University Press, 325–348.

Howard, Amy. 2014. *More than Shelter: Activism and Community in San Francisco Public Housing*. Minneapolis: University of Minnesota Press.

Jackson, Jean E. and Kay B. Warren. 2005. Indigenous Movements in Latin America, 1992–2004: Controversies, Ironies, New Directions. *Annual Review of Anthropology* 34: 549–573.

Jameson, Fredric. 2004. The Politics of Utopia. *New Left Review*, February, 35–54.

Kalb, Don. 2012. Thinking about Neoliberalism as if the Crisis Was Actually Happening. *Social Anthropology* 20 (3): 318–330. https://doi.org/10.1111/j.1469-8676.2012.00215.x.

Kopper, Moisés. 2021. The Politics of Differentiation and the Co-production of the "Model Periphery" in Brazil's Public Housing. *City & Society* 33 (3): 467–491.

Kusiak, Joanna. 2021. Trespassing on the Law: Critical Legal Engineering as a Strategy for Action Research. *Area* 53 (4): 603–610. https://doi.org/10.1111/area.12700.

Law, Sam. 2022. Building Urban Autonomy: The Construction of a Communal Form of Life in Mexico City's Periphery. *PoLAR: Political and Legal*

Anthropology Review, Ethnographic Encounters with Destitute Power, March. https://polarjournal.org/2022/03/31/building-urban-autonomy-the-construction-of-a-communal-form-of-life-in-mexico-citys-peripheries/.

Levitas, Ruth. 2010. *The Concept of Utopia*. Ralahine Utopian Studies 3. Oxford: Lang.

Lomnitz, Claudio. 2003. Times of Crisis: Historicity, Sacrifice, and the Spectacle of Debacle in Mexico City. *Public Culture* 15 (January): 127–148. https://doi .org/10.1215/08992363-15-1-127.

Lyons, Kristina. 2018. Chemical Warfare in Colombia, Evidentiary Ecologies and *Senti-Actuando* Practices of Justice. *Social Studies of Science* 48 (3): 414–437. https://doi.org/10.1177/0306312718765375.

Mathers, Andrew. 2021. Renters Rising! Extending the Analysis of Housing Activism in Europe to the UK. *Araucaria (Triana)* 23 (46): 147–171.

McIvor, Meadhbh. 2020. *Representing God: Christian Legal Activism in Contemporary England*. Simultaneous cloth and paperback. Princeton: Princeton University Press.

Moyn, Samuel. 2012. *The Last Utopia: Human Rights in History*. 1. Belknap Press of Harvard University Press paperback ed. Cambridge, MA: Belknap Press of Harvard University Press.

2018. *Not Enough: Human Rights in an Unequal World*. Cambridge, MA: The Belknap Press of Harvard University Press.

Murphy, Edward. 2016. *For a Proper Home. Housing Rights in the Margins of Urban Chile, 1960–2010*. University of Pittsburgh Press.

Parés, Marc. 2019. Socially Innovative Housing Activism: Local Context and Collective Leadership Practices in Barcelona and New York City. *Housing Studies* 34 (10): 1654–1672. https://doi.org/10.1080/02673037.2019.1566521.

Pérez, Miguel. 2022. *The Right to Dignity: Housing Struggles, City Making, and Citizenship in Urban Chile*. Stanford: Stanford University Press. www.sup .org/books/title/?id=31494&local_ref=new.

Povinelli, Elizabeth A. 2002. *The Cunning of Recognition: Indigenous Alterities and the Making of Australian Multiculturalism*. Politics, History, and Culture. Durham: Duke University Press.

Rose, Nikolas. 2000. Government and Control. *British Journal of Criminology* 40 (2): 321–339.

Schwenkel, Christina. 2020. *Building Socialism: The Afterlife of East German Architecture in Urban Vietnam*. Durham: Duke University Press.

Stavrides, Stavros. 2019. *Common Spaces of Urban Emancipation*. Manchester: Manchester University Press.

Thompson, E. P. 1975. *Whigs and Hunters: The Origin of the Black Act*. London: Allen Lane.

Villinger, Christoph. 2016. Gastbeitrag Mietenbündnis: Wagt die Enteignung! Die Tageszeitung: taz, February 29, 2016, sec. Berlin. https://taz.de/!5278275/.

Wacquant, Loic. 2001. The Penalisation of Poverty and the Rise of Neo-Liberalism. *European Journal on Criminal Policy and Research* 9 (4): 401–412.

2012. Three Steps to a Historical Anthropology of Actually Existing Neoliberalism. *Social Anthropology* 20 (1): 66–79. https://doi.org/10.1111/j.1469-8676.2011.00189.x.

Wright, Robin M. 1988. Anthropological Presuppositions of Indigenous Advocacy. *Annual Review of Anthropology* 17: 365–390.

8

Plurinational Juristocracy and Rights from Below at Bolivia's Gas Frontier

PENELOPE ANTHIAS

8.1 Introduction: In What Justice Can We Believe?

In January 2022 I accompanied a group of human rights activists from Tarija city to conduct a series of workshops in Chiquiacá Canton in the northeast of the Tariquía National Reserve of Flora and Fauna, the site of new hydrocarbon contracts between the Bolivian state oil company YPFB and the Brazilian company Petrobras. The workshop took place in a boarding house for schoolchildren located opposite Chiquiacá's Educational Center. As people arrived, the four workshop organizers, from the activist group Defensores de Tariquía (Defenders of Tariquía) and the feminist nongovernmental organization Mujeres en Acción (Women in Action), asked them to register their name, community, mobile phone number, and identity card number on a form. They then distributed miniature copies of Bolivia's 2009 National Constitution and asked recipients to sign a separate form. I noted some wariness among participants and remembered what I had been told about the "consultation" process in Chiquiacá: that representatives of the state oil company had asked people to sign a form with their identity card numbers in exchange for a free lunch, then used these documents as evidence of their consent for extraction.

On signing in, participants received a package of documents pertaining to the three-part workshop series, which was entitled "Primer of Fundamental Economic, Social, Cultural, and Environmental Rights: Getting to know our rights we defend territory, life and our identity."

A young lawyer led the first activity, asking "What are our fundamental rights?" Community members responded noting various rights such as "the right to life." We looked together at Article 15 in our mini-Constitutions. He explained: "The Constitution is the mother of all the laws. All authorities must submit to it; no one is above it." Following his summary of the previous workshop, an older woman whom I recognized as the vice president of Chiquiacá's Defense Committee, Nelly Coca, raised her hand to speak. "We know all about the Constitution and there are many laws," she said. "The question is: Do they comply with it? And what can one do to ensure that laws are complied with?"

The young lawyer responded indirectly, by elaborating a case intended to illustrate the law's capacity to deal with the justice claims fairly, based on evidence. In this fictional case, a motorist swerved to avoid a stone and hit a motorcyclist. Who's fault was it? It turned out that the motorcyclist had no plates, helmet, or license. The implication seemed to be that the motorcyclist was culpable – something I felt unconvinced of. Nelly responded by mentioning a real case that happened in a nearby community, where a motorist hit and killed a cyclist from a poor family who was cycling somewhere to get help for a sick relative. The motorist was not charged because he had money to pay lawyers, while the family of the cyclist were forced to pay for damage to the vehicle in addition to losing their son. She concluded, reinforcing her original point: "In what justice can we believe?"

This exchange might appear as an abstract discussion of law's incapacity to deliver justice in the context of a society marked by racial and class divisions. And yet, it acted as a proxy for a question that was at the heart of an ongoing struggle over hydrocarbon development in the Tariquía Reserve. This conflict had brought community activists in Chiquiacá into contact with a new set of regional actors – human rights workers, NGOs, lawyers, environmentalists – who were committed to juristocratic forms of politics. Yet, as will become clear, they already had reasons to be skeptical of the promise of law and rights. Nelly's challenge expressed a moment of juristocratic reckoning, in which the radical promise of Bolivia's 2009 Constitution, enshrined in our pocket-sized texts, was being put to the test by a series of unsuccessful constitutional challenges, as well as encounters with police and park guards defending hydrocarbon interests. Still, workshop participants had evidently not given up on the promise of rights as instruments of territorial defense and movement building. Indeed, as Nelly herself declared in a closing speech: "Look: the people who are here, how many of them were in the march? [implying few had joined recent mobilizations against extraction]. Thank God that we're here learning what are our rights are to the Reserve."

***

The role of human rights at extractive frontiers is marked by a paradox. On the one hand, processes of accumulation by dispossession that characterize these spaces frequently act as a catalyst for the mobilization of rights by affected communities. Indeed, the very existence of certain rights, such as the right to prior consultation, is a result of past struggles by those facing dispossession. In this sense, the historical coincidence of neoliberalism and the rise of human rights is not merely a result of elite collusions (Hirschl 2004), but also of on-the-ground struggles by communities whose territories are being opened to investment by transnational corporations. We might say that capitalism and rights are locked in an awkward embrace, part of a common process of territorial expansion.

At the same time, the promise of rights is routinely undermined by the territorial and political imperatives of extraction. The implementation of rights depends on the operation of state power, but postcolonial states are often trapped in relations of economic dependency that render their performance of sovereignty and national development contingent on their ability to secure the resource-accessing claims of transnational corporations. In many cases, communities' rights are from the outset constrained by hierarchical relations between national and international (and in some cases, foreign national) law that protect corporations' right to conquest and future profit. Communities' rights may be protected in law but selectively implemented in practice due to prevailing relations of land, political economy, and social power (Anthias 2018). Of course, "the state" is not a homogenous entity, but an "effect" (Mitchell 1991) and site of contestation between competing interests and governmental projects. The implementation of law and rights – which involves various branches and levels of state power – is itself a terrain of struggle, in which the capacity of local communities to defend their own conceptions of rights comes up against the capacity of extractive interests to bend the law in their favor.

All this makes extractive frontiers privileged sights from which to interrogate the dialectics of what the editors of this volume term "juristocratic reckoning." They define this as a two-part process wherein the law and legal categories become elevated, invested with unusual weight and responsibility, and yet ultimately fail to usher in the utopian future that the juristocratic transformation promises. By exploring how resource frontiers intensify this dynamic, this chapter offers a political ecology account of juristocratic reckoning. That is, I draw attention to the role of conflicts over territory and resources in shaping everyday encounters with the promise and the limits of law. Indeed, I argue that processes of accumulation by dispossession, and the concomitant use of law to facilitate the resource-accessing claims of capital, represents a crucial context for processes of juristocratic reckoning.

Bolivia – the site of a radical experiment in plurinational constitutionalism, which unfolded alongside increased state participation in extraction – offers a fruitful example through which to explore such dynamics. Based on an examination of the unfolding conflict over natural gas development in the Tariquía Reserve, I trace how encounters with the limits of law give rise to extralegal forms of politics – including embodied forms of protest and territorial defense – as well as forms of juristocracy "from below," through which local actors seek to redefine rights beyond parameters set by capital and the state. I argue that community activists see themselves as defending rights *against* the state – that is, as custodians of a juristocratic settlement achieved through popular mobilization that the state is itself violating due to its relations with transnational extractive corporations.

The remainder of this chapter is structured as follows. The first section engages scholarly debates on human rights as instruments of social transformation, arguing for extending philosophical critiques of rights through ethnographies of rights-based struggles. Section 8.3 considers Bolivia's recent history of transformative constitutionalism, arguing that a post-neoliberal juristrocratic settlement encounters its limits at extractive industry frontiers. The final section provides an ethnographic account of juristocratic reckoning in the context of the ongoing conflict over hydrocarbon development in the Tariquía Reserve.

8.2 Rethinking Rights through Ethnographies of Struggle

The concept of juristocracy belongs to a long tradition of leftist skepticism regarding the possibilities of human rights to address the systemic crises and inequalities produced by capitalist development. The term was coined by Ran Hirschl to describe the post-cold war rise of the "new constitutionalism" as an ideology in which political demands were "juridified" in the form of a bill of rights, to be overseen by a strengthened independent judiciary. While such reforms are often associated with democracy, social justice, or universal rights, Hirschl argued that they were in fact part of political and economic elites' attempts to insulate policymaking from the vicissitudes of democratic politics. The international human rights movement from the 1970s coincided with the imposition of neoliberal reforms, which devastated the lives of many people in the Global South (Klein 2007). Critics have argued that human rights promote forms of subjectivity that are compatible with the economic imperatives of neoliberalism (Brown 2004). Nancy Fraser (1995) was among the first to question the long-term consequences of the turn to rights-based recognition as a new framework for "postsocialist" politics. South Africa's post-apartheid transition is taken as a paradigmatic example of failures of law and rights to address not only economic inequalities, but also postcolonial demands for land redistribution and racial justice (Zenker 2014). As Mark Goodale summarizes (in this volume) "the global human rights revolution would prove to be no match for either the deep-seated structures of global, regional, and national economic inequality . . . or the vast spectrum of demands for justice . . . rooted in particular places, particular histories."

A more historically grounded critique of human rights has been developed by decolonial and feminist scholars, who have argued that the "human" in human rights – understood as sovereign, self-interested, and separate from nature – is inextricably linked to the rise of modern capitalism and was shaped through the exploitation and dehumanization of colonized peoples, as well as the denigration of women and working-class populations in Europe (Rivera Cusicanqui 2010). The fact that the earliest discussions of human rights doctrine were debates on the humanity of Amerindians is a reminder that human rights were born of histories of conquest and slavery. Scholars have noted the limitations of rights for contemporary Indigenous struggles for self-determination, due to their compatibility with capitalist development and their tendency to reinscribe notions of sovereignty and property grounded in histories of indigenous dispossession (Watson 2002; Coulthard 2014; Anthias 2018).

In light of such critiques, it is tempting to conclude that human rights have reached their "endtimes" (Hopgood 2013). Indeed, an early iteration of the proposal for this edited volume was entitled "After Law." As discussions at the "After Law" workshop made clear, however, proclamations of an "end of rights" appear out of step with the actual social and legal struggles that many of the contributors study. They are also politically ambivalent in a context where human rights are increasingly under attack from right-wing populism. This volume's revised focus on "juristocratic reckoning," in contrast, recognizes that efforts to redress social inequalities through law and rights routinely encounter their limits, while maintaining an ethnographic openness as to what might emerge from such encounters.

My contribution to this debate starts from an observation that in many parts of the world social movements and communities claiming rights are often among the most vociferous critics of both neoliberal capitalism and colonial histories of dispossession (see also Sieder, this volume). This suggests that law and rights are not merely instruments of elite rule, but are sites of discursive and material struggle by those who are, and have historically been, at the sharp end of liberalism's imbrication of law, capital, and racialized dispossession. As Lara Montesinos Colman (2023: 4) argues:

> We should not assume in advance that rights talk constrains emancipatory change or that human rights operate only within the confines of hegemonic political horizons. Indeed, the very idea that we should decide "for" or "against" human rights only really makes sense when we by-pass the politics of struggle.

Her enquiry into human rights as a "vocabulary of resistance" builds on the seminal work of E. P. Thompson (1975), who showed that law was not only an instrument of class rule, but also a forum in which forms of class conflict were fought out. Law and rights have also played a central role in anticolonial struggles. The historical genealogy of human rights must include not only the Valladolid debate of 1550–1, but also the Haitian Revolution (1791–1804) – the outcome of a slave rebellion that gained its moral grounding in the Rights of Man. The exclusion of African slaves from the French republicans' conception of "Man" did not stand in their way; rather, it was precisely the political ground on which the struggle for independence was fought. One can trace a line of historical continuity between the Haitian Revolution – which triggered independence wars across the Americas – and recent and ongoing struggles over the national bill of rights in Bolivia, led by those who were excluded from the category of "citizen" long after national independence.

In other words, the colonial and capitalist foundations of human rights – which consistently locate certain subjects, on whose labor and territory colonial capitalism depends, outside the category of human – is precisely what makes them an important ground for contestation. It should not be assumed that those mobilizing around a language of rights accept the subjective, normative, or humanist foundations of international human rights discourse. Nor do rights claims require prioritizing legal process over more disruptive forms of protest. Paying attention to the unfolding history of rights from below means recognizing that rights are not only defended in the courtroom but are intrinsic to broader processes of movement building and embodied acts of territorial resistance. Ethnographic research can play an essential role in extending philosophical debates on human rights as instruments of social transformation (Coleman 2023).

This chapter draws on ethnographic research in Bolivia's Tariquía Reserve to highlight resource frontiers as key sites of juristocratic reckoning – that is, for the contestation of existing rights regimes (and their power-infused implementation), and for the emergence of counter-hegemonic conceptions of rights. Resource frontiers are sites where the relationship between law and capitalism is thrown into sharp relief, as the resource-accessing rights of capital are prioritized – both in law and in practice – over local rights to consultation. In Latin America, extractive corporations are increasingly turning to law to criminalize Indigenous territorial defenders and their allies. Resource frontiers are also sites of extralegal violence. As Racher Sieder argues (in this volume), "a combination of legality and violence guarantees the functioning of extractive industries." Struggles that emerge at resource frontiers are fundamentally concerned with recognition, as people rendered sacrificial by capital and the state seek to assert their existence, their humanity, and their right to a say over their own future. Yet rather than a dematerialized politics of recognition, rights claims at resource frontiers are often grounded in struggles to defend territory (understood as an assemblage of more-than-human relations) in the face of the threat of enclosure and dispossession.

I now turn to consider Bolivia's recent history of transformative constitutionalism to highlight how the 2009 Constitution emerged from a reckoning with the limits of neoliberal juristocracy, yet has encountered its own limits in conflicts over resource extraction.

8.3 Bolivia: The Limits of Transformative Constitutionalism, Revisited

In December 2005, following a wave of social protests calling for an end to neoliberalism and the renationalization of the country's gas reserves, former coca growers' union leader Evo Morales swept to power as Bolivia's first Indigenous president. One of his first acts as president was to convoke a Constituent Assembly, with elected representation of Indigenous, peasant, and urban social movements, to rewrite the country's National Constitution. The Magna Carta they produced is arguably the most ambitious example of transformative constitutionalism of this century. It redefines Bolivia a "plurinational state" and recognizes an array of new rights for Indigenous, originary, and peasant peoples, including to "autonomy" (self-governance) in their ancestral territories (Prada 2008). This focus on collective rights has been read as a vernacularization of liberal rights by diverse social actors toward radical, arguably postliberal, ends (Postero 2010). The 2009 Constitution also redefined the relationship between the state and the market, declaring Bolivia's gas reserves "national patrimony" and giving the state a minimum 51 percent share in all new hydrocarbon contracts. The new bill of rights thus incorporates two sets of social movement demands: first, longstanding demands by indigenous movements for territory and self-governance; and second, an anti-neoliberal platform that demanded the restoration of popular sovereignty over Bolivia's hydrocarbon wealth and a more distributive regime of resource governance. It marks a historic moment of transformation in Bolivia, which has been understood locally as a democratic and cultural revolution, a *Pachakuti* (world-reversal or world-renewal), or simply as the "process of change" (Goodale 2019).

The year 2009 was not the first time in recent history that Bolivia has seen modifications to its Constitution. The 1980s and 1990s saw the National Constitution amended twice to define Bolivia as a multiethnic and multicultural nation, and to recognize some limited Indigenous rights.[1] This echoes a broader trend of "multicultural constitutionalism" (Van de Cott 2000) in Latin America during this period. As in other contexts, these constitutional changes accompanied a neoliberal program of state restructuring, which impoverished ordinary Bolivians while enriching transnational companies. The social mobilizations that led up to the election of Evo Morales in 2005 can thus be read as the outcome of a previous moment of juristocratic reckoning, as indigenous, peasant, and workers' movements encountered the limits of the neoliberal multicultural rights regime of the 1990s. This makes Bolivia a kind of rebel offspring of the juristocracy conceptualized by Hirschl – and an important context from which to revisit his critique.

Significantly, rather than turning away from rights and law as instruments of social transformation, Bolivia's Movement Toward Socialism (MAS) government saw a deepening of this investment in juristocracy, through a constitutional text that promised nothing short of decolonizing the state and society. Law was once again privileged as a mechanism for dealing with past and ongoing injustice, through the creation of new legal instruments, new legal protections, and new legally recognized rights. Bolivia's 2009 Constitution has acquired an iconic status as an example of indigenous-led efforts at decolonizing the state in Latin America. Yet

[1] Specifically, it recognized indigenous peoples' rights to intercultural bilingual education, participation in municipal governance, and collective land rights in Native Community Lands.

challenges were apparent from its inception. The combination of a push for social justice to overcome both colonialism and neoliberalism, on the one hand, and the embrace of liberal political institutions to do so, on the other, was a source of a profound tension (Postero 2017). Staunch resource nationalists pointed out that the 2009 Constitution did not represent a true nationalization of gas (Gustafson 2022). Indigenous rights activists critiqued the watering down of more radical indigenous demands for autonomy and land distribution in the final text following pressure from landowning groups (Garcés 2011). A language of pluralistic belonging glossed over a series of exclusions in the refounded Bolivian nation (Goodale 2019).

Of particular relevance to this chapter is the contradiction between the promise of expanded indigenous rights to territory and a model of socioeconomic transformation based on resource extraction (particularly of hydrocarbons), much of which occurs in indigenous-claimed territories. In the gas fields of the Chaco region, these contradictions were evident early on (Anthias 2012). For many Bolivians and international observers, the 2011 conflict over the construction of a highway through the Isiboro Sécure Indigenous territory and national park, or TIPNIS, marked a watershed moment when the MAS government's willingness to sacrifice indigenous rights to an extractivist development model became apparent. Since then, Bolivia has seen a gradual weakening of Indigenous and environmental rights in law. A series of presidential decrees in 2015 weakened rights to prior consultation and opened the way to extraction in protected areas, some of which are also Indigenous territories.

Extractive frontiers have thus emerged as key sights of "post-neoliberal" juristocratic reckoning in Bolivia. In this new phase, it is not so much the tepid nature of liberal rights regimes and their failure to address social and economic inequalities that is at issue, as the impossibility of realizing the radical promise of more plurinational juristocracy in the context of an extractivist development model that requires ongoing colonial processes of accumulation by dispossession. Bolivia has largely addressed the social and economic inequalities that animated social movement critiques of multicultural constitutionalism in the 1990s. However, it has done so at the expense of indigenous rights and the rights of nature.

If socioecological conflicts expose the limits of Bolivia's plurinational juristocracy, then it is also in the context of such struggles that the 2009 Constitution finds its clearest expression. The text is seen by many Bolivians not as a creation or instrument of the state, but as a text authored and approved by the people, via the Constituent Assembly of 2006–8 and the popular referendum of 2009. This shift in the subject of political and legal authority – from the state to the people – implies that if necessary the Constitution must be defended by the people *from* the arbitrary exercise of state power. This shows the importance of seeing juristocracy not only as an instrument of liberal rule, but as an arena of struggle. It is important here to note the role of indigenous sovereignty – a sovereignty that preexists the state – as a political and legal foundation for the 2009 Constitution. For indigenous peoples, the Constitution did not *create* their rights but merely marks the state's formal *recognition* of rights to self-governance that predate the state's existence. What is being violated when these rights are ignored is not merely the Constitution but the indigenous sovereignties that predate and ground it. The 2009 Constitution – with its recognition of indigenous autonomy, indigenous justice, and indigenous "usos y cosumbres" – represents a kind of settlement between the liberal state and indigenous sovereignty – albeit in a form that is unequal and riven with contradictions. This reminds us of the long history of indigenous engagements with rights and law in Bolivia (Ari 2014) and the various imperfect legal settlements that resulted from this, beginning with the notion of "two Republics" (Platt 1984).

In short, extractive frontiers in Bolivia are a key place where the promise of rights is unraveled by the complicity of state power with transnational corporations, but also places where Bolivians emerge as defenders of rights *against* the state in the name of "the people" and, in some cases, specific Indigenous nations or territories. The violation of rights to serve extractive interests leads to critiques of juristocracy in its plurinational formation but, as we will see, not to an abandonment of rights. Rather, extrajuridical forms of protest take on a central role as a means of defending and realizing rights in practice. I now turn to an exploration of these dynamics in the Tariquía National Reserve of Flora and Fauna.

8.4 Mobilizing Rights against Extraction in the Tariquía Reserve

Historically part of the territory of the Guaraní people, the area that now encompasses the Tariquía Reserve saw centuries of intermittent warfare until the late nineteenth century, as efforts at missionization and military subjugation encountered fierce Indigenous resistance. While the reserve still bears many Guaraní place names, today communities of Tariquía identify as *campesinos* (peasants). The territory's history as a national park adds another layer to its complex political geography. Created in 1989, the Tariquía Reserve of Flora and Fauna is the only protected area of the Andean Yungas, and includes subtropical, temperate, and rare cloud forests, along with hundreds of threatened and endangered species. It plays a critical role in regional hydrology and climate, providing water supply and rain cloud effects for Tarija's regional capital and central valley, an important food and wine-producing region.

At least ten campesino communities live inside the nucleus zone of the reserve, with another thirteen in the surrounding areas or buffer zone. While the relationship between local communities and the national park has not always been harmonious, the territory's status as a protected area has had a formative impact on environmental subjectivities in ways that are consequential for responses to hydrocarbon development. In particular, community members contrast the strict environmental restrictions they have been subjected to for the past twenty years (for example, regarding the use of timber for building houses) with the ease with which oil companies have been able to enter the park and conduct environmentally damaging activities – just one example of how oil companies are perceived as "above the law."

Tariquía was reserved as an area of hydrocarbon interest by the Bolivian state oil company YPFB in 2007, shortly after nationalization. In 2011–12 Petrobras conducted studies in two blocks which confirmed the existence of significant hydrocarbon reserves. These are thought to be the most significant recent discoveries in Tarija department, and have acquired a heightened political significance in the context of concerns over the decline in gas exports and production in aging fields in the nearby Chaco region, which has led to a depletion of government reserves and a shortage of dollars. This provides the context for a series of presidential decrees in 2015, which opened up protected areas to hydrocarbon development, modified the process of prior consultation, and watered down environmental norms around air and water contamination. The same year, the state parks agency SERNAP contracted a Dutch consultancy to produce a new National Park management plan for Tariquía, which altered the boundaries of the park's nucleus zone so that planned gas wells would fall outside the area of strict protection. Formal contracts between YPFB and Petrobras were signed in 2018, accompanied by two laws which authorized and then validated these contracts. As this suggests, hydrocarbon companies are not merely "above the law" but are key actors in (re)making state law to facilitate extraction.

Plans for hydrocarbon development in Tariquía have generated strong resistance by affected communities, in which women have played a leading role. In 2017, community members from Tariquía Canton marched to the regional capital Tarija city after learning of the initial hydrocarbon agreements. In 2019, activists from Chiquiacá Canton in the northeast of the reserve staged a five-month blockade of a bridge, which prevented the entry of heavy equipment to drill two planned gas wells. The Tariquía Reserve has thus emerged as a key example of resistance to extractive industry development in Bolivia at a moment when the 2009 juristocratic settlement is being gradually eroded, both in law and in practice, to facilitate extraction. I now turn to examine three ethnographic examples of juristocratic reckoning, which illustrate how the promise of law and rights has been simultaneously invoked and undermined by the threat of hydrocarbon development in Tariquía, and how this has produced forms of juristocratic politics "from below."

8.4.1 *Presenting the Magna Carta*

In June 2019 a cantonal "information meeting" was held in Chiquiacá Canton near the site of a planned gas well. The meeting was open to all residents of the canton and saw the presence of two geologists, as well as the provincial governor and other regional authorities. Sergio, an Argentinian evangelist pastor whose large family are tenants of the property in which the well was to be drilled, attended the meeting with his wife Silvana. The family were part of a group of community members in Chiquiacá who were already organizing to educate themselves and others about the risks of extraction and their rights, following contact with activists in Tariquía Canton. Sergio recounted how he had carefully studied the text of Bolivia's 2009 Constitution in preparation for the meeting, printing and highlighting the most relevant passages and making notes in the margins about articles of particular relevance. He explained his developing interest in the law as a complement to the religious foundations of his activism:

> At the beginning of our involvement in the struggle, the defense, first from our cosmovision as believers we saw that we not only had the endorsement of God in the defense of the environment ... but I also wanted to investigate ... I wanted to understand, to see clearly, to what extent the laws of the country also supported our struggle. So I began to research it in our Constitution.

Flicking through his printed pages, Sergio described how his research made him aware of specific articles relating not only to reserves, but to the environment in general. In particular, he learned of the prohibition of hydrocarbon development in regions with important hydrological resources, such as springs. He concluded: "The more I read, the more I investigated, tried to deepen my knowledge, I found that what they are trying to do was *illegal* – well, at least, it went against the fundamental law of our nation." Sergio viewed the cantonal meeting as a key opportunity to mobilize this knowledge of the Constitution – to share his conclusion that hydrocarbon extraction in Chiquiacá was "illegal":

> When I knew we were going to have this very important cantonal meeting, where they were going to discuss these issues in depth, I decided to organize the principal paragraphs of the plurinational Constitution, to highlight them with the objective of giving – if they allowed me – a brief presentation of the main points.

His brief opportunity to speak only arose after five hours of uninterrupted presentations by authorities regarding various infrastructure projects they were undertaking in the region, as well as data presented "to underplay the impact" of planned gas development. However, his effort to publicly challenge oil companies with reference to the constitutional text was cut short:

> I was able to start to read the rights of citizens, the articles related to the environment, to the reserve and to water, and this moment awakened a bit of opposition and annoyance . . . there was excitement, people who spoke in loud voices, people who started to leave . . . they didn't want to listen, and in that moment the authority who was presiding the meeting asked me . . . he insisted a little bit . . . he asked me that please, please, would I stop and, well, I ceded the microphone – but I was able to read the most important articles of our Magna Carta.

Sergio's account of the meeting, which was corroborated by other community members, shows how activists in Chiquiacá have sought to use rights and law to challenge oil company and state narratives and the legality of planned extraction. The intended audience here is not so much the authorities who organized the event as other community members. The meeting staged a moment of juristocratic reckoning in a double sense. First, it saw state practice challenged with reference to the text of the 2009 Constitution, to which, as Sergio noted, all state organs were supposed to be subject. At the same time, it demonstrated the capacity of state officials to ignore and silence such protestations. Second, the meeting provided the context for a heated exchange between community members regarding the relevance of constitutional rights for shaping local responses to extraction. If in one sense this example demonstrates the political potency of mobilizing rights beyond official spaces of law, then it also represents one of numerous moments in which juristocratic politics encountered their limits. Not only was Sergio silenced by the provincial governor chairing the event, but those in favour of extraction had little interest in hearing a verbatim reading of the Magna Carta following five hours of presentations by state authorities. Yet Sergio insisted that this didn't matter: "When the people made all that fuss and started to leave, I continued unperturbed; I continued reading so that whoever wanted to listen could listen."

This moment forms part of a longer discursive battle in which community activists challenged oil company and state knowledges. Whether anyone's mind was changed by the reading of the Constitution is impossible to say. But such stagings of rights are significant in the sense that they unsettle the assumed relationship between state power and the implementation of the National Constitution. That is, they open up the potential for a decentering political authority away from the state to *el pueblo* – the political subject, author and approver of the 2009 Constitution. As Sergio put it: "What I wanted to show was simply that it was illegal, that we were going to commit an environmental crime and a crime against the National Constitution and I wanted to show the authorities that they were wrong."

8.4.2 The Limits of State Justice

The legality of extraction in Tariquía has not only been challenged in political meetings. Over the course of the conflict, community activists have waged a series of formal legal and constitutional challenges that have contested the legal and constitutional basis for the implementation of the hydrocarbon projects. These encounters with judicial power constitute a broader moment of juristocratic reckoning, in which Tariquía activists and their allies (urban human rights workers, activists, lawyers, and NGOs) have reflected on the possibilities and limits of judicial process at the present political conjuncture in Bolivia.

The first was a constitutional challenge to Supreme Decree DS 2366, signed by Evo Morales in 2015, which permitted hydrocarbon development in protected areas. This was presented to the Plurinational Constitutional Tribunal by a collective of social movements representing communities in protected areas, including the peasant union of Tariquía. As activist and lawyer Juan Carlos (Negro) Aróstegui explained, the legal basis for the challenge was that anyone directly affected by a change to existing legislation in Bolivia has the right to a consultation. This had not happened in the case of the 2015 decree, as residents of protected areas were not consulted about a modification to the 2009 Constitution that affected their rights.

In fact, this was not the first time such a legal challenge had been made. In 2015, shortly after Evo Morales signed the decree, the national ombudsman presented a similar case to the Constitutional Tribunal. The sentence issued by the tribunal was interpreted by human rights activists as legitimizing the 2015 decree. Because a ruling by the Constitutional Tribunal represents the final legal interpretation of the 2009 Constitution, this was seen as a permanent weaking of communities' constitutional right to prior consultation. This led some leading NGOs – notably CEDIB, which has played a key role in the Tariquía conflict – to refuse to support the latest constitutional challenge. In the context of a politicized judiciary and a state committed to new hydrocarbon development, they feared that the resulting sentence would further weaken rights established in the 2009 Constitution. Despite such antecedents, the new constitutional challenge went ahead, coinciding with the unelected right-wing interim government of Jeanine Áñez. Predictably, it floundered at its first hurdle in the departmental Tribunal of Constitutional Guarantees. According to some of those involved, a Santa Cruz tribunal failed to notify Tariquía community leaders in time for the hearing and the judge in Tarija then failed to hear the case. One participant claimed that the judge had called a mutual friend in Palos Blancos complaining that he was under pressure from the Áñez government to reject the case. To date, no sentence has been issued.

A further set of legal challenges have focused on the legality of the hydrocarbon contracts and the laws that authorized them. These cases were assembled in 2018–19 by the Commission of Human Rights of the Departmental Assembly of Tarija – at the time made up of assembly members opposed to the ruling MAS party – following a request for help by community members in Tariquía Canton. The commission's first objective was to access all relevant information pertaining to the new hydrocarbon contracts, none of which had been provided to the departmental assembly. The commission sent letters to the Ministry of Hydrocarbons and the Ministry of Environment requesting details of plans for hydrocarbon development in Tariquía. These requests were met by silence. Finally, after waiting several months, the commission presented a constitutional challenge based on the right to petition. This triggered a response to the initial request for information.

Following its analysis of this information, the commission presented an action of inconstitutionality contesting the laws and decrees that approved the hydrocarbon contracts in Tariquía, on the basis that no legitimate prior consultation had been conducted before approving the contracts, in violation of rights established in the 2009 Constitution. Their complaint referenced both to the timing of the consultation process and the manner in which it was conducted, which is alleged to have involved bribes (the distribution of free stoves and gas cylinders) and the signing of documents under false pretenses (as registration for participation in an information session and free lunch).[2] As the commission's then legal advisor explained:

> What was our main argument? That the Constitution stipulates that there has to be a prior consultation in order to approve contracts and with these incursions of the oil companies there wasn't really a prior consultation, not really; they did a pretense of consultation only in a few communities, which were dominated by MAS.

In March 2019 the commission supported a further legal action in which two leading activists from Tariquía Canton appeared as complainants, defending their constitutional right to prior consultation. This was followed by another in June, presented after the commission discovered that the planned Astillero wells were located in the nucleus area of the reserve according to the original National Park management plan. These cases coincided with the five-month blockade in Chiquiacá and responded to a request from activists to "see what tool we can use from a juridical point of view to defend Tariquía." These legal actions backfired. Following the first's rejection due to a bureaucratic observation, it was sent to Sucre for revision, which meant that the second could not be legally progressed. Javier concluded:

> It was pure malice because it was the way of freezing [the constitutional challenge] so they it wouldn't leave Sucre, where it has taken two or three years and we haven't been able to do anything in this time . . . Juridically they shut the doors; politically it's a legal ruse which isn't illegal, but it's

[2] My documentary *Tariquía No Se Toca* includes news footage of the distribution of gas stoves and community members' accounts of the "consultation" process (Anthias 2022).

> very dirty and very low that they impeded us from protecting [Tariquía residents'] rights.

The work of the commission never regained momentum and it was soon dissolved due to departmental elections. However, leaders from Tariquía continued their legal battle, presenting a further constitutional challenge to interim President Jeanine Añez and Minister of Hydrocarbons Victor Hugo Zamora in February 2020. Despite trying to make political capital from the conflict, the Añez regime saw accelerated progress in the approval of decrees and contracts enabling the entry of oil companies in Tariquía.[3] While the legal challenge was predictably unsuccessful, it gained wide publicity in local media.

These frustrated legal challenges reveal how Tariquía activists and their allies have encountered the limits of formal juristocratic process in the context of a state committed to hydrocarbon development, under two contrasting political regimes. They constitute a moment of juristocratic reckoning in which the promise, limits, and risks of legal strategy are reassessed in light of the intimate relationship between extractivism and judicial power. As Negro put it, the issue was not about the MAS government, but about "transnational corporations and their capacity to influence the state."

It is perhaps surprising that such experiences did not deter activists from pursuing their claims through the law. When I asked why this was the case, Negro admitted that this may have something to do with the interests of the legal profession. Yet he also provided another rationale: the legal cases would generate a record of all the injustices that happed through the law, so that at some undefined future point these could be assessed and the legitimacy of the struggle to defend Tariquía could be recognized. Even when the law failed to achieve justice in the present, it still held the promise of a future perfect form of recognition. Put another way, the legal process was a way of bearing witness. He also expressed a more concrete aspiration. Having exhausted this legal avenue at the level of the nation-state, communities from Tariquía would be in a position to present a complaint to the Inter-American Court of Human Rights. Francisco Romero, a peasant union leader from Tariquía who was one of the plaintiffs in the action of constitutionality, echoed this aspiration. As he put it: "We need that to pass to the next level, which is the International Court of Human Rights; it's a requirement to exhaust the

[3] See https://elpais.bo/tarija/20191128_comunarios-de-tariquia-cuestionan-a-zamora.html.

departmental and national arenas to arrive there." This prospect of some future moment of reckoning, beyond the spatiotemporal frame of the current state, may help to explain why the promise of juristocratic politics was not extinguished by these experiences of state justice. They did, however, serve to push activists toward extralegal forms of politics. Francisco (who is from Tariquía Canton) described how his experience of being ignored and disrespected by a judge led him to focus on strengthening on-the-ground resistance in Chiquiacá, where the oil companies were now focusing their efforts:

> We picked ourselves up off the floor, we organized a Defense Committee, we began attending meetings again, we returned and Chiquiacá was strengthened. When the companies entered [Chiquiacá] we sent help commissions – from Tariquía we left to go there, we went to help.

Activists' experiences of the limits of state juristocracy thus served to propel them toward embodied tactics for defending territory, where constitutional rights could be put into practice.

8.4.3 Mobilizing Rights on the Front Lines of Resistance

As already noted, the conflict over gas development in Tariquía has been punctuated by direct action by communities in two cantons, which have at times drawn support from within the broader region. The use of protests and blockades is commonplace in Bolivia, drawing on a long-established repertoire of tactics of Indigenous anticolonial resistance (Dangl 2019). In Chiquiacá Canton, the first direct confrontations took place in the countryside, when a small group of women challenged oil company personnel who were conducting seismic testing. The women challenged the legality of their operations, given that they didn't have consent from local communities. They presented their own quasi-legal document in support of their claim. As the president of Chiquiacá's Defense Committee recalls:

> We went to the forest, we caught up with them there by the stream – they were working there – and we notified them with an act; we have an act that says that they were going to leave their work, because the community members didn't agree. They left later that day. And the next day they went back by another road – so we couldn't see them. We found out again that they were working and again we went back.

In the forests of Chiquiacá, hydrocarbon workers had little capacity to enforce their understanding of state law over the moral economy and norms of local residents. It was only when they retreated and returned with the support of vanloads of Bolivian police that the power asymmetries between rural residents and extractive corporations in relation to state law were made clear. Community members responded by occupying the bridge over the Quebrada de las Vacas (cow stream). The inevitable confrontation took place early the next morning. As Juanita Mercado recalled:

> Two minivans – or three minivans, I don't remember – arrived full of police. And we were not more than 20, 30 people. And we thought . . . we felled some trees like this, we thought to stop them with those trees. What did they do? They arrived; we had the flag, we had the National Constitution. The flag was there, they trampled on the flag, they took the Constitution from us, they threw it to the ground . . . we had already told them that they were not going to enter Chiquiacá; they said: "no, yes, you lot get out of here and that's it" – the police. We wanted to resist so that they couldn't pass.

Here, the 2009 Constitution was wielded as a physical artefact and visual symbol of community members' defense of the Constitution *against* the state – a performance in which the police unwittingly collaborated. Video footage of this confrontation circulated widely on local news channels and social media. In one particular clip, which is reproduced in the documentary (Anthias 2022). Bolivian police with plastic shields are shown pushing rural women and children and trampling the protesters' national flag. Against this backdrop, the following verbal exchange can be heard:

POLICEMAN:	Now move on, we need to pass. You cannot prohibit the passage of the police, of your Bolivian police. Got it?
ACTIVIST FROM TARIJA:	Don't attack us, we're defending the environment; it's a defense of the environment and it's a right to protest that they have. Because these traitors of the country . . .
POLICEMAN:	You can't prohibit the passage of the Bolivian police; the Bolivian police have to be in all parts of Bolivia, and you cannot prohibit a state entity . . .
ACTIVIST FROM TARIJA:	No, no, no, no, no; the right to life and to the environment is above any other right.
POLICEMAN:	Ladies and gentlemen, please –
LOCAL WOMAN ACTIVIST:	One question . . .
SECOND LOCAL WOMAN ACTIVIST:	How much money do they pay you to come here to destroy the environment?

Here, we see rights enshrined in the Constitution mobilized beyond the courts, in ways that made their defense and violation a public spectacle. The circulation of such footage helped to propagate the narrative that Tariquía residents' rights were being violated. This resulted in tangible forms of support for the blockade in Chiquiacá, with many residents of Tarija city donating tents, warm clothing, and provisions. The blockade continued for five long months, with those involved in the defense taking turns to keep watch overnight. When the blockaders took the decision to conclude the blockade with a seven-day march to Tarija, they were joined by supporters from nearby villages and towns. Crowds welcomed them to Tarija, where they assembled for a town hall meeting. If the bridge over Quebrada Las Vacas became a stage for juristocratic reckoning, then the audience for this extended beyond the territory, sparking a regional conversation about community rights and environmental risks in the context of hydrocarbon development.

This is not to say that the women from Chiquiacá's Defense Committee Canton who led these mobilizations saw their struggle primarily through the lens of rights. When asked what animated their activism, they spoke not of rights but of preserving water, forests, and clean air for future generations. They define their struggle as "the defense" (*la defensa*) and its objective as "to defend" (*defender*). The object here is left implicit. Within the broader discourses of human rights activism, what is being defended is "human rights," as made explicit in the widely used term "human rights defender" (*defensor de derechos humanos*). Footage of the standoff described above would reinforce the idea that it is rights that are being defended. Yet for residents of Tariquía, the object of "defense" takes on multiple other meanings. At different moments it can refer to territory, the environment, the Reserve, our resources, or our children's future. Or, as Nelly Coca's song "Resiste Tariquía" (Resist, Tariquía), performed at the end of my documentary *Tariquía No Se Toca* (Anthias 2022) concludes: "the struggle we have is in defense of our own life." The concept of "defense" thus acts as a site of controlled equivocation (Viveiros de Castro 2004), bringing international and national discourses of human rights into play with local conceptions of territory, sovereignty, and living well. Using their bodies to block the entry of oil companies was an expression of a sovereignty, of an ethics of care, and of a spiritual (religious) obligation to "nature" that precedes and exceeds knowledge acquired in human rights workshops.

Still, wielding their copies of the 2009 Constitution – which affirmed the right to prior consultation, the right to protest, and Indigenous and peasant rights to territory and to the protection of its productive resources (among other rights) – lent their tactics an added legitimacy. As noted above, the Constitution was written with participation of Indigenous and peasant social movements, and enshrines their (more-than-liberal) understandings of territorial sovereignty, justice, self-determination, and living well. Seen in this context, such enactments of rights from below reground Bolivia's plurinational juristocracy in the social struggles from which it emerged. They point to the possibility of a plurinationalism that is based not on a contract of mutual recognition with the state (Lund 2016), but rather on a grounded normativity and self-recognition (Coulthard 2014) which finds expression in the embodied defense of territory.

8.5 The Criminalization of Protest and a Response from IACHR

On October 1, 2024 while this chapter was in production, Petrobras and YPFB entered the community of Saican in Chiquiacá Canton to begin the topographic survey for the Domo Oso X3 gas-well project. Community activists mobilized, confronting the workers and arguing that they lacked authorization from the local communities. They referenced the results of a cantonal vote conducted through the peasant union, in which 292 community members voted "No" to the entry of oil companies, while only 182 voted "Yes." They also argued that the authorizations obtained by the oil companies from supposed property owners were invalid, given the unresolved status of land rights in these areas, which are claimed by conflicting parties and lack legal titles. The next day, the president of YPFB filed criminal charges against twenty community members (later adding another nine), invoking Article 161 ("Obstructing and harming a public official in the exercise of their duties") and Article 303 ("Attacks against freedom of work") of the Bolivian Penal Code. These charges combined carry a maximum sentence of four years in prison.

On November 8, urban environmentalist Gonzalo Torrez Terzo, represented by Juan Carlos Aróstegui, filed an "Action of Freedom" (Acción de Libertad) lawsuit with the Departmental Court of Justice in defence of the twenty-nine community members facing criminal charges. I had just arrived in Bolivia and offered my testimony in the virtual hearing, where my documentary *Don't Touch Tariquía: The Resistance of Chiquiacá* (Anthias 2022) was presented as legal evidence. The lawsuit was rejected on the grounds that the penal process had not yet been concluded. However, the virtual hearing provided a public forum where community activists could denounce violations of their rights and the criminalization of their protest. The lawsuit also forced the oil companies to share sensitive information about the unresolved property rights in the planned extraction sites. As in previous instances, activists speculated that the evidence presented could lay the groundwork for a legal case before the IACHR.

I was doubtful this would ever come to pass, having heard similar hopes expressed since 2017. However, in early February 2025, news broke that the IACHR had accepted a request for an audience on the criminalization of environmental defenders in Tariquía, which is scheduled for March 7. This was not a result of the legal action described above, but rather responded to a request presented by the local peasant union Subcentral Campesina Tariquía, the social movement CONTIOCAP (National Coordinator in Defence of Indigenous Originary and Peasant Territories and Protected Areas) and the NGO Centro de Documentación e Información Bolivia (CEDIB).

Regrettably, this hearing took place several weeks after a public consultation process for the project Domo Oso X3 had been completed by Petrobras and YPFB. Participation of those opposed to extraction was limited, with many fearing legal repercussions and some denied access to free transport provided by oil companies. Those who did attend used their voices to denounce the process as fraudulent, to demand respect for the peasant union vote, and to provide emotional testimonies of the effects of criminalization on them and their families.

These events offer further illustration of how activists in Tariquía continue to engage with the promise of law and rights, despite the criminalization of protest and the ongoing failure of legal actions within the Bolivian justice system. They do so in ways that situate legal and political authority within the organic decision-making processes of peasant communities and hold open the hope of achieving justice beyond the state.

8.6 Conclusion

Critics of human rights have pointed to their historical imbrications with colonialism and capitalism, and their systematic failure to address economic inequalities, and postcolonial demands for land redistribution and racial justice. Yet Bolivia's 2009 Constitution demonstrates the remarkable persistence of juristocracy in Latin America, and its evolution beyond a neoliberal or even (purely) liberal frame. Rather than turning away from the politics of recognition, as a growing number of Indigenous scholars have recommended, Bolivian social movements have overthrown neoliberalism through collective mobilization, then participated in the elaboration of a radical bill of rights that reflects longstanding Indigenous demands for territory and self-governance. In doing so, they have taken transformative constitutionalism to a new level. Ultimately, this experiment has encountered familiar limits. The current neoextractivist development model – which involves greater state participation in extraction and social distribution of rents, but still requires giving transnational oil companies unfettered access to the Bolivian subsoil – has constrained the implementation of plurinational rights in practice, particularly in territories targeted for extraction. The current drive to expand hydrocarbon development into protected areas has heightened such contradictions, producing new alliances between human rights activists, environmentalists, and rural communities.

These dynamics reveal how extractive industry frontiers constitute key sites of juristocratic reckoning, where the promise of rights is simultaneously invoked and undermined as communities' efforts to use rights to defend themselves from environmental dispossession come up against the intimate relationship between extraction and state power. Resource frontiers are also, I have suggested, spaces for the emergence of alternative conceptions and practices of rights from below, in ways that may exceed humanist understandings of both "rights" and "nature." This argument is not specific to contemporary Bolivia. It resonates across many Latin American contexts, where scholars have observed an "eco-territorial" and "eco-feminist" turn of social movements opposing extractivism (Svampa 2019). The particular significance of the conflict over gas development in the Tariquía Reserve is that it constitutes a moment of reckoning for Bolivia's experiment in plurinational juristocracy, which emerged from previous counter-movements against neoliberal extractivism.

Failed constitutional challenges and violent encounters with police have exposed the limits of law and rights as tools against state-led extraction, framing Nelly's question "In what justice can we believe?" Yet the ethnographic examples discussed above also suggest that the locus of political authority has been subtly shifted by the discourse of plurinationalism and the protagonism of social movements within Bolivia's "process of change." Activists in Tariquía (many of whom voted for the MAS party in 2005) see themselves as custodians of the 2009 Constitution against a state that has been corrupted by its relations with transnational oil companies. By wielding the bill of rights in meetings and mobilizations, as well as in court, they have created public stagings of juristocratic reckoning, in which the gap between rights and their implementation is laid bare to local, regional, and national audiences. It is unlikely that their struggle will unsettle the hegemony of an extractivist development model in Bolivia, or prevent further extraction in the Tariquía Reserve.[4] But it does provide important insights into the evolving politics of rights, a decade and a half after Bolivia's new Constitution was approved by popular referendum. More broadly, it demonstrates the value of looking beyond philosophical critiques of rights to learn from real-world struggles, where rights – and their relationship to capitalism, the state, territory, and the nonhuman – are being debated, contested, and reinvented.

References

Anthias, P. 2012. Territorializing Resource Conflicts in "Post-neoliberal" Bolivia: Indigenous Land Titling and Hydrocarbon development in TCO Itika Guasu. In H. Haarstad, ed., *New Political Spaces in Latin American Natural Resource Governance*. New York: Palgrave Macmillan, 129–154.

2018. *Limits to Decolonization: Indigeneity, Territory and Hydrocarbon Politics in the Bolivian Chaco*. Ithaca: Cornell University Press.

2022. Tariquía No Se Toca: La Resistencia de Chiquiacá. Dir. Penelope Anthias. Self-published with English subtitles: www.youtube.com/watch?v=R3SbF-nGZbI.

Ari, W. 2014. *Earth Politics: Religion, Decolonization, and Bolivia's Indigenous Intellectuals*. Durham: Duke University Press.

Brown, W. 2004. The Most We Can Hope For . . . : Human Rights and the Politics of Fatalism. *South Atlantic Quarterly* 103 (2–3): 451–463.

Coleman, L. M. 2023. *Struggles for the Human: Violent Legality and the Politics of Rights*. Durham: Duke University Press.

Coulthard, G. S. 2014. *Red Skin, White Masks: Rejecting the Colonial Politics of Recognition*. Minneapolis: University of Minnesota Press.

[4] At the time of writing, oil companies had entered communities in the south of the reserve and were making renewed efforts to win local support in Chiquiacá, having been prevented from drilling by the 2019 blockade.

Dangl, B. 2019. *The Five Hundred Year Rebellion: Indigenous Movements and the Decolonization of History in Bolivia*. Edinburgh: AK Press.

Fraser, N. 1995. Recognition or Redistribution? A Critical Reading of Iris Young's *Justice and the Politics of Difference*. *Journal of Political Philosophy* 3 (2): 166–180.

Garcés, F. 2011. The Domestication of Indigenous Autonomies in Bolivia: From the Pact of Unity to the New Constitution. In B. Gustafson and N. Fabricant, eds., *Remapping Bolivia: Resources, Territory, and Indigeneity in a Plurinational State*. Santa Fe: SAR, 46–67.

Goodale, M. 2019. *A Revolution in Fragments: Traversing Scales of Justice, Ideology and Practice in Bolivia*. Durham: Duke University Press.

2022. Translocal Dilemmas: Social Mobilization and Justice-Seeking beyond the Boundaries of Law. Draft chapter for international workshop "After Law: Mobilization, Injustice, and Confrontation in the Post-Juristocratic Transition," University of Lausanne, June 6–10, 2022.

Gustafson, B. 2022. *Bolivia in the Age of Gas*. Duke University Press.

Hirschl, R. 2004. *Towards Juristocracy: The Origins and Consequences of the New Constitutionalism*. Cambridge, MA: Harvard University Press.

Hopgood, S. 2013. *The Endtimes of Human Rights*. Ithaca: Cornell University Press.

Klein, N. 2007. *The Shock Doctrine: The Rise of Disaster Capitalism*. Toronto: Knopf Canada.

Lund, C. 2016. Rule and Rupture: State-Formation through the Production of Property and Citizenship. *Development and Change* 47 (6): 1199–1228.

Mitchell T. 1991. The Limits of the State: Beyond Statist Approaches and Their Critics. *American Political Science Review* 85 (1): 77–96.

Platt, T. 1984. Liberalism and Ethnocide in the Southern Andes. *History Workshop Journal* 17 (1): 3–18.

Postero, N. 2010. The Struggle to Create a Radical Democracy in Bolivia. *Latin American Research Review* 45 (1): 59–78.

2017. *The Indigenous State: Race, Politics, and Performance in Plurinational Bolivia*. Oakland: University of California Press.

Prada, R. 2007. Articulaciones de la complejidad. In Á. García, L. Tapia and R. Prada eds., *La Transformación Pluralista del Estado*. La Paz: Muela del Diablo, 201–265.

Prada, Raúl. 2008. Análisis de la nueva Constitución Política del Estado. *Crítica y emancipación: Revista latinoamericana de Ciencias Sociales* 1 (1). Buenos Aires: CLACSO.

Rivera Cusicanqui, S. 2010. The Notion of "Rights" and the Paradoxes of Postcolonial Modernity: Indigenous Peoples and Women in Bolivia. Trans. Molly Geidel. *Qui Parle: Critical Humanities and Social Sciences* 18 (2): 29–54.

Sieder, R. 2022. After Judicialization, after Property? Authoritarian Regression and the Defense of Indigenous Life-Worlds in Guatemala. Draft chapter for international workshop "After Law: Mobilization, Injustice, and Confrontation in the Post-Juristocratic Transition", University of Lausanne, June 6–10, 2022.

Svampa, M. 2019. *Neo-extractivism in Latin America: Socio-environmental Conflicts, the Territorial Turn, and New Political Narratives.* Cambridge: Cambridge University Press.

van Cott, D. L. 2000. *The Friendly Liquidation of the Past: The Politics of Diversity in Latin America.* University of Pittsburgh Press.

Viveiros de Castro, E. 2004. Perspectival Anthropology and the Method of Controlled Equivocation. *Tipití: Journal of the Society for the Anthropology of Lowland South America* 2 (1): 3–22.

Watson, I. 2002. Buried Alive. *Law and Critique* 13: 253–269.

Zenker, O. 2014. New Law against an Old State: Land Restitution as a Transition to Justice in Post-Apartheid South Africa? *Development and Change* 45 (3): 502–523.

9

Law-Washing the Transitional State

The Practice of Property Restitution in Postwar Kosovo

AGATHE MORA

Following the North Atlantic Treaty Organization's (NATO) military intervention and a very wide-ranging United Nations (UN) peacekeeping and administration mission, Kosovo is nowadays the site of the largest civilian mission of the European Union outside EU borders.[1] The armed conflict of 1998–99, which was fought along ethno-national lines, led to mass atrocities and to the destruction of more than half of the available housing stock. During the conflict, Kosovo Albanians (who form the majority of the Kosovan population) were first displaced en masse, then, following international intervention and the retreat of Serbian and Yugoslav forces, Kosovo Serbs fled to Serbia and neighboring countries, and the returning Kosovo Albanians often occupied their abandoned properties.

In the aftermath of the war, to resolve the urgent issue of property rights and thus create preconditions for the return of displaced persons, the UN set up a quasi-judicial, administrative mechanism called the Kosovo Property Agency (KPA).[2] Staffed predominantly by Kosovo Albanian national legal professionals and a few international jurists, the KPA was entrusted to deal with war-related property claims submitted overwhelmingly by Kosovo Serbs.

Throughout Kosovo's internationally supervised postwar transition to (contested) independence, respecting human rights was, and still is, seen as a precondition of international recognition and, potentially, eventual accession to the European Union. The key measure of this is the

[1] EULEX's current mandate ends on June 14, 2025.

[2] The KPA started its activities in 2006 and is, in fact, the second property restitution mechanism put in place by the UN. The KPA incorporated the mandate of the previous mechanism, the Housing and Property Directorate (HPD), which was set up right after the war and only dealt with housing and possession rights.

constitutional protection of minority rights and the implementation of the rule of law. The restitution of property lost during the war to displaced Kosovo Serbs (the former "oppressors") was a cornerstone of achieving this. But what does protecting minority rights and implementing the rule of law mean in practice in such a context?

Relatively powerless and underfunded, the KPA is a paradigmatic example of a contemporary transitional justice mechanism that is understood as a short-term, bridging, technical-legal project rather than a national process of righting past wrongs. With rule of law understood as a tool of good governance, the KPA espoused neoliberal managerial logics of efficiency to organize its mass claims procedure. To "streamline" the process and allow for the "quick" and "efficient" resolution of claims, it created an "assembly line" for the production and processing of case data, and decisions were issued in batches of claims of similar legal scenarios.

In this chapter, I conceptualize the work of the KPA as "law-washing" as a characteristic move of the post-cold war juristocratic phase of international intervention and international law more generally. Law-washing involves the use of legal language and procedures to give the appearance of legitimacy to practices that may be unethical, illegitimate (or even illegal), or morally questionable. For example, corporate lawyers might engage in law-washing by creating policies or procedures that produce "compliance" with fiscal or environmental regulations but are in fact designed to circumvent those regulations or exploit loopholes. Similarly, a government might engage in law-washing by passing laws or regulations that give the appearance of addressing a particular problem, but in reality do little to solve the underlying issue.

In the context of transitional Kosovo, law-washing is the process through which the fiction of a stable, rule of law-abiding polity is produced. It implies hard legal work and that messy realities are hidden behind a clean façade of rightfulness and due process. These messy realities include an enormous amount of bricolage and negotiating within a patched-together legal system, and a real-political context that makes effective property restitution nigh impossible, as very few claimants were able to come back to Kosovo based on their newly reasserted property rights.

Juristocracy, in turn, should not be understood as the precise description of a particular political system, but as a metaphorical or rhetorical device (Bellamy 2007). In a broad sense, juristocracy is a diffuse and transhistorical ideology by which the judiciary assumes a dominant role in decision-making and governance, and where law is "overloaded with expectations" as it used in fetishistic, instrumental ways to tackle a range of social and political issues previously not conceived as legal issues. Following the book's premise, this chapter critically examines how legal practitioners and judges I worked with applied (international or constitutional and property) law in the context of war-related property restitution, while also reckoning with the historical and political context in which this legal framework emerged. I analyze the practice of "notification by publication" in the processing of property claims (which I will describe in a later section) as a prime example of law-washing, when taking stock of the limits of the juristocractic overloading of law with expectations became unavoidable.

Looking at processes of law-washing in Kosovo, a context that is commonly depicted as a permanent state of exception (Pandolfi 2010; Mora 2020), allows us to query conventional understandings of the seeming "normal carrying capacities" of law. Rather than being exceptional, law-washing is in fact an integral aspect of making law in juristocratic times: one that is more readily ethnographically captured in seeming situations of permanent crisis, but that is in fact always present, behind the veneer of "normality."

This chapter is based on over ten years of intellectual involvement and fourteen months of "observant participation" as a research intern at the KPA and the Supreme Court KPA Appeals Panel in 2012–13. Here, I describe law-washing through the techno-bureaucratic processing of war-related property claims. This process is accompanied by a political instrumentalization of law. By techno-bureaucratic processing, I mean the juridification and rendering legal-technical of a complex sociopolitical and historical problem, in this case, the property rights of the Serbian minority in Kosovo. From a legal perspective, mass claims property restitution required the lowering of evidentiary and procedural standards. Yet, paradoxically, such a lowering of standards produced "adherence" to human rights and the rule of law, legitimizing the postwar status quo, and Kosovo's existence as a modern sovereign state.

9.1 Juristocracy and Juridification

Law-washing is a distinct modality of international intervention in the name of human rights, using law to justify certain forms of violence and transitional state-building. It shows clear continuity with older logics of civilizing interventionism that can be traced back to eighteenth- and nineteenth-century liberal rationalism and colonialism, but is a specific product of post-cold war juristocratic times.

Juristocracy, a term first coined by Hirschl (2004), depicts a situation in which law's reach and hegemony attain new heights, where "law-saturated practices" shape social relations in ever more central and ubiquitous ways. The rule *of* law becomes a tool of governance *by* law. Hirschl analyses juristocracy as a tool of interest-based hegemonic preservation (Hirschl 2004: 214), not primarily driven by a genuine commitment to expanding rights, but rather as a means to enshrine the dominant social and political order in law, thereby insulating it from the vicissitudes of everyday politics. He traces the expansion of this new mode of rule to the first decade after the end of the cold war, when foundational nation-building challenges were transferred into the realm of the judicial (Hirschl 2004: 170). As a consequence, law exceeded its previous limits, and was "over-inflated" as a way of coming to terms with no other viable alternatives (e.g., Marxism, see Moyn 2010) and western ideological dominance.

Similarly, Martti Koskenniemi's analysis of international law in the late twentieth and twenty-first century diagnoses its "fall" into the pervasive hold of a form of "managerialism . . . the idea that global problems may be overcome through technical expertise, rather than political struggle" (Koskenniemi 2007; Lang & Marks 2013: 438). It is surely no coincidence that such pessimistic diagnoses coincide with the rise of big international legal bureaucracies and international courts that seek solutions to social and political problems by legal and increasingly bureaucratic and technical means. Liberal triumphalism and the "end of history" meant a lot of faith was put in technocratic rule to find solutions to enduring social, political, and economic claims.

The picture that I draw of transitional state-building as law-washing in Kosovo is a particularly salient illustration of the rise of juristocracy as the ideological handmaiden of juridification in the aftermath of the cold war (Goodale, this volume, p. 125). The transposition of social and political problems in the domain of law has often been called "juridification." Juridification judicializes contentious social problems while dispersing political responsibility for their solution by making them fall under the remit of seemingly apolitical, technical experts (Blichner & Molander 2005; Eckert et al. 2012). This "turn to law" is thus accompanied by a process of "rendering technical," by which power relations and power struggles are depoliticized, especially in the context of international cooperation, through technical, "best practice" solutions (Ferguson 1994; Mora 2023).

While juristocracy in the Global North is a product of post-cold war politics, juridification and techno-politics predate it. Already in a 1940 address, the prominent international law scholar Hans Morgenthau warned interwar liberal international lawyers that "fundamentally political questions such as constituting new orders could [not] be approached in the technical manner of 19th century liberal rationalism, with its belief that a social world can be known and manipulated in the manner of nature" (quoted in Bhuta 2008: 519). In fact, Nehal Bhuta's postcolonial critique of liberal reformism as a political technology draws a direct line from colonial state-building projects in Africa and Asia that "were laboratories for the liberal reformist fantasy that whole peoples could first be grasped as objects of knowledge, and then reconstituted as political subjects through long-term intervention and oversight" (Bhuta 2008: 519).

So, the United Nations Administration Mission in Kosovo (UNMIK)'s intervention in Kosovo should also be seen in continuity with a liberal-rational colonial project of techno-politics. This includes the humanitarian and "mission civilisatrice" impetus to intervention, which was also a key justification for colonialism in the eighteenth and nineteenth centuries. Similarly, a critique from a Latin American perspective shows that what Hirschl terms juristocracy predates the end of the cold war, where political issues – especially regarding the status of indigenous populations – were transposed into the realm of law (Sieder, this volume).

What is specific to the post-cold war period, however, is the "unprecedented ideological hegemony achieved by the liberal democratic states of the West, and the geopolitical hegemony of the United States" (Bhuta 2008: 521), which had the effect of legitimizing new forms of liberal, state-building interventions. In this moment, "democratization, good governance and now, state-building, [emerge] not only as normative ideals, but forms of expertise characteristic of politics-as-technology" (Bhuta 2008: 521). This idea of politics-as-technology leads to the rise of juristocracy, by which these normative ideals, now almost uncontestably hegemonic, become enshrined in law. This, in turn, leads to what Goodale and Zenker (this volume) call "law in excess": the overloading of law with expectations and objectives.

9.2 Juristocratic Transitology

The Kosovo war can be seen as the apotheosis of juristocracy, an international military intervention conducted in the name of human rights that fundamentally changed the face of international law.

Although not sanctioned by the UN Security Council, the NATO intervention and bombing of Belgrade was *violence justified by law in the name of law.*[3] The Kosovo conflict was seen as a "moral or ethical issue, a matter of rights or principles" (Koskenniemi 2002: 161). Whereas cold-war politics were about "a calculation of military force and balance of power," the Kosovo war had become "a matter of moral ideals, self-determination, democracy and human rights" (Douzinas 2000; Koskenniemi 2002: 161). Following the international community's abject failure to protect civilian lives a few years earlier in Bosnia and Herzegovina, the bombing of Serbia by NATO forces was envisaged in humanitarian terms, to "save" the Kosovo Albanian population from Serbian violence. Through this, the international intervention in Kosovo became a determining factor in shaping "what "we" [in the Global North] hold as normal and what as exceptional, and through that fact, about what sort of international law we practice" (Koskenniemi 2002: 162). At the same time, NATO's intervention in 1999 normalized international intervention and brought it within the purview of international law (through, e.g., the indictment of Slobodan Milošević in The Hague).

The NATO military intervention, conducted to prevent further serious human rights violations and civilian deaths, was followed by unparalleled UN participation in postwar peace-building and reconstruction (the only comparable case being East Timor, see Wilde 2008: 11). Very quickly after the end of the war, the UN passed Resolution 1244, which established UNMIK. A keystone of international intervention was the establishment and promotion of the rule of law, that is, the safeguarding of human rights and the promotion of "good governance" via the strengthening of institutions, and a short-term technical-legal approach to "transition."

The goal was to transform Kosovo into a functioning, sovereign, "modern," multiethnic state compatible with possible future EU accession criteria. Thus, it could act as a buffer state on the EU's outside borders, but also mitigate tensions with Serbia and avoid territorial divisions along ethnic lines (i.e., not to reward ethnic cleansing by the

[3] Samera Esmeir makes a similar point about the war in Iraq as a post-cold war site of "transition to democracy" and a "zone of intervention" (Esmeir 2007: 101). She writes that post-cold war "juridico-democracy ... declares the confinement of its violence to the sphere of means employed to the end of eradicating all other violence threatening security. It promises an endpoint of non-violence alongside its own *instrumentalized* violence, and proposes itself as an alternative to other non-juridical formations of violence that themselves anticipate nothing but further violence" (Esmeir 2007).

kind of ethnic federalism established in Bosnia and Herzegovina). While this was the long-term goal, the international territorial administration operated from the beginning in a logic of exceptionality derived from the humanitarian catastrophe of mass displacement that justified the institu tionalization of "interim" governance mechanisms (Sahin 2013).

And in the perspective of these international custodians of Kosovo's sovereignty, the country was not simply transitioning from conflict to peace, but rather was a blank slate waiting to be filled: Where there were no institutions, no infrastructures, and no coherent legal framework the rule of law would now be established. In that logic, safeguarding human rights became the most appropriate tool and ultimate goal of transition. This transformed the thornier questions of sovereignty and living together after conflict into technical issues – and these required international solutions, because of the perceived failure of governance of former Yugoslav and Serbian institutions (Sahin 2013: 25).

The legal apparatus and regulations of transition added a new layer of legal uncertainty to what was clearly not the blank slate imagined by the ideologues of transition, but rather a complex, historically grown judicial system and a complicated palimpsest of property laws still eminently relevant to current property relations – from Ottoman Empire *tapija* titles, to the land concessions of the Yugoslav kingdom, to usage and occupancy rights of the Socialist Federal Republic of Yugoslavia, to the discriminatory laws of the Milošević era. Rather than mitigating existing issues, the ambiguities of transition compounded these. Procedural rules were created from scratch, and UNMIK regulations were written in a "very poor, unprofessional" and "superficial" manner, according to judges I spoke to.

A good example of this is that UNMIK failed to provide a list of discriminatory laws that needed repealing, which meant that judges had to decide for themselves and on a case-by-case basis, which laws would apply when and how. Legal professionals relied on "flimsy regulations" and "cryptic rules." The new, supposedly efficient instruments created by the international territorial administrations to make a "new start" in effect compounded the judicial quagmire.

Kosovo's contested declaration of independence on February 17, 2008 represented a next step in the tortuous road of transition. It did not, however, solve the problem of sovereignty, nor announce the end of international supervision and a regime of emergency. Rather, internationally supervised institution-building became the yardstick to assess Kosovo's statehood (Pandolfi 2010; Sahin 2013). The new Constitution, written with active support from the US and the EU, exemplifies this: On the one hand, it created the framework for an effectively existing, EU-compatible state; on the other hand, the Constitution still included "transitional provisions" that gave the international community a continued role in the country's institutions, especially the judiciary. As a mark of this ongoing institutionalization, the European Rule of Law Mission in Kosovo (EULEX) replaced UNMIK in 2008.

National courts, in this context, were scripted as being incapable of dealing with the requirements and standards of human-rights-compatible, technically "correct" rule of law. One solution, then, was to "build capacities": International legal professionals were flown in to help draft new legislation, train "locals," do "MMA" (monitoring, mentoring, and advising), and, with their "neutral and disinterested professionalism," oversee and adjudicate "ethnically sensitive" cases. Another approach was to create special courts and quasi-judicial institutions that would stand outside the national (read: supposedly inefficient, corrupt) judiciary and tackle the most pressing and contentious property questions: the privatization of socialist immovable assets (the Privatization Agency of Kosovo, PAK) and war-related property restitution (the Kosovo Property Agency, KPA). Their mandates were limited in time and scope to find quick solutions to pressing issues without addressing underlying questions of historical discrimination and injustices, or the future of Kosovo as a sovereign state.

These interim, technical-legal governance mechanisms themselves helped perpetuate a permanent state of exception. One example, which I discuss in greater detail elsewhere (Mora 2020), is the paradox whereby the European Convention on Human Rights is directly applicable in Kosovo, as it is enshrined in the 2008 Constitution, but Kosovo has no access to the European Court of Human Rights, as it is not a state party to the European Convention on Human Rights. This also works at the level of legal practice, where the gap between "ordinary" applications of legal principles and some of the legal solutions used in the everyday in Kosovo is justified in the same language of transitional exceptionalism, as we shall see in the case of the KPA and its notification practice.

The fact that things do not seem to work as well as they should under transitional conditions of exception, however, is not an aberration or a wrinkle to be ironed out over time. It is, in fact, absolutely essential to what "transition" actually does. Transition works as an ideological device justifying a state of exception, built on the premise that the challenges of postwar reconstruction are such that things *could never* work as they would under "normal" circumstances. The international law scholar Ruti Teitel thus writes that in such "hyper-politicized" conditions, "the law operates differently, and often is incapable of meeting all of the traditional values that are associated with the rule of law, such as general applicability, procedural due process, and more substantive values of fairness or analogous sources of legitimacy" (Teitel 2014: 4). "What is fair and just in extraordinary political circumstances," Teitel furthermore suggests, "[is] to be determined from the transitional position itself" (Teitel 2003: 54–55). The problem with this perspective is that it furthers the idea that law's ethical or moral standards must *necessarily* be lowered in situations of transition. It thus participates in the normalization of the state of exception, allowing for a gap between ethical legal standards such as due process standards that would ordinarily apply and everyday legal practice "in transition" to grow and flourish. Of course, a gap between theory and practice always exists, but short-sighted, technocratic measures of transitional governance create legal inadequacies in the name of law; the law becomes a "front" of good governance through processes of law-washing. In other words, law-washing leads to a "hollowing out" of the law, in which legal norms and procedures become detached from their underlying moral or ethical foundations.

Judge Irina, a formidable EULEX civil judge in secondment from Bulgaria whom I shadowed in 2013 gave me an example of such "hollowing out." She explained that the Kosovan judiciary, partly run by EULEX, was good at "processing" cases, but not good at "finalizing" and implementing them. Instead of solving property cases, she explained to me over coffee one day, the Supreme Court "quashes and returns [them] back to District and Municipal Courts with a very short judgement . . . It's not even very clear why they return back." Then:

> District court judges send their cases back to municipal courts with new numbers, even if they are actually very old. They say: "we're only three judges, with not enough courtrooms." They keep the cases with the judges, in their wardrobes. They don't know what they have in there. The norm at Municipal and District level is thirty cases per month. We are far from achieving that. They used to finalize the easy cases, but the more complicated property cases remain pending because no one dares to take a decision.

For Irina and other (national and international) legal professionals I interviewed and worked with, this epitomizes a major issue of internationally supervised governance in Kosovo: UNMIK and EULEX set up huge legal bureaucracies that are very good at "processing" cases and showing that "something is being done," but not good at all at *solving* problems. Irina emphasized: "Stacking up cases in wardrobes is not the job we [EULEX] were supposed to do."

While the problem is perhaps more visible in ethnically sensitive, or in war-related property cases, it also goes beyond exceptional scenarios. Irina gave the example of a friend who, at the time, was a EULEX civil judge and sat in the municipal court of Podujevo in the northeast of the country. The judge mostly dealt with divorce proceedings, and her decisions were very seldom executed. In one case, the father had received legal custody; the mother visiting rights every weekend. The mother came back to see the judge several months later, crying: she had not been allowed to see her child at all. The judge, who was by that time on the brink of a mental breakdown, then took it on herself to drive to the father's house, take the child, and bring them to their mother. She then went to pick up the child on Sunday evening and brought them back to their father's house.

For Hilmi Jashari, a chain-smoking, congenial human rights lawyer and former Kosovan Ombudsperson, whom I've known since 2012, the nonfinalization and nonexecution of decisions was a major issue across the judicial system. In an interview for the magazine *Kosovo 2.0*, Hilmi made plain:

> We conducted a national study where we found that a high number of cases are hardly executed. Despite the fact that they are determined by court decisions. According to our research, the number of unexecuted cases [in 2019] on the national level is 117,000. This creates a defect within the system – when court decisions are not implemented. The state undermines the whole of the justice system because it has no effect. This also makes people lose their trust in the system. (Rama 2019)

The limitations or problems of transition and reconstruction are produced by the structural conditions of exception, which are owed to the confluence of two emergencies: the war, and the transition. It would, however, be misplaced to see this situation as a "failure of implementation." Rather, it is an essential feature of how the legal bureaucracies of UNMIK and EULEX have understood and framed postwar issues to govern the transition.

In this context, I develop the notion of law-washing as a framework to reckon with the effects of the overloading of law with expectations in the post-cold war juristocratic moment. Law-washing allows me to conceptually grapple with the gap between the promises and achievements of law in Kosovo's postwar transition to statehood. Law-washing, as I show, describes the processes by which decision-makers abdicate political responsibility for eminently political problems by demonstrating adherence to the rule of law and human rights – adherence which is produced by technocratic measures that evacuate human rights of their radical potential.

9.3 Property Restitution as Techno-politics

The KPA is empathetically not a national process of "dealing with the past" and righting wrongs. It is an ultimately relatively powerless, underfunded, and temporarily delimited institution that is paradigmatic for the kind of short-term, bridging, technical-legal solutions that define post-cold war, internationally supervised and funded humanitarian emergency and postconflict transition situations. With rule of law conceived of as a tool of "good governance," neoliberal managerial logics prevailed, leading to the set-up of the KPA as a mass claims mechanism. The internal organization of its data collecting and processing technologies created an "assembly line" of case processing, allowing for the bundling of claims of similar legal scenarios and the "quick" and "efficient" adjudication of claims.

To streamline the claiming process and ensure efficiency, the KPA adopted several managerial techniques to create a "mass claims" processing system. Such mass claims mechanisms have been in use since at least the 1980s. This approach supposedly ensures "effective remedies to claimants within a reasonably prompt period of time and in a manner which was economical and consistent" (Cordial & Rosandhaug 2008: 29). One of the three KPA commissioners (i.e., judges) described the mass-claims mechanism as such:

> A mass claims process can be broadly understood as a process designed to deal with a high number of claims that arise out of the same extraordinary situation or event and are filed with the decision-making body within a limited period of time; thus, claimants in a mass claims process are generally in the same situation, having suffered the same or similar losses within the same period of time ... In view of the high number of claims and their similarity, a mass claims process must be organised in a fair and efficient manner to ensure that claimants are treated equally and all the claims are resolved within a reasonable period of time. (HPCC/RES/7/2003, in Heiskanen 2006: 29)

Other mass claims mechanisms usually sought to provide "fair and just" compensations to claimants (Holtzmann & Kristjánsdóttir 2006; Das & van Houtte 2008). The KPA, however, as Heiskanen put it, provided the "simple form of relief [that is] property restitution" (Heiskanen 2006: 30). This, Heiskanen implies, is a good thing. Proponents of such ad hoc arbitration mechanisms argue that the requirements of mass-claims processing, such as lower procedural and evidentiary standards, make sense from a cost–benefit viewpoint without necessarily undermining the quality of judgments (Das 2006; van Haersolte-van Hof 2006; Das & van Houtte 2008). Yet, as I show in the next section, this can have extremely problematic consequences.

A precedent for Kosovo was the South African post-apartheid restitution model, which was, because of its overreliance on oral hearings and adversarial proceedings, seen as too slow (Das 2004: 436). In Kosovo, the drafters of the KPA mandate thus opted to make the institution rely almost exclusively on written submissions and evidence. They installed a hybrid system, whereby cases would be bundled into batches of similar types by KPA lawyers, and decided on the basis of "Standard Operation Procedures (SOP)" [*sic*]. Only contested claims, or especially tricky uncontested ones, were read and adjudicated as individual cases by one of the three commissioners.

An in-house IT system and tailor-made applications designed specifically for each unit at HQ and the regional offices were a further central element in improving the efficiency of the KPA. These, in turn, helped produce specific institutional logics and procedures to the case processing, the consequences of which I address elsewhere (Mora 2023).

The KPA was a bridging solution designed to resolve war-related property disputes in this difficult period of "transition." The KPA mandate defined war-related property loss as falling within a strictly delimited time window of February 27, 1998 to June 20, 1999. This had the effect of excluding many if not most of Kosovo Albanian potential claimants, as these had largely lost their properties to discriminatory practices in the years leading up to open war (except for properties in the Serbian-dominated areas north of the Ibar River). This was intentional: the international community wanted to ensure the return of displaced Kosovo Serbs to promote the establishment of Kosovo as a multiethnic *Rechtsstaat* through the stated logic of "property rights are human rights."

But it was also to exclude the thornier question of older, historical underlying injustices that took place before the conflict from the process. The exclusive focus on private *ownership* meant that more recent ownership titles superseded older (socialist) *occupancy* rights, and issues of discrimination in property allocation and fraudulent property transactions in the 1990s, which had centrally contributed to the conflict. By framing the right to property as a universal human right, community-based conflicts and cleavages were removed from the agency's remit. And this wilful blindness was justified by invoking human rights and "neutral" rule of law principles.

The regulation that set up the KPA (UNMIK reg. 2006/50 and related administrative directions, transformed into national law in 2008) was not a restitution law that reflected (and legitimized) one specific political reading of history, but rather an extraordinary measure of transition. This meant the KPA (as a constitutionally independent agency) was given administrative and legal leeway to implement its mandate within the allotted period of funding, so long as it did it in a "reasonable" manner judged from the "exceptional" circumstances of transition.

In what follows, I look into how the KPA informed the public about properties for which a claim had been submitted, highlighting the practice of "notification by publication" as a key instantiation of law-washing. This, as I show next, reveals the limitations and consequences of the juristocratic use of law "in excess."

9.4 Wrong Notifications

Large patches of high grass strewn with wildflowers were broken up irregularly by mounds of earth. This land had not been worked in a long time. Perhaps some of the larger mounds hid the remnants of a house, or of a cowshed. Perhaps they hid other debris of war that had been deposited there by returning neighbors in need of a dump pit. In the adjacent parcel stood a recently built one-room brick house that looked inhabited. We walked for about twenty minutes in search of the two claimed plots of land. Under a scorching sun, a GPS device donated to the KPA by the Norwegian Development Cooperation and a hand-drawn map guided our progress. I was given huge rubber boots to wear over my sandals, which made me walk like Charlie Chaplin in *The Tramp* and gave me blisters. The men on the team cracked jokes about me in Albanian as we walked. Finding claimed lots was not always easy, and KPA field officers and regional cadaster agents, with the help of GPS devices and cadastral and hand-drawn maps, spent most of their working days driving around in white UN 4x4s and walking, alone or in pairs, along half-hidden paths across Kosovo, carrying wooden poles and large KPA notification stickers.

We had four claimed properties to find and "notify" that day. Lirim, the head of our group of four (with two cadaster experts and myself) was a burly, self-confident man aged 37. He had a wife and two primary-school-aged children with whom he lived on the outskirts of Pristina. During the war he had fled to Germany where he had become a cook and where, unexpectedly, he had learned rudiments of Hindi. Laughing, he told us horror stories of his job as a KPA field officer: such as having a (thankfully malfunctioning) hand grenade thown at him by a former soldier of the Kosovo Liberation Army (the Kosovo Albanian separatist militia of the 1990s), who was very unhappy about being considered an "illegal occupant"; or being threatened at gunpoint by a Kosovo Albanian policeman for similar reasons. In these stories Lirim portrayed himself as the good guy, fighting impunity within the Kosovo Albanian community, despite expressing deep personal resentment against the Serbs who occupied Albanian lands in the north of the country.

Notification was a crucial step in the quasi-judicial administrative procedure meant to give back property rights to persons (mostly Kosovo Serbs) who had lost possession of land, houses and/or commercial spaces during the 1998–9 war. The KPA's original internal regulations (SOPs) specified that all claimed properties had to be physically inspected by KPA staff. A wooden pole and sticker with the claim number and explanations about how to become involved in the claim process had to be planted on each parcel claimed. For many lawyers and judges I worked with, this was key to ensure that potential respondents (the current occupants, or other family members, for example), could take part in the legal process.

We did not make any inauspicious encounters that day, but perhaps too busy telling heroic stories, or simply too unbothered with procedure, Lirim went about notifying properties in a somewhat unconventional manner. After having compared the printed cadastral information to the actual situation on site and collected the grid reference for both parcels, Lirim proceeded to drive a wooden pole into the ground of the first parcel. He then pasted a sticker on which he had written the KPA code for both parcels and other relevant information and took a couple of photographs of the pole. Contrary to KPA notification instructions, he then removed the pole that he had just planted and photographed and walked to the second plot with it. There, he replanted it, took a second set of pictures, and removed the pole from the earth again. No evidence remained that the KPA had "notified" the plots.

I turned to look at Lirim's two colleagues to observe their reactions. One of them also noticed and somewhat clumsily asked Lirim to explain himself. The fact that I was present added a significant level of formality to the entire situation. Back at the KPA Pristina headquarters, I recounted the story to the head of the notification unit and to the KPA director. Both of them expressed shock and seemed extremely uncomfortable.

Perhaps wary of what might happen if this became known to the Supreme Court or to donors, they gave me reassurance that this was an isolated incident, which they attributed to individual "incompetence." But both also alluded to more structural issues to do with notification practices that had occurred before 2009, which, they said, made the present situation quite problematic. Lirim received a warning and stopped talking to me, and I went poking further into notification issues.

The issue of "wrong notifications," as KPA staff called it, had reached a critical point in 2009, as it became evident that more than 30 percent of claims that had been notified since 2006 had been done so incorrectly. These were notifications performed on the wrong field or plot of land, or that had not followed the SOP. The problem was such that many KPA lawyers, KPA international donors, and the Supreme Court KPA Appeals Panel saw the credibility of the whole KPA adjudication process in jeopardy. How could property restitution ever be made to work when the actual, physical location of these properties was uncertain? If the current occupants were not correctly informed about the legal proceedings, how could they constitute themselves as respondents to cases? All cases were checked, those that had been wrongly notified were reopened and renotified, and the decisions for already adjudicated cases were quashed, at great cost and reputational damage to the institution.

The "notification fiasco" of 2009 led the KPA to revise its notification procedure. An alternative, "notification by publication" method was introduced, to save time and reassure the agency's international donors. According to the new method, instead of physically checking and identifying plots and buildings, and informing occupants and other possible respondents in person of the opening of the claims process, claims were now published in Kosovan and Serbian newspapers and other media, and lists of claims were affixed on municipal notice boards. However, this new notification procedure was arguably even more problematic than the wrong notifications, as it was now the responsibility of potential respondents to identify the notified property as one they had a claim to, and take note of the existence of the claiming process. Many potential respondents, moreover, did not have access to newspapers or municipal offices, especially those living in rural and remote areas in Serbia. Although this procedure was mostly used for single-party agricultural cases, out of the 42,749 claims processed by the agency, about 30,000 cases were eventually notified in this way.

The KPA mandate required solutions that were both efficient and "reasonable," and that took into account the limitations of a mass-claims mechanism and the exceptional circumstances of transition. Because the KPA was an independent, administrative agency understood to be tackling extraordinary issues of transition, they were entitled to develop and evaluate their own due process solutions.[4] This gave the KPA commissioners the authority to determine what qualified as "reasonable efforts" and to decide when those efforts had been successfully met, without being bound by general rules; and they ruled that notification by publication constituted a "reasonable effort."

The Appeals Panel team and certain KPA lawyers had mixed reactions to the introduction of the new method and the KPA commissioners' opinion on the matter. They acknowledged that notification by publication was not illegal, but raised concerns about the practice's reasonableness and fairness. They thought that notifying properties through publication was inadequate to ensure access to justice for potential respondents. Physical notification was, according to them, a fairer and much more effective way of reaching them. No one at the KPA was aware of any cases that had been challenged by a responding party on the basis of a notification made through publication. The KPA appeals panel judges even took the unusual step of publishing a differing opinion that stated that, for them, notification by publication was "insufficient."

I asked Bardhana, a national Kosovo Albanian KPA lawyer in her early thirties whose desk was next to mine in the case-processing offices what she thought of all this. She reflected:

[4] Due process here is understood based on Article 6 of the European Convention on Human Rights, which provides for access to and exclusivity of claims proceedings, the impartiality of adjudication, and the fairness, timeliness, finality, and implementation of decisions (van Houtte & Yi 2008: 83). However, the same article serves to allow for "specific circumstances" of emergency to "lead to some flexibility" (van Houtte & Yi 2008: 70). As Olivier Corten notes, Article 6 is an important doctrinal reference in international human rights law that interprets "reasonableness" as "ambiguous" and "context-dependent" (Corten 1999: 613).

> KPA is faster than the courts. But for me, there are serious violations of human rights when we notify by publication. . . . KPA could have done better. Pressure is no excuse. The goal should be to do the job well, not just to get it over with. I don't think the KPA claims reflect the real situation, especially in uncontested cases because of the notification by publication. I've never seen a claim where people actually responded to notification by publication. A lot of these claims are not properly adjudicated because of that. It doesn't solve the situation. (Mora 2020: 91)

However, KPA and Supreme Court staff also acknowledged the challenges of operating in a transitional context and the inherent limitations of a temporary mass-claims, quasi-judicial mechanism. In the end, the ability of the Appeals Panel to overturn the legal opinions and decisions taken by the KPA commissioners was very limited, if inexistent. The panel lacked the resources to conduct its own investigations and hearings, and it was uncertain whether the judges on the Appeals Panel had the power to quash and return cases to the KPA if they did not align with the judges' perspectives. The state of exception justified "necessary adjustments" and a lowering of due process standards. Marianne, the German head judge on the KPA appeals panel, summatively put it: "rough remedies are better than no remedies at all." Legal practitioners and judges simply do "what [they] can with what [they] have" (Mora 2020: 90). Marianne thought that "notification by publication [was] not good enough," "but sometimes," she said, contritely, "it is necessary." She went on: "It's not a criticism, a mass claims mechanism leads to rough justice. You cannot afford to go into details."

9.5 Concluding Thoughts

Juristocratic exceptionalism, itself justified and normalized by international law, produces a gap between the promises of the law and the achievements of the law: The lowering of due process standards in war-related property restitution cases produces not fast-track fairness or justice as hoped, but adherence to the letter of the law and thus to human rights from a purely technical-legal, proceduralist perspective.

As Jessica Greenberg has observed for the European Court of Human Rights, the "efficacy" of international human rights bureaucracies is an epistemic and semiotic construct. In such a context, legal procedural constraints *produce* rather than hinder a sense of efficacy and ethics (Greenberg 2020). Human rights are thus "made real" by these legal bureaucracies through procedural conformity first and foremost. Change is deemed to have happened when actors involved decide that the benchmark – very often from a procedural standpoint – has been reached, and this is not necessarily something that is observable or made tangible outside the realm of law. Such a narrow, proceduralist (or managerialist, à la Koskenniemi) understanding of human rights not only erases historical and other kinds of violence; it also locks these erasures into place through measures that more often than not fail to address harm and provide justice substantively and extralegally. In such cases, "efficacious" human rights work is just as likely to undermine and obstruct substantive change for claimants and other beneficiaries.

Achievements in the form of proceduralist, technical-legal human rights solutions only make sense within the relatively hermetic realm of EULEX–KPA judicial practice, solely through epistemic measurements of "efficacy" and the language of the exceptional. In such heightened situations of bureaucratization of human rights, the notion that their efficacy should have anything to do with justice and the social world at large is lost. Irina, the EULEX civil judge, was about to leave Kosovo. She had lost sense of "the bigger picture," as she put it, and was not very optimistic about the fate of the rule of law mission. She expressed cynicism about the solutions offered: "they are not just often enough," she told me. Practices of law-washing result in the hollowing out of the law's critical substance, where legal standards and procedures lose their connection to their fundamental moral or ethical foundations.

Rather than serving as load-bearing walls of democracy, human rights and the rule of law become wallpaper for political gain; being seen to "implement" the rule of law legitimizes Kosovo's claim, backed by the EU and the United States, to recognition as a modern, sovereign state. So, in parallel to the juridification of politics, law-washing also participates in the politicization of law, in which the idiom of the rule of law acquires new political capital and political deals are brokered through formal adherence to the law. This, in turn, helps cement the political status quo as all political actors involved – Kosovan and Serbian politicians and EU representatives – are thereby able to show compliance with the rule of law. By ticking the box of compliance, they satisfy the requirements of state-building on the path to EU accession, while washing their hands – literally, through law – of the insolvability of Kosovo's definitive status.

References

Bellamy, R. 2007. *Political Constitutionalism: A Republican Defence of the Constitutionality of Democracy*. Cambridge: Cambridge University Press.

Bhuta, N. 2008. Against State-Building. *Constellations* 15 (4): 517–542.

Blichner, L. C. and Molander, A. 200). What is Juridification? University of Oslo, Centre for European Studies Working Paper Series, 14.

Cordial, M. and Rosandhaug, K. 2008. *Post-Conflict Property Restitution: The Approach in Kosovo and Lessons for Future International Practice*. Leiden: Martinus Nijhoff.

Corten, O. 1999. The Notion of "Reasonable" in International Law: Legal Discourse, Reason and Contradictions. *International and Comparative Law Quarterly* 48 (3): 613–625.

Das, H. 2004. Restoring Property Rights in the Aftermath of War. *International and Comparative Law Quarterly* 53 (2): 429–443.

2006. The Concept of Mass Claims and the Specificity of Mass Claims Resolution. In International Bureau of the Permanent Court of Arbitration, ed., *Redressing Injustices through Mass Claims Processes: Innovative Responses to Unique Challenges*. Oxford: Oxford University Press.

Das, H. and van Houtte, H. 2008. *Post-War Restoration of Property Rights under International Law. Volume 2: Procedural Aspects*. Cambridge: Cambridge University Press.

Douzinas, C. 2000. *The End of Human Rights* Oxford: Hart.

Eckert, J., Donahoe, B., Strumpell, C. and Biner, Z. O. eds. 2012. *Law against the State: Ethnographic Forays into Law's Transformations*. Cambridge: Cambridge University Press.

Esmeir, S. 2007. The Violence of Non-Violence: Law and War in Iraq. *Journal of Law and Society* 34 (1): 99–115.

Ferguson, J. 1994. *The Anti-Politics Machine:"Development," Depoliticization, and Bureaucratic Power in Lesotho*. Minneapolis: University of Minnesota Press.

Greenberg, J. 2020. Law, Politics, and Efficacy at the European Court of Human Rights. *American Ethnologist* 47 (4): 417–431.

Heiskanen, V. 2006. Virtue Out of Necessity: International Mass Claims and New Uses of Information Technology. In Holtzmann, H. M. and Kristjansdottir, E., eds., *International Mass Claims Processes: Legal and Practical Perspectives*. Oxford: Oxford University Press.

Hirschl, R. 2004. *Towards Juristocracy: The Origins and Consequences of the New Constitutionalism*. Cambridge, MA: Harvard University Press.

Holtzmann, H. M. and Kristjánsdóttir, E., eds. 2006. *International Mass Claims Processes: Legal and Practical Perspectives*. Oxford: Oxford University Press.

Koskenniemi, M. 2002. The Lady Doth Protest Too Much: Kosovo, and the Turn to Ethics in International Law. *Modern Law Review* 65 (2): 159–175.

2007. Constitutionalism as Mindset: Reflections on Kantian Themes about International Law and Globalization Critical Modernities: Politics and Law beyond the Liberal Imagination. *Theoretical Inquiries in Law* 8 (1): 9–36.

Lang, A. and Marks, S. 2013. People with Projects: Writing the Lives of International Lawyers. *Temple International and Comparative Law Journal* 27 (2): 437–453.

Mora, A. 2020. Black Hole State: Human Rights and the Work of Suspension in Post-war Kosovo. *Social Anthropology* 28 (1): 83–95.

2023. "Property Rights Are Human Rights": Bureaucratization and the Logics of Rule of Law Interventionism in Postwar Kosovo. *PoLAR: Political and Legal Anthropology Review* 46 (1): 82–96.

Moyn, S. 2010. *The Last Utopia: Human Rights in History*, Cambridge, MA: Harvard University Press.

Pandolfi, M. 2010. From Paradox to Paradigm: The Permanent State of Emergency in the Balkans. In Pandolfi, M. and Fassin, D., eds., *Contemporary States of Emergency: The Politics of Military and Humanitarian Interventions*. New York: Zone.

Rama, L. 2019. Hilmi Jashari: The Problems that Face Kosovo Citizens Today Are the Product of Systemic Failure. *Kosovo 2.0*, 26.12.2019.

Sahin, S. B. 2013. How Exception Became the Norm: Normalizing Intervention as an Exercise in Risk Management in Kosovo. *Journal of Balkan and Near Eastern Studies* 15 (1): 17–36.

Teitel, R. G. 2003. Transitional Justice Genealogy. *Harvard Human Rights Journal* 16 (69): 69–94.

2014. *Globalizing Transitional Justice: Contemporary Essays*. Oxford: Oxford University Press.

van Haersolte-van Hof, J. J. 2006. Innovations to Speed Mass Claims: New Standards of Proof. In International Bureau of the Permanent Court of Arbitration, ed., *Redressing Injustices through Mass Claims Processes: Innovative Responses to Unique Challenges*. Oxford: Oxford University Press.

van Houtte, H. and Yi, I. 2008. Due Process in International Mass Claims. *Erasmus Law Review* 1 (2): 63–85.

Wilde, R. 2008. *International Territorial Administration: How Trusteeship and the Civilizing Mission Never Went Away*, Oxford: Oxford University Press.

10

After Judicialization?

Law, Authoritarian Regression, and the Defense of Indigenous Life-Worlds in Guatemala

RACHEL SIEDER

10.1 Introduction

> [C]ertain histories of juristocratic reckoning are imbued with what might be thought of as an "iconic indexicality," in which their supposed historical significance itself enters into the process of juristocratic elevation and then unraveling.
>
> (Goodale and Zenker, Introduction, this volume, p. 4)

The late-twentieth-century recognition of indigenous peoples as collective subjects of human rights would seem to represent a textbook case of what the editors of this volume term "iconic indexality." International human rights instruments approved at the turn of the twenty-first century held out promises of recognizing difference, repairing colonial harms, and reckoning with the slow violence of environmental damage that has translated into genocide for so many indigenous peoples. A paradigm shift occurred as struggles that had been fought out over centuries, first through colonial legalities and later through the laws of nation-states, were transposed to the idiom of human rights. A shared transborder language for framing "indigeneity" and indigenous claims coalesced as international human rights law steadily codified and

Rachel Sieder is Senior Research Professor at the Center for Research and Graduate Studies in Social Anthropology, CIESAS, in Mexico City. She is also an Associate Research Professor at the Chr. Michelsen Institute, Bergen, and a Global Fellow at LawTransform, The Center for Law and Social Transformation, Bergen. This chapter is part of the project "PluriLand: Theorizing Conflict and Contestation in Plural Land Regimes" (project number 300851).

expanded the collective rights of indigenous peoples, first through ILO Convention 169, approved in 1989, and then the 2007 UN Declaration on the Rights of Indigenous and Tribal Peoples. In the Americas the evolving jurisprudence of the Interamerican Court of Human Rights and the American Declaration on the Rights of Indigenous Peoples, approved in 2016, came to be central to indigenous peoples' juridified struggles for self-determination. Their resort to law generated new legal principles and hybrid judicial interpretations in domestic and international law, through iterative processes that Stuart Kirsch has termed "looping effects" (Kirsch 2018). In diverse processes of norm creation and diffusion,[1] indigenous individuals, communities, and their allies in civil society organizations lodged multiple appeals before national courts and the Interamerican system in ever-expanding processes of judicialization aimed at turning the human rights promises of indigenous and native peoples' self-determination into concrete guarantees and policies.

Judicialization was accompanied by broader dynamics of juridification, as sociolegal mobilization encouraged many individuals and communities to see themselves as part of broader collectives united across ethno-linguistic communities and national borders by the novel legal category of "indigenous peoples." However, the judicial expansion of indigenous peoples' rights faltered by the second decade of the twenty-first century. In addition to the "implementation gap" pointed to decades earlier by the first United Nations special rapporteur on indigenous rights (Stavenhagen 2002), powerful elites across the region increasingly turned to law and "lawfare" to systematically criminalize indigenous territorial defenders and their allies and renew processes of legalized and violent dispossession.

Yet rather than seeing indigenous rights as a case of juristocratic excess and failure, in this chapter I argue that processes of defense against old and new forms of colonial dispossession and erasure, and the complex roles that law plays in these, should be understood in the *longue durée*. Indigenous people have engaged with hegemonic forms of law in different ways since conquest and although these engagements acquired new dimensions and intensity during "the age of human rights" (Goodale 2022), rarely was law viewed as a panacea or an alternative to political

[1] On iteration, see Eckert et al. who suggest that all situated forms of engagement with legal norms and institutions are necessarily interpretative acts that constitute both self and law (Eckert et al. 2012: 11–13).

organization or other forms of resistance. The strategic resort to law is accompanied by a keen awareness of its historical role in old and new forms of colonial violence and dispossession. Colonial laws remade indigenous worlds by constituting land as an alienable object – "property"– displacing alternative understandings to justify racialized inequalities grounded in systemic violence. The late-twentieth-century turn to law by indigenous peoples never supplanted other horizons of justice premised on alternative lifeworlds; indeed, the juristocratic shift and its centering of "self-determination" served to amplify claims and histories conceived prior to and beyond human rights law. In other words, human rights constitute one more phase of this *longue durée*, wherein dominant forms of law shape but never completely define indigenous subjectivities.

In this chapter I draw on my ongoing collaborations with Mayan lawyers' organizations that have litigated key cases of indigenous peoples' collective rights in Guatemala to consider the uses of law in an increasingly hostile context of state capture and authoritarian regression. In the first section, I briefly discuss the role of the courts and law in ongoing processes of authoritarian regression and state capture, pointing to the links between indigenous peoples' legal mobilization, court decisions to uphold their constitutional and human rights, vested interests in extractive "development" projects, and the current wave of criminalization and violence unleashed upon territorial defenders. In the second section, I engage with recent theoretical discussions on competing ontologies of land or territories, and the enduring connections between racialized imaginaries, the making of property rights, and colonial dispossession of indigenous people. In the third section, I consider the generative possibilities of judicialization initiatives that seek to challenge these racialized imaginaries and dominant forms of property or "legal land ontologies" (Di Giminiani 2018). I argue that even though litigation may stand little chance of success in the courts, it represents an attempt to inscribe alternative understandings and historical claims within the judicial-political sphere, potentially shaping broader political imaginaries. I describe a specific claim for ancestral land rights to the territory of Los Copones, in the Ixcán region of Guatemala, to show how judicialization linked to processes of community political organization can strengthen localized forms of self-determination, defeat in court notwithstanding. I conclude by suggesting that even in a context of renewed authoritarianism and "juristocratic reckoning," the legal defense of indigenous lands and territories continues to hold emancipatory potential.

10.2 Authoritarian Regression, Violence, and Criminalization

In their edited volume, *The Limits of Judicialization: From Progress to Backlash in Latin American Politics*, Sandra Botero, Daniel Brinks and Ezequiel González-Ocantos consider why the judicialization of politics in Latin America has generally failed to guarantee greater rights protection. They observe that the late-twentieth-century project of progressive constitutionalism based on multiple international human rights treaties represented, in effect, a revolutionary charter. Given the acute levels of socioeconomic inequality and ingrained structural racism across the region, the belief that equality and democracy could somehow be engineered through constitutionalized human rights seemed utopian at best. Yet sustained efforts to combat corruption, racism, and impunity through strategic litigation led to significant victories in court, which social movements and progressive forces leveraged in attempts to achieve broader political change. Pro-rights rulings were a result of various factors. These included sustained social mobilization, the consolidation of legal expertise within social movements, donor support for legal services NGOs, "rule of law" institutional reforms in the 1980s and 1990s, and an incipient transformation of judicial culture whereby some judges and public prosecutors came to see themselves as defenders of human rights (González-Ocantos 2016). In numerous high-profile cases, courts in Latin America were instrumental in the impeachment of incumbent presidents, they convicted former military rulers of genocide and gross violations of human rights and confirmed same-sex marriage rights and women's sexual and reproductive rights. And as I underline in this chapter, they also endorsed – at least in declaratory terms – the collective rights of the region's indigenous peoples to preserve their distinctive ways of life. However, in many contexts, progressive legal victories – or processes of juristocratic reckoning – have contributed to a sustained backlash.

Botero, Brinks, and González-Ocantos explain how the institutional and cultural changes that empowered the courts and placed them at the heart of political disputes in the 1980s and 1990s – what they call the "judicialization superstructure" – often fell short of the promise of greater accountability and rights protection. They signal various reasons: first, progressive court rulings failed to take persistent state weakness into account, meaning that policy changes recommended by the courts often exceeded state capacity to implement them. Second, judicial corruption, nepotism, and other "intra-institutional pathologies" diminished the transformative potential of courts and public prosecutors' offices. Third, the inability of courts and activists to embed change in strong support structures sometimes generated political and social backlash that frustrated efforts at social transformation. This was particularly the case where social movements had become "NGO-ized" and successful litigation was disconnected from broad-based popular support. As a result, and despite notable and rightly celebrated successes in court, the impact of judicialization across Latin America has been relatively limited and has provoked aggressive responses from conservative forces. This is clearly the case with respect to the judicialization of indigenous peoples' collective rights claims to resist the encroachments of extractive development projects within their ancestral territories. Botero, Brinks, and Gonzalez-Ocantos conclude that in some cases judicialization has done more harm than good, especially when the expectations of those who promote it have been fulfilled too well, specifically in fighting corruption. This has hastened the (re)capture of judicial institutions by conservative forces.

10.2.1 Human Rights, Extractive Industries, and the Criminalization of Protest

Rural Maya, Xinca, and Garifuna communities in Guatemala facing the socioenvironmental consequences of mines, hydroelectric dams, or monoculture crop expansion have mobilized through networks of legal professionals and civil society organizations to defend themselves and their territories before different courts and administrative instances. For nearly two decades, in common with indigenous peoples throughout Latin America, they resorted to the figure of free, prior, and informed consultation (FPIC) to juridify and judicialize their resistance to extractive projects. FPIC was established as a collective human right of indigenous peoples in ILO Convention 169 (ratified by Guatemala in 1997) and extended to a formulation of "FPIC for consent" by the UN Declaration on the Rights of Indigenous and Tribal Peoples. Litigation initiatives before the courts appealed to the international standards for FPIC established through the jurisprudence of the Interamerican human rights system, which has confirmed, inter alia, that all consultations should be carried out according to the self-determined governance procedures of the affected peoples (IACHR 2021). The first cases of FPIC were presented to Guatemala's constitutional court in 2007, and after 2008 the court issued several rulings ordering the temporary suspension of large-scale extractive projects until consultation was carried out.[2] In some instances, these rulings were issued after the license to the company in question had been issued by the Ministry of Energy and Mines but prior to the project's initiation, in other cases the extractive project was already in operation when the court ordered its suspension.

These legal victories for the indigenous rights movement failed to change governmental development policies, but they did temporarily delay the implementation of important extractive projects, seemingly providing at least some respite for communities under threat and sending a signal to others that litigation in defense of collective human rights could have concrete effects. Yet in practice, the right to consultation proved largely declaratory. Guatemala's constitutional tribunal has always insisted that indigenous consultations are not binding and do not entail a right to veto. Consultation is effectively understood, at best, as an administrative requirement for the installation and operation of projects, rather than as a mechanism to ensure consent or much less "self-determination," the principle and promise which lies at the heart of the 2007 UN Declaration on the Rights of Indigenous and Tribal Peoples and the jurisprudence of the Interamerican system of human rights (IACHR 2021). Most nominally "pro-rights" sentences issued by the constitutional court failed to even stipulate that the mandated consultations be carried out in accordance with the self-government arrangements of the affected communities, in line with international standards. In her research on courts and indigenous peoples in Guatemala, Braconnier has argued that a distinction should be drawn between progressive and transformative court judgments (Braconnier 2021). As she notes, there is no contradiction between apparently progressive court rulings that formally recognize indigenous peoples' rights to FPIC and the continuation of the colonial project of racialized extractive capitalism. Few effective mechanisms exist to ensure that government institutions and private companies comply with judicial decisions. Mineral extraction has continued notwithstanding temporary suspensions of mining operations ordered by Guatemala's constitutional court. Despite doctrinal and jurisprudential advances, in practice, domestic and international legal systems protect private contract rights between

[2] The most significant FPIC rulings include: La Puya (795-2016, 1380-2016); San Juan Sacatepéquez (1031-2009, 1925-2014); Oxec (90-2017, 91-2017, 92-2017), and the San Rafael mine (4785-2017).

governments and corporations more than the collective rights of indigenous peoples to self-determination.

Legal attempts to uphold indigenous peoples' human rights have run up against transnational webs of corruption involving government elites and companies, which in turn have fueled increased confrontations and the murder, harassment, and criminalization of indigenous community leaders, a pattern repeated across Latin America and indeed worldwide.[3] For example, in March 2022 a leak of thousands of documents shared by the hacking collective Guacamaya Roja revealed the operations of the Russian-owned, Swiss-incorporated mining giant Solway Investment Group, whose subsidiary CGN-Pronico has long operated a controversial nickel mine (named Fenix) in El Estor in the department of Izabal, an area predominantly inhabited by Q'eqchi' Maya fishermen and peasants. The leaked company documents showed how CGN-Pronico had bought off local police, paying for their gasoline, vehicle repairs, food, rent of local offices, and "violence prevention programs." The company also monitored and tracked journalists, categorized local leaders and communities according to whether they were in favor or against the mine, and repeatedly tried to expel Q'eqchi' communities from their ancestral lands. The documents also revealed that CGN-Pronico hid negative scientific studies showing high levels of heavy metals in lake Izabal and surrounding soil, something residents had long pointed to as the probable cause of numerous health problems. The company brought pressure on successive presidents and government agencies to ensure favorable environmental assessments and secured political loyalties through donations and kickbacks.[4]

In 2018 Q'eqchi' members of the local artisanal fisherman's union filed a constitutional action of *amparo* against the Ministry of Energy and Mines for failing to guarantee the right to FPIC prior to issuing the original mining license in 2005. In 2020 the constitutional court ordered that a process of pre-consultation be carried out, reaffirming in principle the rights of indigenous peoples to participate in the formulation, application, and evaluation of development projects directly affecting them. The court also reduced the territorial circumscription of the original

[3] See, for example, A/HRC/39/17 Report of the Special Rapporteur on the rights of indigenous peoples presented to the 39th Session of the Human Rights Council, September 2018. Available at: www.ohchr.org/Documents/Issues/IPeoples/SR/A.HRC.39.17.pdf. Last consulted November 1, 2023.

[4] See https://forbiddenstories.org/case/mining-secrets. Last consulted November 1, 2023.

license and ordered the suspension of CGN-Pronico's operating rights until the full consultation process was concluded. It was not until the following year that the Ministry of Energy and Mines initiated administrative measures to give effect to the judicial ruling, and in any case – as the leaked documents later confirmed – the mine continued to operate. In October 2021, following several weeks of a blockade organized by Q'eqchi' villagers at the mine's entrance to protest the lack of implementation of the court's ruling, the Guatemalan congress ratified a state of siege in the municipality of El Estor, allowing the government to suspend constitutional guarantees of freedom of action, legal detention, and rights to assembly and demonstrations. During the month of the state of siege, and the following month's "state of exception," community leaders and local journalists were harassed, threatened, detained, and their houses ransacked.

The case of CGN-Pronico in El Estor is just one example among many of the juridification of socioenvironmental conflicts, characterized by the increasingly repressive use of law to systematically displace indigenous peoples and peasants and criminalize protests by people, groups, and organizations that question the operations of extractive industries (Montoya, Sieder & Bravo 2021). Companies and their allies in government promote legal actions against activists for moral or material damages supposedly sustained by the companies and their representatives. Indigenous authorities and community members are subjected to systematic campaigns of defamation and harassment, including sexual violence against women, and indicted on charges of terrorism and illicit association to commit crimes. Criminalization involves extended periods of pre-trial detention, high bail requirements, and the constant postponement of hearings, only for many cases to eventually be dismissed on the grounds of insufficient evidence, sometimes years after the initial arrests. The suspension of fundamental rights of participation, association, and expression through the declaration of localized states of siege facilitates the militarization of indigenous territories, as demonstrations and protests are violently suppressed by the police or members of the armed forces under the cover of the "rule of law."[5] A combination of legality and militarized violence guarantees the functioning of extractive industries,

[5] See Report of the UN Special Rapporteur on the rights of indigenous people on her mission to Guatemala, A/HRC/39/17/Add.3, September 10–28, 2018. https://undocs.org/en/A/HRC/39/17/Add.3. Last consulted November 1, 2023.

revealing the networks and overlaps between state and private actors that facilitate dispossession.

Persecution of indigenous activists and journalists in Guatemala has extended to the entire judicial apparatus. Since 2015, when former army general President Pérez Molina was forced to resign by massive anti-corruption demonstrations, and subsequently imprisoned on charges of illicit association and corruption following investigations supported by the United Nations International Commission against Impunity in Guatemala (known as CICIG), powerful political and economic sectors redoubled their efforts to secure a pliant a judiciary and public prosecutors' office (Braconnier 2021). The CICIG was eventually forced out of the country by President Jimmy Morales, who had been investigated by the commission and accused of accepting a million dollars in illegal campaign donations. The constitutional court prevented Morales' efforts to expel the head of the CICIG, Ivan Velásquez, from the country in 2017. But when Guatemalan prosecutors from the office of the special prosecutor against corruption (known as the FECI), which had been created to work alongside CICIG, successfully petitioned the supreme court in 2018 to authorize a congressional vote to remove the president's legal immunity so he could stand trial, Morales immediately revoked the CICIG's mandate and by 2019 its operations had ceased (Bowen 2022). The country's corrupt and criminal political elite captured the processes of nomination to the high courts to guarantee impunity – operations documented by the FECI in the judicialized cases known as "parallel commissions."[6] In April 2021 Gloria Porras, the constitutional court justice who ordered the suspension of CGN-Pronico's operations in El Estor, fled the country after congress refused to renew her mandate. Justice Porras was known for her stance in favor of indigenous peoples' collective rights and the fight against corruption. Once she lost her immunity she was effectively forced into exile, like many other Guatemalan judges and public prosecutors who face criminal charges because of their efforts to defend human rights and secure accountability.[7] In short, backlash and authoritarian regression is directly related to attempts by citizens' groups and members of the judiciary to hold the

[6] See Adriana Beltrán, "Detrás de la lucha por secuestrar el sistema de justicia de Guatemala," WOLA – Washington Office on Latin America, July 20, 2020. Last consulted November 1, 2023.

[7] See Jonathan Blitzer, "The Exile of Guatemala's Anti-corruption Efforts," *The New Yorker*, April 29, 2022.

powerful to account and guarantee human rights in the postwar period. In the case of indigenous peoples' collective rights, the backlash reflects long-run patterns of the defense of property regimes established through violent racialized dispossession.

10.3 Indigenous Territorial Defense: A Long Game

The juridification of socioenvironmental conflicts in the ancestral territories of native and indigenous peoples involves the mobilization of conflicting imaginaries and legalities. States claim permanent sovereign rights to adjudicate subsoil resources and land, rights grounded in legacies of colonial dispossession and legalities that negate the legitimacy of legal orders whose origins lie in the precolonial period (González-Serrano, Montalván-Zambrano & Viaene 2022). By contrast, indigenous people claim rights to their ancestral territories, to determine their own forms of government, development, and life, and protect themselves from the devastating environmental and cultural impacts of extractive projects. As signaled above, these rights are set out in international human rights instruments and multiple claims have been codified in these terms. As Bens and others have underlined, when native communities engage postcolonial states through dominant forms of law, they effectively "become indigenous," insisting that their rights originate from their own systems of law (Bens 2020). While they do not exist outside of colonial and capitalist dynamics, indigenous peoples have always exercised and defended different sovereignties over their territories.

Judicialized disputes over indigenous peoples' human rights highlight the gaps between hegemonic capitalist frames of land-as-property, and alternative understandings or ontologies of land and territory. In addition to highlighting the gaps between "the *experience-near* formulation of indigenous knowledge and practices and the *experience-distant* language of jurisprudence" (Kirsch 2018: 23), judicialized socioenvironmental territorial disputes reveal the limits and frictions of legal translation. Di Giminiani has referred to the different understandings mobilized in these contexts as "land ontologies"; his research on land titling programs in Mapuche territories in Chile suggests that interactions between different frames expose the limits of commensuration between territories inhabited in multiple ways by different groups and actors, and the hegemonic legal framework of property, which constructs an abstract thing called "land" as something alienable which can be bought and sold (Di Giminiani 2018).

> Indigenous land ontologies are predicated upon an intersubjective relation – in other words, a relation between two subjects, land and people, both endowed with sentient abilities. Legal land ontologies, in contrast, are founded upon the principles of property theory according to which land is an object of possession that can be standardized within a regime of value. (Di Giminiani 2018: 9)

In contrast to binary readings of state domination versus indigenous resistance, Di Giminiani emphasizes the complex ways in which indigenous politics are enmeshed in state forms of ordering – including different forms of property law – and at the same time informed by alternative understandings of the relations between humans and nonhuman entities, in turn shaped by histories longer than those of the nation-state and capitalism.

> Territories undergo continuous cycles of regeneration put in motion by political action as much as embodied experiences in the environment, two actions that are enmeshed since dwelling in specific ways is a political act itself and politics is also made of affects and bodily experiences. (Di Giminiani 2018: 8)

The political actions and embodied experiences of many grassroots indigenous activists engaged in territorial defense in Guatemala are shaped by three factors: First, the climate of criminalization, dispossession, and authoritarian backlash described in the previous section; second, human rights discourses which over three decades have reaffirmed indigenous peoples' rights to self-determination and ancestral lands; and third, accelerating climate change which increasingly threatens the very viability of rural life in many parts of the country, fueling accelerated out-migration. These contentious dynamics are underpinned by historical patterns of state formation forged through racialized structural violence.

In *Theft is Property: Dispossession and Critical Theory*, Nichols builds on the theoretical contributions of North American, Canadian, and Australasian indigenous scholars who analyze the nature and effects of settler colonialism. Land is a central element in the material constitution of group differences, and its legal ordering is central to colonial patterns of appropriation and capital accumulation. Focusing on North America, Nichols analyzes the historical constitution of "land" as an alienable object ("property") codified in law, and the ways this has displaced alternative ontologies of territory.

> "Land" is not a material object but a mediating device, a conceptual and legal category that serves to relate humans to "nature" and to each other in a particular, proprietary manner. (Nichols 2020: 83)

Nichols' central point is that "It is thus not (only) about the *transfer of* property but the *transformation into* property. In this way, dispossession creates an object in the very act of appropriating it." (Nichols 2020: 31). Specific racial subjectivities and forms of ordering have underpinned the development of property law in colonized territories, something Bhandar conceptualizes as "racial regimes of ownership." In her book *Colonial Lives of Property: Law, Land, and Racial Regimes of Ownership*, she signals the need to interrogate, deconstruct, and historically contextualize property laws, stating that:

> Laws of property . . . reflect and consolidate language, ways of seeing, and modes of subjectivity that render indigenous and colonized populations as outside history, lacking the requisite cultural practices, habits of thought, and economic organization to be considered as sovereign, rational, economic subjects. (Bhandar 2018: 3)

By inviting us to denaturalize "land" and property law, Nichols and Bhandar underline the fact that prior to conquest, indigenous and native peoples never "possessed" (or therefore conceived of) *land* in the sense of capitalist commodification. While territory was often the focus of disputes between competing groups, it was animated by multiple ontologies and understood as a complex sentient landscape involving obligations and duties on the part of human beings, rather than something that one has a proprietary *right* to. Anthropologists have long documented the ways in which indigenous epistemologies and ontologies regarding territory tend to be relational, forms of documentation which have acquired a new urgency in the face of accelerated extractivism and climate crisis (de la Cadena 2015; Li 2015). Today, elements of such relational ontologies animate legal disputes over territory and extractive projects, even as conflicts are framed in dominant legal languages, including property and human rights. As I have argued elsewhere, indigenous rights juridification necessarily involves multiple, overlapping, and conflicting frames which may or may not be commensurable (Sieder 2020a).

Colonial orders of dispossession operate in both material and conceptual registers (Nichols 2020). The judicialization of indigenous rights claims has raised important questions about the ways in which alternative understandings of territory are mobilized, disputed, translated, and truncated in legal encounters, as well as how these legal encounters in turn shape political actions and embodied experiences within the territories in dispute. In the following section I discuss legal actions taken by Mayan lawyers' collectives in Guatemala in defense of indigenous peoples' collective rights. I then focus on a specific land claim presented on behalf of the Maya Q'eqchi' communities of Los Copones, Ixcán. I highlight how processes of judicialization have sought to unpack the ways in which certain notions of property and race have been historically co-produced in Guatemala, naturalizing both territorial dispossession and the enslavement of Mayan people during the development of the agro-export economy in the late nineteenth and early twentieth centuries (McCreery 1994). Although constrained by the legal forms of Guatemalan constitutional and civil law, the judicialization processes I describe here go beyond human rights, constituting attempts to destabilize dominant racialized frames that derive from historical and ongoing processes of colonization. The contestations and frictions produced by the interaction of different forms of knowledge point to the limits, but also the politically generative possibilities of such legal encounters.

10.4 Litigating Alter-Worlds?

Is it possible to contest extractive projects through sociolegal mobilization without accepting dominant legal ontologies of private property and state control over subsoil resources? Can indigenous people and their representatives use state law and at the same time dispute legal land ontologies grounded in colonial dispossession? And what does it mean to attempt such actions through the courts in a time of authoritarian regression? One of the most notable features of counterhegemonic legal action in Guatemala is the role of different associations of Mayan lawyers, including the Association of Mayan Lawyers and Notaries of Guatemala Nim Aipu, the Indigenous Peoples Chambers (*Bufete de los Pueblos Indígenas*), and the Association of Popular Legal Chambers of Rabinal (*Asociación Bufete Jurídico Popular de Rabinal*). These collectives were formed in the first years of the twenty-first century, following earlier initiatives in the wake of the 1996 peace accords to open spaces for indigenous people within the legal academy and judiciary.[8] While they litigate to guarantee rights to FPIC and defend criminalized community leaders, they do not limit their arguments to state law and human rights but rather defend indigenous peoples' rights to self-determination, including that of exercising their own forms of law – or land ontologies, in Di Giminiani's terms. By insisting on the prior existence and legitimacy of

[8] For the antecedents of these associations, see González-Serrano and Vaiene (2022).

indigenous peoples' governance systems, and their prior occupation of disputed lands, Mayan lawyers question the legitimacy of the prevailing property regime, putting critical and decolonial perspectives on law into action. As Maya-Kaqchikel lawyer Wendy López, of the *Bufete de los Pueblos Indígenas* told me: "we want to show the state that indigenous peoples are the owners of the earth, we don't need (formal title)."[9]

In contrast to most nonindigenous lawyers, these legal professionals continually experience structural and interpersonal racism in their engagements with the state legal system. Several Mayan women lawyers who have increasingly assumed a prominent role in strategic litigation for indigenous peoples' rights observed that their very presence in the courts revealed the workings of structural racism and gender discrimination. For example, when they appear at state tribunals in indigenous dress, court officials often mistake them for victims, seemingly unable to conceive of the fact that indigenous women can be legal professionals. The lawyers understand their litigation initiatives as just one element of long-running political struggles. In 2019 one colleague told me:

> By this point I'm tired and frustrated. We've been working since 2007 for the defense of territory using the figure of [free, prior, and informed] consultation. The good thing is that people are often very clear about how to defend their territory, they see legal action as a form of support, but not as the end of their processes.[10]

She reflected:

> I don't see what else we can do, the space [for litigating] consultation has been reduced, we need to explore other options. The thing that renews my energies is the reconstitution of [ancestral] authorities and territorial recovery. We need many resources, but we are moving forward.[11]

While indigenous peoples' collective action in recent decades has been at least partially focused on the national courts, it frames a set of claims and arguments based on alternative conceptions of sovereignty that question capitalist understandings of property and Westphalian notions of sovereignty. Through legal battles articulated in the languages of human rights, transnational moral grammars of indigenous lifeworlds have been

[9] Prensa Comunitaria 169 and Fundación MAG, forum: "Los abogados y la múltiple acción jurídica," July 15, 2021.

[10] Interview with Lucía Xiloj, Asociación Bufete Jurídico Popular de Rabinal, November 2019.

[11] Ibid.

mobilized in struggles against environmental and cultural destruction. These struggles are being amplified by global efforts to confront the climate crisis, at the same time as they are a response to the drastically reduced prospects for the physical survival of many communities.

Indigenous lawyers' associations in Guatemala conceive of litigation as just one element in claiming collective rights. Strategic litigation is always viewed as part of broader political processes to strengthen community defense and collective organization for self-determination in everyday lived practice. Well beyond claiming "recognition" from states within neoliberal multicultural models (Povinelli 2002; Hale 2005), the aim of litigation is twofold: to denounce the colonial bases of the dominant economic, political, and legal system, and to contribute to building alternative futures that go far beyond specific legal actions. In their analysis of the work of indigenous lawyers in Guatemala, González-Serrano and Vaiene describe "a dialectical exercise and an ontological encounter within law" in which indigenous lawyers act as bridges between the state's legal institutions and codes, on the one hand, and indigenous practices and concepts on the other (González-Serrano & Vaiene 2022: 101).

While litigation mobilizes arguments framed in terms of constitutional and human rights law, and in some cases civil law, the use of special expert witness reports represents an attempt to place alternative world-views within the state legal arena. These reports include anthropological or cultural interpretations, but also historical analyses; for example, detailing the processes whereby indigenous peoples were dispossessed of their territories when legal title was granted to nonindigenous settlers. Grounded in specific localized contexts, these analyses acquire broader resonance through the legal category of indigenous peoples. By foregrounding alternative understandings of history and the relationship between human beings and their lived environments, the deployment of special expert witness reports before the courts constitutes what might be best understood as moral pedagogies with political effects that extend far beyond the judicial arena. Irrespective of the outcome of litigation, special expert reports have often placed radically different histories and ontologies within the public sphere.

While I and other nonindigenous professionals have provided such reports to the courts, Mayan lawyers' collectives in Guatemala have prioritized collaborations from Mayan professionals, including several distinguished anthropologists, who have assumed a central role in legal and political battles to defend indigenous people. In one well-documented example Maya K'iche' anthropologist and journalist Irma Alicia Velásquez Nimatuj provided a key report for the case of Sepur Zarco, which set a global precedent wherein a domestic court found members of the military guilty of the crime against humanity of forced sexual slavery during an internal armed conflict (Crosby & Lykes 2019; Posocco 2022). Velásquez Nimatuj's collaborative research with Maya Q'eqchi' women survivors of Sepur Zarco explored the relationship between the community's struggle for land title and security of tenure in their ancestral lands, the forced disappearance of the women's husbands, and the women's subsequent enslavement and sexual torture over many years. By documenting the cultural and economic impacts of these intersectional forms of violence, Velásquez Nimatuj's legal deposition clearly underlined the relationship between racialized land dispossession and gender violence (Velásquez Nimatuj 2019).

10.4.1 The Reaffirmation of Ancestral Presence: The Copones Case

Collective rights litigation in defense of indigenous self-determination involves extended collaborative processes between communities resisting different forms of colonial violence, indigenous lawyers' associations, and allied indigenous and nonindigenous professionals. Through the systematization of community histories and collective memory, preparing documentation for legal cases has strengthened political processes of community defense. Anthropological and psychosocial special expert witness reports tend to privilege the voices of indigenous community members, and the litigation strategies of Mayan lawyers also foreground the testimony of affected community members. This emphasis on the experiences and worldviews of indigenous plaintiffs counterbalances the need to recur to state property records to document indigenous territorial dispossession. As Di Giminiani notes, in claims for ancestral land, claimants are:

> paradoxically, forced to prove the consistency of demanded territories as property through technologies of legal documentation, such as deeds of property, archival sources, and maps, initially designed to validate land dispossession. (Di Giminiani 2018: 5)

Los Copones refers to a judicialized claim for recognition of collective title to ancestral indigenous lands, a right guaranteed in general terms by article 67 of Guatemala's Constitution, ILO Convention 169, and the UN

Declaration on the Rights of Indigenous Peoples, but which to date has not altered Guatemala's highly unequal and racialized land tenure regime.[12] The thirty-six communities of Los Copones are Q'eqchi' Maya, located in the northern municipality of Ixcán. Q'eqchi' Maya have inhabited this region for over two centuries. The *amparo* writ presented to the constitutional court in 2015 against the national property registry was a test case which sought recognition of these communities' ancestral possession of the lands known as the finca Patio de Bolas Copón.

The legal claim was supported by several special expert witness reports and amicus curiae. An anthropological-historical special witness report reconstructed the history of Los Copones, demonstrating that the form of community organization in evidence among the Q'eqchi' inhabitants of this region represented a continuity with a prehispanic form of supra-communal governance in the Mayan altiplano, the *amaq'* (Vásquez Monterroso 2017). The study showed how over the course of two centuries the geographical and social conformation of the *amaq'* changed in response to shifting ecological conditions and external threats. The dispersed settlements at the edges of the Chixoy and Copón rivers multiplied and expanded to become the thirty-six communities that today make up Los Copones.

During the late nineteenth century, decentralized and dispersed forms of Q'eqchi' territorial organization in these lowland regions facilitated the absorption of entire communities within the agro-export plantation model. However, what Vásquez Monterroso defines as the *amaq'* of Copones predated the colonization of those lands for the coffee economy. In his report for the court, Vásquez Monterroso drew on oral histories, details of visits of nineteenth century surveyors contained in the land registry, and the writings and maps of settler landowners, ethnographers, and explorers of the region to establish the continuous occupation of Q'eqchi' Maya in the area since around 1760 and possibly even earlier.[13] Effective indigenous possession meant that the denunciation in the late

[12] The Constitution of the Republic states that the lands of indigenous communities "shall enjoy special protection from the State, preferential credit, and technical assistance, which guarantee their possession and development, in order to ensure a better quality of life for all inhabitants ... indigenous communities and others that have lands that historically belong to them and that they have traditionally administered in a special way, will maintain that system" (Article 67).

[13] Diego Vásquez Monterroso (unpublished 2015). "Antigüedad de la presencia Q'eqchi' en la región de 'Los Copones,' Ixcán, Guatemala." Anthropological special expert report presented as part of the litis. Document in authors' archives.

nineteenth century of these lands as "*tierras baldías*" or unclaimed and un-utilized land, was false. The report included an official document of one of the engineers originally sent to measure the territory, who noted the presence of Q'eqchi' peasants and their dwellings. It also included maps published in 1900 by the German ethnographer and landowner Karl Sapper, which indicated that the Q'eqchi' population in the region inhabited territories that were not yet included in the state's property register.

Guatemalan government policies at the end of the nineteenth century promoted a form of racial capitalism that favored commercial export agriculture over indigenous subsistence production, allowing individuals and municipalities to lay claim to untitled lands – evidently, indigenous communities' ancestral lands had never been registered as property. In 1893 the militias of Chinique in the department of Quiché lodged a claim for title of the finca Patio de Bolas Copón, comprising some 356 *caballerías* (16,425 hectares). At the start of the twentieth century title was awarded to the municipality of Chinique and its neighbors ("*vecinos*") in recompense for the support that Chinique's *ladino* (nonindigenous) militias had given to the revolution of Justo Rufino Barrios which cemented the hegemony of the Liberal agro-export model after 1871.[14] The titling process signaled the importance of the Chinique militias to departmental and national politics: In effect, following the denunciation of lands as "*baldías*" (unoccupied and unproductive) the recognition of these claims depended on the executive (the *Jefe Político* of the department, and the president), who rewarded their allies.[15] Previously autonomous indigenous communities were thereby converted into "*fincas de mozos colonos*" or plantations with indentured labor, with inhabitants subjected to forced labor requirements to benefit those who were awarded formal land title,[16] even though all the existing evidence points to the prior and historical occupation by Q'eqchi' Maya. As the historical expert witness report presented to the court stated:

[14] The first land grant of 200 caballerías was made in 1904; the remaining 165 caballerías in 1905.

[15] Juan Carlos Sarazúa Pérez (unpublished 2015). "Titulación y condiciones sociales. Patio de Bolas Copón, 1871–1906." Historical special expert report presented as part of the litis. Document in authors' archives.

[16] The 1877 *Reglamento de Jornaleros* obligated peasants to work for large landowners in productive activities, and in roadbuilding for the state; the 1934 *Ley contra la Vagancia* strengthened the forced labor regime.

> The titling of lands to militias was . . . a political recognition of their members to the cost of populations whose ancestral lands [used for] crop rotation or religious centers, were taken away. This [legal] recognition shows how violence is deeply inscribed in contemporary state institutions, as well as state bias to ensure the titling of many territories.[17]

The most influential nonindigenous family of Chinique, the Urizars, and other prominent militia families now converted into landed local elites, periodically demanded agricultural labor from the Q'eqchi' inhabitants of Los Copones and payment to occupy their subsistence plots. This prompted further displacement of Q'eqchi' peasants, some of whom moved north to try and escape the forced labor regime.[18] The Urizars exercised absolute power over the indigenous inhabitants of the region during the most lethal years of the internal armed conflict in the early 1980s; acting as military commissioners in support of the army they were implicated in the murder of numerous community leaders.[19] Conflict between the Urizars and the municipal authorities of Chinique continued throughout the twentieth century and into the twenty-first. By the mid-1980s, the inhabitants of Los Copones discovered that the legal owners of their lands were not in fact the Urizars but the municipality of Chinique. The families in the community of Margaritas Copón refused to continue working for the Urizars, who sent armed men to threaten them. The community authorities subsequently came to an agreement with Chinique's municipal authorities to leave 30 caballerías (1350 hectares) to the Urizars and pay rent to remain on their lands. The special expert reports detailed the trickery involved: instead of legal rental agreements, the Q'eqchi' Maya peasants handed over "rent" in exchange for worthless pieces of paper which stated they had made voluntary contributions to the festivities of Chinique's patron saint.

Around the time of the peace settlement in 1996, the communities of Los Copones formed an association to negotiate purchase of the finca Patio de Bolas Copón with Chinique's municipal authorities. Yet despite more than a decade and a half of negotiations, and considerable sums of money spent, their efforts came to nothing. By the twenty-first century

[17] Juan Carlos Sarazúa Pérez (2015). Document in authors' archives: 29 (my translation).

[18] Ruth Del Valle Cobár (unpublished 2015). "Efectos psicosociales de las violaciones de derechos humanos de las comunidades de Patio Bolas Copón," Psychosocial special expert report presented as part of the litis. Document in authors' archives.

[19] Ibid.

corrupt state officials and organized crime also began to dispute their territories, located as they are within regions now subject to intensive development of megaprojects, particularly hydroelectric dams. These new threats, combined with a growing awareness of their collective rights as indigenous peoples, prompted the Maya Q'eqchi' inhabitants of Los Copones to seek out the Association of Mayan Lawyers and Notaries of Guatemala Nim Aipu and to judicialize their struggle for territory, seeking legal recognition as indigenous communities with a claim to their ancestral lands.

10.4.2 *Legal and Other Framings*

On behalf of the communities of Los Copones, Nim Ajpu presented an *amparo* writ to the constitutional court against the national property registry, alleging that the process whereby the finca Patios de Bolas Copón had been titled was based on false claims that the lands were "*baldío*" or unoccupied. As part of the process of preparing the legal submission, representatives of the different communities legally registered themselves before the local municipal authorities as a Great Council of Ancestral Authorities, further cementing supracommunal coordination and collective identity as indigenous peoples. The ancestral authorities in each of the thirty-six communities oversee the internal boundaries of the territory, which is divided into family plots which can only be passed down to future generations, not sold. While the ancestral authorities originally dealt only with matters pertaining to territory, by 2022 they were resolving all kinds of problems and disputes, strengthening powers of self-governance.

As part of the preparation for litigation, the centuries-long historical battle by the Q'eqchi' Maya inhabitants of Los Copones for title to their lands was inscribed not only in special expert witness reports, but also in a book entitled *Aquí nacieron mis padres, y aquí vivirán mis nietos. Historia de las comunidades Q'eqchi' de Los Copones* (My parents were born here, and my grandchildren will live here. History of the Q'eqchi' communities of Los Copones), published in 2016. Mayan lawyers and anthropologists had organized numerous workshops since 2010, and in 2015 community researchers carried out interviews in Q'eqchi' with the elders of all the thirty-six communities. The results were translated into Spanish and written up with the support of a members of a local NGO. As members of the Great Council of Ancestral Authorities insisted, the aim of this publication was for the new generations of Los Copones to know the history of their ancestors' struggle. Local teachers now use the book in community schools, with children enacting dramatizations of the fight for land and the racial violence suffered by their parents and grandparents. Legal discourses form part of this narrative, but the principal emphasis is on historical constructions of justice:

> We know that it is not easy for a State that has been neglecting us for more than 500 years to recognize our rights as indigenous peoples, but we are not discouraged, because we know that we are right. Our Mayan grandparents and grandmothers always lived on these lands. Here they built their great cities. Here they created science and technology. They taught us to plant corn, beans, squash, chili. They left us a spirituality that makes sense only if it is related to nature. We have the right to these sacred lands because we work, suffer and care for them.[20]

The constitutional writ cited violation of the Guatemalan Constitution, the International Convention on the Elimination of All Forms of Racial Discrimination, the American Convention on Human Rights, ILO Convention 169, and the UN Declaration on the Rights of Indigenous Peoples. It extensively referenced the jurisprudence of the Interamerican Court of Human Rights, including the 2006 sentence of *Sawhoyamaxa* v. *Paraguay* which stated: "The members of indigenous peoples who have left or lost possession of their traditional lands due to causes beyond their control, maintain rights to property of those lands even if they lack legal title."[21] The claimants argued that their right to file for a constitutional writ of protection was justified by the "permanent and ongoing violation of the rights of indigenous peoples to the access, use, enjoyment, possession and dominion of their property."[22]

The legal action called for the cancellation of the original registry of the property made to the municipality of Chinique, and any subsequent registration of the lands in question deriving from this original action. It stated that "the lack of effective, specific, and regulated procedures for the titling of indigenous communal lands causes generalized uncertainty which is incompatible with the standards set out in article 25 of the American Convention on Human Rights [citing the 2001 case *Comunidad Mayagna (Sumo) Awas Tigni vs. Nicaragua*]."[23]

[20] Puente de Paz et al. (2016: 77) (my translation).
[21] Acción Constitucional de Amparo, p. 5.
[22] Acción Constitucional de Amparo, p. 6.
[23] Acción Constitucional de Amparo, pp. 8–9.

Running to seventy-three pages, the *amparo* writ referred extensively to the three special expert reports presented to the court (anthropological, historical, and psychosocial). The plaintiffs directly appealed to the magistrates, stating:

> The judicialization of our demand for the recognition of our ancestral property is a defense mechanism and an exercise of our human rights that have been systematically and permanently violated by the State, and we seek in this way to reestablish those rights, trying to demonstrate the historical truth of our being a community, of our spiritual relationship with Mother Earth, of that deep love we have for the abundant life with whom we share that space. We have carried out several studies and we have legal certainty of our property.[24]

In effect, the *amparo* writ called on the Guatemalan state not only to void the original grant of property rights made at the turn of the nineteenth century, but to make effective its constitutional and treaty obligations to respect and protect indigenous peoples' collective human rights to their land and territories by issuing a title of collective property to the communities of Los Copones. Referring to a thematic audience at the Interamerican Commission of Human Rights held in 2011, when the government of Guatemala had recognized the absence of agrarian legislation referring to the ancestral collective property rights and therefore the absence of this figure within the country's civil code, the petitioners argued that the matter could not be resolved within civil law procedures.

The *amparo* writ was first admitted by the Appeals Court in the city of Quetzaltenango, where the representative of the property registry asked that it be dismissed as inadmissible, arguing that the registration of the finca Patio de Bolas Copón had met the legal requirements at the time of its inscription. The official also argued that the claim was a matter for civil, not constitutional law.[25] The *amparo* writ was subsequently rejected. In its sentence the court recognized the lack of legislation to

[24] Acción Constitucional de Amparo, p. 31. "La judicialización de nuestra demanda por el reconocimiento de nuestra propiedad ancestral, es un mecanismo de defensa y un ejercicio de nuestros derechos humanos que han sido vulnerados de forma sistemática y permanente por el Estado, y buscamos por esta vía reestablecer esos derechos, tratando de demostrar la verdad histórica de nuestro ser comunitario, de nuestra relación espiritual con la madre tierra, de ese profundo amor que le tenemos a la abundante vida con quien compartimos ese espacio. Hemos realizado varios estudios y tenemos certeza jurídica de nuestra propiedad." (Original in Spanish.)

[25] Informe circunstanciado emitido por la autoridad impugnada, October 5, 2015. Expediente 09002-141934103.

uphold the state's obligations to guarantee indigenous peoples' constitutional rights and human rights as defined by the Interamerican system, but affirmed that remedy lay exclusively with the national legislature. It also argued that the fact that the Maya Q'eqchi' inhabitants of the finca Patio de Bolas Copón had entered negotiations to buy the land from the municipality of Chinique meant that they accepted the latter's legitimate title. The court called on the parties to continue with these negotiations.

The plaintiffs appealed and the case was sent to the constitutional court. In its sentence of November 9, 2020 the court stated that constitutional writs were not the appropriate route to denounce violations of rights to property caused by supposedly illegitimate administrative acts. The court's judgment mentioned ancestral indigenous land rights but defined these as rights to private property and determined that the case should be processed through civil law channels, arguing that these constituted the most effective mechanisms for resolving property disputes. The Association of Mayan Lawyers and Notaries Nim Aipu has sent the case to the Interamerican Commission of Human Rights, arguing that domestic remedies have been exhausted and the collective human rights of the indigenous communities in question to their ancestral lands have not been guaranteed.

10.5 Conclusions

In this chapter I have suggested that the current "juristocratic reckoning" with the promise of indigenous rights should be understood as part of a much longer story of indigenous engagements with racialized colonial legalities. In the late nineteenth and early twentieth centuries, Q'eqchi' Maya in Guatemala engaged with dominant forms of law when they had no rights as citizens and were legally inscribed by dominant elites as forced labor for the agricultural export economy. In the late twentieth century their engagement with dominant legalities coincided with the codification of indigenous peoples' collective rights in international and domestic law. As I have indicated, judicialization to demand indigenous rights to self-determination expanded in Guatemala in the first two decades of the twenty-first century, spearheaded by indigenous lawyers' associations. Yet recent experience has shown that judicial decisions affirming indigenous rights are not transformative of the underlying structures of racial capitalism and dispossession. The resort to hegemonic forms of law to dispute existing understandings of property poses complex challenges, particularly in a context of authoritarian regression and backlash. In the face of state capture and systematic repression, indigenous lawyers hold out scant hope of securing progressive decisions through the courts. Yet they argue that law and legal categories still matter for the ongoing struggles of indigenous peoples, even if the prospects for winning in court are narrowing or disappearing. This is because legal engagements and framings form part of much wider and long-run processes of territorial defense, community organization, and subject formation. Judicialization processes such as the case of Los Copones described here open new possibilities for critically interrogating colonial histories of dispossession as part of a broader emancipatory politics. In this sense, the impact of indigenous lawyers and special expert reports resonate beyond the judicial arena. As I have argued elsewhere (Sieder 2011, 2020a, 2020b) juridification is much more than the use of state law or international human rights law against the state – it also includes the ongoing mobilization, reframing, and continuity of legal and political orders that go beyond racialized colonial legalities, envisioning justice in different registers.

References

Bens, Jonas. 2020. *The Indigenous Paradox: Rights, Sovereignty and Culture in the Americas*. Philadelphia: University of Pennsylvania Press.

Bhandar, Brenna. 2018. *Colonial Lives of Property: Law, Land, and Racial Regimes of Ownership*. Durham, NC: Duke University Press.

2019. Property Abolitionism: Race, Colony, Body, Land. The Disorder of Things blog, May 10, 2019: https://thedisorderofthings.com/2019/05/10/property-abolitionism-race-colony-body-land. Last consulted November 1, 2023.

Botero, Sandra Daniel Brinks and Ezequiel González-Ocantos, eds. 2022. *The Limits of Judicialization: From Progress to Backlash in Latin American Politics*. Cambridge: Cambridge University Press.

Bowen, Rachel E. 2022. Backlash against State Strengthening Reforms: The Rise and Fall of the CICIG in Guatemala. In Sandra Botero, Daniel M. Brinks and Ezequiel A. Gonzalez-Ocantos, eds., *The Limits of Judicialization: From Progress to Backlash in Latin American Politics*. Cambridge: Cambridge University Press, 115–138.

Braconnier, Ana. 2021. Disputing Extractivism at the Court: Elite Countermobilization and Backlash in a (Still) Colonial Guatemala. PhD thesis, Department of Government, University of Texas in Austin.

Crosby Alison and M. Brinton Lykes. 2019. *Beyond Repair? Mayan Women's Protagonism in the Aftermath of Genocidal Harm*. New Brunswick, NJ: Rutgers University Press.

de La Cadena, Marisol. 2015. *Earth Beings: Ecologies of Practice across Andean Worlds*. Durham, NC: Duke University Press.

Di Giminiani, Piergiorgio. 2018. *Sentient Lands: Indigeneity, Property, and Political Imagination in Neoliberal Chile*. Tucson, AZ: University of Arizona Press.

Eckert, Julia Brian Donahoe, Christian Strümpell and Zerrin Özlem Biner, eds. 2012. *Law Against the State: Ethnographic Forays into Law's Transformations*. Cambridge: Cambridge University Press.

González-Ocantos, Ezequiel A. 2016. *Shifting Legal Visions: Judicial Change and Human Rights Trials in Latin America*. Cambridge: Cambridge University Press.

González-Serrano, María Ximena and Lieselotte Viaene. 2022. La acción jurídica indígena en Guatemala Voces de resistencia y conexión. In *Aguas Turbias Extractivismo (neo)liberal, acción jurídica indígena y transformación del Estado en Guatemala, María Jacinta Xon and Lieselotte Viaene (Coords.)*, Guatemala: Catafixia, 89–126.

González-Serrano, María Ximena, Digno José Montalván-Zambrano and Lieselotte Viaene. 2022. Hacia la descolonización del régimen extractivo: patrones y límites de la judicialización en conflictos mineros. *Íconos: Revista de Ciencias Sociales* 72: 97–116.

Goodale, Mark. 2016. Dark Matter: Toward a Political Economy of Indigenous Rights and Aspirational Politics. *Critique of Anthropology* 36 (4): 439–457.

2022. *Reinventing Human Rights*. Stanford: Stanford University Press.

Hale, Charles R. 2005. Neoliberal Multiculturalism: The Remaking of Cultural Rights and Racial Dominance in Central America. *PoLAR Political and Legal Anthropology Review* 28 (1): 10–28.

IACHR (Interamerican Commission on Human Rights). 2021. Derecho a la libre determinación de los Pueblos Indígenas y Tribales. OEA/Ser.L/V/II. Doc.413/21 Available at: www.oas.org/es/cidh/informes/pdfs/LibreDeterminacionES.pdf. Last consulted November 1, 2023.

Kirsch, Stuart. 2018. Dilemmas of an Expert Witness in the Amazon. Working Paper #428, Kellog Institute for International Studies, Notre Dame, IN.

2012. Jurifidication of Indigenous Politics. In Julia Brian Donahoe Eckert, Christian Strümpell and Zerrin Özlem Biner, eds., *Law against the State: Ethnographic Forays into Law's Transformations*. Cambridge: Cambridge University Press, 23–43.

Li, Tania. 2015. *Unearthing Conflict: Corporate Mining, Activism, and Expertise in Peru*. Durham, NC: Duke University Press.

McCreery, David. 1994. *Rural Guatemala. 1760–1940*. Stanford University Press.

Montoya, Ainhoa, Rachel Sieder and Yacotzin Bravo Espinosa. 2022. Juridificación multiescalar frente a la industria minera: experiencias de Centroamérica y México. *Iconos Revista de Ciencias Sociales* 72: 57–78.

Nichols, Robert. 2020. *Theft is Property: Dispossession and Critical Theory*. Durham, NC: Duke University Press.

Posocco, Silvia. 2022. Sepur Zarco, Guatemala: "Bodying Forth" and Forensic Aesthetics of Witnessing in the Courtroom and beyond. *Feminist Anthropology* 3 (1): 12–27.

Puente de Paz, Acodet and Asociación de Abogados Mayas. 2016. *Aquí nacieron mis padres, y aquí vivirán mis nietos. Historia de las comunidades Q'eqchi' de Los Copones*. Guatemala: Fotopublicaciones.

Sieder, Rachel. 2011. Building Mayan Authority and Autonomy: The "Recovery" of Indigenous Law in Post-peace Guatemala. In A. Sarat, ed., *Studies in Law, Politics, and Society*, Vol. 55. Leeds: Emerald, 25–57.

2020a. "To Speak the Law" Contested Jurisdictions, Legal Legibility, and Sovereignty in Guatemala. *PoLAR* 43 (2): 334–351.

2020b. The Juridification of Politics. In Marie-Claire Foblets, Mark Goodale, Alison Dundes Renteln and Olaf Zenker, eds., *The Oxford Handbook of Law and Anthropology*. Oxford: Oxford University Press, 701–715.

Sieder, Rachel and Santiago Bastos. 2015. Pueblos indígenas en Guatemala: rearticulación comunitaria y disputa de legalidades en la democracia neoliberal. In Laura Raquel Valladares de la Cruz, ed., *Nuevas violencias en América Latina: Los derechos indígenas ante las políticas neoextractivistas y las políticas de seguridad*. UAM: Mexico, 141–183.

Stavenhagen, Rodolfo. 2002. Indigenous People and the State in Latin America: An Ongoing Debate. In Rachel Sieder, ed., *Multiculturalism in Latin America: Indigenous Rights, Diversity and Democracy*. New York: Palgrave Macmillan, 24–44.

Vásquez Monterroso, Diego. 2017. *La construcción de un amaq' moderno: los Copones, Ixcán, Quiché (1760–2015)*. Guatemala: Universidad Rafael Landívar.

Velásquez Nimatuj, Irma Alicia. 2019. *"La justicia nunca estuvo de nuestro lado"Peritaje cultural sobre conflicto armado y violencia sexual en el caso Sepur Zarco, Guatemala*. Bilbao: UPV/EHU-Hegoa.

11

"A Dead Child Is Better than a Missing One"

Religiosity, Technology, and Aspirations for Justice beyond Law

KAMARI MAXINE CLARKE

While attending a conference in Mexico City during fieldwork in 2018, I heard a speech by a mother who had lost three of her sons to forced disappearances linked to drug cartels. We listened as she pledged to the audience that she would not rest until she knew the fate of her sons, that she was determined to locate their remains. After months of inaction by lawmakers, continuing her search required this mother to sidestep the prosecutor's office and other state institutions that had been her recourse for justice. She had turned instead to alternatives offered by science and technology. Partnering with community-based and nongovernmental organizations, she trained herself in the use of new technologies – geospatial technologies, ground sensing, crowdsourcing – that are increasingly used today to track the remains of loved ones.

In rejecting the traditional criminal justice and legal processes that had failed her, this mother affirmed that she was prioritizing not juridical resolutions but, rather, a pathway toward memorialization and closure. As she spoke, her voice cracked and her face wavered even through moments of great declarative agency; her search was threaded with pain. In responding to the mother's plight, a prosecutor in the audience offered a technocratic lament, citing the difficulties that families of the missing face in overcoming admissibility of evidence issues related to information they have unearthed about remains. For the prosecutor, the law's rules set the conditions for justice, and within this framework one mother's personal mission can be cast as futile at best, a costly diversion at worst.

In reflecting on both narratives – the mother's rejection of legal processes and the prosecutor's loyalty to them – as an ethnographer and theorist, I was struck by the productive tension between the two convictions: on the one hand, a vision of science and technology offering up tools to facilitate an elusive process of personal and collective mourning, and on the other, a confidence in the power of evidentiary procurements to enable judicial justice. Each narrative enabled a very different perspective on the missing and on human remains and their purposes. The contrast between these underlying interests and the mechanisms on which their subjects pinned their hope and faith continued to haunt me over subsequent years as I partnered with a team of researchers to interview family members who had lost loved ones in Mexico and in a field site I have worked for many years, Nigeria.

Amid broad recognition in both these countries of a collapse in the state's ability to provide security or justice, growing numbers of survivors appear to be turning away from the pursuit of legal justice mechanisms and toward a kind of grassroots quest for closure. In the process, some are building new alliances, not with judicial actors but rather with NGOs and research scientists who offer access to new technologies that might help locate the disappeared and even mitigate future violence via Early Warning Early Response (EWER) programs. Once the purview of the state and its legal systems, these functions of "search and secure" are being taken up in unlikely collaborations between ordinary local survivors and international technocratic networks capable of operating independently of nation-states. This trend points toward a large-scale recognition of the evacuation of the biopolitical state that appears increasingly inept, its politico-legal remedies accomplishing little in the wake of compounded violence and tragedy. As judicial solutions appear increasingly ineffective and meaningless for impacted communities, what does this foreshadow about more globalized futures as people engage reckon with justice "after law"?

The dynamics in Mexico and Nigeria highlight tensions between two crises: the crisis of extrajudicial killing through unmitigated vigilante violence and the seeming collapse of the postcolonial state experiment (Lomnitz 2024). Since 2006, when Mexico began a war on drugs, more than 40,000 people remain "disappeared" as violence between organized criminal groups and the Mexican government has escalated. At least 26,000 unidentified human bodies are stockpiled in regional morgues (Arteta 2019). State institutions have been largely unable to identify remains, investigate, or follow up on cases, and some of the most prominent cases have drawn accusations of cover-ups by state actors. One of the most haunting concerns a group of missing students from Ayotzinapa Rural Teachers' College in Iguala, Guerrero, Mexico. On September 26, 2014 forty-three male students went missing. Official Mexican government reports state that the students disappeared while en route to commemorate the anniversary of the 1968 Tlatelolco Massacre of student activists, and that they were later mistaken for a drug gang, taken into custody, and killed. In light of public questions about the plausibility of the government's findings, and with little progress being made by law enforcement, the Inter-American Court conducted a six-month investigation and determined that the government's explanation was not viable. Remains have never been found and no one has been arrested in conjunction with the disappearances. Nationwide protests and international condemnations have fueled the resolve of a coalition of family members, concerned citizens, lawyers, scientists, and technologists to carry on an independent search for bodily remains. Family members and advocates have formed more than seventy collectives; participants receive forensic training and scour morgues, jails, and potential burial sites in search of loved ones. Many are now working under the umbrella of a united national group, Movement for Our Disappeared in Mexico, a social mobilization that stretches across the country (Wilkinson 2019). Supported by the Truth & Justice Commission established in 2018 by President López Obrador and by allies such as the Argentine Forensic Anthropology Team (EAAF), these collectives are successfully finding evidence of clandestine graves and are exhuming bodies in several of Mexico's most violent states. Encouraged by their successes, they are demanding and innovating more access to technologies and to platforms to share their findings.

In Nigeria, the focus of this chapter, thousands of citizens have been victims of violence and disappearances related to the radical insurgency campaign Boko Haram. Based in northeastern Nigeria, Boko Haram is a jihadist terrorist organization founded by Mohammad Yusuf in 2002. Translated as "western education must be forbidden," Boko Haram was initially conceived in opposition to perceived western influences in Nigerian culture with the goal of forming an Islamic state in Northern Nigeria. Following a 2002 raid by the Nigerian government leading to the death of its leader, the organization accelerated its use of violence and has brought the northeastern region into turmoil through destruction of government buildings, churches, and civilian centers, as well as killings and disappearances of civilians of all ages. Moreover, as part of its counterinsurgency campaign, Nigerian police have engaged in unlawful killings, torture, and enforced disappearances throughout the country. Boko Haram became internationally known as a result of the abduction and disappearance of more than 250 schoolgirls from Chibok, Nigeria, in April 2016. The

#BringBackOurGirls campaign mobilized a global social movement of activists, politicians, and celebrities. Locally, the intervention effort took the form of family members and civil society organizations collaborating with investigators, legal experts, and scientists to deploy scientific crisis-tracking technologies to identify the girls and attempt to prevent future violence. This mobilization created a precedent for efforts that are ongoing, and which are gradually changing the terrain of governance in Nigeria.

The violence in Northern Nigeria has become endemic and reflects a range of motives and actors far more complex than is generally acknowledged in analyses of Boko Haram. In Nigeria's Kaduna and Plateau States, our research team spoke with people who attributed the abduction and killing of their loved ones to a scourge of criminal activity waged by bandits intent on ransom, theft of occupied land, and forced displacement of villagers. This criminal activity unfolded largely with impunity in light of the marked absence of police or other security services. When we asked surviving loved ones about the search for forensic evidence that could allow for the pursuit of justice through the court system, they answered time and time again with expressions of futility, echoing a pervasive stance that such activity would be pointless.

As in Mexico, Nigerians we spoke with understood the institution of policing and its legal protocols to be sites of oblivion. Police stations were viewed as places where reports are sent to die and courts as empty theatres where legal professionals meet failure before even attempting success. A powerful Yoruba proverb reverberated throughout interviews: *Ọmọ ẹni kú sán jù ọmọ ẹni nú lọ* (a dead child is better than a missing one). While this sentiment – that it is better to know that one's child is dead than to agonize indefinitely – may be universal among families seeking closure when loved ones have disappeared for long periods, in places like Mexico and Nigeria the sheer scale of the crisis of vigilante and extrajudicial killing has made the proverb prophetic: Due to a dire combination of extreme, protracted violence and the failure of state responses, entire communities are organizing at a collective and even cultural level to seek evidence of the death of loved ones.

In this context, we are seeing that when states fail to provide security or justice, people respond to crises by brokering their own solutions. Whereas legal institutions have traditionally shaped the process of recovering and interpreting human remains within the framework of the modern nation-state, contemporary recovery efforts in places like Nigeria and Mexico are challenging the state's perceived monopoly on this function, with important consequences for the relationship between state power and technology. In *Reframing Rights: Bioconstitutionalism in the Genetic Age*, Sheila Jasanoff (2011) argues that certain types of bodies (victims, perpetrators, pro-accountability interveners) are being reshaped in the contemporary period (Agathangelou, A. M. (forthcoming). Race, racism, and global power. Bristol University Press; Foucault 1977, 1988; Jan Rupp 1992). Arguing that there is a fundamental transformation underway in the relationships among biology, law, and biotechnology, she introduces the concept of "bioconstitutionalism," naming the ways in which "radical shifts in the biological representation of life necessarily entail far-reaching reorderings in our imagination of the state's life-preserving and life-enhancing functions – in effect, a repositioning of human bodies and selves in relation to the state's legal, political, and moral apparatus" (Jasanoff 2011: 4). Jasanoff helps us to rethink how the waning of the law's reach repositions bodies and reframes rights (Pottage 2017), yet as useful as this intervention is, Jasanoff is less interested in the ways in which quotidian applications of science intersect with religious frameworks, and how these synergize toward the construction of new processes for social repair beyond or outside of the mechanism of law. This chapter, focusing on the imbrication of religion, technology, and justice in Nigeria, begins to address that gap.

In pondering the future of social justice by considering new ways in which people are engaging with the postcolonial state experiment, this chapter asks who is equipped to uncover – and, in effect, to save – the biological body. What new and traditional resources are local communities bringing to bear as they forge post-juristocratic landscapes in the shadow of state absence, and what are the implications of their efforts beyond their geographic borders? Drawing on ethnographic cases, I suggest that the post-juristocratic is best seen as a *state of reckoning* in which law's aspirational possibilities are inundated with fissures that render transparent its challenges. As citizens sidestep the law's constraints, leaping beyond its inefficacy, they are gathering new forms of agency and alliance that point toward the possibility of broader, perhaps globalized, alternative futures for law and justice. Nigeria presents a particularly apt case study in this respect. The state of insecurity around life and death in Nigeria – the so-called Giant of Africa – illuminates how threats to both bodily security and economic infrastructure necessitate a collective reckoning around the very terms of life. Here, I explore the possibility that contemporary emergencies may not only signal the waning into oblivion of the postcolonial state but may also be ushering in a new post-juristocratic state form that relates to the biological and juridical subject in novel ways.

Of central importance to this emergence is what I call a *transformation of senses* around knowing and locating the body. Whereas the (post) colonial state had attempted to cede the authority to locate and interpret bodies to legal domains, contemporary movements using tools that exceed legality are privileging and reviving alternative domains: new technologies and (re)newed forms of religiosity. Together, these twin forces appear to be facilitating a reinterpretation of what it means to pursue justice – and, indeed, what it means to be human – that may gradually negate the authority of the nation-state's institutions, unmask its performances, and transgress its borders. To adequately theorize this turn toward new cosmologies of justice, I first provide a historical and contemporary account of the role of religion in the Nigerian case study.

Since 2009, even as extreme violence has proliferated, there has been a large-scale embrace of evangelical and fundamentalist sects of both Christianity and Islam in Nigeria. These sects, often linked to transnational networks, reject traditional hierarchies of religious authorities who have historically acted as faith mediators. Astonishing numbers in Nigeria are turning, in a kind of democratizing moment, toward direct experiences of spiritual fervor and the promises of prosperity and justice they are purported to bring. This shift provides a glimpse of a future in which evangelizing modalities of religious faith are expanding and thriving even as traditional religious canons are in decline. I suggest that the move toward new and innovative religious practices is concurrent with the move toward communities directly assuming agency over new technologies, and that each strategy is fundamentally linked to a desire to address persistent insecurity in the face of proliferating violence and the failure of state governance to act. Ultimately, this shift may have profound implications for the future of democracy, governance, the state, and justice. The Nigerian case offers insights into the emergence of new possibilities for mitigating harm and procuring restorative options through religious and technological tools that are perceived to empower ordinary people to unearth and cope with past, present, and future loss – with or without institutional sanction or support.

11.1 Nigerian Pentecostalism as a Social Technology of Power

The presence of Christianity in Nigeria can be traced back to the fifteenth century when early missionaries attempted to evangelize the west coast of

Africa (Adewale & Abu 2013: 122). In the first wave, Portuguese missionaries worked to convert communities in Benin and Warri, where indigenous cosmologies mapped relatively well on to Christian frameworks. Later, Catholics attempted to Christianize people in the Borno and Hausaland regions of what is now Northern Nigeria, an effort that eventually fizzled out (Galadima & Turaki 2001: 92). These missionary activities unfolded alongside the evolution of the slave trade, and continued after abolition in 1807: The modern missionary movement began when British Anglican institution the Church Missionary Society (CMS) saw an opportunity in a population of Africans already exposed to Christianity through the experience of enslavement (Adewale & Abu 2013: 122). Former slaves turned theologians became trailblazers in propagating Christian missions throughout the region, particularly in Yorubaland (now southwestern Nigeria). Ultimately, the CMS's efforts helped build the cultural infrastructure that would facilitate further colonization of the region by Britain.

Anglicanism remained the dominant form of Christianity in Nigeria until the twentieth century when Pentecostalism launched "renewal" missions across Africa (Lindhardt 2014). In Nigeria, this development is traced to a 1910 local charismatic movement led by a deacon who separated from the Anglican Church to establish the Christ Army Church. Charismatic units grew rapidly and formed independent churches characterized by fervent prayer styles, with followers known by the Yoruba word *Aladura* (praying people). By the start of the 1950s, Pentecostalism was spreading even more widely in Nigeria. Martin Lindhardt (2014) argued that the growth of Pentecostalism was due to efforts to break away from western missionary control. To him, this inherent anticolonialism accounted for the popularity of many African-initiated churches focused on prophecy and healing. In the 1960s, after Nigeria's independence from the British government, and through the period of the Biafran civil war into the 1970s, a second wave of Pentecostal expansion emerged in Nigeria, this one characterized by student-organized revivals on college campuses (Lindhardt 2014). Today, Nigeria has the largest population of Pentecostals in Africa, with a 2006 study reporting that three out of ten Nigerians identify as either Pentecostal or charismatic (Unah 2017).

Given its scale, Pentecostalism has influenced popular culture even beyond the domain of the faithful, impacting a broader collective imagination with regard to a range of personal, political, socioeconomic, and moral issues (Obadre 2022). Thus, Nigerian Pentecostalism functions as a kind of emergent technology of knowledge during a time of endemic societal crisis. Through its charismatic and transcendent modes of worship, the religion continually reinforces an understanding that supernatural forces undergird the manifestation of all phenomena. In engaging with these forces, Pentecostal worshippers are in essence seeking a kind of power with which to access social, political, or economic capital and agency over their profoundly uncertain daily realities (Adelakun 2022). Against the background of a history of authoritarian and increasingly ineffective governance by the state, Nigerians are increasingly turning to this option, and it is an option that offers them a sense of power amid a context of disempowerment.

For Nimi Wariboko (2014) and Obadre (2022), Pentecostals are split between the visible and the invisible worlds. To extract knowledge from the invisible realm is to explain, predict, and control the visible world. Power is thus an important identity marker for Nigerian Pentecostals. And some would argue that Pentecostals' fixation with supernatural power creates real-life consequences through actions undertaken to manipulate the material by channeling the invisible. The Pentecostal religion developed in Nigeria in the context of various crises of modernity, development, and identity, and that context is reflected in its tremendous popularity as a mechanism for gaining agency in the face of forces one cannot control (Vaughan 2016). Ruth Marshall (2019) similarly insists that Pentecostalism has transcended its status as a mere identity within Christianity by promising processes of conversion and transformation that have the power to reconstitute the lived social worlds of the faithful. Within this cosmology, believers are no longer passive subjects of large institutions but are transformed into holders of power. This transformation is embodied in moments of heightened spiritual prowess when, for example, Pentecostals vigorously summon powers from the Holy Spirit to violently attack enemies and obstacles blocking their progress or causing them suffering (Adelakun 2022). It is also woven into two of the bedrock principles of Nigerian Pentecostal culture: the preaching of prosperity and its corollary, the doctrine of giving.

There are two schools of thought regarding the emergence in Nigeria of the prosperity gospel: the proclamation that the will of God is for Christians to live in material prosperity. The first argues that prosperity gospel ideology was exclusively an American phenomenon aggressively exported to Nigeria, while the second argues that it is an inherently African ideology nurtured and propagated on African soil. Bridging these approaches, Omavuebe (2021) has argued that the Nigerian prosperity gospel is a hybrid theology that integrates elements of the American prosperity gospel ideology, originating in the American New Thought movement, and Nigerian revivalism. In referencing specific biblical scriptures, evangelists of this gospel assert that Christians can expect affluence through faith (Amadi 2013). For example, Deuteronomy 8:18 states, "But thou shall remember the Lord thy God, for it is he that giveth thee power to get wealth," and Psalm 112:1–3 states, "Blessed is the man that feareth the Lord, wealth and riches shall be in his house." Pentecostal pastors employ these and other passages to emphasize the claim that God expects every Christian to be materially prosperous. As scholars have argued, people living in conditions of poverty whose options are severely limited by structural forces may be especially attracted to such a perspective (Amadi 2013). In a moment of widespread economic hardship and threats to basic security, the prosperity gospel has rendered Nigerian Pentecostalism enormously marketable (Eyo et al. 2020).

A twin doctrine to the prosperity gospel – also widespread in Nigerian Pentecostalism – is the doctrine of giving, which urges members to tithe to the church in order to sow seeds of future prosperity. While most wealth gathered through this doctrine is accumulated – and often spectacularly consumed – at the level of church leadership, Pentecostal churches also hold special giving ceremonies through which some wealth is redistributed to the poor and needy. This structure creates a compelling tether between tithing members and the church organization, and it has undoubtedly improved the financial status of many Pentecostal churches in Nigeria, enabling them to carry out several projects that have enhanced the socioeconomic well-being of many people. In the context of a society in which state institutions have failed to provide basic social welfare, massive churches have filled some of the void through projects like financial empowerment programs for members, grade schools and universities, media outlets, employment, clothing and food drives, micro-loans, and outreach to orphanages and hospitals (Asuquo 2020). This quasi-state function was especially prominent during the COVID-19 pandemic, when Nigeria's major Pentecostal churches – including RCCG, Living Faith Church, Mountain of Fire, Deeper Life Church, and Foursquare – came out in force to assist the government in distributing relief to citizens. Such activity in turn increases the popularity of these churches, growing the base of members who tithe. Modest estimates hold that there is one Pentecostal church for every twenty households in urban areas of south, southeast, and southwest Nigeria (Eyoboka 2004). Particularly in these regions,

Pentecostalism is in a strong position to continue its transformation of social consciousness writ large, and its increasing role fulfilling functions traditionally carried out by the state. In the northern region, a similar phenomenon is unfolding through the rise of Islamic fundamentalism.

11.1.1 Stance of Resistance: The Rise and Resilience of Islamic Fundamentalism in Nigeria

Uthman Dan Fodio's Jihad of 1804–8 marked the beginning of Islamic fundamentalism in Northern Nigeria, and this region has experienced some level of religious conflict ever since (Agai 2014). The goal of the Jihad included the spread of Islamic compliance as inscribed in the Holy Quran (2:190–191): "Fight for the cause of God those that fight you but do not transgress limits; for God loveth not transgressors. And slay them wherever you catch them, and turn them out from where they have turned you out." Dan Fodio called on his followers to use force to take over lands occupied by *infidels* (Dar al-Harb), and transform them into lands of the faithful (Dar al-Islam) (Agai 2014). Islam succeeded in Northern Nigeria in part due to the region's relative defiance of British colonialism and in part due to the stark differentiation it offered from Christian influences in the south. Britain carried out its colonial project through indirect rule, which systematically empowered local leaders and, in the case of Nigeria, favored leaders in the Christian south. As a result, Christian values and jurisprudence were elevated while Islamic values and judicial principles were relegated to "figurehead" status within the colonial state, a reality that the retreat of British colonial rule only exacerbated (Žebrauskaitė n.d.).

Nigeria's independence in 1960 brought about a form of secularization that undermined political Islamism, the framework that asserts Muslims should be ruled by the laws of God rather than those of the state. Despite the pressure to conform to an idealized secularism, the long-lasting Islamic tradition uniting Northern Nigeria with the rest of North Africa and separating it culturally from southern Nigeria has prevailed. Yet it is important to acknowledge that the northern region is not monolithic. For example, Muslim communities in north-central Nigeria have long joined their southern neighbors in agitating against a perceived Islamization of public institutions (Žebrauskaitė n.d.). Today, many moderate Muslims and Christians believe that extremists in Northern Nigeria are intent on Islamizing the entire country. This perception has grown gradually and is based on events including the adoption of criminal Sharia law in 1999 by twelve northern states (Ostien 2011), the inclusion of Nigeria as a member of the organization of Islamic conference in 1986, and the country's new status as a beneficiary of the Islamic Development Bank in 2005.

The growth of Islamic fundamentalism in Nigeria, as well as elsewhere in Africa, is rooted in a response to the conditions of colonization that continue to manifest in severe quality of life disparities (Žebrauskaitė n.d.). In Nigeria, specifically, differential policies by the British Empire translated into better access for southern communities to colonial infrastructure around education, medicine, bureaucracy, and science. Today, benefits from natural resource wealth and economic growth are distributed unequally, with the Muslim majority in the northern regions often left behind. According to data published in EduCeleb, the 2017 national literacy rate was 65.1 percent (Amoo 2018), with southern states ranked above the national average and all northern states falling below, with a far greater gender gap. The enduring legacy of this history has made the region vulnerable to extremist political leaders.

The Jama'atu Ahli's Sunna Lidda'awati Wal-Jihad sect, also known as Boko Haram, was established in 1995 with the aim of purifying Islam through a struggle against Christians, the Nigerian government, and certain Muslims deemed to not be living according to Islamic law. The militarization of Boko Haram can be traced to July 2009 when, over four days, members of the sect burned churches and killed Christians across the region. In subsequent years, Boko Haram has carried out many terrorist attacks and kidnappings targeting both Christians and moderate Islamic clerics and Muslim politicians (Agai 2014). Islamic fundamentalism continues to gain momentum as groups like Boko Haram call for socioeconomic justice for the ordinary people of Northern Nigeria who feel they have been systematically excluded from economic benefits enjoyed in the south. Boko Haram's propaganda portrays the Nigerian state as decadent, corrupt, and irrelevant, calling for its destruction and the establishment of a pure and just Islamic society (Anugwom 2018). Dire socioeconomic conditions, particularly in the northeast region where Boko Haram concentrates its recruitment efforts, have produced a generation of young men searching for a pathway toward greater economic security and for belonging and purpose (Anugwom 2018). The rise of Islamic fundamentalism has thus been linked to the extreme poverty that millions of Nigerians endure (Abumere 2016).

Having introduced the evolution and current broad appeal of evangelical Christianity and fundamentalist Islam in Nigeria, I turn now to a consideration of the core beliefs about death that each cosmology offers before returning to a consideration of how technology aligned with religiosity is transforming Nigerians' beliefs about loss, justice, and the state.

11.2 Death and Afterlife in Yoruba Cosmology, Christianity, and Islam

In historic Yoruba cosmologies of southern Nigeria, death is not seen as the end of life but rather as a transition from one form of existence to another. It marks the end of an existence that is known and the beginning of one that is unknown. Scholars of African religion have argued that immortality is the dream of many Africans, and it is understood that this state can only be achieved in the afterlife. But the Yoruba also believe that participation in the afterlife is dependent on the nature of one's death. The desirable goal of becoming an ancestor after death cannot be achieved if an individual did not live a meaningful life, or if his or her life was cut short through an accident or "unnatural" death (Ekore & Abass 2016). A person who is missing or disappeared is in an especially precarious position. It is regarded as great mental torture if one's loved one, relation, or friend is declared missing or lost. In fact, this tragedy is treated almost as a taboo, with a belief that death would actually be preferable to disappearance.

For many Yoruba, no "Ebo" (sacrifice) or "Ogun" (medicine) can stop a person from dying when their time has come. A disappearance frustrates this clarity and is often described as a state of limbo between the finality of death and the hope that one may sustain in the face of injury or illness. In Yoruba cosmology, death in old age is an occasion of celebration rather than mourning. The assumption is that the elderly await death eagerly knowing that burial rites will reunite them with their ancestors. When a person is disappeared, it is not possible to perform these rites. Hence, in popular Yoruba worldviews, a lost individual attracts shame and mental torture while death attracts fame and treasure, allowing for closure and even celebration for the living who remain. Within Yoruba cosmology, the failure to locate remains and provide a proper burial can lead to the individual becoming a wandering ghost, unable to live properly after death (Ekore & Abass 2016). A missing individual cannot be accepted into the ancestral realm, and in this tortured state may even become a force of danger for those who are still alive.

In Northern Nigeria, traditional cosmologies are similar. The destiny of a person's soul is tied to both their sociopolitical status and the determination of whether those around them have carried out the proper funeral rites. Despite the emergence and dominance of Islam, "[t]he Hausa world view exhibits a strong belief in the existence of spirits and their interaction with human beings" (Danfulani 1999: 413) and considers the appearance of spirits to be a manifestation of God's power. Thus, everyone is "entitled to a ceremonial burial in order that his soul might finally be dismissed to join the company of his forefathers, and that his living relatives might be cleansed from the pollution of death" (Ogbuagu 1989: 88).

For Muslims following Islamic religious and Arabic cultural traditions, the deceased are to be buried as soon as possible after death, their bodies washed and dressed in cloth. This practice follows the Prophet Muhammad's guidance: "Hurry up with the dead body for if it was righteous, you are forwarding it to welfare; and if it was otherwise, then you are putting off an evil thing down your necks" (Sahih al-Bukhari 1315). Among many Hausa, engaging in the proper rites and homilies is key to death's journey, and maintaining the corporeal body is important for the long journey in which the deceased is made to account for their lifetime deeds (Pilaszewicz 1988: 53). Following such a journey, it is believed that two angelic figures appear to the deceased and interrogate them to determine whether they will face punishment or redemption (Hiskett 1982: 42). Various Hausa beliefs about death can found in homiletic songs and poetry, inspired by Arab and Islamic traditions, which provide religious guidance on how to live a life that allows passage into heaven and a reminder of the day of judgment. Homiletic verses depict the temporal world as the negative, transient opposite of the eternal afterlife, and reflect an understanding that death not only is inevitable but can come for anyone (Pilaszewicz 1988).

In the Christian tradition, death can be considered both a punishment for sin and a passage toward redemption. As with Yoruba and other indigenous African cosmologies, Christianity asserts the continuity of life after death. Death is the portal to a new existence in either heaven or hell, with souls routed to one or the other based on a final judgment of their sins and/or belief (Vogt 2004). In Christian rhetoric death is often described as a kind of sleep from which one can be resurrected (as in the case of Jesus) (Atari 2021). Christian sects, including Pentecostalism, hold that the faithful will be woken from death and granted eternal life. Many Christians describe death as an opportunity to access higher glory and eternal life. It is a state that has been conquered by Christ, and this same transcendence is accessible to Christians through belief in his status as savior. This belief is reflected in passages from scripture such as "O death where is your victory? Where, O death is your sting? The sting of death is sin, and the power of sin is the law. But thanks to God, he gives us the victory through our Lord Jesus Christ" (1 Corinthians 15:54–57; see also Ayodeji 2013) and "Everyone who believes in me will never die" (John 11:26) (see also Ayodeji 2013).[1] Christianity espouses a confidence in reunion after death with the Holy Trinity (Jesus, God, the Holy Spirit) as well as with faithful loved ones. Both traditional Yoruba and Pentecostal Christian frameworks therefore speak to the ways that religious worlds shape ways of coping with loss and the possibility of death without the guarantee of certainty.

Islam's concept of death shares similarities with those of Christianity and African traditional religions. In Islam, death is seen not as the termination of life, but rather as the continuation of life in another form, and this worldly life is understood as a test and preparation ground for the afterlife (Leaman 2006: 27). In Islam, death is predetermined by Allah, who knows each person's exact time of death. Death is accepted as wholly natural and merely marks a transition between the material realm and the unseen world (Turner 2011: 125). Islam further teaches that no one has the power to take a human life because all lives ultimately belong to Allah. Within this understanding, one can take another's life if their appointed time of death has come. Some hold that true believers and the righteous welcome death when it arrives, eschewing notions that death is painful or an experience to fear (Hughes 1995: 79). The Quran itself mentions that certain individuals, such as martyrs, are alive despite their apparent death (2:154).

Certain Muslim traditions argue that it is possible to contact the living dead by sleeping in graveyards (Diem & Scholler 2004), and visiting the graves of holy persons or prophets is a common practice among some Muslim sects. The Quran discusses death and its inevitability on several occasions, including the frequently quoted verse, "Every soul shall taste death and only on the Day of Judgment will you be paid your full recompense" (3:185). In general, death is not a taboo subject in a Muslim society and is by contrast a matter upon which one is encouraged to reflect frequently (Campo 2009: 185). In fact, aversion to death and

[1] Ayodeji 2013: 508–515.

love for the world are seen as two aspects of ignorance. The faithful are encouraged to eschew worldly enjoyment in light of the larger reality of death and afterlife. And when spiritual leaders counsel Muslims regarding terminal illness or bereavement, this understanding of death – as inevitable and even to be welcomed – is emphasized.

11.2.1 Technologies of Prediction: How Twenty-First-Century Nigeria Harnesses Religiosity and Technology to Challenge the State's Monopoly on Managing Violence

The proliferation of evangelical and fundamentalist forms of Christianity and Islam in Nigeria, mapped against Yoruba cosmologies, troubles the secular ("western") political values that the British colonial state in the region attempted to impose and that the postcolonial state has failed to secure. It is critical to understand this broader context as the backdrop for the current uptick in grassroots and civil society movements that compete with and even bypass the state functions of security and justice in the face of extreme violence, mass disappearances, and enduring instability. Just as fundamentalist religion offers hope to the economically disenfranchised, new technologies offer a strategy around which to mobilize community-based efforts to locate loved ones' remains and even to prevent ongoing cycles of violence. More specifically, just as religion and the hope of future redemption enables people to cope with loss, certain technologies are likewise future-oriented and are, in fact, embedded within their own particular cosmology of death. Technology projects involve the assignment of interpretive meaning from past abhorrent events toward future possibilities. While doing so may not alleviate the suffering of loss, these projects presume that their anticipatory potential can help to alleviate future suffering. The power of technologies such mobile-phone-based apps, location searching with geospatial technology imagery and other forensic searchers allows for the assigning to future violence an interpretive code from past violence that transfers symbolic value from images of the past to material codes deemed capable of predicting the future. These material effects drawn from visual codes are used to justify action that is rationalized as life preserving. These technologies do not gain their value from observed destruction and harm. As an act of decoding that is anticipatory, their power lies in a decoding potential. They gain their strength from proleptic possibilities and at the core is the production of knowledge and a counter-production of new forms of expertise. Like religious tools, these technological tools produce knowledge that has the potential to usurp the role of the welfare state. However, the challenge is in what is called user-generated content (UGC) and the widespread forms of knowledge production that can emerge. The opening of new forms of expertise through the seeming inactivity of state institutions in various sites in the Global South provides a space for understanding not only the transformation underway but also the extent to which we are entering a post-juristocratic phase in the contemporary period.

I turn now to an analysis of efforts underway in the contemporary Nigerian context, where community-based technology projects are already numerous and far reaching. Two prominent examples – the "Eyes on Nigeria" project (backed by Amnesty International and the American Association for the Advancement of Science [AAAS]) and the 2001–3 Village Monitoring Project – have sought to go beyond judicial modalities, engaging partners including community-based organizations in an effort to provide training, establish warning indicators, and create and share knowledge networks capable of anticipating, verifying, and ultimately stopping violent action by insurgents.[2] These projects hinge on broadening access to hand-held tools that can be used to download information and disseminate the data derived from geospatial technologies.

"Geospatial technologies" refers to technologies that acquire, manipulate, and store geographic information. The term *geospatial* entered the lexicon during the late 1980s, but its roots can be traced to the early cold war. Today, geospatial technologies encompass a vast array of tools including geographic information systems (GIS), global positioning systems (GPS), geofencing, aerial photography, cartography, satellite imaging, photogrammetry for multidimensional cartographic modeling, multi- and hyperspectral imaging, and renderings from LiDAR survey data. In particular, remote sensing – a subset of geospatial technologies that collects images and data from space-based and airborne cameras and sensor platforms – is lauded for its supposed ability to overcome obstacles to detecting and reaching sites on the ground in a timely fashion

[2] In addition to Eyes on Nigeria, they include the Search for Common Ground (SFCG), the Community Action for Popular Participation (CAPP) by Mercy Corps, Plateau Peace Practitioners Network and the Women Peace & Security Network in Plateau State, Women Empowerment Foundation and Gender Awareness Trust in Kaduna state, West Africa Network for Peace Building (WANEP) in Zamfara state, and Community Centre for Excellence in Taraba state.

(LeBlanc et al. 2014; Abate et al. 2019;). Geospatial outputs from multiple sensors are seen as offering forensic advantages in that they can be interpreted in tandem to help analysts fill in data gaps (Blau et al. 2018). Furthermore, the speed at which remote sensing technologies retrieve data has been useful in shaping responses to rapidly developing humanitarian crises in cases where earth observation satellites are used to monitor conflict zones (Marx & Goward 2013). As a result, geospatial technologies employing remotely sensed imagery have been used to substantiate warnings around escalating conflict, to report human rights abuses, and to make predictions about future atrocities aimed at motivating state-based preemptive action. These technologies are used in human rights work to uncover and interpret gravesites, and to establish evidence and augment it through expert testimony in trials (Thompson 2008; Edelman & Aalders 2018). By tracking patterns captured by satellite images, rapid response networks empower themselves with intelligence that has the potential to prevent attacks.

Since 2011, there has been a particular expansion in scientifically driven technological possibilities aimed at finding bodies, discovering the nature of violence, and new domains of memorialization. And though digital tools (such as video capture through social media and geothermal satellite documentation) initially promised to provide evidence to courts, if ever the law was seen as the key site for addressing violence, this is increasingly no longer the case. Today these technologies are being deployed for the purposes of countering violence – sometimes state violence – outside of the courts. One such modality – "Early Warning and Early Response" (EWER) – is increasingly playing a role once occupied by the security state.

Yet even as the transnational alliances that make these new applications of technology possible appear to offer new hope for survivors, they also connect to broader histories and contemporary economies of power, in some ways resembling colonial dynamics. Recent analyses underscore the extent to which geospatial satellite experts are not on the sidelines offering counsel to political projects, but are in fact central to shaping the social and physical landscapes that legitimize institutions (Carroll 1996). In the US, for example, nominally neutral think tanks are leveraged for political purposes (Smith 1993; Medvetz 2014). Yet deploying expert knowledge in the Global South can have unintended outcomes as (post)colonial assumptions play out in particular cultural contexts (Mitchell 2002). Knowledge processes are often carried out by a small number of transnational experts, whose interpretation of data and knowledge-making processes speak to the particular techniques, practices, and assumptions (Graeter 2017) that undergird technologies used to *see* data. By reflecting on the roles of such agents and the practices involved, we see how seemingly objective practices, often carried out by regionally uninvested technocrats, reveal the circumscribed ways that scientists generate and validate knowledge (Latour & Woolgar 1986; Latour 1988), socialize new experts (Matoesian 1999; Mertz 2007), represent specialized knowledge in broader society (Lynch & Woolgar 1990; Collins & Evans 2007; Coopmans et al. 2014; Randalls 2017), and imbue knowledge within institutional structures (Good 2004, 2007; Carr 2009) and political movements and processes (Epstein 1996; Collier 2017; Newman 2017).

Today, commercial entities selling satellite data are able to profit from a narrative of technology's "mechanical objectivity" and transparency (Harris 2006; Daston & Galison 2007), and legal professionals seek to translate technical data into knowledge that can be mobilized as evidence to facilitate particular justice outcomes. These simplified narratives around the objectivity (and obviousness) of technical data are continually complicated by counter-narratives about which forms of truth (and whose suffering) are legible and "countable" within particular spheres (Joyce & Stover 1992; Rosenblatt 2015; Weizman 2017).

The historical antecedents of such technological expertise have been clearly theorized as tools and methodologies for exercising imperial conquest, exploitation, and control (Harley et al. 2001; Edney 2019). The US and Soviet governments monopolized the early development of satellite-based surveillance technology. Regular systematic satellite monitoring of the Earth's surface first entered the civilian sector with the 1972 launch of the US's *Landsat 1,* an Earth Resource Technology Satellite (ERTS) that was used to study and monitor changes in land use and land cover, a mission that continues to this day (Davis 2007). In the 1980s, the Reagan Administration rolled out a broad agenda of privatization and increased commercial access to satellite technology and its outputs (Lambright 1994). In the late 1990s, the US Global Positioning System entered civilian life, bringing applications for the investigation of crimes, enforcement of laws, and the offering of evidence in a wide range of civil matters (Elmes et al. 2014). And by 2001, Google Earth had become among the first platforms to give civilians free access to satellite archives.

Advances in satellite technology by commercial entities picked up speed over the following decade, bringing new opportunities for the public to influence law enforcement and the pursuit of justice in connection with environmental abuses, criminal investigations, and practices such as geofencing, or the triggering of specific actions on location-aware devices when they cross defined spatial boundaries. As the privatization of satellite technology continued, nongovernmental human rights groups were among those interested in working with commercial providers of satellite data (Wang et al. 2013). Among these providers' many customers are governments and investigators, leading to a dramatic increase in the use of satellite evidence.

In many of today's armed conflicts, such as in Syria, Libya, and Ukraine, repeated and ongoing violence occurs far from sites that are readily monitored. Investigators often lack access to locations where violence takes place, and they are increasingly turning to satellite images as well as photos, video, and text messages posted to social media using mobile phones, which in turn may be curated by witnesses (and sometimes also by perpetrators). Because the options for intervening in and procuring evidence of such violence are limited, international courts and tribunals are, with the help of the United Nations Institute for Training and Research (UNITAR) Operational Satellite Applications Programme (known as UNOSAT) as well as NGOs or governments, increasingly turning to satellite evidence to help make arrests and secure convictions. But far larger numbers are turning such possibilities in new directions.

In the first decade of the twenty-first century, private companies based primarily in the US, Canada, and Europe began to make remotely sensed imagery much more accessible by launching satellites that can capture imagery at increasingly higher resolutions and launching constellations of satellites capable of more comprehensive coverage of the Earth with a shorter revisit cycle. Prominent human rights groups such as Human Rights Watch and Amnesty International became customers of private data providers such as Digital Globe, with the aim of collecting and publicizing data about human rights abuses and pursuing the prosecution of crimes against humanity (Freeman 2018). Since then, there has been a growth in the use of digital evidence in domestic, regional, and international criminal courts such as the International Criminal Tribunal for the former Yugoslavia (ICTY) and later at the International Criminal Court (ICC). Related NGO projects contracted out data analysis projects to identify war and conflict zones. Meanwhile, corporations launched endeavors to connect directly with users and collect "crowdsourced" data and analysis, such as Google's Crisis in Darfur project (Levinger 2009; Wang et al. 2013); these projects were celebrated in their time as innovative, groundbreaking, and demonstrating great promise for preventing future mass atrocities. A decade later, NGO projects more commonly focused on Early Warning Early Response notifications and procurement projects that allow those victimized to memorialize their loved ones. These technologies have enabled civil society activists and families of the disappeared to challenge technology's imperial relation to knowledge and to (re)imagine their own roles at the intersection of data science, legitimate action, and social justice.

While certain geospatial technology projects are increasingly seen as not only imperialist but also exclusive and of little use to the families of those victimized by violence, new uses of these technologies mark an emerging and consequential shift in the logic and practices of international justice, with members of civil society participating in journalism, fact-finding, archiving, documenting, and managing a range of projects. In this vein, the past twenty years have seen an unprecedented rise in the number of citizen documentarians of human rights atrocities (Belloni 2001; van Schaak 2019). Humanitarian and public interest law groups have also increased attempts to professionalize civilian documenting of crimes against humanity (Leyh 2017), and literature, guides, handbooks, training, software, and programming on best practices for documenting serious crimes against humanity have begun to shape the investigation and prosecution of these crimes, and the possibilities and promises of justice itself (Subotic 2012). However, it is difficult to assess whether or to what extent crowdsourced geospatial evidence-gathering projects have prevented atrocities, as monitoring agendas had hoped. Instead, we are seeing strategies being put in place to usurp state-based projects and to produce user-generated content (UGC) that can serve the needs of those most directly affected by the losses. An examination of two such projects illustrates this point.

11.2.2 The Nigerian Village Monitoring Project

Northern Nigeria has seen frequent clashes between Christian sedentary farmers (and the vigilante security networks acting on their behalf) and predominantly Muslim nomadic Fulani herders. The effects of climate change on the Lake Chad basin are significant underlying triggers of conflict: the Fulani herders are migrating to new areas in the region in search of fodder and water for cattle as resources become more scarce. The migration patterns of nomadic communities have begun to signal security concerns beyond the immediately impacted regions. Key

Northern Nigerian states, including Kaduna and Plateau, are divided into northern and southern regions, exacerbating breaks in communal and familial lines, and fueling a climate of hate speech and religious misrepresentation that continues to justify and normalize violence. These crises continue to split communities along religious and geographic lines, a phenomenon that only foreshadows further intensification of the conflict. Zamfara State in Northwest Nigeria offers an example of the scale of the conflict: thirteen out of fourteen local government areas in the state have experienced armed group violence between 2014 and 2020. In late 2015, attacks by herder-allied armed groups, vigilantes, and criminally motivated groups spread from Zamfara to other states (primarily Kaduna, Katsina, Sokoto, and Niger) with varying intensity. Violence in these states has been concentrated in areas near their borders with Zamfara, or close to the forests where multiple armed groups have made camps.[3] Conflicts are occurring against a backdrop of stark and prolonged economic hardship. Zamfara State is one of the seven states that form the Northwest geopolitical zone of Nigeria with a combined estimated population of 35,794,944 (PADEAP Nigeria n.d.). The region is dominated by Hausa and Fulani ethnic groups and about 80 percent of the population is comprised of small-scale entrepreneurs, farmers, pastoralists and agro-pastoralists (International Crisis Group 2020). Across these sectors, communities share a common experience of high levels of poverty, illiteracy, and violence. Since the 1980s the region has experienced a fairly continual state of conflict, including instances of election violence, extremist and terrorists attacks, and sectarian clashes. Despite economic and population advantages relative to adjacent states, Zamfara has only a 29.7 percent literacy rate and the country's highest number of children not in school.

Complicating this situation in the north has been the rise of "opportunistic violence" as armed groups of young men across the north-central, northwest, and southern parts of the country engage in cattle rustling. In late 2017, state governments within the western and southern parts of Nigeria began to set up community policing strategies to address growing security challenges around their states, including those relating to the (perceived) threats associated with the movement of cattle herders.

[3] In Kaduna, the attacks have happened mostly in the Birnin-Gwari, Igabi, Giwa, Kajuru, and Chikun local government areas; in Taraba state, they have occurred mostly in Wukari and Donga; and in Plateau State in two Local Government Areas (LGAs): Riyom and Barkin Ladin.

Local civil society initiatives have continued to emerge to address problems between these levels of governmental intervention and attempts to mitigate ever-growing inequality and insecurity concerns in the region. Participation by key stakeholders from affected communities has remained low, however, and interventions have therefore been limited in their effectiveness. Some responses to these conflicts have taken technological approaches focused on making violence more visible to governmental and nongovernmental entities. Yet government and civil society efforts at various levels, ranging from the creation of legal and policy frameworks to programs on the ground, have been inadequate to protect civilians. A recognition of the failure to contain violence once it erupts has led to an investment of resources in EWER approaches, which involve the application of various technologies to capture daily images which are then integrated into an algorithm that uses big data to detect property destruction. Data uploaded from mobile devices also feeds into these systems.

The Nigerian Village Monitoring Project is one EWER intervention currently in play. Through a collaboration with a number of universities, government, and Nigerian civil society organizations, this program aims to prevent and mitigate violence against civilians in at-risk areas in Northern Nigeria through continuous monitoring and analysis of geospatial data and through an alert notification system that can provide near real-time notice of village burning incidents. The project is in the process of establishing baseline data that it will use to train an algorithm to detect the presence of burnings in geospatial satellite imagery. This optical structure shapes how anomalies are detected: the choice to capture daily imagery of the landscape further solidifies that which is concretized within the system's optic. The project works via processes of visual zooming and circumscription of land, property, and place: as such, it engages in a form of space-making along longitudinal and latitudinal coordinates that renders structures legible, thereby enabling observational optics to take shape. Given the limitations of existing EWER structures and the slow responses of state security actors, the project focuses on mobilizing individual and collective civilian engagement as a more effective strategy for turning the tide of violent conflict in Northern Nigeria. By training civil society early responders, establishing community-derived warning indicators, and sharing knowledge across EWER networks, the program seeks to anticipate, verify, and intervene in violent action. As such, it aims to engage civil society (especially women-led networks) to serve as peacebuilders and conflict mitigators trained in early detection, warning, and response to violence. This project and others like it all share an assumption that violence against civilians can be reduced through the successful build-out of accurate EWER technology and well-trained community response networks capable of detecting and mobilizing around potential and current attacks. Though the project receives some government support, then, it nevertheless shifts the responsibility for actually responding to ongoing and potential violence onto nonstate actors.

11.2.3 *The Eyes on Nigeria Project*

Between February 2008 and February 2010, approximately 375 structures were destroyed in the Njemanze neighborhood of Port Harcourt, in Nigeria's southern Niger Delta region, resulting in the displacement of an estimated 13,800 people.[4] Satellite images captured in February 2008 showed intact structures in the neighborhood; these images were compared to images taken in February 2010 showing the destruction. Eyes on Nigeria was launched on March 18, 2011, and focused on a range of communities such as Okerenko and the Njemanze neighborhood of Port Harcourt as well as the northern city of Jos. The project was tasked with documenting human rights violations including forced evictions, policing and justice issues, conflict in the Niger Delta, communal conflict, and industrial gas flaring.

The project was a collaboration between Amnesty International and the Geospatial Technologies and the Human Rights Project of the American Association for the Advancement of Science (AAAS).[5] It employed satellite and geospatial technologies, eyewitness accounts, cartographic techniques, and geolocated photography and video (created by Amnesty International researchers) to collect data for analysis, planning, and presentation, using an interactive platform housed on the Eyes on Nigeria website. The project used high- and moderate-resolution satellite images to corroborate witness accounts and provide a picture of human rights issues in Nigeria. Its goal was to mobilize three million global activists to hold the Nigerian government accountable.[6] To accomplish this goal, the project made a number of choices in terms

[4] www.amnesty.org/en/documents/AFR44/017/2010/en/. Satellite images: www.aaas.org/resources/eyes-nigeria-technical-report/forced-evictions.
[5] www.aaas.org/news/geospatial-technology-allows-observers-keep-eyes-nigeria.
[6] www.aaas.org/resources/eyes-nigeria-technical-report/overview.

of how to frame the data it collected – selecting, categorizing, and recontextualizing information in ways that reflected the project's structural, optical, and discursive frameworks.

Satellite imagery used in the city of Jos documented the extent of damage after four days of violence between Muslims and Christians in January 2010. An initial baseline satellite image from June 2007 was compared to a second image taken five days after the end of the conflict on January 27, 2010, for damage assessment. Based on the image analysis, it was determined that the damage covered an area of approximately one square kilometer, involving multiple city blocks. Structures that appeared intact in the images from June 2007 appeared to have no roofs in the images used for damage assessment in January 2010. The cause of the damage could not be assessed using the images, but witness media reports indicate that fires may have been involved in the roof collapses.[7]

The project also gathered fire-based evidence concerning industrial gas flaring. Although gas flaring (in which the natural gas from petroleum extraction is burned off in the atmosphere) it is generally performed for economic reasons, it has high potential for adverse environmental impacts (such as localized acid rain as well as increased greenhouse gas emissions). Moderate Resolution Imaging Spectroradiometer (MODIS) instruments housed on NASA's Terra and Aqua Earth-Observing Satellites (orbital satellites capable of detecting thermal infrared wavelengths) were used to monitor gas flares in the Niger Delta. MODIS data's infrared hotspot detection combined with on-the-ground research provided insight into the increased temperatures in areas surrounding gas flares. Despite the Nigerian government's attempts to reduce the practice of gas flaring since 2008, the images and analysis indicate that the practice has only slightly decreased.[8] By establishing a widespread community of practice in which geospatial technology was put in the service of detecting potential attacks, those engaged in Eyes on Nigeria and other similar projects sought and continue to seek to analyze and provide alerts for on-the-ground early response teams in relevant communities in order to mitigate attacks on civilians and enhance protection of target communities.

As these two cases illustrate, Nigerian officials, civil society actors, ordinary citizens, and transnational human rights partners are increasingly turning to technology in their efforts to develop solutions to

[7] Satellite images: www.aaas.org/resources/eyes-nigeria-technical-report/communal-conflict.

[8] Satellite images: www.aaas.org/resources/eyes-nigeria-technical-report/gas-flaring.

persistent forms of violence that the state has both failed to contain and, in some cases, has fueled or itself perpetrated. This trend is unfolding at the same time as Nigerian communities are gravitating in large numbers toward new forms of religious practice, which are themselves tools for making sense of profound daily and future insecurity. Both trends – the turn to technological solutions and the turn to spiritual solutions, in both cases outside of state institutions – evidence how people are coping in the absence of faith in the security of the state or the effectiveness of its justice apparatus. Local communities are claiming agency to innovate and construct alliances both among themselves and with national and transnational partners – whether human rights and technology organizations or transnational faith movements. By theorizing these activities, we begin to glimpse a new kind of democracy emerging, one that no longer builds power to petition the state for reform, but rather returns us to earlier centuries through which to strategically mitigate or even bypass the framework of the state in pursuit of its aims.

11.2.3.1 Beyond Security, Beyond Law: Making Sense of a Post-juristocratic Transition

In this chapter I have brought into conversation analyses of two interlinked trends in Nigerian society, both of which are calling into question the legitimacy and future viability of the postcolonial state form: fervent religiosity that privileges redemption in the afterlife, and geospatial technologies that empower ordinary survivors with a means to make both meaning and prophecy out of death and disappearance. I close by grappling with how these challenges may be signaling a post-juristocratic transition away from the authority of (western) law as the arbiter of justice and the source of solutions to extreme violence.

Such a transition would mark a significant shift away from the ideal of the welfare state that underlies postcolonial state institutions, despite these forms having lacked the conditions for success. Emerging out of the nineteenth century's rapid social transformation and growing political mobilization of workers and demands for democratization, the welfare state is characterized by generous social programmes and public spending aimed at reducing income insecurity and providing minimum standards of income and services (Amenta 2003, 92). Prior to its emergence, societies globally attended to the provision of social and economic support through a variety of institutions, such as the family, the church, and the local community, but with the welfare state, this responsibility fell on the state. A central part of this involved the role of the judiciary.

The term "welfare state" was first used to describe Britain under the Labour party after the World War II, when pre-war systems of social insurance were transformed. Beyond the UK, social security emphasized employment-based social insurance and involved healthcare coverage for the employed population and their dependents, while public health services covered care for the uninsured (Huber & Bogliaccini 2021). After independence, states throughout Global South introduced broader and more generous social programmes and expanded public social spending in order to reduce income insecurity and to provide minimum standards of income and services (Amenta 2003: 92). The 1940s saw a significant expansion of welfare in Latin American countries, and Colombia, Guatemala, and Mexico had achieved social security health coverage for over 60 percent of the population by 1980. But the trajectory of the welfare state was different on the African continent.

The development of the state as a provider of economic and political security for its citizens was irrevocably shaped in Africa by colonialism. In economic terms, this has made it hard for countries like Nigeria to escape what has been called the "circle of poverty" (Cookey 1980: 26). Britain exercised sovereign power over Nigeria from the middle of the 1800s to the middle of the 1900s. British colonial-era economic policy was based on *vent-for-surplus* theory, which asserts that when a country produces more than it can consume it produces a surplus. In other words, British colonial-era economic policy was not intended for promoting the economic development of British colonies. Instead, surplus agricultural production in Nigeria was exported to British consumers in return for British manufactured goods. Contemporary African political leaders and economic development planners still adopt economic development policies reminiscent of the colonial era (Mustapha 2003), policies that are often at variance with local practical realities. The colonial framework emphasized extraction without benefit to local producers of economic value (Mustapha 2003). Moreover, in the postcolonial era, Nigerian firms have remained largely controlled by transnational companies headquartered in Europe or, increasingly, in China.

Just as postcolonial economic policy has failed to provide for broad social welfare, so postcolonial criminal justice systems have failed to deter, prevent, and adjudicate violence. The police forces established in Nigeria since British colonial rule have been consistently repressive, corrupt, and inefficient (Alemika 1993: 187). This alienation of the police from the people and the perennial crisis of performance suffered by the police in Nigeria are partly explained by the inherited and sustained colonial legacy of repressive policing in the society to sustain governability in the face of widespread opposition and legitimation deficits (Das 1983: 54; Alemika 1993: 187). Repressive police work becomes more visible wherever and whenever there is a preponderance of deviance, disenchantment, and dissension among citizens. Contemporary police forces in Nigeria have been variously criticized for eroding the liberty, security, human rights, and welfare of the citizens, and accused of brutality, corruption, political repression and partisanship, bribery, and political payoffs.

As such, since the transition from military dictatorship to democracy in 1999 and the subsequent emergence of new categories of crime (including kidnapping for ransom, cattle rustling, illegal oil bunkering, oil pipeline vandalization, and Islamic terrorism), Nigerians have had little recourse to the kinds of protections and remedies that a welfare state might be able to provide. This has fueled a proliferation of informal and vigilante security actors. As vigilantes assume the role that the state had reserved for policing, communities are organizing to assume the roles disavowed by postcolonial law.

As this chapter has discussed, violence in Africa has propelled citizen engagements driven by both local knowledge about the political landscape in which people suffer harm and new innovations through which to validate the claims of civil society engagement (James 2010; Smith 2016; Clarke 2019). Members of civil society have participated in journalism, fact-finding, archiving, and documenting human rights atrocities (Belloni 2001; van Schaak 2019), and with the participation of witnesses and those victimized by violence, personal narratives have been brought in to complement geospatial data to make the stories this evidence tells stronger and more holistic (Madden & Ross 2009; Forensic Architecture & SITU Research, 2014). In a range of sites around the world, everyday citizens have become involved in collecting social media documentation of violence: citizen scientists have taken active roles in the processes of locating and excavating clandestine graves, and identifying exhumed bodily remains of the disappeared (Bishr & Kuhn 2007; Rubin 2014).

These developments reflect a significant change in how citizens across the globe relate to the state in the sphere of justice. Recently, sociolegal scholarship concerned with legal consciousness and the promise of the law has tracked the experiences of civilians (witnesses and victims), including their perceptions of the process of justice and subsequent disappointments over outcomes (Stover 2005; McEvoy 2007; Leebaw 2008). Scholars of transitional justice have situated these experiences within the larger politics of engagements with international legal institutions, exposing the impacts of failures to hold offenders accountable, with respect to both legal mechanisms (Haslam 2011; Cronin-Furman 2013) and public morality (Hansen & Sriram 2015). Ethnographies focused on truth commissions and civil engagement in transitional justice explore both the embodied emotions and practices around the drive to achieve "justice" and the ways in which institutions fall short of this achievement (Lundy & McGovern 2008; Hayner 2011).

Technological developments are fueling this shift, with new platforms and media expanding beyond traditional notions of space and situated movements (Auge 1995; Juris 2005, 2012) and bringing in new stakeholders to preexisting politics (Flyverbom 2011). Ethnographers have documented this phenomenon in a wide range of movements, including anti-globalization politics (Smith & Smythe 1999; Juris 2012), environmental movements (Washbourne 2001), transnational solidarity for political autonomy and anti-imperial resistance (Olesen 2004), consumer and food activism (Schneider et al. 2018), and women's and children's rights (Berridge & Portwood-Stacer 2015). As the skills needed to operate digital communication technologies become more widely attainable, digital activism has moved into the mainstream (Karatzogianni 2015). Scholars have described the ways that new communication technologies have shaped social movements as a new form of bio-constitutionalism (Jasanoff 2004, 2011; Agathangelou 2017) and with the recent emergence of "discursive activism," or "hashtag activism," we are seeing new globalized forms of social organizing (Ristovska 2016; Brown et al. 2017; Clarke 2017; Ray et al. 2017). These new forms of organizing involve new kinds of actors: anthropologists of social movements have recently directed attention to the expanding role of NGOs in the actions of social movements (Fisher 1997; Bornstein 2009; Bornstein & Sharma 2016), as well as to the frustrations, failures, and the reproduction of former colonial relations arising from such collaborations. Exposing these conflicts has led to a rise in engaged anthropology of social movements as a movement itself, in which anthropologists participate in the projects of their subjects depending on their various needs (Goldstein 2014; de Leon 2015).

Tracking how technology provides a new platform for the pursuit of social justice illuminates a range of benefits and methodological challenges. While such technologies are opening new possibilities around which new domains of knowledge and expertise are taking shape, they also present new risks: questions about misinterpretation, misrepresentation, and malfeasance remain at the heart of the knowledge-producing enterprise. In considering whether and how new technologies and platforms are democratizing access to the means of producing judicial knowledge and evidence, it becomes all the more important to understand more comprehensively the interactions and interrelations that are produced through using these new tools, and how and to what effect new constituencies are gaining access to them.

These developments speak to a change in the fiction of the welfare state amidst the reality that, while countries in the Global South are seeing some of the highest numbers of violent deaths since the World War II, reliance on legal institutions for contemporary solutions is on the decline (Albiston 2010; Aiyede 2016). The juridical power of local, state, regional, and international law to intervene and address the enabling conditions of violence is elusive at best. I, therefore, close by suggesting that while the entrenchment of modernity's legal formations always and already structures the conditions in which contemporary juristocratic formations take shape, the failure of state institutions in Nigeria to secure lives and livelihoods, including via its legal mechanisms, is leading to a post-juristocratic reality.

Under these conditions, new competitors to the state – nongovernmental organizations, scientists, democratizing evangelicals – are inserting themselves in Nigerian locales and struggling to gain authority over the management of violence. In response to the perception of state complicity or incapacity, people are becoming involved in the management of violence through the use of video capture technologies, crowdsourcing, and early warning projects, as well as forms of religiosity that are producing new possibilities for the good life. As such, a rethinking of Ran Hirschl's analysis of "juristocracy" (Hirschl 2004) must involve a reckoning not only with the "post-juristocratic transition" taking shape in the contemporary period but also with how this turn away from the juridification and judicialization of social, economic, and political life involves much more than uncertainty concerning the future. Though legality is always already central, these developments require that we consider the new formations that are increasingly supplanting the roles that juristocratic forces once played. New digital technologies and contemporary forms of religious fervor have come together to provide new quotidian tools for managing insecurity and reckoning with contemporary crises in and beyond the law.

References

Abate, D. et al. 2019. A Review of Remote Sensing Applications for Precision Agriculture in Smallholder Farming Systems of Sub-Saharan Africa. *Remote Sensing* 11 (14): 1667. https://doi.org/10.3390/rs11141667.

Abumere, F. I. 2016. The Rise of Islamic Fundamentalism (Boko Haram) and Poverty in Nigeria. The Project of Culture and Religion Society.

Adelakun, A. A. 2022. *Performing Power in Nigeria: Identity, Politics, and Pentecostalism*. Cambridge University Press.

Adewale, O. O. and O. F. Abu. 2013. Christianity in Nigeria before Pentecostalism. *Academic Journal of Interdisciplinary Studies* 2 (2): 121–122.

Agai, J. M. 2014. The Rise of Islamic Jihad in Northern Nigeria and its Implications on the Jos-Plateau Religious Conflicts. *Social Sciences* 3 (3): 67–73.

Agathangelou, A. 2017. The Time of and Temporal (Un) Civility of the City: MENA Urban Insurgencies and Revolutions. In Suzanne Hall and Ricky Burdett, eds., *The Sage Handbook of the 21st Century City*. London: Sage, 349–375.

Aiyede, E. R. 2016. Seeking Redress beyond the State: Vigilantism, Informal Justice and the Politics of Law Enforcement in Nigeria. *African Affairs* 115 (459): 600–622.

Albiston, C. R. 2010. *Institutional Inequality and the Mobilization of the Family and Medical Leave Act: Rights on Leave*. Cambridge: Cambridge University Press.

2015. Legal Cynicism and (Subcultural?) Tolerance of Injustice: The Absence of Efficacy in Legal Institutions and Violent Crime in a Mexican City. *Law & Society Review* 49 (1): 121–154.

Alemika, E. E. 1993. Colonialism, State and Policing in Nigeria. *Crime, Law and Social Change* 20: 187–219.

Amadi, F. A. 2013. Understanding the Practices that Define Pentecostal Christianity in Nigeria. *European Scientific Journal* 9 (32): 297–309.

Amenta, E. 2003. What We Know about the Development of Social Policy: Comparative and Historical Research in Comparative and Historical Perspective. In James Mahoney and Dietrich Rueschemeyer, eds., *Comparative Historical Analysis in the Social Sciences*. Cambridge University Press, 91–130.

Amoo, A. 2018. Young Adult Literacy Rate in Nigeria (State by State). https://educeleb.com/young-adult-literacy-rate-in-nigeria/.

Anugwom, E. E. 2018. Islamic Fundamentalism and Religious Conflicts in Nigeria: Reflections on the Boko Haram Insurgence. *Politics and Religion Journal* 12 (2): 225–243.

Arteta, I. 2019 (May 15). ¿ Hay 26000 cuerpos sin identificar en México? Segob no lo sabe, solo tiene estimaciones. Animal Político. www.animalpolitico.com/2019/05/cuerpos-sin-identificar-mexico-segob/.

Asuquo, O. O. 2020. Pentecostalism and Development: The Role and Prospects of Prosperity Gospel in the Socio-economic Development of Nigeria. *Predestinasi* 14 (1): 35–40.

Atari, M. 2021. Death in Christianity. In *Encyclopedia of Evolutionary Psychological Science*. Springer, 1847–1850.

Augé, M. 1995. *Non-places: Introduction to an Anthropology of Supermodernity*. Verso.

Ayodeji, O. 2013. Christians' Perception of the Concepts of Death and Judgment: A Multimodal Discourse Analytical Study of Selected Editions of Christian Women Mirror Magazine. *International Journal of English and Literature* 4 (10): 508–515.

Belloni, R. 2001. The Role of Information Technology in Human Rights. *Human Rights Quarterly* 23 (2): 547–574.

Berridge, S. and L. Portwood-Stacer. 2015. Introduction: Feminism, Hashtags and Violence against Women and Girls. *Feminist Media Studies* 15 (2): 341.

Bishr, M. and W. Kuhn. 2007. Geospatial Information Bottom-Up: A Matter of Trust and Semantics. In S. Fabrikant and M. Wachowicz, eds., *The European Information Society: Leading the Way with Geo-information*, Proceedings of the 10th AGILE International Conference in Geographic Information Science. Aalborg: Springer, 365–387.

Blau, S., J. Sterenberg, P. Weeden, F. Urzedo, R. Wright and C. Watson. 2018. Exploring Non-invasive Approaches to Assist in the Detection of Clandestine Human Burials: Developing a Way Forward. *Forensic Sciences Research* 3 (4): 320–342.

Bornstein, E. 2009. The Impulse of Philanthropy. *Cultural Anthropology* 24 (4) 622–651.

Bornstein, E. and A. Sharma. 2016. The Righteous and the Rightful: The Technomoral Politics of NGOs, Social Movements, and the State in India. *American Ethnologist* 43 (1): 76–90.

Brown, M., R. Ray, E. Summers and N. Fraistat. 2017. # SayHerName: A Case Study of Intersectional Social Media Activism. *Ethnic and Racial Studies* 40 (11): 1831–1846.

Campo, J. E. 2009. *Encyclopedia of Islam*. Facts On File. Inc.: New York.

Carr, S. 2009. Anticipating and Inhabiting Institutional Identities. *American Ethnologist* 36 (2): 317–336. https://doi.org/10.1111/j.1548-1425.2009.01137.x.

Carroll, P. 2006. *Science, Culture, and Modern State Formation*. University of California Press.

Clarke, K. M. 2017. Rethinking Sovereignty through Hashtag Publics: The New Body Politics. *Cultural Anthropology* 32 (3): 359–366.

2019. *Affective Justice: The International Criminal Court and the Pan-Africanist Pushback*. Duke University Press.

Collier, A. 2017. *Shadow Banking and the Rise of Capitalism in China*. Springer Singapore.

Collins, H. and R. Evans. 2007. *Rethinking Expertise*. University of Chicago Press.

Cookey, S. J. S. 1980. Colonialism and the Process of Underdevelopment in Nigeria: A Review. *Journal of Asian and African Studies (Leiden)* 14 (1–2): 19–31.

Coopmans, C., J. Vertesi, M. E. Lynch and S. Woolgar, eds. 2014. *Representation in Scientific Practice Revisited*. MIT.

Cronin-Furman, K. 2013. Managing Expectations: International Criminal Trials and the Prospects for Deterrence. *International Journal of Transitional Justice* 7 (3): 434–454.

Danfulani, U. H. D. 1999. Factors Contributing to the Survival of the Bori Cult in Northern Nigeria. *Numen* 46 (4): 412–447.

Das, D. 1983. Conflict Views on Policing: An Evaluation. *American Journal of Police* 3: 51.

Daston, L. and P. Galison. 2007. *Objectivity*. Princeton University Press.

Davis, C. H. 2007. Landsat and Beyond: Sustaining and Enhancing the Record of Earth's Changing Landscapes. *Photogrammetric Engineering & Remote Sensing* 73 (9): 1005–1010.

de Leon, J. 2015. *The Land of Open Graves: Living and Dying on the Migrant Trail*. University of California Press.

Diem, W. and M. Schöller. 2004. *The Living and the Dead in Islam: Epitaphs as Texts* (Vol. 1). Otto Harrassowitz Verlag.

Edelman, G. J. and M. C. Aalders. 2018. Photogrammetry Using Visible, Infrared, Hyperspectral and Thermal Imaging of Crime Scenes. *Forensic Science International* 292: 181–189.

Edney, M. H. 2018. Map History: Discourse and Process. In A. Kent and P. Vujakovic, eds., *The Routledge Handbook of Mapping and Cartography* (1st ed., pp. 68–79). Routledge. https://doi.org/10.4324/9781315736822-7

Ekore, R. I. and B. Lanre-Abass. 2016. African Cultural Concept of Death and the Idea of Advance Care Directives. *Indian Journal of Palliative Care* 22 (4): 369–372.

Elmes, G. A., D. Barry and R. Owen. 2014. The Impact of GPS on Crime Investigation: A Case Study of the United States. *Journal of Criminal Justice* 42 (6): 570–579.

Epstein, S. 1996. *Impure Science: AIDS, Activism, and the Politics of Knowledge* (Vol. 7). University of California Press.

Eyo, U., E. Essien and G. Ekong. 2020. Beyond Prosperity Gospel and Socio-economic Insecurity in Africa: Ethical Implications of Spiritualizing Poverty. In E. Essien, ed., *Handbook of Research on the Impact of Culture in Conflict Prevention and Peacebuilding*. IGI Global, 440–463.

Eyoboka, S. 2004 (March 14). Eminent Clerics React to Nigeria being the Most Religious Nation of the World. Vanguard, p. 17.

Fisher, W. F. 1997. Doing Good? The Politics and Anti-politics of NGO Practices. *Annual Review of Anthropology* 26: 439–464.

Flyverbom, M. 2011. *The Power of Networks: Organizing Global Governance.* Edward Elgar.

Foucault, M. 1977. *Discipline and Punish: The Birth of the Prison*, trans. Alan Sheridan. New York: Vintage.

1988. Technologies of the Self. In L. H. Martin, H. Gutman and P. H. Hutton, eds., *Technologies of the Self: A Seminar with Michel Foucault.* University of Massachusetts Press, 16–49.

Freeman, L. 2018. Satellite Imagery and Human Rights: A Necessary Partnership. *Journal of Human Rights Practice* 10 (1): 1–21.

Galadima, B. Y. and Y.Turaki. 2001. Christianity in Nigeria. *African Journal of Evangelical Theology* 20 (1): 85–101.

Goldstein, D. M. 2014. *The Spectacular City: Violence and Performance in Urban Bolivia.* Duke University Press.

Good, A. 2004. *Worship and the Ceremonial Economy of a Royal South Indian Temple.* Edwin Mellen.

2007. *Anthropology and Expertise in the Asylum Courts.* Routledge.

Graeter, S. 2017. To Revive an Abundant Life: Catholic Science and Neoextractivist Politics in Peru's Mantaro Valley. *Cultural Anthropology* 32 (1): 117–148.

Hansen, T. O. and C. L. Sriram. 2015. Fighting for Justice (and Survival): Kenyan Civil Society Accountability Strategies and Their Enemies. *International Journal of Transitional Justice* 9 (3): 407–427.

Harley, J. B., D. Woodward and G. M. Lewis. 2001. *The History of Cartography: Cartography in the Traditional African, American, Arctic, Australian, and Pacific Societies.* University of Chicago Press.

Harris, C. 2006. The Omniscient Eye: Satellite Imagery, "Battlespace Awareness," and the Structures of the Imperial Gaze. *Surveillance & Society* 4 (1–2).

Haslam, E. 2011. Subjects and Objects: International Criminal Law and the Institutionalization of Civil Society. *International Journal of Transitional Justice* 5 (2): 221–240.

Hayner, P. B. 2011. *Unspeakable Truths: Transitional Justice and the Challenge of Truth Commissions.* Routledge.

Hirschl, R. 2004. *Towards Juristocracy: The Origins and Consequences of the New Constitutionalism.* Cambridge, MA: Harvard University Press.

Hiskett, M. 1982. *The History of Islam in West Africa.* Longman.

1984. *The Development of Islam in West Africa.* Harlow: Longman.

Huber, E. and J. Bogliaccini. 2021. Latin America. In Francis G. Castles, Stephan Leibfried, Jane Lewis, Herbert Obinger, and Christopher Pierson, eds., *The Oxford Handbook of the Welfare State.* Oxford: Oxford University Press, 644–655.

Hughes, T. P. 1995. *Thomas Patrick Hughes Dictionary of Islam*. Asian Educational Services.

Idowu, D. L. 2022. *Performing Power in Nigeria: Identity, Politics, and Pentecostalism. Abimbola Adelakun*. Cambridge, UK: Cambridge University Press.

International Crisis Group. 2020. *Violence in Nigeria's North West: Rolling Back the Mayhem*. International Crisis Group.

James, E. C. 2010. Ruptures, Rights, and Repair: The Political Economy of Trauma in Haiti. *Social Science & Medicine* 70 (1): 106–113.

Jasanoff, S., ed. 2011. *Reframing Rights: Bioconstitutionalism in the Genetic Age*. MIT.

2004. *States of Knowledge: The Co-production of Science and Social Order*. Routledge.

Joyce, C. and E. Stover. 1992. *Witnesses from the Grave: The Stories Bones Tell*. New York: Ballantine.

Juris, J. S. 2005. The New Digital Media and Activist Networking within Anti-corporate Globalization Movements. *Annals of the American Academy of Political and Social Science* 597 (1): 189–208.

2012. Reflections on #Occupy Everywhere: Social Media, Public Space, and Emerging Logics of Aggregation. *American Ethnologist* 39 (2): 259–279.

Karatzogianni, A. 2015. *Firebrand Waves of Digital Activism 1994–2014: The Rise and Spread of Hacktivism and Cyberconflict*. Springer.

Lambright, W. H. 1994. The Reagan Administration's Commercial Space Policy: A Critical Assessment. *Space Policy* 10 (2): 103–116.

Latour, B. 1988. *The Pasteurization of France*. Trans. Alan Sheridan and John Law. Cambridge, MA: Harvard University Press.

Latour, B. and S. Woolgar. 1986. *Laboratory Life: The Construction of Scientific Facts*. Princeton University Press.

Leaman, O., ed. 2006. *The Qur'an: An Encyclopedia*. Routledge.

LeBlanc, S. G. et al. 2014. Remote Sensing for Environmental Site Screening and Watershed Evaluation in the Great Lakes. *Environmental Management* 54 (6): 1350–1364. https://doi.org/10.1007/s00267-014-0340-2.

Leebaw, B. A. 2008. The Irreconcilable Goals of Transitional Justice. *Human Rights Quarterly* 30: 95.

Levinger, B. 2009. Satellite Imagery and Human Rights: A New Tool for Human Rights Organizations. *Human Rights Quarterly* 31 (1): 194–220.

Leyh, B. 2017. The Professionalization of Civilian Documenting of Crimes against Humanity. *Journal of Human Rights Practice* 9 (2): 187–207.

Lindhardt, M. 2014. *Pentecostalism in Africa: Presence and Impact of Pneumatic Christianity in Postcolonial Societies*. Brill.

Linus, U. 2017. Young Nigerians are Connecting with Pentecostal Churches. Will They Return to Catholicism? *American Magazine*. www.americanmagazine.org.

Lomnitz, C. 2024. *Sovereignty and Extortion: A New State Form in Mexico*. Duke University Press.

Lundy, P. and M. McGovern, 2008. Whose Justice? Rethinking Transitional Justice from the Bottom Up. *Journal of Law and Society* 35 (2): 265–292.

Lynch, M., and S.Woolgar. 1990. *Representation in Scientific Practice*, 1st ed. MIT.

Madden, F. and S. Ross. 2009. The Role of Narrative in International Criminal Trials. *Journal of International Criminal Justice* 7 (5): 959–981.

Marx, A. and S. Goward. 2013. Remote Sensing in Human Rights and International Humanitarian Law Monitoring: Concepts and Methods. *Geographical Review* 103 (1): 100–111.

Matoesian, G. M. 1999. The Grammaticalization of Participant Roles in the Constitution of Expert Identity. *Language in Society* 28 (4): 491–521.

Marshall, R. 2019. *Political Spiritualities*. Chicago University Press.

McEvoy, K. and R. Rebouche. 2007. Mobilizing the Professions: Lawyers, Politics, and the Collective Legal Conscience. In J. Morison, K. McEvoy and G. Anthony, eds., *Judges, Transition, and Human Rights*. Oxford: Oxford University Press, 275–314.

Medvetz, T. 2014. *Think Tanks in America*. University of Chicago Press.

Mertz, E. 2007. *The Language of Law School: Learning to "Think Like a Lawyer."* New York: Oxford University Press.

Mitchell, J. P. 2002. Corruption and Clientelism in a "Systemless System": The Europeanization of Maltese Political Culture. *South European Society & Politics* 7 (1): 43–62.

Mustapha, A. R. 2003. Colonialism and Environmental Perception in Northern Nigeria. *Oxford Development Studies* 31 (4): 405–425

Newman, J. 2017. *Governing Public–Private Partnerships*. McGill-Queen's Press-MQUP.

Obadre, E. 2022. From Man of Letters to the Man of God: The Social Origins of Clerical Authority in Nigeria. Nigeria in the World seminar series at the Harvard Weatherhead Center for International Affairs, 39.

Ogbuagu, S. C. 1989. The Changing Perception of Death and Burial: A Look at the Nigerian Obituaries. *Anthropologica* 31 (1): 85–101.

Olesen, T. 2004. Globalising the Zapatistas: From Third World Solidarity to Global Solidarity? *Third World Quarterly* 25 (1): 255–267.

Olowu, A. 2013. Christians' Perception of the Concepts of Death and Judgment: A Multimodal Discourse Analytical Study of Selected Editions of Christian Women Mirror Magazine. *International Journal of English and Literature* 4 (10): 508–515.

Omavuebe, A. 2021. Evaluating Nigerian Prosperity Gospel as a Mixed Ideology. *Missiology: An International Review* 49 (4): 389–401.

Ostien, P., ed. 2011. Sharia Implementation in Northern Nigeria 1999–2006: A Sourcebook. The Centre for Islamic Legal Studies. Draft Harmonised Sharia Penal Code Annotated 2011.

PADEAP. n.d. PADEAP Nigeria. www.padeap.net/en/who-we-are/our-offices/nigeria/item/13-padeap-nigeria.html.

Pottage, A. 2017. Rev. of Reframing Rights: Bioconstitutionalism in the Genetic Age. *New Genetics and Society: Critical Studies of Contemporary Biosciences* 36 (2): 188–190. https://doi.org/10.1080/14636778.2017.1318532.

Pilaszewicz, S. 1988. Images of the Temporal World in Hausa Verse. *Africana Bulletin* 35: 67–80.

Randalls, S. 2017. Assembling Climate Expertise: Carbon Markets, Neoliberalism and Science. In Vaughan Higgins and Wendy Larner, eds., *Assembling Neoliberalism: Expertise, Practices, Subjects*. Springer, 67–85.

Ray, R., M. Brown, N. Fraistat and E. Summers. 2017. Ferguson and the Death of Michael Brown on Twitter: #BlackLivesMatter, #TCOT, and the Evolution of Collective Identities. *Ethnic and Racial Studies* 40 (11): 1797–1813.

Ristovska, S. 2016. Strategic Witnessing in an Age of Video Activism. *Media, Culture & Society* 38 (7): 1034–1047. https://doi.org/10.1177/0163443716635866.

Rosenblatt, A. 2015. *Digging for the Disappeared: Forensic Science after Atrocity*. Redwood City, CA: Stanford University Press.

Rubin, J. S. 2014. Transitional Justice against the State: Lessons from Spanish Civil Society-Led Forensic Exhumations. *International Journal of Transitional Justice* 8: 99–120.

Rupp, J. C. 1992. Michel Foucault, Body Politics and the Rise and Expansion of Modern Anatomy. *Journal of Historical Sociology* 5 (1): 31–60.

Schneider, T., K. Eli, C. Dolan and S. Ulijaszek, eds. 2018. *Digital Food Activism*. London: Routledge.

Smith, J. A. 1993. Idea Brokers: *Think Tanks and the Rise of the New Policy Elite*. Simon & Schuster.

Smith, M. 2016. *Boko Haram: Inside Nigeria's Unholy War*. I.B. Tauris.

Smith, P. J. and E. Smythe. 1999. Globalization, Citizenship and Technology: The MAI Meets the Internet. *Canadian Foreign Policy Journal* 7 (2): 83–105.

Stover, E. 2005. *The Witnesses: War Crimes and the Promise of Justice in the Hague*. University of Pennsylvania Press.

Subotic, J. 2012. The Power of Documentation: The International Criminal Tribunal for the Former Yugoslavia and the Production of Evidence. *Human Rights Quarterly* 34 (4); 1005–1034.

Thompson, R. A. 2008. *An Introduction to Criminal Evidence: A Casebook Approach*. Oxford University Press.

Turner, C. 2011. *Islam: The Basics*. Routledge.

Unah, L. 2017. Young Nigerians are Connecting with Pentecostal Churches. Will They Return to Catholicism. *American Magazine*. www.americanmagazine .org.

Van Schaack, B. 2019. *Innovations in International Criminal Law Documentation Methodologies and Institutions*. https://doi.org/10.2139/ssrn.3329102.

Vaughan, O. 2016. *Religion and the Making of Nigeria*. Duke University Press.

Vogt, C. P. 2004. Practicing Patience, Compassion, and Hope at the End of Life: Mining the Passion of Jesus in Luke for a Christian Model of Dying Well. *Journal of the Society of Christian Ethics* 24 (1): 135–158.

Wang, S., A. D. Smith and D. M. White. 2013. Crowdsourcing Geospatial Data for Disaster Response: A Case Study on the Use of Social media in the 2010 Haiti Earthquake. *World Medical & Health Policy* 5 (4): 353–369.

Wariboko, N. 2014. *Nigerian Pentecostalism* (NED-new ed.). Boydell & Brewer.

Washbourne, N. 2001. Information Technology and New Forms of Organising?: Translocalism and Networks in Friends of the Earth. In Frank Webster, ed., *Culture and Politics in the Information Age*. Routledge, 143–155.

Wilkinson, D. 2019. *Mexico: The Other Disappeared*. Human Rights Watch. www .hrw.org/news/2019/01/15/mexico-other-disappeared.

Weizman, E. 2014. *Forensis: The Architecture of Public Truth*. Sternberg.

2017. *Forensic Architecture: Violence at the Threshold of Detectability*. Princeton University Press.

Žebrauskaitė, G. n.d. Islamic Fundamentalism and the Case for Intercivilizational Dialogue in Nigeria and Cameroon. Retrieved from http://unav.edu.

INDEX

www.ingramcontent.com/pod-product-compliance
Lightning Source LLC
LaVergne TN
LVHW011807200926
848484LV00005B/1090
9781009499545